Mexico Today

Mexico Today

AN ENCYCLOPEDIA OF LIFE IN THE REPUBLIC

VOLUME 2
I–Z

Alex M. Saragoza, Ana Paula Ambrosi,
and Silvia D. Zárate, Editors

 ABC-CLIO

Santa Barbara, California • Denver, Colorado • Oxford, England

Library of Congress Cataloging-in-Publication Data

Mexico today : an encyclopedia of life in the republic / Alex M. Saragoza, Ana Paula
Ambrosi, and Silvia D. Zárate, editors.
     v. cm.
  Includes bibliographical references and indexes.
   ISBN 978-0-313-34948-5 (hbk. : acid-free paper) — ISBN 978-0-313-34949-2 (ebook)
  1. Mexico—Civilization—Encyclopedias.   2. Mexico—Social life and customs—
Encyclopedias.   3. Mexico—Politics and government—2000—-Encyclopedias.
4. Mexico—Economic conditions—1994—-Encyclopedias.   I. Saragoza, Alex.
II. Ambrosi, Ana Paula.   III. Zárate, Silvia D. (Silvia Dolores)
  F1210.M6175   2012
  972.08›42—dc23

                                       2011050155

ISBN: 978-0-313-34948-5
EISBN: 978-0-313-34949-2

16 15 14 13 12   1 2 3 4 5

This book is also available on the World Wide Web as an eBook.
Visit www.abc-clio.com for details.

ABC-CLIO, LLC
130 Cremona Drive, P.O. Box 1911
Santa Barbara, California 93116-1911

Contents

Alphabetical List of Entries

Topic Finder

Below are the entries for *Mexico Today* listed under broad topics. For more detailed access, consult the index at the back of volume 2.

Business and Economy

Agriculture

Airlines

Banking

Beverage Industry

Debt, Foreign

Economic Crash of 1994–1995

Economy, Informal

Economy, U.S.-Mexican Border

Energy

Foreign Direct Investment

Foreign Trade

Global Market and Multinational Corporations

Income

Labor Force and Labor Movements

Land Distribution and Land Reform

Maquiladoras

Mining

Monetary System

North American Free Trade Agreement

Peasantry

Petróleos Mexicanos

Tourism

Transportation

Cities and States

Aguascalientes

Baja California Norte

Baja California Sur

Campeche

Chiapas

Chihuahua

Coahuila

Colima

Durango

Guanajuato

Guerrero

Hidalgo

Jalisco

Mexico, State of

Mexico City

Michoacán

Morelos

Nayarit

I

Immigration and Emigration

While Mexican history has been influenced by the movement of people into the country, most historical and political focus has been on Mexicans leaving the country. In particular, emphasis has been on the impact of Mexican citizens moving from Mexico to the United States. According to the Pew Hispanic Center, "12.7 million Mexican immigrants lived in the United States in 2008, a 17-fold increase since 1970." Of those immigrants, 55 percent are estimated to be undocumented ("Mexican Immigrants in the United States, 2008" 2009).

U.S. attitudes toward the role of the Mexican immigrant changed dramatically with the onset of the Great Depression of the 1930s. With unemployment rapidly rising (eventually reaching 25 percent in 1933), there was growing pressure for Americans to hold the jobs that remained, although relatively few Americans were willing to do the type of labor—agricultural work—that generally employed large numbers of Mexicans. Mexican workers were among the first to be laid off, and there was growing criticism that they were a welfare burden. The idea of repatriating Mexican workers was a popular though misguided solution to the unemployment problem and to the notion that Mexicans posed a welfare burden. Local and state governments sponsored repatriation, some going voluntarily, but most under pressure. Community groups, charitable agencies, and Mexican consular officials also helped finance repatriation. The U.S. federal government had little involvement in repatriation activities but increased its efforts at formal deportation—the removal of an alien who has violated some law. The time and expense of a formal deportation proceeding often led federal officials to encourage deportable aliens to depart voluntarily. Repatriated immigrants received assistance from the Mexican federal government once they reached the border. Repatriates were permitted to bring their possessions into Mexico without paying any duties. The Mexican government also provided free rail transportation from the border to the interior. There were also offers of government land for repatriates, but these "colonization" schemes involved only about 5 percent of the repatriates and were generally unsuccessful. Repatriation peaked in 1931; by 1935 an estimated 500,000 had been repatriated. Among the repatriates were a number of children born in the United States of Mexican parents who were thus U.S. citizens.

The U.S. economy did not show substantial improvement until the late 1930s when the buildup to and the outbreak of World War II substantially increased the demand for American products. From 1938 to 1941, the United States went from having an unemployment problem to anticipating major labor shortages after U.S. entry into the conflict in December 1941. To deal with the labor shortages in agriculture, the U.S. and Mexican governments in 1942 created the Bracero Program. Under the arrangement, the Mexican government permitted the recruitment of Mexican laborers to work in the United States, with the U.S. government guaranteeing the workers' transportation, living expenses, and repatriation costs. The U.S. government, in turn, was to subcontract the Mexican workers to individual employers. The employers had to furnish housing and medical care, as well as reimburse the U.S. government for transportation costs. The 1942 agreement regulated the flow of bracero workers until 1947; from 1942 to 1947, more than 200,000 braceros entered the United States. The program continued after 1947, but the U.S. government was no longer a guarantor of work contracts. Problems with U.S. employers adhering to contracts led to the reinstatement of the U.S. government as the contract guarantor in 1951. The U.S. government continued in that role throughout the remaining years of the bracero agreement. The demand for bracero labor remained strong throughout the 1950s, but entered a pronounced decline in the early 1960s as mechanization of agriculture accelerated. The Bracero Program officially came to an end on December 31, 1964. During the life of the program, almost 5 million Mexican workers found employment in U.S. agriculture.

Supporters of the Bracero Program claimed—or hoped—that providing a legal mechanism for immigration would reduce the growing problem of illegal immigration from Mexico into the United States. There was little indication that the Bracero Program had that desired effect. One of the earliest criticisms of the program was that many braceros were originally illegal immigrants whose status had been legalized by receiving a work contract. During the life of the Bracero Program (1942–1964), the number of illegal aliens apprehended (approximately 5 million) was almost exactly the same as the number of legal workers imported under the system. Critics further claimed that the number of illegal aliens apprehended was considerably less than the number of Mexican workers illegally entering the United States.

Despite the end of the Bracero Program, Mexico continued to be a major source of legal immigrants to the United States. Changes in immigration laws, however, reduced Mexico's special status under earlier legislation. Until 1965 Mexico as a Western Hemisphere nation was exempt from any quota restrictions on legal immigration. In 1965 new legislation established a quota of 120,000 immigrants per year for the Western Hemisphere. In 1976 Mexico came under general restrictions limiting any single nation to a maximum of 20,000 immigrants a year. One of the most important changes involving immigration law took place in 1986 with the passage of the Immigration Reform and Control Act (IRCA). IRCA combined two important features: an amnesty provision for illegal immigrants and sanctions for employers who knowingly hired illegal aliens. Under the amnesty provisions, more than 1 million Mexicans illegally in the United States became legal residents with a

New braceros receive registration packets for temporary employment in the United States in 1943. (Howard R. Rosenberg, "Snapshots in a Farm Labor Tradition" *Labor Management Decisions,* Winter-Spring, 1993.)

process for becoming full citizens if they wished. Further changes in immigration laws in 1990 raised Mexico's annual quota to 25,620. Immigration legislation has also typically contained provisions providing for preferential admission of close relatives of U.S. citizens or those who have permanent resident status. Such preferences favor the legal admission of additional Mexicans not covered by the quota systems. The Legal Immigration and Family Equity Act, which went into effect in December 2000, continued and expanded on policies that favored legal Mexican immigration. The net effect of all of this legislation has been to make Mexico an important source of legal immigration to the United States.

Although Mexico figures prominently in terms of legal immigration, the focus in recent decades has been on illegal immigration from Mexico into the United States. Mexico experienced a series of economic and financial crises beginning in the 1970s at the same time that its population was expanding rapidly. The Mexican economy could not generate enough new jobs to absorb new entries into the workforce much less reduce the high rate of existing unemployment. These economic conditions pushed ever larger numbers of Mexicans north to find employment. The Mexican government publicly indicated that it considered this migration to be an important social "safety valve" for Mexico and had no intention of trying to stop it. Mexican workers entering the United States were violating U.S. law but were not doing anything illegal by Mexican standards. Those apprehended by U.S. authorities were typically returned to the border where they could easily recross into the United States. Since the passage of IRCA in 1986, employer sanctions have been in place, but these sanctions have been poorly enforced and do not impose any major legal penalties on the illegal immigrants themselves. Although IRCA caused a brief decline in illegal immigration from Mexico, the flow of illegal immigrants soon returned to pre-1986 levels, with U.S. officials making more than 1 million apprehensions a year.

In the late 1980s and early 1990s, discussions relating to the North American Free Trade Agreement (NAFTA) raised the issue of the flow of Mexican workers into the United States. Mexican officials hoped that NAFTA's provisions for a freer flow of goods and capital would also include a freer flow of labor. NAFTA, however, did not call for any major changes in immigration restrictions. With Vicente Fox's assumption of the presidency in 2000, there was renewed emphasis on reaching a new agreement on immigration. Fox came from the Mexican state of Guanajuato, which had a long history of sending large numbers of illegal workers to the United States. Fox called for a legalized, orderly, and circular flow of workers from Mexico to the United States and back. Fox met with President George W. Bush at Fox's ranch in Guanajuato in February 2001. The two agreed to the creation of a high-level commission on migration headed by the U.S. secretary of state and the Mexican minister of foreign relations. The events of September 11, 2001, however, shifted the emphasis to tighter control of immigration into the United States rather than easing controls. U.S. officials specifically cited the porous U.S.-Mexican border as a major security problem. A downturn in the U.S. economy after a lengthy period of prosperity also undercut support for more liberal immigration policies. The discussions of the special commission failed to produce any tangible results, and President Bush's push for Congress to pass immigration reform measures in 2006 and 2007 also failed. Instead, the Bush administration successfully sponsored the Secure Fence Act of 2006, which expanded border enforcement efforts. Following his election in 2008, President Barack Obama indicated his hope for immigration reform, but his administration as of this writing has not introduced any meaningful initiatives toward that end.

In contrast, the importance of remittances has prompted Mexican politicians to recognize the significance of immigrants in the United States. In 2005, for example, monies sent to Mexico from the United States reached a high point approaching $25 billion, more than the earnings generated by the Mexican tourist industry and second only to the foreign earnings from oil revenues. As a consequence, the Mexican government developed a program to utilize remittances toward improvement projects for the sending communities. Although the results have fallen short of expectations, the spending afforded by remittances has boosted local economies and has lessened poverty among an enormous number of Mexican households. During the U.S. recession of 2007–2010 the value of total remittances declined, but their importane to the Mexican economy remained. Moreover, in another show of the importance of immigration, the Mexican government has allowed Mexican citizens to vote in federal elections, and various states have passed legislation permitting their residents to vote in state and local elections (in both cases by casting their votes at Mexican consulates). In addition, 27 of Mexico's 31 states have established state agencies to assist immigrants in the United States. Most important, the federal government has also established an office to provide different types of programs for its citizens abroad, especially those in the United States.

New trends are evident in the nature of the flow of illegal immigrants to the United States. In the 1940s and 1950s, workers came from rural backgrounds generally seeking seasonal employment in American agriculture, primarily in the upper Midwest, the Pacific Northwest, and, most dramatically, in the Southwest, notably California. Those trends began to change in distinct ways in the 1960s, with the large-scale migration of rural people to Mexico's cities. As a result, more and more Mexican immigrants arrived from more urbanized backgrounds and with increasing concerns for improving not only their income but also their comparative material well-being. At the same time, the low-wage, low-skill service sector of the U.S. economy began to expand rapidly, particularly in California. As a consequence, a growing proportion of Mexican immigrants found employment in the restaurant, entertainment, and hospitality industries as cooks, waiters, food processors, custodians, hotel maids, and maintenance workers. By the 1970s, the vast majority of Mexican immigrants were working in nonagricultural jobs. Through such jobs, networks developed that facilitated an acceleration of the shift of immigrants toward areas with service-sector employment: ski resorts, beachside hotels, amusement parks, gaming sites, retirement communities, and the like. Thus, Mexican immigrants could be found working in Reno, Las Vegas, Anaheim, Seattle, San Diego, Scottsdale, Palm Springs, and many other cities in the western half of the United States. The relative ease in finding long-term nonagricultural employment combined with periodic spikes in border enforcement led to more Mexican immigrants staying for much longer periods of time than in the past. Moreover, the regional origins of Mexican immigrants have diversified, as opposed to the greatest numbers coming from western Mexico from states such as Guanajuato, Jalisco, Michoacán, and Zacatecas. Currently, virtually all of the states in Mexico have contributed to the flow of immigrants to the United States, most of them undocumented. Historically, Mexicans were the least likely of the major immigrant groups to seek U.S. citizenship. There is now a greater trend toward seeking citizenship, primarily because of the surge of nativist legislation since the early 1990s, as immigrants feel a sense of security with the acquisition of citizenship and its consequent civil rights protections. Furthermore, on the U.S. side of the border, there has also been a change in the destination points for Mexican immigrants. For example, there has been a clear slowing of the migratory flow to southern California, long a primary receiving site for Mexican immigrants, and

Arizona's Tough Immigration Bill

On April 19, 2010, the Arizona state legislature passed Arizona Senate Bill 1070 (SB 1070), the Support Our Law Enforcement and Safe Neighborhoods Act, and Arizona governor Jan Brewer signed the bill into law on April 23. The act, which provides for broader policing of illegal immigration by state and local law enforcement in Arizona, ignited a firestorm of controversy in the wake of its passage. On July 28, a day before it was scheduled to go into effect, U.S. district court judge Susan Bolton temporarily blocked key parts of the new law, including a provision that would require police to check a person's citizenship or immigration status at the time of a traffic stop, detention, arrest, or other police action if there is reasonable suspicion that the person is not a U.S. citizen or legal immigrant. Judge Bolton also put on hold a component that would make it a state crime for an immigrant to be without papers indicating legal immigration status. Though the law also includes several other provisions that attempt to crack down on illegal immigration in other ways, these elements provoked the most controversy, as critics charged that they mandate or reinforce racial profiling by police and will lead to unconstitutional infringement of the civil rights of many U.S. citizens. Supporters of the law claim that inadequate federal immigration enforcement has made such state-level measures necessary due to economic and safety concerns associated with illegal immigrants.

There has been significant public outcry against SB 1070, particularly by advocacy groups concerned about the prospect of targeted profiling of Hispanics, and boycotts have been organized in an effort to economically ostracize Arizona—even the governments of major U.S. cities like Los Angeles and San Francisco have terminated or stopped pursuing contracts with Arizona-based firms. Legal challenges to the law on constitutional grounds have also been filed by such civil rights groups as the American Civil Liberties Union, the National Association for the Advancement of Colored People, and the Mexican American Legal Defense and Educational Fund. On July 6, 2010, the U.S. Justice Department officially joined the fray and filed suit against the state of Arizona and Gov. Brewer, aiming to block enforcement of the new immigration law on the grounds that it usurps the federal government's authority on immigration policy. Even after Judge Bolton issued her injunction in response to this legal challenge, which Gov. Brewer has appealed in federal court, protesters against the law, in an act of civil disobedience, gathered in Phoenix on the morning it went into effect and blocked a street near city hall.

Arizona's new law and the events surrounding it have reenergized the national debate over immigration reform and drawn attention to a larger movement taking place in many states to expand upon federal efforts to combat illegal immigration. Several other state legislatures have had similar initiatives introduced or have passed laws like SB1070, including Mississippi, Indiana, and Alabama, among others.

Alex M. Saragoza, Ana Paula Ambrosi, and Silvia D. Zárate

a notable increase in a migratory flow to the South. Since the 1990s, spurred in part by the anti-immigrant legislation in California (Proposition 187), more and more Mexican immigrants have moved to nontraditional destination sites, such as North Carolina, Georgia, Arkansas, Tennessee, Nebraska, and Alabama, among other states. These states have been traditionally antiunion and have attracted companies and businesses looking to lower their labor costs.

As enforcement efforts have intensified, unauthorized immigrants increasingly depend on the services of so-called coyotes (professional smugglers of people) and take extraordinary risks in crossing the border. Recently, given the monies carried by immigrants to pay coyotes, the commerce in human smuggling has attracted the attention of drug gangs as a means of expanding their criminal activities. This trend has added an additional dangerous obstacle to undocumented immigrants, which has added another incentive for immigrants to return to Mexico much less frequently than in the past. (One of the outcomes of the border enforcement strategy of the Clinton administration that focused on the California-Mexico border, Operation Gatekeeper in 1994, induced many more immigrants to cross through the very rugged and extremely dry area along the Arizona-Mexico border, often with fatal results.) While officials in Mexico and the United States increasingly see migration as a permanent part of the bilateral relationship, there are a number of experts who believe that this migration must be viewed in a global context and not simply as a bilateral problem involving Mexico and the United States. As the economy has worsened as a result of the 2007–2010 recession, there has been a wave of nativism, with calls from local and state officials for the federal government to pursue a much tougher policy of enforcement at the border. Arizona passed a law in 2010 allowing law enforcement officers, for instance, to ask drivers to show proof of legal residence, although the law has been blocked by U.S. federal courts. Nonetheless, a number of other states have moved toward similar or more draconian measures, such as Georgia, Indiana, and Alabama.

Migration into Mexico While Mexican migration has typically been thought of in terms of outflows of population, migration into Mexico has also played an important role. For most of the 19th century, Mexico offered little to attract substantial foreign immigration. Chronic political instability scared off many potential immigrants. Mexico was also experiencing major financial and economic problems; in particular, the landholding system of Mexico, which concentrated land in the hands of a relatively small number of people, discouraged immigration. In attracting foreigners, Mexico found it difficult to compete with other hemispheric nations such as the United States, Canada, Brazil, and Argentina. Early government efforts to promote immigration proved unsuccessful or even disastrous as in the case of Texas in the 1820s and 1830s. The government of Porfirio Díaz (1877–1880, 1884–1911) viewed immigration as a key component in its larger program of modernization. The government provided land and financial support for a number of rural colonization schemes that were almost uniformly unsuccessful. There were also changes in land, mining, and immigration laws aimed at attracting more foreigners to Mexico. While these changes led to a growing foreign role in the economy, they did not bring in significant numbers of immigrants; certainly they did not attract enough immigrants to produce the "civilizing" effect on Mexican society envisioned by Díaz's policy makers. The Mexican census of 1895 indicated that the largest group of foreigners in Mexico were the Guatemalans, not the Europeans the Porfirian elite hoped to attract. The few immigrants who came tended to resist assimilation and tried to isolate themselves from the Mexican population; such foreign "enclaves or colonies" contributed little to the "uplifting" of Mexican society envisioned by the government. Díaz himself became disenchanted with the results of his efforts to promote immigration; in the closing years of his regime, he moved to a more restrictive immigration policy.

The outbreak of revolution in 1910 led to a lengthy period of political, economic, and social upheaval that not only discouraged immigration but also led to an exodus of foreigners from Mexico. The pronounced nationalist theme of the revolution often took on an antiforeign character, especially directed against U.S. and Spanish citizens. World War I (1914–1918) further interrupted international migration. The 1920s brought some political stability and national reconstruction, including a modest increase in immigration. The onset of the Great Depression of the 1930s caused further interruption in immigration to Mexico. Faced with a declining economy and the need to absorb some 500,000 Mexican workers repatriated from the United States, the Mexican government moved to a more restrictive immigration policy. The Mexican government wanted to block the influx of indigent immigrants who would only add to the country's financial and economic problems. This more restrictive policy had its exceptions. The administration of President Lázaro Cárdenas (1934–1940) did admit some Jewish refugees fleeing Nazi persecution in Europe and refugees from the civil war in Spain (1936–1939). The Spanish refugees in particular had an important influence on Mexico's cultural and intellectual life, as many remained permanently in Mexico. The advent of World War II led to further changes in immigration and to the partial breakdown of the foreign enclaves that had developed in earlier years. In particular the Mexican government—urged on by the United States—cracked down on activities by the Germans, Italians, and Japanese, even seizing their business operations after Mexico officially entered the war against the Axis powers. During the postwar period, there were further changes in Mexico's attitude toward immigration. Postwar administrations abandoned the idea that immigration could and should play a major role in economic development and modernization. The Ley General de Población (General Law of Population) passed in 1947 downplayed immigration and emphasized natural population growth as the key to Mexico's economic development. Instead of trying to attract foreign immigrants, emphasis was on promoting the return of Mexican nationals working outside the country, especially in the United States.

The law wanted to admit immigrants who could make an immediate, positive impact on the economy, not those who might compete with Mexicans for jobs. With both its population and its economic problems growing rapidly, Mexico further restricted immigration in 1973. The new legislation made it difficult for immigrants to get permanent work authorization; some groups such as foreign retirees and tourists were specifically prohibited from working while in Mexico. The Mexican government did admit political refugees, even permitting them to work; but this policy encountered problems in the 1980s when political and military upheavals in Central America sent large numbers of refugees into southern Mexico.

According to various sources, there are easily more than 1 million foreign citizens residing in Mexico. Of that number, nearly 1 million are U.S. citizens. (Many Americans have second homes in the country, live in Mexico for varying periods of time, and return periodically to the United States.) Those figures are dwarfed by the number of persons born in Mexico and living in the United States. Mexico is also an important transit point for non-Mexican workers; the Mexican government estimates that as many as 200,000 foreign workers a year pass through Mexico en route to a third country, usually the United States. In January 2002 officials in the Mexican state of Hidalgo detained 42 undocumented persons traveling through Mexico to the United States. Of the group, 25 were from Honduras, 14 from Guatemala, and 3 from El Salvador. The migration of workers—in a variety of forms—will continue to play an important role in Mexico's future.

The issue of immigration, specifically among those who are undocumented, has become highly politicized in the United States. There has been a large increase in legislation passed at the local and state levels of government that reflect concerns over the rights and status of undocumented immigrants in the United States; most have been nativist in character, from the imposition of fines on landlords who knowingly rent to unauthorized entrants to the barring of undocumented students at public colleges and universities. Several of these measures have been blocked by the courts or went unsigned by governors, rendering them null and void at least temporarily. Yet, the tenor of these legislative efforts has been decidedly anti-immigrant in nature, and they usually target immigrants from Latin America, primarily Mexicans. One key aspect of the political fallout from 9/11 has been the use of national security by nativists as a rationale for cracking down on the crossing of unauthorized immigrants into the United States, in addition to earlier nativist complaints based on alleged loss of jobs for U.S.-born workers, purported health risks to the American public, and putative increases in crime rates. Partisan politics has added to the heated debate on immigration, as candidates have exploited the issue for or against their opponents. As the 2012 presidential race develops in the United States, it is more than likely that the question of immigration, especially over the undocumented, will play a role in the campaign. For a large proportion of Hispanic voters, immigration has become a major issue that will pressure the Democratic Party in particular to take a cautious if not positive stance toward immigration reform, including initiatives to provide a path to legalization for undocumented immigrants presently in the United States. On the other hand, the Republican Party, generally speaking, has been much less enthusiastic toward accepting a change in immigration policy to accommodate what many within the party call "amnesty" for "illegals." Republican strategists are split on how to handle the issue, given the potent Hispanic vote in key electoral states. In short, immigration represents a complicated public policy issue that will not be easily resolved and will continue to be a thorn in relations between Mexico and the United States.

Don M. Coerver

See also Foreign Policy; Fox Quesada, Vicente; Income; North American Free Trade Agreement; Peasantry; Poverty; Social Structures, Class, and Ethnic Relations

Further Reading

Cardoso, Lawrence A. 1980. *Mexican Emigration to the United States, 1897–1931: Socio-Economic Patterns.* Tucson: University of Arizona Press.

Chomsky, Aviva. 2007. *"They Take Our Jobs"! And 20 Other Myths about Immigration.* Boston: Beacon.

Hoffman, Abraham. 1974. *Unwanted Mexican Americans in the Great Depression: Repatriation Pressures, 1929–1939.* Tucson: University of Arizona Press.

Massey, Douglas S., Jorge Durand, and Nolan J. Malone. 2002. *Beyond Smoke and Mirrors: Mexican Immigration in an Era of Economic Integration.* New York: Russell Sage Foundation.

"Mexican Immigrants in the United States, 2008." April 15, 2009. Pew Hispanic Center. http://pewresearch.org/pubs/1191/mexican-immigrants-in-america-largest-group.

Mexico, Consejo Nacional de Población [National Council on Population]. http://www.conapo.gob.mx/.

Overmyer-Velasquez, Mark. 2011. *Beyond la Frontera: The History of Mexico-U.S. Migration.* New York: Oxford University Press.

Regan, Margaret. 2010. *The Death of Josseline: Immigration Stories from the Arizona-Mexico Borderlands.* Boston: Beacon.

Reisler, Mark. 1976. *By the Sweat of Their Brow: Mexican Immigrant Labor in the United States, 1900–1940.* Westport, CT: Greenwood Press.

Income

Inequality marks the distribution of income in Mexico. In general, poverty afflicts about half of the Mexican population, and roughly one-fifth of the Mexican poor are considered to be in extreme poverty. On the other hand, a small proportion of the economically active population (10 percent) controls about 40 percent of the income of the country. If the economically active population is divided in quintiles, the two middle sectors earn about 35 to 40 percent of total national income. Thus, the majority of Mexican income earners, about 60 percent, receive approximately 20 percent of the remaining income. However, these overall figures disguise important variations, whereby six fundamental factors must be taken into account to have a better understanding of income distribution in the country.

First, there is an important distinction between income and wealth. Income is generally related to wages or salaries. Wealth, in addition to income, also includes assets of various sorts, such as savings, real estate, stocks, bonds, annuities, and additional sources of income apart from wages or salaries. In the case of Mexico, inequality is evident in terms of income earnings and in the distribution of wealth. Thus, the people most likely to be very wealthy are also the people most likely to have high incomes (as opposed to situations where individuals may have large estates and be wealthy in terms of landownership, but may have modest incomes due to the lack of high profits generated by their property).

Second, the gaps in income are strongly related to urban or rural differences as well as to geographic region. Poverty is particularly evident in rural Mexico, and more so in the countryside of the southern region than in northern or central Mexico. The states with the highest levels of poverty are generally in the south, for example, Oaxaca, Chiapas, and Quintana Roo. In urban areas, there is also severe poverty, particularly in the country's largest cities. Mexico City, for instance, possesses large numbers of extremely poor people, with insufficient access to basic needs such as adequate housing, sanitation, health care, and nutrition. For the very poor, mobility is also constrained by limited access to the means of socioeconomic improvement, such as adequate schooling; this is especially true in the poorest of rural areas.

In contrast, the very wealthy are much more likely to live in major cities, such as Monterrey, Nuevo León, Guadalajara, Jalisco, and most dramatically, Mexico City.

The middle-income sectors of Mexico are found throughout the country, though as a proportion of the population, the middle class is more visible in rural areas than in highly urbanized parts of the country. This is due to the fact that the working class is much more numerous in urban areas.

The geography of income distribution is also affected by the impact of globalization, international trade networks, and remittances from immigrants, particularly from those in the United States. Northern Mexico, for example, has been most positively impacted by the development of industry and manufacturing tied to exports to the United States and to other countries, notably after the onset of the North American Free Trade Agreement (NAFTA) in the early 1990s. Tourism, to give another example, affects Mexico unevenly. The coastal strip along the Yucatán Peninsula attracts large numbers of tourists, which generates service jobs for Mexicans in that area. In contrast, the state of Chiapas in southern Mexico has been basically untouched by new industrial or manufacturing investment, and tourism in that state has yet to have a major impact on local economic opportunities.

Remittances from Mexicans living abroad, primarily immigrants in the United States, have served to lessen poverty in those rural areas with high rates of migration. For instance, in 2007 about $25 billion was sent to Mexico from immigrants in the United States, providing economic relief for many poor families in rural Mexico. Still, rural Mexicans generally have limited access to good schools and teachers and other avenues of economic mobility.

In contrast, the urban middle class and the very affluent have access to the best schools in the country, primarily private, given the concentration of better educational resources in urban areas. Education is a key path to overcoming poverty, but that pathway for mobility reflects largely the same inequity found in income distribution.

A third factor in income distribution is type of employment. Formal employment derives from the private sector, which generates the most jobs. The public sector (primarily government workers) also produces a large proportion of jobs in Mexico. However, a substantial proportion of work takes place in the informal sector, such as domestic service, street vending, selling of artifacts and secondhand goods, temporary casual labor, and related types of labor. The people involved in the informal sector are generally paid low wages in cash or are self-employed, and most are not covered by basic health insurance or benefit plans. There is no unemployment insurance in Mexico.

A fourth issue to consider in understanding income inequality in Mexico is the importance of the business cycle, that is, the swings in the Mexican economy. In general, economic crisis tends to lessen the magnitude of income inequality, as the gap between the different income groups narrows, usually due to the erosion of income for middle-class sectors as a result of high inflation rates. For example, the economic downturn of the mid-1990s served to lessen the severity of income inequality. On the other hand, periods of economic growth have generally meant an overall increase in income inequality in Mexico due to the imbalance of the distribution of the benefits of economic prosperity.

A fifth factor is related to this last point, given the limited access to capital and credit in Mexico. The large swings in the Mexican economy, with a deep recession in the mid-1990s for instance, have made financial institutions reluctant to offer easy access to loans for housing, new business ventures, expansion of small to medium size enterprises, applying updated technology in agribusiness firms, or educational advancement. Those with sufficient assets and/or income, on the other hand, find that capital is generally easier to acquire, enabling the wealthy to leverage their position to extend their economic advantages. For example, beginning in the 1980s and on into the early 1990s, the Mexican government began to privatize a significant number of its enterprises. The people most able to bid for formerly government-controlled companies were those Mexicans who were already very wealthy. They had the means to gain vast amounts of capital in order to compete for assets previously in the hands of government. Thus, inequality in wealth distribution was exacerbated by the processes of privatization in Mexico. The dividends generated by the newly privatized companies also added to the inequity of income and wealth distribution.

A final consideration is the tax structure in Mexico. For decades, the government failed to levy a reasonable tax burden on the wealthy and on corporations, and tax collection enforcement was lax and inconsistent. As a result, wealthy Mexicans in particular were able to accrue large sums of income that were often turned into assets of various sorts and/or into investment capital. The current situation of income inequality reflects to a large extent the legacies of that long period of time in which government policy facilitated income inequality, though there were a few occasions in which government actions reduced the assets of the very wealthy—but those actions failed to change the basic disparities in income distribution and the sources of that inequality.

Mexico has endeavored to lessen poverty in the country through various means, such as the expansion of government social welfare programs, greater investments in public schooling, improvements in infrastructure, and efforts to better utilize remittances. Consequently, progress in lessening poverty in the country has taken place. Rates of extreme poverty have diminished since 2000 for many rural Mexicans in particular, but such progress has been less the case in urban Mexico. (The recession in the United States, especially during 2008–2009, led to a contraction of the Mexican economy, and poverty rates spiked as a consequence; remittances also declined as a result of recessionary conditions across the border.) On the other hand, recent tax reforms, including higher tax rates on the wealthy and on corporations, offer the promise of more government revenues to combat the root causes of poverty in Mexico and to reduce over time the wide disparities in income. There has also been an effort to provide more equitable access to low-interest loans as a means of stimulating the housing industry, which would allow lower middle-income earners to begin to build assets and credit resources.

Politics will play a major role in whether Mexico will undertake decisive policy initiatives to lessen income inequity. In the 2006 presidential elections, the candidate of the left-of-center party ran on a platform based to a large extent on issues related to the lack of equitable income distribution, and he came within a whisker of winning that election. The razor-thin margin of victory prodded the winner, President Felipe Calderón (2006–2012), to push for more social spending on the poor and for the tax reforms noted earlier. To what extent Mexico will in fact lessen income inequality substantially will depend on the reforms and policies of the Mexican government. Basic changes in income distribution will also depend decisively on the ability of Mexico to sustain a stable economy.

Alex M. Saragoza

See also Debt, Foreign; Feminism; Immigration and Emigration; Maquiladoras; North American Free Trade Agreement; Peasantry; Poverty; Racism; Social Structures, Class, and Ethnic Relations

Further Reading

Levy, Santiago, and Michael Walton, eds. 2009. *No Growth without Equity? Inequality, Interests, and Competition in Mexico.* New York: Palgrave MacMillan.

Ruiz, Ramon Eduardo. 2010. *Mexico: Why So Few Are Rich and the People Poor.* Berkeley: University of California Press.

Indigenous Culture

The term "indigenous" has been often used to refer to what is local or native (commonly referred to as *indio* in English Indian or *indígena* in Spanish). In this respect, when speaking of Mexico's indigenous cultures the term refers to descendants of the first settlers of the geopolitical entity known as Mexico. Like most of the countries of the American continent, Mexico was inhabited by several different local groups before the arrival of Europeans in the 16th century. The Spanish Conquest, colonial system, and imposition of Catholicism failed to erase native belief systems. Instead a variety of adaptations of ideas, beliefs, and practices involving the original cultural forms of indigenous peoples ensued. For decades, scholars used the concept of syncretism to explain this process. However, the term preferred in Spanish is *transculturación* ("dynamic exchange of beliefs and practices among cultural systems"), which is more akin to the concept of contact cultures or even cultural hybridization than that of syncretism, which implies a complete merging of two cultures into a distinctive third culture.

Today, 12 percent of the country's 120 million people belong to one of the different ethnic groups, speaking up to 60 different indigenous languages. The members of those communities currently identified as indigenous are bounded by shared social and cultural beliefs and practices that constitute a specific "ethnic identity." Their group identity is self-defined and also recognized by the rest of Mexican society as distinct. Some Mexicans even consider such ethnic identity to be "alien" to mainstream Mexican culture. The rich cultural diversity within Mexico has been valued in different ways throughout Mexican history. For example, the Mexican government, particularly since the 1920s, has invested enormously in the conservation of important native archaeological sites, their history and their traditions. Paradoxically, the indigenous communities of Mexico are among the most politically marginalized, and their integration into Mexican society is a source of debate.

There are three points that need to be taken into consideration for an understanding of indigenous culture in Mexico. First, a historical review of the nation's multiethnic development shows how 19th-century and postrevolutionary nationalism took advantage of the notion of "indigenous culture" to construct the "official" concept of a Mexican national identity and, at the same time, subjected indigenous peoples to public policies aimed at assimilating them into mainstream mestizo (mixed-blood) society and culture. Second, the cultural reproduction of these different ethnic groups and the strategies they employed to cope with external changes that resulted in complex and varying responses must be acknowledged. Finally, the intricacies of interethnic relations, often overlooked, illuminate some of the current issues raised by Indian-based political movements like the Ejército Zapatista de Liberación Nacional (Zapatista Army for National Liberation, EZLN), the guerrilla movement that arose in Chiapas in 1994.

The eruption of the EZLN marked a turning point in the way in which indigenous groups were understood in contemporary Mexico. With ski masks, machetes, and rifles, the Zapatistas claimed five centuries of oppression and demanded that the indigenous voice of Mexico be heard. The Zapatista position was based on the notion of an autonomous self-definition for Indians and their right to be considered distinct political subjects. This indigenous movement questioned the prevailing political order, making itself visible to the world through different discursive strategies that have influenced other indigenous groups in Mexico and Latin America.

Indigenous cultures in historical perspective Mexican national history begins in primary school textbooks with the migration of different Náhuatl-speaking groups from the north to the fertile and prosperous central highlands of Mexico's plateau between the 12th and 13th centuries. According to the origins myth of Mexico-Tenochtitlán later propagated by Aztec rule, these groups were prompted to migrate and resettle by prophecies of a promised land, which they would recognize upon the sighting of an eagle devouring a serpent, atop a cactus that stood on a rock in the middle of a lake. This image became in time the national emblem. By 1428, Mexico-Tenochtitlan had become the most important cultural center in Mesoamerica through conquest and domination. Using economic and military action, the Aztecs brought groups to the west and the northeast of the Aztec capital under their rule.

With the retelling of the story of the origin of Mexico-Tenochtitlán Náhua identity is privileged as the founding indigenous culture of Mexico. Náhua culture was dominant over the other indigenous groups of Mesoamerica until 1521, when the Spanish and their Indian allies crushed the Aztec empire and established Spanish colonial rule. However, indigenous cultures in the period prior to the conquest were limited to the central region of the country or entirely subject to Náhuatl-speaking peoples. Archaeological research and material culture remains document that other groups occupied parts of the territory. Among these indigenous groups were the Tlapanec, Mixtec, Zapotec, and Mixe of the western coastal region; the Tarascan and Otomí of the central and northwestern regions; the Cuicatec and Mazatec of the central portion of the country; the Popoloca on the eastern coast (in what today is the state of Veracruz); the Yucatec Mayans in the Yucatán Peninsula; the Tzitzil, Tzeltal, Tojolabal, Zoque, Jacaltec, Quiché, Cakchiquel, and Chorti of the southwest (in what today is the state of Chiapas and the country of Guatemala); and the Tototac, Tepehuas, and Cuextecas of the Northeast.

According to Luis Villoro (1950), the official attitude toward indigenous populations can be summed up through the 20th century concept of *indigenismo* (a cultural, political, and anthropological school of thought dedicated to the study of the indigenous cultures and their appraisal). Public policy regarding Indians has existed since the 16th century when religious officials debated the prospect of Indians having souls and thus being redeemable through conversion to Catholicism or lacking them and therefore deserving being treated as animals and slaves. This theological controversy pitted Cardinal Juan Ginés de Sepúlveda against Friar Bartolomé de Las Casas in Valladolid, Spain, in 1550. Las Casas defended the rights of the Indians and won the debate, establishing the responsibility of Spain to convert them and condemning abuses made on the Indians by the *encomienda* ("trusteeship labor system") in New Spain. For some time Las Casas believed that slaves should be imported from Africa as a source of labor instead of exploiting the Indians so terribly.

Colonial society was divided into different pseudoracial categories known as *castas* ("castes") that accommodated every possible combination between Indians, Africans, and Spanish and descendants of these mixes. Class differences also cut across racial boundaries and reaffirmed different positions in the social hierarchy.

Official Spanish colonial policy toward Indians was premised on their integration as Spanish subjects, i.e., their assimilation. Indigenous groups reacted to and coped with the processes of adaptation differently depending on a number of factors. The two most important factors were the religious orders that settled in specific indigenous areas and the negotiated agreements between local Indian groups and Spanish authorities. The Indians adopted some Spanish customs and beliefs and also kept some of their own in a transformative process. They did not fully assimilate to Spanish culture, but rather constructed new social structures, cosmologies, and power relations within their communities, which led to new ethnic identities. Struggles and resistance by Indian peoples also took place. There were areas where colonial rule was particularly oppressive and cruel and sometimes aided by the local priests, provoking Indians to defend themselves. Land tenure and settlement strategies were also important as a means of dominance over the indigenous populations. Indians who had lived in dispersed settlements were grouped and reorganized into towns and granted land tenure but were "trusted" to a Spanish guardian through commendation ceremonies.

The 19th century was a period of intense conflict in Mexican history. The struggle for independence from Spain began in 1810 and ended in 1821. The birth of Mexico as a nation-state actually intensified the problems of the Indians. Communally held lands, which helped indigenous communities sustain a sense of ethnic identity, were challenged by the new order. Liberal ideology and the creed of private ownership argued against communal holding and held that such practices were backward and unsuitable for a modern economy. Haciendas, large land holdings in the hands of very few rich criollos ("persons of 'pure' Spanish descent"), became the rule, sometimes at the expense of communal lands. For Indians independence meant a change of power in which their everyday situations remained much the same or became even worse. However, it is also in this period that the historic Indian began to be revalorized as an ideological response to the Spanish colonial legacy. The splendor of ancient Indian civilizations became part of the nationalist discourse with which the leaders of independence attempted to unify the newborn nation and give it a national identity. But while the historic Indian was being redeemed, the living one was despised and more oppressed than ever. Abuses of indigenous populations lead to ethnic struggles and uprisings. The bloodiest and longest lasting rebellions began in 1847 and ended in 1901 in the south and north of the country: the Guerra de Castas (Caste Wars) in the Yucatán Peninsula, and the Yaqui rebellion in the north.

By the time of the Mexican Revolution of 1910 the situation of the indigenous population was not much better. They had been systematically ignored and regarded only insofar as they were considered a hindrance to national integration. With the proclamation of the new constitution in 1917, it became apparent to politicians and the military alike that something had to be done with the living Indians. Their material culture was considered an asset (Indian art, dance, music, and dress) that made Mexico unique and different in the eyes of foreign nations. This valorization implied a certain continuity with the majestic past embodied in the great ruins dispersed throughout the territory, but it was also an obstacle for the consolidation of a truly new Mexican identity. The postrevolutionary order predominantly viewed indigenous cultures as inferior and backward. From the 19th century to at least the middle of the 20th century the concept of "evolutionism" was employed in assimilating the Indians into the larger mestizo society. In order to achieve greater evolution, most government-sponsored programs were concerned with incorporation and "deindianization." During the 20th century, Mexico faced three key issues regarding its indigenous communities that became known as the question of *indigenismo:* first, how best to integrate indigenous communities into Mexican society; second, what government programs and policies would best serve these communities and their interests; and third, to what extend would Mexico incorporate its indigenous heritage into the construction of a national identity. One way to achieve the goal of homogenization and integration was extending the use of Spanish as a national language and not allowing the Indians to speak their own language. Throughout the 20th century, the indigenous populations were subject to different indigenist policies.

The official agency that dealt with the promotion and defense of indigenous peoples' cultural, legal, and political rights was the Instituto Nacional Indigenista (National Indigenous Institute, INI), founded in 1948. In 2003, the Comisión Nacional para el Desarrollo de los Pueblos Indígenas (Commission for the Development of the Indigenous peoples, known for its initials in Spanish as CDI) replaced the INI. Indigenous cultures have gained recognition of their diversity and right to self-determination even under constitutional law. However, this acknowledgment of the value of indigenous cultures remains more symbolic than tangible in changing attitudes and establishing different power relations with the state and non-Indian civil society. Mexico seems to be moving slowly away from the paradigm of viewing indigenous cultures as traditional, immobile, and unchangeable. Still, ambiguity is a common attitude toward indigenous cultures, which are regarded on the one hand as profoundly rich and a proud heritage, but on the other as ultimately backward.

Indigenous peoples have moved away from the stereotypes formed in the early 20th century and transformed their cultures while at the same time maintaining their own cultural specificities. The most salient outward signs of indigenous identity (ethnicity) are dress, language, means of production, and economic activities. Most indigenous cultures are still agrarian societies, use traditional ethnic dress, and speak an Indian language. Today language is one of the strongest aspects binding indigenous cultures and in some places is being revitalized and used in modern literary forms.

In the 21st century certain indigenous groups continue to fight for an autonomous self-definition. The governments of Ernesto Zedillo (1994–2000), Vicente Fox (2000–2006), and Felipe Calderón (2006–2012) recognized the "indigenous problematic" and addressed it in their political agendas. Nevertheless, these efforts have failed to resolve the question of the status of indigenous people in Mexico.

Deborah Dorotinsky Alperstein

See also Archaeological Sites; Art Market; Cultural Policies; Culture and the Government; Ejército Zapatista de Liberación Nacional and the Indigenous Movement; El Museo Nacional de Antropología; Folklore Culture; Folk Music; Indigenous Peoples; Nationalism and National Identity; Racism; Social Structures, Class, and Ethnic Relations

Further Reading

Gossen, Gary H., ed. 1986. *Symbol and Meaning beyond the Closed Community: Essays in Mesoamerican Ideas.* Albany: Institute for Mesoamerican Studies, University at Albany, State University of New York.

Hidalgo, Margarita, ed. 2006. *Mexican Indigenous Languages at the Dawn of the Twenty-First Century.* Berlin; New York: Mouton de Gruyter.

Martínez Novo, Carmen. 2006. *Who Defines Indigenous?: Identities, Development, Intellectuals, and the State in Northern Mexico.* New Brunswick, NJ: Rutgers University Press.

Peña Martínez, Francisco de la. 2002. *Los hijos del sexto sol: Un estudio etnopsicoanalítico del eovimiento de la mexicanidad.* Mexico City: Instituto Nacional de Antropología e Historia.

Stanford, Thomas. 1966. *A Linguistic Analysis of Music and Dance Terms from Three Sixteenth-Century Dictionaries of Mexican Indian Languages.* Austin: Institute of Latin American Studies, University of Texas at Austin.

Villoro, Luis. 1950. *Los principales momentos del Indigenismo en México.* Mexico City: El Colegio de México.

Indigenous Peoples

Twelve percent of Mexico's 120 million people belong to one of the ethnic native groups that represent approximately 60 different indigenous languages. Indigenous groups are commonly classified linguistically in Mexico, as opposed to by tribes. All of the Indian languages spoken in Mexico belong to 11 linguistic families: Algic, Yuto-Náhuatl, Cochimi-Yumana, Seri, Oto-Mangue, Maya, Totonaco-Tepehua, Tarasca, Mixe-Zoque, Chontal from Oaxaca, and Huave. The following is an annotated listing of the indigenous groups classified in contemporary Mexico that includes an estimated number for each group from Mexican census figures, their commonly known name in Spanish, and their term of self-identification.

Aguacatecos, Cakchiqueles, Ixiles, Kekchíes, Tecos, Quichés   From the 16th century until Mexican independence in 1821 Chiapas was a province of the Capitanía (a territory that is under the governance of a military capitan) of Guatemala. In 1824, the province was incorporated into the Mexican Republic. Members of these ethnic groups of Maya origin still move between Guatemala and Mexico, particularly since 1981, when thousands of Indians fled Guatemala due to the violence generated by internal civil strife during that decade. These new Maya groups appeared in the 2000 census and were considered refugees; in 1984 and 1985 several communities were resettled in the states of Quintana Roo and Campeche.

Amuzgo   Members of this group identify themselves with different names. For example, those from the community of San Pedro Amuzgos call themselves Tzjon Noan, which in their language means "peoples of the thread," and their linguistic family belongs to the Otomangue branch. This group of about 40,000 is found primarily along the border of the states of Guerrero and Oaxaca.

Chatinos   Self-identified as Kitse Cha'tnio, Chatinos are concentrated in the southern Sierra Madre in the state of Oaxaca and number around 40,000 people.

Chichimeca Jonaz   This tiny group of less than 2,000 members refers to themselves and to any other person of Indian origin as Úza Indian, or Ézari Indians. Members of this group live mainly in the municipality of San Luis de la Paz in the state of Guanajuato.

Chinantecos   Self-defined as Tza ju jmí, or "people of ancient word," this group is clustered in the northeastern part of the state of Oaxaca. Specialists agree that there are various Chinantec dialects, and those who speak the Chinantec languages number around 134,000.

Chochos   They call themselves Runixa Ngiigua, meaning "those who speak the language," and less than 600 remain in the state of Oaxaca.

Choles   This group straddles the area along the border of the states of Chiapas and Tabasco. Chol speakers call themselves Winik, a Maya dialect meaning "men" or "the men who make corn." Their population is estimated to be about 160,000.

Chontales from Oaxaca   Chontal is the name by which this group has been known since pre-Columbian times, derived from Chontalli, a Náhuatl word that means foreigner. Sometimes they have been called Tequistlatecos to distinguish them from a totally different group, the Chontales from Tabasco State. They name themselves as Slijuala Xanuc, meaning "dwellers of the mountains." Speakers of Chontal from Oaxaca number about 5,000 and are concentrated in the southeastern part of the state. Their languages are part of the Tequistlateca family, Hokano branch, like many North American indigenous languages.

Chontales from Tabasco   They refer to themselves as Yokot'an or Yokot'anob. This Maya-speaking group of about 40,000 resides primarily in the state of Tabasco.

Cochimí, Cucapá, Kiliwa, Kumiai, Paipai   These five groups, which share a common origin, are found in the northern part of Baja California. They are named according to the specific area from which they originate. The entire collection of these very small linguistic groups numbers less than 700. Cochimí and Kumiai are called dwellers of the plateau, Cucapá are known as river people, and Paipai and Kiliwa are called Southerners. Cochimí call themselves M'Ti-pa; Cucapá self-identify as Es-pei; and Kiliwa refer to themselves as Ko'Lew, or "hunting man." Kumiai designate themselves as Ti'pai, and their language is known as Kamia, Kmuyai, or Kemiaia. Paipai name themselves Akiwa'al or Akiwa Alax.

Coras   This group self-identifies as Nayeri, although each Cora community receives a different proper name as a group; for example, those from Mesa del Nayar call themselves Yohke. The Coras are concentrated in the northeast of the state of Nayarit (which they share with other ethnic groups like the Huicholes, Mexicaneros, Tepehuanes, and mestizos), and their population is estimated at about 15,000 nationwide. The Cora language derives from the Yuto-Náhuatl linguistic branch and together with Huichol, it composes the Cora-Chol linguistic family.

Cuicatecos   This ethnic group was apparently named by the Mexicas from a nahua word, *cuicatl,* which means song, after the group's area of residence, called Cuicatl, or "place of the song." The languages of the Cuicateros are Dvacu, Ndudu, Induudu Yu, or also Davaacu Yañ'e Yu, and they derive from the Mixtec family, Otomangue branch. The overwhelming majority of this group of about 13,000 is found in the state of Oaxaca.

Guarijíos   This group refers to themselves as Mucurawe or Maoragü, meaning "those who grab the land." Numbering less than 2,000 in population, they are found along the boundary between the states of Sonora and Chihuahua. Their language belongs to the Taracahita family, Yuto-Náhuatl branch.

Huastecos   They identify themselves as Teenek, meaning "the men from here." A branch of the Mayan language, Huasteco is the only one from this linguistic family separated geographically from the territory usually occupied by Maya-speaking peoples (Yucatán Peninsula, Chiapas, and Guatemala). This group is concentrated in the northeastern part of the state of San Luis Potosí. There are about 150,000 Huasteco speakers nationwide.

Huaves   Huazantecos, or Huave, is a term used pejoratively by Zapotec Indians to designate "those who rot in humidity," making the Huave reluctant to identify with this appellation. They prefer to call themselves Mero 'Ikooc, and less than 15,000 are clustered long the Pacific coastal area of the state of Oaxaca known as the Gulf of Tehuantepec. Huave has no linguistic relationship to any other Meso-american language.

Huicholes   They identify themselves as Wirrarica, plural Wirraritari. Approximately 16,000 Huicholes are spread among the states of Jalisco, Nayarit, Zacatecas, and Durango. Their language is known as Huxarica or Tejí Niukiyari; it belongs to the Yuto-Náhuatl branch, Cora-chol linguistic family. Huicholes are famous for their ritual activities, which according to some experts help them maintain a very vital ethnic identity. Traditional Huichol attire, such as their beautifully embellished hats and dresses, and artwork are highly valued.

Ixcatecos   The name of this group derives from an area named Ixcatlán by Náhuatl speakers, meaning "place of cotton." The Ixcatec language belongs to the Otomangue branch, Popoloca family, and less than 400 speakers of this remain in the state of Oaxaca.

Jacaltecos   This dialect, Abxubal, belongs to the Maya linguistic branch, Macro-Kanjobal family. The Spanish name of this group probably derives from two Ñáhuatl terms, *xahcalli* and *teco,* meaning "owner of the hut or house." The Jacaltecos originally migrated from Guatemala due to the violence there in the 1980s, and they have settled in Mexico as refugees. Fewer than 600 Jacalteco speakers can be found in Mexico.

Kanjobale   Originally from Guatemala, this group of about 9,000 arrived in Mexico through migration as refugees. Their language belongs to the Macro-Kanjobal family, Maya branch.

Kikapúes   Self-identified as Kikaapoa, meaning "those who walk on the land," this group is found along the U.S.-Mexican border. Most live on the American side, and less than 200 are found in Mexico.

Lacandones   The name of this group in Chorti language derives from the term *tacam-tum*, meaning "the great boulder" or "standing boulder." Lancandon was used during colonial times to designate most of the non-conquered peoples that fled into the jungle. Present-day Lacandones call themselves Hach-winik, meaning "true men." Hach Tan or Hach T'an, the Lacandones language, belongs to the Maya branch of the Yucatec linguistic family. The 1,000 or so speakers of this language are originally from the Guatemalan Petén and the Yucatán Peninsula, and they migrated to the jungles of the state of Chiapas, where they interact with other ethnic groups, like the Choles and Tzeltales.

Mam   This group's name derives from Quiché *mam*, meaning "father, grandfather, or kin." About 8,000 Mam speakers are clustered along the border of Mexico and Guatemala.

Matlatzinca   Mexicas named this group Matlatzincas for the mainstay of their livelihood: fishing on the lagoons of the Lerma River region. Once a dense population, this group was devastated by the impacts of Spanish colonialism and the dislocation caused by changes in the 19th century. Only a handful of this group survives in the community of San Francisco in the municipality of Temascaltepec. The Matlatzinca dialect has practically disappeared; only very old people and a few children can speak this language that belongs to the Otomangue branch of the Otopame linguistic family.

Mayas   With about 700,000 spread through the states of Campeche, Yucatán, and Quintana Roo, this ethnic group is among the largest in Mexico.

Mayos   This group identify themselves as Yoremes, meaning "the people who respect tradition," and they are found primarily in parts of the states of Sinaloa and Sonora. There are about 30,000 speakers of Chaita or Yoreme from the Yuto-Náhuatl branch.

Mazahuas   Self-identified as Jñatjo, they number about 130,000 and represent one of the largest ethnic groups in Mexico. Concentrated in the State of México, the Mazahua speak a language from the Otopame linguistic family, Otomangue branch.

Mazatecos   Mazatec is a tonal language characterized by its many local variants. Mazatecos call themselves Ha Shuta Enima, which means "those who work the land, humble people of traditions." Approximately 200,000 speakers of Mazateco, or O Chota Te Ho, are found mainly in the state of Oaxaca, but they are also present in the states of México, Puebla, and Veracruz as well as Mexico City. Their language is from the Popoloca linguistic family, Otomangue branch.

Mexicaneros   They are a small Náhuatl-speaking group mainly found in the state of Nayarit, though some live in the state of Durango.

Mixes   This group of about 120,000 name themselves Hayuuk Jä'äy, meaning "people of adorned language." They are concentrated in the state of Oaxaca and their language, known as Ayuuk or Ayook, is from the Mixe-Zoque linguistic family. They are well known as gifted musicians.

Mixtecos   Naming themselves Ñuu Savi, meaning "peoples from the rain," Mixtecos are mainly found in the Mixteca region of the state of Oaxaca. A large number also live in the neighboring state of Guerrero; it is estimated that their population is about 450,000. Many Mixtecos migrate seasonally to work as agricultural or construction workers both within Mexico and in the United States.

Motozintlecos or Mochos   This tiny group of less than 200 call themselves Mochos, which in their language means "there is none." The term Motozintlecos comes from the name of the town Motozintla in the state of Chiapas. The language of this group, Mocho, or Qatok, is classified as part of the Maya linguistic branch, Macro Kanjobal family. Although the people were thought to be extinct, researchers from the Museum of Anthropology in Mexico City discovered in 1967 that there were still a few speakers of this dialect.

Otomíes   Concentrated in the Mezquital Valley, they name themselves Hñä HÑü, meaning "those who speak a nasal language," while those from the adjacent region call themselves N'hyühü. Most of the country's 290,000 Otomíes are clustered in communities in the states of Puebla, Hidalgo, Veracruz, México, and Querétaro. The language of the Otomíes derives from the Otomangue branch, Otopame linguistic family.

Pames   Self-identified as Xi'ui, meaning "Indian" (that is, those that are non-mestizo descendants), the Pames speak a language that is part of the Otomangue branch of the Otopame linguistic family. Of the nation's 8,000 or so Pames, most live in the states of Querétaro and San Luis Potosí.

Pápagos   The Pápago name themselves Tohono O'otham, meaning "people of the desert." The term Pápago has been used since the 19th century to differentiate them from the Pimas. The Papagos straddle the border between the Mexican state of Sonora and the U.S. state of Arizona. Less than 400 remain on the Mexican side of the border, in contrast to the 20,000 or so that call the Sells reservation in the United States their home. The Pápago language, also known as High Pima, Himeri, or Tono-ooh'tam, is classified in the Pimana linguistic family, Yuto-Náhuatl branch.

Pimas Self-named O'ob, meaning "the people," the less than 800 Pima Yecoras that have survived live in the states of Sonora and Chihuahua (at one time there were three distinct Piman groups). The Pima language derives from the Yuto-Náhuatl branch, Pimana linguistic family.

Popolocas This group is found in the state of Puebla, scattered in three distinct areas, and speaks separate variants of the Popoloca language. Approximately 15,000 speakers remain in Mexico. Popoloca is a Mexica term, alluding to all those peoples who did not speak Náhuatl languages, and it held a pejorative connotation of barbarity and lack of intelligence. Popoloca is a tonal language from the Otomangue branch, Popoloca linguistic family.

Populucas This group tends to identify themselves with the name Populuca, rather than with the terms Núntaha 'yi, Tuncapxe, Yaac avu, Nuntajuyi, or Anmati, words that denote their linguistic affiliation. They have also been called Olmecas, Zoque-Populucas, and Mixe Populucas. The Populuca language derives from the Mixe-zoque branch. The 40,000 or so Populucas regard themselves as "sons of *Homshuk*," the god of maize.

Purépechas They call themselves P'urhépechas, which means "the people," and their population of about 120,000 is concentrated in the mountainous lake region of the state of Michaocán. Their language, P'urhé, also known as Porhe, Tarasco, Purhépecha, or Purépecha, has no linguistic relation to any of the other indigenous languages spoken in Mexico.

Seris The Seris call themselves Konkaak, which means "the people." In present-day Mexico less than 500 Seri speakers can be found along the desert coastal edge of the state of Sonora and on Tiburon Island. Their language is from the Hokano branch, Tequistlateca linguistic family, and still possesses much vitality, as they make up new words in Seri to name new cultural elements that have entered their lives.

Tacuates Numbering no more than about 2,000, the Tacuates are concentrated in the southwestern part of the state of Oaxaca in the Mixteca coastal region. Specialists dispute the origins of the term Tacuate; some propose that it derives from the Náhuatl term *tacoatl,* for "land of serpents," and that mispronunciation in Spanish turned it into Tacuate. Other experts believe that Tacuate comes from the Mixteco language and has a pejorative connotation.

Tarahumaras They name themselves Rarámuris, meaning "foot runners," and are found primarily in the region where the three states of Chihuahua, Durango, and Sonora come together. There is some disagreement about the number of this group, with estimates ranging from about 80,000 to 100,000 Tarahumaras in Mexico. The language is from the Yuto-Náhuatl Taracahita linguistic branch.

Tepehuanos   This group was divided into two communities during the colonial era and that division has continued into present-day Mexico, with one group concentrated in the state of Chihuahua (the Ódami) and the other in Durango (self-identified as O'dam, meaning "people"). The term Tepehuano is a Náhuatl word meaning "people from the mountains" and was adopted during the colonial era. Tepehuano speakers number approximately 25,000, and the language belongs to the linguistic branch Yuto-Náhuatl or Yuto-Náhuatl, Pimana family.

Tepehuas   This group refers to itself as Kitndkanmakalkaman, or "we are the ones from the Tepehua language," or Hamauspini, "owners of the hills." Their language is also known as Chahuindi, Hamasipini, or Lhimak'alhk'ama. Part of the Tototano-Tepehua linguistic family, together with Totonaco, the language is spoken by about 9,000 people scattered among the states of Veracruz, Puebla, and Hidalgo.

Tlahuicas   This very small linguistic group of less than 500 is found in the state of México in the community of San Juan Atzingo. The Tlahuica, or Runujinara in their own language, speak Atzinca, which is part of the Otomangue branch, Otopame linguistic family, but has affinities with the Mtlazinca language.

Tlapanecos   Náhuatl-speaking peoples named them Tlapaneco due to their main site of concentration, Tlapa. The group, however, prefers to be called Mbo Me'phaa, meaning "he who is a resident of Tlapa." This group is found mainly in the coastal area of the state of Guerrero and on the southern range of the Sierra Madre, where about 100,000 are concentrated. Their language, known also as M'phoa or Me'Phaa, is a tonal dialect and belongs to the Subitiaba-Tlapaneca linguistic family of the Otomangue branch.

Tojolabales   This group calls itself Tojolwinik'otik, or "true or legitimate men," but they are commonly referred to by one of the names of their language, Tojolabal, Chanabal, or Chaneabal. Located primarily in and around the municipality of Las Margaritas in the state of Chiapas, the Tojolabales form a community of about 38,000. Their Mayan language is part of the Macro-Kanjobal linguistic family.

Totonacas   This group's name literally means "three hearts," and it alludes to the three religious centers guiding their culture: Tajín, Cempoala, and Castillo de Teayo. Together with the Tepehua language, Totonaca belongs to the Totonaca-Tepehua linguistic family. There are approximately 240,000 speakers of the language in the states of Puebla and Veracruz.

Triquis   Triqui is a Spanish corruption of the dialect Driqui, which in Triqui language means "supreme lord." It was used by the Indians to name their lords, but the Spanish applied the term to identify the group, though they call themselves Tinujei, meaning "my brother." They are clustered in the Mixteca region of the state of Oaxaca. The tonal Triqui language, also known as Trique, Drique, Drique, Driqui, Nanj n'n, Tinujei, Sii man, Chuman'a, and Nanjn'i, belongs to the Mixteca linguistic family, Otomangue branch.

Tzeltales   Self-identified as Winik Atel, meaning "working men," this group's language belongs to the Maya linguistic branch, Macro-Tzeltal linguistic family. The language is also known as C'op and Tzendal. It is considered one of the richest indigenous languages of Mexico, as it has no dialectal variants of significance and is spoken by nearly 300,000 people. The Tzeltales are concentrated in the state of Chiapas, where large numbers have settled in the Lacandon rain forest.

Tzotziles   They call themselves Bats'il winik, or "true men." Their language is classified as Bats'il kop, Batz'il c'op, Chamula, Huixteco, Quelen, Totik, or Jchi'iltic and belongs to the Maya branch, Macro-Tzeltal linguistic family. There are approximately 300,000 Tzotziles in the country, but most are located in the central highlands of the state of Chiapas.

Yaquis   Long known for their defiance and resistance to outsiders (*yori* in their language), the country's 13,000 or so Yaquis are concentrated in the state of Sonora. Their language, Cahita, Yaqui, or Yoreme, is part of the Taracahita linguistic family, Yuto-Náhuatl branch. The Yaqui call themselves Yoreme, a term meaning "person or man."

Zapotecs   The term Zapoteca derives from the Náhuatl Zapotecatl language, which the Spanish adopted as a means of referring to this group. They call themselves Binnizá, meaning "people who came from the clouds," Bene Xon, or Ben'zaa, depending on the specific region in the state of Oaxaca from which they originate. They are the largest ethnic group in the state, numbering about 450,000. There are several Zapotec languages that belong to the Chatina-Zapoteca linguistic family, Otomangue branch.

Zoque   They refer to themselves as O'de Püt, "people of language," and number about 50,000, located primarily in the states of Oaxaca and Chiapas. Their language comes from the Mixe-Zoque linguistic family.

Zoques de Chimalapas   This is the name given to the Zoques living in the Chimas region of the state of Oaxaca. They call themselves Angpøn in their own language, which is a dialect related to the Mixe and its variants, known as the Mixe-Zoque linguistic family.

Deborah Dorotinsky Alperstein

See also Indigenous Culture

Further Reading

Comisión Nacional Para el Desarrollo de Los Pueblos Indígenas. www.cdi.gob.mx.

J

Jalisco

The official coat of arms of Jalisco. (Corel)

Of Mexico's 31 states, Jalisco is undoubtedly one of the most important in the country's history. Jalisco sits in the rich agricultural basin called the *bajío* in the center-west of Mexico. Among the largest states in Mexico (ranked sixth in size), Jalisco is bordered to its west by the Pacific Ocean and is surrounded by the neighboring states of Colima, Michoacán, Guanajuato, San Luis Potosí, Zacatecas, Aguascalientes, and Nayarit. Because of its size, the state possesses a highly diverse climate and topography and corresponding biodiversity as well. Two mountain ranges traverse the state, and it also has an extensive temperate plateau as well as a tropical coastal area. Jalisco boasts the largest and easily most famous lake, Lake Chapala, which has been the site of numerous films and television shows. Rainfall is moderate in much of the state, feeding the various streams and providing ample water for agricultural pursuits. Since its founding, Jalisco has been identified as the breadbasket of Mexico because of its abundant agricultural production. It is also associated with iconic aspects of Mexican culture, notably the liquor tequila, as well as mariachi music and the national dance of Mexico, the Jarabe Tapatío. (The term "Tapatío" refers to people who are native to the state of Jalisco.)

The state is ranked fourth in population in the country, though the capital of Guadalajara is by far the largest city and dominates the demographic distribution of the state. Of the state's six million or so residents, the metropolitan area of Guadalajara holds about four million, or two-thirds of the state's total population. The state has an extensive rural area, marked by sizable indigenous populations of Purépecha-, Náhuatl-, and Huichol-speaking groups. Since the 1940s, however, the density of the rural population of the state has been depleted by decades of out-migration to Jalisco's urban areas and to other cities in Mexico. In addition, Jalisco has sent large numbers of immigrants to the United States since the turn of the 20th century.

The configuration of the economy of the state has changed over time. Early in its history Jalisco was known primarily for its agricultural production, livestock raising, and related economic activities, such as textiles, tanneries, and milling. Adjacent to the enormously rich mining areas of north-central Mexico, such as

Zacatecas, Jalisco was a crucial source of food products for the huge population of miners in the region and its key cities, such as Zacatecas, Durango, and Guanajuato. Moreover, Jalisco also supplied an important amount of foodstuffs for Mexico City. At present, Jalisco is the largest producer of corn (maize) and second largest source of poultry and beef products in Mexico. The state also produces pork, eggs, and milk products, in addition to sugar, vegetables (especially tomatoes), and its signature liquor from maguey plants, tequila. Hay and sorghum are also produced in large quantities.

Beginning in the 1940s, the state's economy became more diversified, adding a sizable industrial and manufacturing base, spearheaded by those related to its traditional economy, such as food processing. More recently, the state has developed a strong industrial and technology component, anchored by the early establishment of an IBM plant in 1975 in Guadalajara. Since that time, IBM has been joined by other high-tech manufacturers, such as Hitachi, Siemens, General Electric, and Hewlett-Packard. These plants make components for computers and assemble related products.

The service sector of Jalisco is based on the significance of commerce and tourism. As a major hub of Mexico's domestic economy since colonial times, Jalisco has always had a robust commercial trade sector, led by the centrality of Guadalajara as a business center for the region as a whole. Not surprisingly, transportation-related enterprises have also played an important economic role, including hotels and restaurants. As tourism developed in the area after the 1920s, Guadalajara in particular became a key attraction, as the city's fame for its folk arts (leather products, lacquerware, pottery, and textiles), traditional music, and dance, as well as for its cuisine, drew visitors to Jalisco. By the 1970s, the rising attraction of Puerto Vallarta added to the tourist industry of the region, where Guadalajara served as the gateway to the coastal resort area. The rapid expansion of "PV" (as the beach resort is often referred to by foreign tourists) after the 1980s has expanded the commercial ties between Guadalajara and the state's coastal area.

The signing of the North American Free Trade Agreement had a large-scale impact on the state's economy. For example, from 1994 to 2007 (before the onset of the recession of 2007 in the United States), the value of exports from Jalisco to the United States and Canada increased more than 9 times, from $3 billion to over $27 billion. In brief, the service sector, combined with tourism, represents almost 50 percent of the state's gross domestic product (GDP), while manufacturing is about 25 percent. Transportation-related businesses generate about 12 percent of Jalisco's GDP. Agriculture, despite its importance, is responsible for only about 10 percent of the state's GDP, in light of the value of production of the other sectors of the state's economy. Unfortunately for Jalisco, with its huge proportion of exports to the United States, the economic downturn that began in 2007 in the latter country has had adverse effects, especially for the industrial sector. Moreover, competition from Asia, especially China, had already undercut the assembly plants located in the state, particularly in Guadalajara, leading to an increase in underemployment and unemployment. For years previously, the city had drawn workers from elsewhere in Mexico, but that attraction has dramatically slowed, particularly as China rose as a site for low-wage labor. As a consequence, the so-called maquiladoras (foreign-owned factories where imported parts are assembled by lower-paid workers into products for export) have shed thousands of jobs in the state since the early 2000s. With increasing Asian competition, the robust growth of Jalisco has slowed considerably, and its recovery will depend in large measure on the resurgence of the U.S. market for Mexican goods and services.

The per capita income of Jalisco is among the highest in Mexico, given the large number of executives and professionals associated with the industrial and high-tech companies in

Agave cactus grows in a field field near Tequila, Jalisco, Mexico. (Elena Elisseeva | Dreamstime.com)

the state, especially in Guadalajara. The relatively high incomes in the state are also due to the extensive number of tourist businesses that require white-collar employees. For those who work in the larger established firms, wages are generally above the norm for Mexico. Assembly plants also employ an enormous number of women, adding to the household incomes of many families. Jalisco also contains numerous wealthy individuals associated with agribusiness. Yet, the aggregate statistics on income disguise huge disparities between rich and poor in Jalisco. Rural poverty is deep and entrenched, as a host of small farmers attempt to sustain themselves on tiny plots of land, inducing many people from rural areas to immigrate to the United States or to migrate to the country's urban centers. Not surprisingly, Jalisco is one of the largest recipients of remittances from immigrants in the United States, usually ranking in the top five of states receiving monies from its natives living in that country. One year prior to the U.S. recession that began in 2007, remittances to Jalisco were valued at more than $1 billion. In this sense, immigrants from Jalisco lessen the disparities that underlie the social structure of the state. In addition, large numbers of young migrants from the countryside contribute to the income of rural households in Jalisco, which serves to reduce the inequalities that provoke out-migration from the state. In light of these socioeconomic circumstances, it is not surprising to find a large informal sector, especially in the metropolitan area of Guadalajara, as thousands of people try to eke out a living as street vendors, sellers of various goods to tourists, and the like. It is estimated that nearly 50 percent of households in Jalisco are below the poverty line; extreme poverty is especially evident in the remote rural areas of the state.

A key source of the income gaps in Jalisco can be traced to the poor public schooling in Mexico in general and in states such as Jalisco in particular. The drop-out rate is particularly high and is acute in the rural areas of the state. Ironically, higher education in the state is considered among the best in Mexico, but the pipeline between colleges and universities and the public schools is at best mediocre. In addition, a large proportion of students who begin college-level studies do not complete their degrees.

In spite of the underlying inequities in Jalisco, the state remains the third most important in Mexico in terms of GDP, mainly due to the enormous economic resources of the metropolitan area of Guadalajara. As a result, Jalisco has been and continues to be a pivotal state in the country's electoral politics. As of 2010, politics in Jalisco indicate the longstanding conservative bent of its residents, punctuated by the extraordinary strength of Catholicism among the state's population. For example, of the state's 21 congressional delegates in 2010, 18 belonged to the right-of-center Partido Acción Nacional (National Action Party, PAN); 2 of its 3 senators also hailed from the same party, as did the governor of the state (the three previous governors of the state have also been from PAN). The gubernatorial candidate of the left-of-center party, the Partido de la Revolución Democrática (Democratic Revolution Party, PRD), was a very distant third in the election of 2006, though the party's presidential candidate came close to winning the presidency in that same year. Most political analysts expect Jalisco to remain a bastion of PAN. The former dominant party, the Partido Revolucionario Institucional (Institutional Revolutionary Party, PRI), has made a comeback of sorts in the state, due in large measure to the weakening economic conditions in Jalisco as the state's businesses face stiff competition from Asia in particular, while also battling the negative effects of the U.S. economic slump that began in 2007.

Despite that recent economic slowdown, Jalisco has sustained a lively social and cultural life, highlighted by the second most important city of the nation, Guadalajara. The capital of Jalisco crackles with a host of museums, galleries, performance centers, and artistic venues that are enriched by the city's premier universities, notably the Universidad de Guadalajara and the Universidad Autonoma de Guadalajara, among others. For decades, the city has also been a very popular attraction for visitors, both international and domestic. In addition, as the home state of Mexico's best known liquor, tequila, the state receives thousands of tourists who visit each year to taste the intoxicating drink. Furthermore, Jalisco is also home to its own famed culinary style, and it is the area that has been associated with Mexico's national musical form, the mariachi, and its accompanying dance form, the

Jarabe Tapatío. The popularity of the resort town of Puerto Vallarta—particularly with visitors from the United States—has also boosted Jalisco's tourist traffic (the growth of PV has also seeped across to the neighboring state of Nayarit, which has led to the development of Nueva Vallarta).

In economic orientation, patterns of immigration, and tourist industry, the prospects for Jalisco hinge to a large extent on the United States, the major market for the state's exports, invariable destination for its immigrants, and source of most of its international visitors. Even the state's illicit drug trade centers on the consumption of illegal substances north of the border. The overall sensitivity of the state to economic swings in the United States makes for an unsettled future. The state's economic foundation has been gradually undermined by overseas competition, particularly its most vulnerable sectors, such as apparel-making plants, though its high-tech component has generally been able to maintain its position. Nonetheless, the health of the U.S. economy will continue to be crucial to Jalisco in the long term; the decline in the value of remittances due to the U.S. recession that began in 2007 serves to underscore the significance of the United States to Jalisco. Any sustained economic slump north of the border will have negative impacts that will likely translate into political tensions and/or an erosion of support for PAN. For Jalisco, like much of Mexico, the prosperity of the United States will figure decisively in future events and developments in the state.

Alex M. Saragoza

See also Beverage Industry; Folk Music; Immigration and Emigration; Maquiladoras; North American Free Trade Agreement; Tourism

Further Reading

Alba Vega, Carlos. 2002. "Regional Policy under NAFTA: The Case of Jalisco." In *NAFTA in the New Millennium,* edited by Edward Chambers and Peter Smith. La Jolla, CA: Center for U.S.-Mexican Studies, University of California, San Diego.

Gobierno del Estado de Jalisco. www.jalisco.gob.mx.

Navarrete, Carlos Alberto. 2009. *Identidad panista: Entre tradicion y modernidad; El proceso de institucionalizacion del Partido Accion Nacional en Jalisco.* Zapopan: Colegio de Jalisco.

Schmidhuber de la Mora, Guillermo. 2009. *Jalisco: Del origen a la globalizacion.* Mexico City: Plaza y Valdes.

Valenzuela-Zapata, Ana Guadalupe, and Gary Paul Nabhan. 2003. *Tequila: A Natural and Cultural History.* Tuscon: University of Arizona Press.

Judicial System

In February 2008, the Mexican Congress approved a major constitutional change in the country's judicial system, and the amendment was signed into effect by President Felipe Calderón in June of that year. Among the most important changes were those in the principles and administration of justice in criminal trials. After the reforms of 2008, criminal cases are conducted through oral arguments, as opposed to the past reliance on paper trials, where judges reviewed the evidence presented by prosecutors and made a determination of innocence or guilt. More fundamentally, unlike the previous legal tradition, innocence is now presumed until a defendant is proven guilty, similar to the legal concept used in the United States in criminal trials. Mexico's criminal justice system is in the process of a complete overhaul, as the reform measures radically change the procedural rules in criminal proceedings. Most other aspects of the country's judicial system, however, remain basically the same.

Structure   The federal and state courts represent the two fundamental arms of the judicial system of Mexico. Each of these systems is subdivided according to jurisdiction and the type of case that is involved. In the federal system, Supreme Court justices are appointed from a list submitted by the president and approved by the Mexican Senate. The Supreme Court handles civil cases dealing with constitutional issues and major felonies, such as proceedings against illegal drug organizations, as well as penal affairs. The Supreme Court is composed of 11 justices, i.e., a chief justice and 10 associate justices. On staggered terms, justices each serve one 15-year term and cannot be reappointed. Selected by the other members of the court, the chief justice serves a four-year term and can serve again in that capacity, but the terms cannot be consecutive.

In addition, there are two types of federal circuit courts; 12 of those courts are composed of three magistrates and address civil and criminal cases. So-called unitary circuit courts that rule on appeals also exist (9 as of 2011). Each unitary circuit court consists of one magistrate. Within the federal court system, district courts deal with commercial and civil law cases (there are 68 district courts). The circuit, unitary, and district courts are dispersed throughout the country based on population and regional considerations.

State courts follow a pattern similar to that of the federal system of justice. Each state, however, has jurisdiction over the specific organization of its courts and its provisions, leading to variations in the administration of the law by state courts. In general, each state has a supreme court, courts of first instance, justices of the peace, and police judges. There are also courts of special jurisdictions, such as those that attend to family-related cases, such as divorce, spousal abuse, child custody cases, and the like.

Mexico also has a large system of administrative law courts that have jurisdiction over specific matters. For example, the Federal Boards of Conciliation and Arbitration are particularly significant, as they oversee and rule on labor disputes of various sorts, including conflicts regarding wages and benefits. The Federal Tribunal on Elections is also very important, ruling over electoral disputes involving federal offices, for example, deputies (congressmen) and senators, as well as presidential electoral disputes. Mexico has had a number of recent controversial electoral cases that have compelled rulings by the Federal Tribunal on Elections as the process of democratization has advanced since the late 1990s. It is likely that the Federal Tribunal on Elections will continue to play a major role in federal elections for the foreseeable future.

There are also agrarian courts that deal with disputes involving lands distributed by the federal government. Tax courts handle fiscal disputes between companies and individuals and the Mexican Treasury Department (similar to the U.S. Internal Revenue Service).

The Council of the Federal Judiciary is responsible for the administration, supervision, and discipline of federal judges and their courts, with the exception of the Supreme Court and the Federal Tribunal on Elections.

The judicial system of Mexico addresses the five major legal codes of the country: the Civil Code, the Code of Civil Procedure, the Penal Code, the Code of Penal Procedure, and the Code of Commerce (business law). The Civil Code covers family law, property, contracts, trusts and estates (probate), and related aspects of the law. The Penal Code involves the definition of crimes and sentencing.

Politics and the courts   From the 1920s to the 1990s, the federal judiciary was fundamentally influenced by the political dominance of one party, the Partido Revolucionario Institucional (Institutional Revolutionary Party, PRI). Consequently, the executive branch of government overshadowed both the legislative and judicial spheres. The president in effect had a "rubber-stamp" Congress composed overwhelmingly of members of his party, allowing him to choose judges and/or have them dismissed (usually through their resignations). Judicial appointments were to a large extent a form of patronage. Moreover, because the PRI also controlled state politics, the state courts were similarly subject to the reach of the dominant party. Judges were basically extensions of the PRI, so that court cases with political overtones were in fact usually mediated by PRI officials. In this sense, corruption characterized much of the federal and state court systems when it came to cases that held political implications. Charges of malfeasance, for example, against a federal or elected official were usually dismissed. Similarly, state judges often rendered decisions favorable to those with political connections to powerful bosses of the PRI. At the municipal level, it was common for local magistrates to make decisions regarding individuals and/or enterprises based on their links to influential PRI members. As a result, the public came to disdain the courts, particularly in cases involving politicians or elected officials, and held the generalized perception that judges and the administration of justice were subject to political influence.

Since the late 1990s, however, the Supreme Court has acquired a growing measure of credibility, probity, and evident independence from the political process. In an unprecedented move, the Supreme Court has adopted a policy of much greater transparency in major controversial cases, including the broadcasting of their proceedings. The court has also undertaken an investigation into human rights abuses and has made rulings on same-sex marriages, abortion rights, and other controversial issues with apparent disregard for the political implications involved.

The process of litigation in Mexico provides judges with extraordinary latitude, as they usually control the process of evidence gathering. Judges are further empowered by Mexico's lack of a tradition of jury trials. There is no principle of punitive damages; people who bring suits to court must pay for attorney fees. Litigation is expensive, and judicial rulings usually take a long time, as judges have much discretion in adjudicating cases. As a result, legal disputes are often negotiated or are subject to arbitration rather than a court proceeding.

Criminal justice system   By far, the criminal justice system is the most disputed segment of the judicial system in Mexico. Until the reform measures of 2008, abuses, mismanagement, and procedural laxity marked the organization and administration of criminal legal proceedings. For example, trials were closed to the public, judges rarely saw defendants, and written evidence presented by prosecutors, based on police reports, was not subject to jury trials. Oral arguments by defense counsel were often circumscribed by judges. Most importantly, the operating principle of criminal proceedings was guilty until proven innocent.

Under the reform measures, a specific judge will be assigned to a case from its onset until the sentencing stage; in the past this was not consistently done and judges were not always present at evidentiary hearings. With the new principle of innocent until proven guilty, it is expected that fewer people will be kept in detention. With open trials, the influence of confessions will be less, given past abuses frequently made by police to gain confessions and/or the mismanagement of evidence by prosecutors, which regularly occurred. Victims will be given greater opportunities to present evidence at trials. In addition, through the reform legislation witness protections were established for testimony against those charged with illegal drug trafficking; defendants who cooperate with authorities will be eligible for reduction of sentence and other incentives. Given the abuses of the past by authorities in bringing charges against defendants, a national public security system will be put into place that will require the training, evaluation, and certification of approximately half a million police officers in the various arms of law enforcement in the country. This aspect of judicial reform also covers the criteria and universal identification for the hiring of law enforcement officers, so as to avoid the movement of unqualified or sanctioned law enforcement personnel from one police force to another. It is expected that these measures will lessen the level of corruption among police forces in the country.

On the other hand, judicial reform faces a number of major challenges. First, these reforms will be costly, with estimates as high as $2 billion, though some experts suggest that the final tally will be as much as $5 billion. Second, key actors in the judicial process will have to undergo retraining, prosecutors and judges as well as defense lawyers, in understanding the implications of the changes in the law for procedural matters. Third, the economic constraints of the Mexican government will slow the implementation and process of the reforms. The changes will need to filter down from the federal judiciary to the state courts and then to municipal legal officials. Public defenders will have to be completely retrained to adapt to the alterations made in criminal proceedings. Law schools will also have to make appropriate changes in curriculum for the preparation of students interested in the practice of criminal law. The reform legislation stipulated that the changes must be completed within eight years.

Certain elements of the criminal justice system will continue as before. For example, suspects will have the right to counsel, the right to confront their accusers, and the right to avoid self-incrimination. Suspects can be arrested and imprisoned for up to 80 days without charges; the latter practice has received a great deal of criticism in the past. Human rights advocates in particular made efforts to include changes to the detention process, but they were rebuffed largely due to concern that major criminals, such as drug lords, would find ways to evade authorities if detention procedures had strict release stipulations. On the other hand, provisions that would allow law enforcement officers to search homes without a warrant were eliminated from the reform legislation.

Before the reform, one authoritative study concluded that the majority of prisoners in Mexico had been convicted of nonviolent crimes of theft or burglary of items worth less than $600. The same study found that less than 5 percent of robberies involved amounts more than $7,500. Many students of the criminal justice system of the past argued that most prisoners were poor, ignorant of their rights, undereducated with little if any understanding of the judicial process, and often intimidated by law enforcement officers into confessing to crimes. As a result, according to experts, about 80 percent of inmates received convictions from judges who never saw them. In effect, the people most likely to be imprisoned were those without the means to receive a fair trial. In short, class distinctions played a key role in the administration of justice and served to undermine the credibility of the court system among the Mexican public in general, especially among those of modest incomes.

The social cost of the past has been a general lack of respect for the judicial system. In this regard, the country faces an enormous challenge, as it will take years of concerted and consistent effort by the courts to earn the trust of the Mexican people in the equitable rule of law and the nation's system of justice.

Alex M. Saragoza

See also Corruption; Election, Presidential, 2000; Election, Presidential, 2006; Feminism; Income; Law Enforcement; Peasantry; Politics and Political Parties; Social Structures, Class, and Ethnic Relations

Further Reading

Beatriz Magaloni. 2008. "Enforcing the Autocratic Political Order and the Role of the Courts: The Case of Mexico." In *Rule by Law: The Politics of Courts in Authoritarian Regimes,* edited by Tom Ginsburg and Tamir Mustafa. New York: Cambridge University Press.

Contreras Acevedo, Ramiro. 2005. *La reforma judicial y las alternativas para la administracion de justicia en Mexico.* Guadalajara: Universidad de Guadalajara.

Uildriks, Niels. 2010. *Mexico's Unrule of Law: Implementing Human Rights in Police and Judicial Reform under Democratization.* Lanham, MD: Lexington Books.

L

Labor Force and Labor Movements

Background   The origins of Mexico's contemporary workforce are rooted in the country's past, particularly since the turn of the 20th century. The Mexican Revolution of 1910 and its outcomes decisively shaped the composition of the nation's workforce and its organizational characteristics. The postrevolutionary order led to the formation of a one-party state by 1929 in which labor unions represented a key constituency. Yet over time, the labor movement became largely subservient to the dominant party and its economic policies, in spite of periodic instances of workers' resistance. With the collapse of the one-party regime in the late 1990s, Mexican labor entered a new era, marked by the efforts of workers to overcome the problematic consequences of the past. In this regard, Mexican labor faces six major challenges. First, the Mexican economy has failed to produce sufficient employment for its working-age population. Second, and related to the first point, the country has a long history of labor migration to the United States that has tended to undermine labor organizing in Mexico itself. Third, for decades the labor movement was under the thumb of the one-party state, which led to large-scale corruption among unions; independent labor actions were usually suppressed, activist labor leaders were jailed if not killed, and workers' protests against probusiness governmental rulings were often violently repressed. Fourth, neoliberal policies since the 1980s have generally favored the private sector to the detriment of the interests of labor. Fifth, economic globalization has meant increasing volatility in labor markets, such as sudden changes in employment rates, dislocation of companies, and wage fluctuations, among other negative effects for workers. Sixth, particularly after the 1980s, the structural changes of the Mexican economy have been a gendered process, which has led to an increasing proportion of female workers. These characteristics of Mexico's contemporary labor force reflect historic trends in the country's political economy.

The beginning of the Mexican workforce can be found in the industrialization process actively pursued during the regime of President Porfirio Díaz (1877–1880, 1884–1911). Despite Díaz's efforts to promote national industry, only about 15 percent of Mexico's workforce was made up of nonagricultural workers by 1910. These industrial workers had to deal with unfavorable working conditions, and there were no organizations or government agencies to provide them with assistance. Therefore, as in many other industrializing societies, Mexican workers formed mutual aid groups, which offered some protection in the absence of a more formal social and economic network. The Díaz administration permitted the development of mutual aid societies, especially if they had ties to the government. However, the administration strongly opposed the development of true independent unions that could represent and bargain collectively on behalf of the workers.

The Partido Liberal Mexicano (Mexican Liberal Party, PLM) led some of the earliest efforts to organize Mexican workers. The PLM advocated government regulation of working conditions, an eight-hour workday, a guaranteed minimum wage, and the abolition of child labor. The Díaz administration refused to tolerate such a radical group and forced the PLM leadership into exile in the United States. Even with its leaders in exile, the PLM inspired major strikes by copper workers in Cananea, Sonora, in 1906 and by textile workers in Rio Blanco, Veracruz. In both cases the Díaz regime used force to break the strikes.

The outbreak of the Mexican Revolution in 1910 gave workers new opportunities to organize for political and economic purposes. The first major labor organization to develop in the wake of the revolution was the Casa del Obrero Mundial (House of the World Worker, COM). The COM had strong anarchist tendencies and lacked the centralized control to form a national labor organization. Due to its radical tendencies, the COM was suppressed by the first two presidents after the revolution (Francisco Madero and Victoriano Huerta). The ouster of Huerta in July 1914 ushered in a chaotic period of civil war among revolutionary factions. The COM returned to action and eventually decided to align itself with the revolutionary faction known as the Constitutionalists under the leadership of Venustiano Carranza and Alvaro Obregón. The COM even provided troops for the Constitutionalists—known as the Red Battalions—who played an important role in the eventual victory of the Constitutionalists over the forces led by Emiliano Zapata and Francisco "Pancho" Villa. However, shortly after assuming power, Carranza disbanded the Red Batallions and undermined the COM that they posed a potential threat to his consolidation of power.

The passage of the Constitution of 1917 provided a new direction to the labor movement in Mexico. Article 123 of the constitution guaranteed a number of benefits for workers, including the right to organize and bargain collectively. Convinced that labor unionization was unavoidable, Carranza, as the first president elected under the new constitution, decided to promote labor organization but also to ensure that the organization was under government control, reluctantly accepting the labor provisions of Article 123. In 1918 the federal government sponsored a national convention of labor leaders that led to the founding of the Confederación Regional Obrera Mexicana (Regional Confederation of Mexican Workers, CROM). The person elected to head the new organization as its secretary-general was Luis Morones, a former member of the COM, who had risen to prominence as a labor leader in Mexico City. In the growing struggle for power between Carranza and Obregón during 1919–1920, the CROM sided with the eventual winner, Obregón. In return for CROM support, Obregón provided a number of benefits for the CROM. The CROM received funds directly from the government and was also permitted to extract "contributions" from federal employees. The government gave the CROM control of the federal committees for arbitration and conciliation; these committees rendered decisions on recognition of unions and the legality of strikes and helped to resolve labor-management disputes. The government also intervened to block the rise of rivals to the CROM. In effect, competing labor organizations were pushed aside or suppressed.

As a result, the CROM expanded and its leadership prospered under the protection of the government. The peak of the CROM's power and influence came during the administration of President Plutarco Elías Calles (1924–1928). Calles appointed Morones to the cabinet-level position of minister of industry, trade, and labor, the government ministry charged with supervising labor affairs. The power of the CROM was so great that Morones himself considered campaigning for the presidency in 1928. However, the CROM soon disintegrated after it unsuccessfully opposed efforts by Calles to form an official party in the aftermath of Obregón's assassination in 1928 (shortly after he won re-election).

The decline of the CROM did not immediately lead to the rise of another national labor organization to assume its position in the alliance with the government. The authoritarian and corrupt rule of Morones and the post-1928 decline of the CROM led to a series of defections from the organization. Two former CROM leaders were particularly important: Fidel Velázquez Sánchez and Vicente Lombardo Toledano. Velázquez broke with the CROM in January 1929, establishing the Federación Sindical de Trabajadores del Distrito Federal (Federated Union of Workers of the Federal District, FSTDF). Lombardo broke with the CROM in 1932, creating what he called the "Purified" CROM in 1933, a collection of unions that had splintered from the CROM. In 1933 Velázquez and Lombardo combined efforts to establish a new national labor organization, the Confederación General de Obreros y Campesinos de México (General Confederation of Workers and Peasants of Mexico, CGOCM). The CGOCM was the basis for an even larger labor organization, the Comité Nacional de Defensa Proletaria (National Committee for Proletarian Defense, CNDP), founded in 1935. The CNDP played a prominent role in the growing power struggle between former president Calles and President Lázaro Cárdenas (1934–1940). Both Calles and Cárdenas tried to mobilize labor support until February 1936, when labor leaders formed a new and larger national labor organization, the Confederación de Trabajadores de México (Mexican Workers' Confederation, CTM). The new organization selected Toledano as secretary-general and Velázquez as organizational secretary. The CTM represented some 3,000 organizations with approximately 600,000 members. With CTM support, President Cárdenas brought a definitive end to the conflict with Calles.

A series of strikes by railroad, electrical, and petroleum workers during 1936–1937 tested the budding alliance between the CTM and the Cárdenas administration as well as the ability of the CTM to contain the labor movement within government-approved bounds. When the interests of the workers clashed with the interests of the government, the CTM leadership made it clear that it would side with the government. This show of loyalty was rewarded in 1938 when the alliance was institutionalized with the reorganization and renaming of the official party. The new official party was called the Partido de la Revolución Mexicana (Party of the Mexican Revolution, PRM). The PRM was divided into four sectors along corporate lines: agrarian, labor, military, and popular. Cárdenas assigned the dominant role in the labor sector to the CTM. He organized the peasants into a separate group, the Confederación Nacional Campesina (National Peasant Confederation, CNC). Government employees also ended up in a labor organization beyond the CTM's control, the Federación de Sindicatos de Trabajadores al Servicio del Estado (Federation of Unions of Workers in Service to the State, FSTSE). Both the CNC and the FSTSE were established in 1938, when the CTM was incorporated into the official party. The early presidents who emerged from the Revolution of 1910 found it difficult to control a mobilized peasantry demanding immediate land distribution. The formation of the CNC led to the incorporation of large segments of Mexico's peasant labor force into the organization, a process greatly facilitated by Cárdenas's agrarian reform measures, particularly his administration's huge land-distribution program. President Cárdenas was able to concentrate power and support and to advance the distribution of land, primarily through the use of the *ejido,* or communal landholding system. The CNC succeeded—when previous attempts had failed—in organizing the peasantry because it could count on the support of the official party, the government, and an active program of agrarian reform. As a consequence, the CNC became the principal intermediary between the government and rural labor. Government programs such as land distribution, rural credit, and irrigation were conducted through the CNC.

Beginning in the 1940s, official unions affiliated with the Partido Revolucionario Institucional (Institutional Revolutionary Party, PRI), previously the PRM, facilitated Mexico's economic growth by accepting low labor wage increases, thus eliminating a major source of inflation and discouraging industrial conflict. The demands of World War II and later the government's postwar development policy both required that workers' wages be kept low and that labor peace be maintained. During the war the CTM attempted to follow a no-strike policy and signed a labor industrial pact pledging to work with business in pursuit of government development policies. The apparent willingness of the CTM leadership to accept this development model and to sacrifice workers' wages to help business and the government, led to massive defections from the CTM by unionized workers in key sectors, such as in the oil industry, railroads, and mining. In this context, the long-simmering rivalry between Lombardo and Velázquez for control of the CTM came to a head during 1947–1948 with the expulsion of Lombardo and his followers for their "communistic" views. With Velázquez's approval, the government continued its policy of undercutting labor unions that represented potential rivals for the CTM. During the PRI regime, the government used repression and rigged elections to put pro-CTM leaders into office in independent-minded unions. The alliance between the government and the CTM tightened, leading to the subordination of labor to the government's developmental model, as the CTM used coercion, bribery, and violence when necessary to restrain wage demands and to discipline dissident workers.

In 1950 Velázquez returned to his position as secretary-general of the CTM, a position he would hold until his death in 1997. Velázquez ensured the dominant position of the CTM by maintaining close ties to both the government and the official party. The relationship between the Velázquez-led CTM on the one hand and the government and the official party on the other was not static. The economic boom of the 1950s and 1960s gave way to a series of economic crises that began in the 1970s. In the 1980s, economic problems forced the government to abandon its post-war development policies and shift toward a market-guided approach to development. The government's efforts to promote productivity and efficiency in the industrial sector meant the reversal of many labor gains. Velázquez sometimes criticized this new approach, but nevertheless he steadfastly kept the CTM behind the government's policies, even to the detriment of the workers' standard of living. The government generally supported the CTM against rival union organizations but also had to show some flexibility in the face of the changing economic situation. During the 1970s, an increasing number of militant union movements broke away from the control of traditional union bosses. Opposition to the CTM flared among workers, forcing the PRI regime to make concessions to dissident labor groups. For example, the government permitted the development of a non-CTM labor organization, the Unidad Obrera Independiente (Independent Worker Unity, UOI) to organize workers in the automobile, textile, chemical, and transportation industries. The UOI was used to block organizational efforts by a more radical and more independent labor organization, the Frente Auténtico del Trabajo (Authentic Labor Front, FAT). Although the government generally favored the CTM, the government was prepared to let non-CTM labor organizations develop as long as they operated within the existing state-labor coalition.

As Mexico's financial and economic problems continued into the 1990s, there were new efforts in the labor movement to establish national organizations to rival the CTM. These dissident groups were especially concerned about the shift toward neoliberal policies begun by the PRI controlled government in the 1980s. In 1995 dissident labor leaders established the Foro Sindicalismo ante la Nación (Labor Forum before the Nation), more commonly referred to as the Foro. The Foro was mildly critical of the government's economic policies and called for the creation of a rival organization to the CTM. The Foro played a key role in the creation of the Unión Nacional de Trabajadores (National Workers' Union, UNT). The UNT pushed for the reversal of the market-guided economic policies, the protection of government social programs, and the independence of unions from both government and PRI control. As the UNT was organizing, Velázquez died in 1997 after a half century at the head of the CTM. The death of Velázquez called into question the role of the CTM in the government-labor alliance and the close connection between the CTM and the PRI, as the dominant party faced plummeting electoral support. In short, the 1990s was a period of flux within organized labor as the Mexican political economy underwent wrenching changes.

Relations between labor and the PRI shifted during the presidency of Carlos Salinas de Gortari (1988–1994), as he further weakened the traditional unions during his sexenio. Shortly after taking office, as a measure to legitimize his power after a highly questioned election, Salinas hit the official oil workers' union by having its powerful chief, Joaquin Hernandez Galicia, arrested on corruption charges. Salinas also undercut the public schoolteachers' union, Sindicato Nacional De Trabajadores de la Educacion (National Union of Education Workers, SNTE), transferring authority over education from the central government to the states and forcing the union to negotiate separate contracts with each state government. Furthermore, the government's privatization program eliminated hundreds of union jobs, and the role and power of the CTM declined substantially. The CTM, however, remains the most important labor organization in Mexico. Furthermore, the reforms introduced by President Salinas reduced the role of the government in the agricultural sector, reducing the importance of the CNC as a mediator between the government and the peasantry. The changes introduced in 1992 under Salinas in particular struck at the traditional role of the CNC. The Agrarian Law of 1992 ended land redistribution as a basic policy of the government and gave *ejido* members the right to sell, rent, mortgage, or sharecrop their land. The *ejidos,* in effect, could choose to dissolve, with *ejido* members receiving individual title to former communal lands. These changes affected some of the basic functions previously performed by the CNC, especially land redistribution and mediation between the government and *ejido* members. For Salinas and his neoliberal political allies, the CNC was no longer a useful political tool of the PRI.

But the political and economic crises of the 1990s engulfed the PRI. The once-dominant party lost its congressional majority in 1997, and in 2000 its presidential candidate was defeated. Seven decades of PRI rule ended when Vicente Fox of the right-of-center PAN took office. Until 2000, the CTM and other official unions such as the CNC, had been able to count on the support of the government and of the PRI as the official party. Official unions had been able to rely on the government to use a combination of co-optation and harassment to divide and weaken its rivals. But when the PRI lost the presidency in the 2000 elections, labor sectors could no longer depend on the government to perform those functions. As a result, a new and ambiguous political situation confronted organized labor. The PRI attempted to retain support among labor bosses, but major defections took place. Notably, Elba Esther Gordillo, head of the teachers' union, began to form strategic political alliances, including PAN, in order to advance her union's objectives. Currently, the status of the labor movement in Mexico remains unsettled, as neoliberal policies have generally benefited the private sector at the expense of organized labor. Workers' actions have fragmented, as a viable and strong national labor organization has failed to materialize to date. Nonetheless, in the face of a very difficult political context, union activists continue to struggle to improve workplace conditions, wages, and benefits, though with differing results.

Labor force Mexico's workforce was estimated in the 2010 census at around 48.9 million. A little more than half of the working-age population (ages 14 years and over) had actually entered the formal labor market, of which 62 percent are employees. Almost 29 percent of the total labor force work in the informal sector. Agriculture, forestry, fishing, and mining (Sector Primario) employed 13 percent of the economically active population, according to the 2010 census; manufacturing, mining, construction, and energy sectors (Sector Secundario) employed 24 percent; and the service sector (Sector Terciario), which includes transportation and communications, tourism, education, and financial services, among other economic activities, employed 61 percent of the workforce.

Historically, real wages in Mexico have been subject to agreements involving government officials, the private sector, and labor union chiefs. During the PRI regime, these sectors had the understanding that while the government was in control of macroeconomic policy, business groups would refrain from political opposition while gaining political access to business opportunities; and labor leaders would control wage-increase demands in exchange for additional patronage and government support. As a result, PRI governments were able to use their control of the labor union movement to hold down wages and reduce inflation. Subsequent economic crises after 1980 have resulted in a constant increase in the unemployment rate and a decline in the average worker's purchasing power. The average minimum wage in 2010 was $58 pesos per day (approximately $4.30).

Labor legislation The Federal Labor Act of 1970 authorizes the government to regulate all labor contracts and work conditions, including minimum wages, work hours, holidays, paid vacations, employment of women and minors, occupational hazards, profit sharing, collective bargaining, and strikes. The act sets the minimum employment age at 14 years. And although the law mandates a minimum wage, noncompliance among employers reaches high percentages, especially in the countryside. The maximum legal workweek is 48 hours, with a maximum workday of 8 hours. The Secretaría del Trabajo y Previsión Social (Secretary of Labor and Social Welfare) is the government ministry responsible for the labor unions' official recognition, and the labor code stipulates that strikes are illegal if unauthorized by the secretary of labor.

Labor unions   Corruption, a corporatist structure, and paternalism have traditionally characterized the labor movement in Mexico. Most labor unions had a strong political relationship with the PRI in the 71 years of the party's hegemonic regime. Organized labor became an integral component of the regime, providing political support to the official party and controlling wage-increase demands. More than 90 percent of production workers in industrial enterprises belong to labor unions. However, almost half of all Mexican workers are either unemployed or underemployed and are therefore not subject to being organized. Labor unions are mostly representative of workers in urban areas. Agricultural workers are mainly organized under the CNC. The CTM is the country's largest labor organization. Most labor unions were affiliated with the PRI through the CTM, which is associated with some independent unions in an umbrella organization called Congreso del Trabajo (Congress of Labor, CT). The CT is composed of more than 30 organizations encompassing more than 80 percent of the unionized workforce. The CT mediates between labor unions and the government. The second organization within the CT, after the CTM, is the FSTSE, established in 1938 as an umbrella organization for labor unions within the federal system and government-related organizations. Among other important labor organizations are the CROM, the Confederación Revolucionaria de Obreros y Campesinos (Revolutionay Confederation of Workers and Peasants, CROC), the Federación Nacional de Sindicatos Independientes (National Federation of Independent Unions, FNSI), and the Confederación de Obreros y Campesinos (Confederation of Workers and Peasants, CTC).

Ana Paula Ambrosi

See also Government; Immigration and Emigration; Maquiladoras; Partido del Trabajo; Partido Revolucionario Institucional; Salinas de Gortari, Carlos

Further Reading

Barry, Tom. 1995. *Zapata's Revenge: Free Trade and the Farm Crisis in Mexico.* Boston: South End Press.

Caulfield, Norman. 1998. *Mexican Workers and the State: From the Porfiriato to NAFTA.* Fort Worth: Texas Christian University Press.

Collier, Ruth Berins. 1992. *The Contradictory Alliance: State-Labor Relations and Regime Change in Mexico.* Berkeley: University of California Press.

Hellman, Judith Adler. 1988. *Mexico in Crisis.* 2nd ed. New York: Holmes and Meier.

La Botz, Dan. 1988. *The Crisis of Mexican Labor.* New York: Praeger.

Levy, Daniel C., Kathleen Bruhn, and Emilio Zebadúa. 2001. *Mexico: The Struggle for Democratic Development.* Berkeley: University of California Press.

Middlebrook, Kevin J. 1995. *The Paradox of Revolution: Labor, the State, and Authoritarianism in Mexico.* Baltimore: Johns Hopkins University Press.

Roxborough, Ian. 1984. *Unions and Politics in Mexico: The Case of the Automobile Industry.* Cambridge: Cambridge University Press.

Labor Party

See Partido del Trabajo

Land Distribution and Land Reform

The history of land tenure and land policy in Mexico is a complex one. Agrarian reform, a prominent theme of the Mexican Revolution, is key to contemporary Mexico and has made the term *ejido* (land granted to a specific group for communal cultivation, or communal landholding) commonplace. The ongoing importance of the agrarian question is evident in the numerous peasant revolts and conflicts that are a part of Mexico's history, including the Zapatista rebellion that emerged during the last decade of the 20th century. At the heart of Mexican agrarian reform and land policy has been the debate over the existence of and right to communal property as well as Mexico's ongoing attempt to grapple with the legacy of *latifundio,* or large-scale landholding.

The concept of communal land was embraced by both pre-Hispanic cultures and the Spanish conquerors of Mexico. Only grants to Spaniards were recognized as private property. Land grants to Spaniards as well as Spanish policies that enabled Spaniards to acquire Indian lands contributed to the growth of large landholdings or *latifundio,* and the large estate, or hacienda, became a permanent fixture of the Mexican economy.

The Catholic Church also contributed to the concentration of land during the colonial era so that by the time of Mexican independence, the Church had become Mexico's principal landowner. In the 19th century land distribution favored the wealthy, while Indians and peasant communities struggled to secure their livelihood. Simultaneously, Mexican leaders in the liberal tradition began a long debate over the future of communal and corporate landholding.

Mexico's struggle for independence that began in 1810 provided evidence that the agrarian question had become a significant one in Mexican society. Immediately after independence, however, liberal leaders determined that the key to Mexico's progress lay in the creation of an economy based on private property and the yeoman farmer. Although the Catholic Church was often able to protect its lands by, for example, selling to trusted friends, many Mexican peasants saw their lands, both family and communal, threatened.

The period from 1876 to 1910, presided over by Porfirio Díaz, was one of impressive economic growth and national integration. The agrarian question was central to Díaz's plans for transforming Mexico, as he envisioned the expansion of Mexico's agrarian export sector and sought the enhancement of the country's rural economy through the incorporation of vacant or untitled lands. To this end

Díaz passed laws in 1875, 1883, and 1884 that provided for the transfer of such *terrenos baldíos* to private ownership. Communities and private owners were given the opportunity to present the title or deed that would protect their lands from such transfers, but most lacked such papers.

Despite enhancing Mexico's economy, by 1910 Díaz's regime intensified land concentration where 87 percent of Mexico's rural lands into the hands of less than 1 percent of its landowners. Thus, the problem of *latifundio* persisted. Approximately 90 percent of the rural population was landless. Not surprisingly, such grievances were an important part of the Mexican Revolution and were central to the crafting of the postrevolutionary Mexican state. Peasants demanded the return of communal lands seized by large-scale commercial producers since the 1880s.

When Francisco I. Madero called for revolt, he included in his revolutionary Plan of San Luis Potosí a pledge to restore to their original owners lands unjustly taken. Yet, Madero's commitment to true agrarian reform was always in doubt, leading to the movement of Emiliano Zapata, a small-scale landowner from the central Mexican state of Morelos. In the 1911 Plan of Ayala, Zapata pledged to help those Mexicans needing land through the restoration of lands previously taken from villages and through the expropriation of hacienda properties. Zapatista calls for reform included the occupation of several large haciendas by Zapatista soldiers.

By 1915 Pancho Villa and Venustiano Carranza, both important revolutionaries from the north, had added their voices to the agrarian debate. And ultimately it was Zapata's vision of rural Mexico that triumphed. Article 27 of the Constitution of 1917 established the *ejido* as the primary form of land tenure. The Constitution established three different forms of land tenure in Mexico: private (worked by owners), public, and social. Social property was subdivided into communal land and *ejidos* (worked and used by ejidatarios). The Mexican state assumed responsibility for restoring lands taken from peasants and granting *ejidos* to peasant communities that needed them.

Despite the strength of Article 27, its implementation varied widely and was dependent upon the political outlook of each Mexican president and the political exigencies faced. The presidency of Lázaro Cárdenas (1934–1940) represented the heyday of agrarian reform. Unlike his predecessors, Cárdenas embraced the idea of the *ejido* and increased state support for *ejidatarios* through such measures as the Ejido Credit Bank. Cárdenas also sealed his reputation as champion of the Mexican campesinos (peasants) by distributing twice as much land as his predecessors. By the end of his term, 49 million acres had been distributed to the benefit of more than 700,000 peasants. Much of the country's arable land was redistributed to peasant farmers (smallholders, or *minifundistas*), who benefited from the agrarian reform program, while the share of land held by large estates fell.

In 1939 Cárdenas established the Confederación Nacional Campesina (National Campesino Confederation, CNC), bringing together local peasant groups into a national organization beholden to him. At the same time, Cárdenas's agrarianism encouraged the continued growth of landowner resistance and militancy. The decline in Mexico's agricultural productivity, a by-product of the initial disruption caused by agrarian reform, motivated a post-1940 shift away from the *ejido* and back to the idea of small-scale privately owned plots.

For the next 25 years, legal reforms increased the amount of agricultural land an individual small landowner could hold, while continuing the protection for cattle ranchers and the cattle industry. Most importantly, as the Mexican government embraced industrial development and agricultural modernization, financial support of the *ejidal* sector declined. By the mid-1960s this policy, along with Mexico's steady population growth, contributed to a situation in which the country could no longer feed itself. From 1964 to 1976, Mexico experienced another wave of agrarian reform as Presidents Gustavo Díaz Ordaz and Luís Echeverría sought to revive the agrarian sector, bolster the country's agricultural productivity, and respond to a new wave of peasant mobilization. The amount of land distributed under these two leaders was twice that distributed under Cárdenas and included a significant portion of northern Mexico, where *latifundio* was especially persistent. Little was solved, however, and it was increasingly obvious that in Mexico the problem of *latifundio* had been replaced by that of *minifundio:* plots too small to meet domestic demand, much less for export.

By the 1980s as Mexico wrestled with a general economic crisis and attempted to respond to international pressures to open its economy, the limits of the *ejido* became especially apparent. It was left to Carlos Salinas de Gortari, president from 1988 to 1994, to make the changes necessary to end Mexico's long history of agrarian reform. Continuous decline in agricultural production and productivity and the rise in food imports motivated President Salinas to change the land tenure system. In 1992 Salinas announced constitutional reforms to Article 27, granting *ejidatarios* formal legal titles to the lands previously held in trust for them by the government and thus providing the opportunity to sell or rent such lands if the majority of members of their *ejido* agreed. This reform was intended to overcome the low productivity resulting from the fragmentation of *ejidos* and overturn the trend toward smaller farming units. President Salinas also encouraged investment and joint ventures with private capital. Land reform was effectively ended, as no further land would be redistributed, and the Mexican agricultural sector was expected to embark upon a new era of growth and productivity.

Predictably, Salinas's determination to end the redistribution of land sparked criticism and protest. The most visible resistance came in the form of the Zapatista uprising in the southern state of Chiapas. This rebel movement began in 1994 and included as part of its agenda the defense of Article 27. Despite changes to the

Constitution, however, Mexico experienced no significant change in landholding patterns during the last years of the 20th century, and the *ejido* is still a significant part of the rural landscape. Whether agrarian reform is truly dead is a question left to the 21st century.

Suzanne B. Pasztor

See also Agriculture; Ejército Zapatista de Liberación Nacional and the Indigenous Movement; Peasantry; Salinas de Gortari, Carlos

Further Reading

Craig, Ann L. 1983. *The First Agraristas: An Oral History of a Mexican Agrarian Reform Movement.* Berkeley: University of California Press.

DeWalt, Billie R., Martha W. Rees, and Arthur D. Murphy. 1994. *The End of Agrarian Reform in Mexico: Past Lessons, Future Prospects.* San Diego: Center for U.S.-Mexican Studies, University of California, San Diego.

Gledhill, John. 1991. *Casi Nada: A Study of Agrarian Reform in the Heartland of Cardenismo.* Albany, NY: Institute for Mesoamerican Studies.

Harvey, Neil. 1990. *The New Agrarian Movement in Mexico, 1979–1990.* London: Institute of Latin American Studies.

Markiewicz, Dana. 1993. *The Mexican Revolution and the Limits of Agrarian Reform.* Boulder, CO: Lynne Rienner.

Randall, Laura, ed. 1996. *Reforming Mexico's Agrarian Reform.* Armonk, NY: M. E. Sharpe.

Sanderson, Steven E. 1981. *Agrarian Populism and the Mexican State: The Struggle for Land in Sonora.* Berkeley: University of California Press.

Sanderson, Susan Walsh. 1984. *Land Reform in Mexico, 1910–1980.* Orlando, FL: Academic Press.

Simpson, Eyler N. 1937. *The Ejido: Mexico's Way Out.* Chapel Hill: University of North Carolina Press.

Tannenbaum, Frank. 1929. *The Mexican Agrarian Revolution.* New York: Macmillan.

Law Enforcement

Mexico's strategy against crime has been to combat the consequences of a flawed institutional design instead of changing the structural and institutional problems inside its law enforcement agencies that are effectively, although mostly unintentionally, abetting crime. Confusing organization, which has produced jurisdictional chaos, separation between investigative and policing responsibilities, deplorable working conditions, militarization of public security, and a general distrust by citizens, are the main features that characterize law enforcement in Mexico.

The complex structure and dynamics of crime-fighting institutions in Mexico have been instrumental for the steady increase in the numbers and severity of crime that the country has experienced in the last two decades. Different police forces often compete for authority and territory. These forces also have jurisdictions that may be clearly defined in the law but not in reality. In other words, despite continuous efforts from these same institutions to prevent growth of criminal activity, the organizational structure, hierarchy, and internal informal practices have facilitated corruption, impunity, and the reproduction of criminal activity.

Separation of functions and the many different levels of police that coexist in the country provoke at best a struggle for power and at worse complete chaos. As Benjamin Reames states, Mexican police "stands out for its confusing organization and inefficient use of personnel." Assorted coordination efforts between different police forces have not been effective, and sometimes have been detrimental to their goal of deterring crime.

Mexico, much like the rest of Latin America, separates the enforcement and investigative functions of its po-

Mexican State policeman guards a tourist attraction in Acapulco. Because of violence in Mexico police officers have been deployed to protect visitors. (iStockPhoto)

lice forces into two distinct organizations: (1) preventive police, who are in charge of maintaining order and public security in cities and towns and can only assist the Ministerio Público (Office of the Public Prosecutor) at its request, and (2) judicial police, the investigative arm that acts under the authority of the Ministerio Público. All police forces (federal, state, and municipal) are organized this way, and, depending on their jurisdiction, they will enforce *fuero federal* ("federal law") or *fuero común* ("local law"). As of August 2009, Mexico had 390,781 policemen ascribed in different enforcement bodies. According to Zepeda Lecuona, Mexico counts 366 policemen for each 100,000 individuals, above the United Nation's average of 225.

As mentioned, apart from its functional separation, police forces may be federal, state, or municipal, which adds another layer of jurisdictional complexity. In 2010 there were around 3,000 distinct police forces in the country. Recognizing this, the president recently sent a bill to Congress that will ascribe all municipal corporations into 31 state police forces, in an attempt at increasing command centralization.

Parallel to the police structure, there is a growing number of private security agencies that, as of August 2009, counted 127,278 guards combined. In October

2008 in Mexico City alone, the Department of Private Security had 435 businesses registered, which included a total of 12,514 members and 9,208 firearms. In total, they report catering to 8,116 Mexico City residents.

All these organizations are stepping on each other's toes, not only creating organizational chaos and incompetence but contributes to police corruption and abuses against the public. The system is skewed in a way that greatly advantages the wealthy and powerful and punishes those who cannot afford to defend themselves. But, contrary to general opinion, not all is explained by corruption. According to one survey, the judicial police's low capacity to investigate has had the direct effect of making most crimes go unpunished and penalizing only those who are caught in flagrante delicto. Police inefficiency thus also ensures that most of those punished are petty offenders and poor citizens who cannot afford a defense. But even among people in that social sector, only a small percentage actually have trials and, if found guilty, are convicted. In other words, in Mexico the cost of committing a crime is very low.

Moreover, policemen's working conditions are deplorable, creating a fertile environment for corruption by disenfranchising most of them from the corporation. For most, low salaries provoke corruption and for some even justify it. On average, in 2010 police officers had a monthly pay of around 6,229 pesos, roughly $500 a month, or about half of what is earned by a factory operative. Some policemen have proposed that the police force should help them find a second job to compensate for low salaries. In turn, there is a widespread lack of respect for the police force, leading at times to outright confrontations between policemen and citizens frustrated by the public safety problem and the abuses that many law enforcement officers commit, which range from bribes to extortion.

In addition, as a reaction to the increased violence of the "drug war," the military has slowly been taking over public security matters. This has had three main consequences. First, because the logic of the police differs from the logic of the army, it has been a cause of increased human rights abuses. Second, the effort by the military to disband corruption networks inside law enforcement has in effect further discredited police forces and has pushed corrupt officers further underground, making it more difficult to root them out. Third, and most important, the use of the army to combat crime has escalated, the violence of the drug war. As a result, cities like Tijuana and Laredo are among the most dangerous in the world. And finally, by using the army to replace many of the country's local police forces to fight against organized crime, the federal government has contributed to a further fragmentation of the lines of authority and jurisdiction in fighting crime.

Moreover, inside police agencies there is an informal de facto system parallel to the institutional hierarchy that encourages corruption that not only puts citizens in danger, but also the policemen themselves. Policemen are forced to pay for their bulletproof vests, bullets, and flashlights among other basic equipment. It is not surprising that, for a monthly fee, some policemen will provide private security for businessmen, politicians, or their families. Some will provide the same service for criminals.

In addition, despite continuous efforts from different tiers of the Mexican government to prevent and eradicate crime, the common perception among its citizens is that crime has intensified in the last two decades. The general opinion is that not only has criminal activity worsened but that it has accelerated.

According to Consulta Mitofsky, an independent Mexican polling firm, in August 2009, 68 percent of Mexicans thought that public security was "worse/equally bad as last year." CIDE's Encuesta de Victimización y Desempeño Institucional revealed that 40 percent of Mexico City's residents were concerned about their public safety, and 30 percent thought that they would be victims of crime sometime during the next year.

One explanation could be that, as the country has become more democratic, the news media have helped uncover cases of corruption, crime, and lawlessness that would have previously remained unknown, fostering citizens' perceptions of increased crime. But it is not only the perception of crime that has grown. When asked if at least one member of their household had been a victim of crime, there was a 65 percent increase in affirmative responses from 2007 to 2008 (from 23 to 38 percent). During 2008, 14 out of every 100 people were victims of a crime in Mexico City. Furthermore, the constant media attention to drug trade–related killings and mayhem has only added to concerns over crime among the Mexican public.

Moreover, many citizens will never report a crime, either because of fear and a lack of confidence in the authorities, a sentiment of futility (that nothing will come from the report), or the amount of time it takes to report a crime. A striking 12 percent of respondents in a national survey said that if they were victims of a crime, like a house robbery, the crime would not be reported to the authorities; and only 30 percent answered that the crime would likely be brought to the attention of law enforcement.

Civil organizations have tried to encourage the reporting of crimes by improving the means by which citizens can report certain crimes. For example, the Instituto Ciudadano de Estudios Sobre la Inseguridad (Citizens' Institute for Studies on Public Safety, ICESI) takes a victimization survey every year in an attempt to produce comparable data, albeit based on opinion polls. Denuncia Ciudadana (Citizen Complaint), a program established by a civil organization in Mexico City, helps victims of house or small business robberies by sending a lawyer and a psychologist to the scene and letting the victims report the crime via webcam. They have to reiterate their report afterward by going to the precinct, but even if they do not go, the crime is "recorded" and therefore can be counted to assess the number of robberies and their geographical distribution. But these efforts, albeit praiseworthy, are still done on a relatively small scale and have had a modest impact.

The set of electoral reforms that began in the late 1970s transformed the conditions in which the Mexican presidential system operated, progressively changing the configuration of power throughout the country. Perhaps one of the most important consequences of this progressive erosion of executive power was that in 2000, for the first time in 70 years, the Partido Revolucionario Institucional (Institutional Revolutionary Party, PRI) did not win the presidential election. As a result, the president's leadership of the PRI affiliates waned, and the opposition adjusted its tactics in response.

It is important to note that before 2000 the Mexican political system worked through a complex interaction between the president and different fractions inside the party, organized social sectors, and vested interests spread around the country that implied a continuous negotiation and systematic exchange of privileges. These constituencies included members of crime-fighting institutions, but as the distribution of power in Mexico changed after 2000, the patronage system also had to be redrawn. As a consequence, the informal, politicized channels of influence within law enforcement agencies were ruptured, opening spaces for more and different sources of corruption.

When the PRI lost the presidency, party operatives lost their control structure and their informal channels of influence. An institutional process based on the functioning of informal pacts and patronage fell apart. What remained were institutions ill-equipped to handle democratic negotiation, much less to coordinate between different tiers of government that have different agendas and jurisdictional goals.

Dolores Bernal

See also Armed Forces; Corruption; Crime and Punishment; Domestic Violence; Feminism; Income; Politics and Political Parties

Further Reading

Arango Duran, Arturo, and Cristina Lara Medina. 2007. "Las estadísticas de seguridad pública en México. Situación y perspectivas." In *Aproximaciones empíricas al estudio de la inseguridad. Once estudios en materia de seguridad ciudadana en México,* coordinated by Luis González Placencia, José Luis Arce Aguilar, and Metzli Álvarez. Ciudad de México: Porrúa.

Bergman, Marcelo, Rodolfo Sarsfield, and Gustavo Fondevila. 2007. *Encuesta de Victimizacion y Eficacia Institucional.* Mexico City: CIDE.

Consulta Mitofsky and México Unido Contra la Delincuencia. 2009. "A un ano de la firma del Acuerdo Nacional for l Seguridad, la Justicia, y la Legalidad." Mexico, DF: Consulta Mitofsky.

Cornelius, Wayne A., and David A. Shirk, eds. 2007. *Reforming the Administration of Justice in Mexico.* Notre Dame, IN: University of Notre Dame Press.

Davis, Diane E. 2006. "Undermining the Rule of Law: Democratization and the Dark Side of Police Reform in Mexico." *Latin American Politics and Society* 48(1) (April 2006): 55–86.

Instituto Ciudadano de Estudios Sobre la Inseguridad, AC. 2009. *Sexta Encuesta Nacional sobre Inseguridad.* Mexico, DF: Instituto Ciudadano de Estudios Sobre la Inseguridad.

Mondragon y Kalb, Manuel. 2008. *Comparecencia del C. Secretario: Glosa del Segundo Informe de Gobierno, 2007–2008.* Mexico DF: Secretaria de Seguridad Publica.

Reames, Benjamin Nelson. 2007. "A Profile of Police Forces in Mexico." In *Reforming the Administration of Justice in Mexico,* edited by Wayne A. Cornelius and David A. Shirk, 117–132. Notre Dame, IN: University of Notre Dame Press.

Zepeda Lecuona, Guillermo. 2010. *La policía mexicana dentro del proceso de reforma del sistema penal.* Mexico City: CIDAC.

Literature, Contemporary

The 1960s represented a watershed period in Mexican history that held decisive consequences for the literature of the country. Against the backdrop of social movements against oppressive regimes, eruptions of concerns over civil rights, assassinations of major figures, and national liberation struggles, Mexico confronted its own internal problems of social disparities, political repression, economic troubles, and a questioning of the prevailing cultural ideology promoted by the entrenched ruling political party. These grievances sharpened with the enormous investment made by the Mexican government to stage the 1968 Olympics. The monies spent on presenting a modern, cosmopolitan image to the world contrasted with the everyday inequities that framed the lives of much of the country's population. These festering problems eventually exploded into a social conflict between the dominant political order and various segments of Mexican society, in which students took a central role. A decisive confrontation occurred in October 1968 between the Mexican army and a large number of protesters, largely university students, workers, and their families, who had gathered at the plaza of Tlatelolco in Mexico City. In the midst of the rally, the military began firing into the crowd. Hundreds were killed, and hundreds more were wounded and/or jailed. The event was the culmination of a growing discontent with the dominant order, leading to a decisive break from the previous era—a break that would be reflected in the writing of Mexican novelists, essayists, playwrights, and poets.

During the presidency of Miguel Alemán (1946–1952) in particular, Mexican leaders made a concerted effort to modernize the country. This effort, however, generated a crucial question for Mexican authors that revolved around the theme of national identity. In that era, distinct groups of intellectuals responded to the question in varied ways. The Universidad Nacional Autónoma de México (National Autonomous University of Mexico, UNAM) and its School of Philosophy and Literature became the center for the Hiperion group, led by Leopoldo Zea (1912–2004), Luis Villoro (1922–), and Emilio Uranga (1921–1988). In his early publications, Leopoldo Zea dwelled on the melancholy and pessimistic character of the Mexican and his country's preoccupation with imitating European models of behavior and culture. For Zea, the Mexican Revolution represented a singular

Mexican writer and philosopher Luis Villoro at his studio in Mexico City, 2007. (AP/Wide World Photos)

moment, when Mexicans attempted to reject European norms and tried to forge an identity of their own. Much of Mexican writing followed suit, raising issues concerning the nation's distinctiveness and its origins. But it was discussion among a small slice of the country's population, as the literary debate over national identity circulated primarily among the middle and upper classes of Mexico.

In books, journals, newspapers, and magazines, the country's writers weighed in on the question of national identity. Among those literary voices, that of Octavio Paz was especially important. Paz cofounded various publications, such as the magazine *Taller* (*Workshop,* 1938–1941), in which poets like Efraín Huerta and Neftalí Beltran were also involved. In his seminal work *Laberinto de la Soledad* (*The Labyrinth of Solitude,* 1950), Paz explored a number of issues about the putative character of Mexicans and their culture, such as the basis for incidences of violence and significance of tradition. Although Paz participated in the discussion of Mexican identity, he argued for an autonomous literature shorn of simplistic nationalistic purposes. Paz emphasized the aesthetic value of literature and the need for Mexico to broaden its literary concerns to include a more critical stance toward the prevailing political order dominated by one party.

Paz reached a broad range of people due to his amazing flexibility with various genres and literary venues. He was an intellectual committed to revolutionizing the arts in Mexico through art itself, as well as to participating actively in the political culture of the country. When he was appointed to an ambassadorship (to India),

Paz nonetheless did not shy away from condemning the killings at Tlatelolco and resigned from his diplomatic post. In 1990 he was the first Mexican to receive the Nobel Prize in Literature.

The events of 1968 made for a divide in Mexico's literary history, as both writers and readers were transformed by Tlatelolco and its widespread ripple effects. Increasingly, politics became a subtext of much of Mexican literary production. Moreover, Mexican writers began to be more experimental and unconventional in expression and to broaden the understanding of culture, thereby blurring the distinction between "high" and "popular" culture. Several authors were involved in this pioneering turn in literary work, notably José Revuletas, Agustín Yañez, Juan Rulfo, Juan José Arreola, Rosario Castellanos, Ricardo Garibay, Carlos Fuentes, Octavio Paz, Jorge Ibargüengoitia, Elena Poniatowska, Sergio Galindo, Sergio Pitol, José Emilio Pacheco, Jorge López Páez, Juan García Ponce, Salvador Elizondo, Vicente Leñero, and Juan Vicente Melo. Many of these authors published before the 1960s, but their work contributed to the discussion precipitated by the events of 1968 and became part of the so-called Boom in Latin American literature.

The Boom was a literary movement with a distinct Latin American tenor that held national, hemispheric, and international repercussions, with its most prominent authors attaining worldwide acclaim, including Carlos Fuentes (1928–) of Mexico, Gabriel García Márquez (1927–) of Colombia, Julio Cortázar (1914–1984) of Argentina, and Mario Vargas Llosa (1936–) of Peru. Perhaps the most famous style that emerged from this movement was magical realism, for which García Marquez received particular attention. In Mexico, Carlos Fuentes assumed a central place in the country's literary life with the publication in 1958 of *La Región más Transparente* (*Where the Air Is Clear*), a novel that challenged the established notions of national identity and the underlying political structure that sustained conventional thinking. Fuentes charted a different course for literature in his highly influential nonfiction work *La Nueva Novela Hispanoamericana* (1969) (*The New Hispano-American Novel*), arguing for a Latin American writing that would be different from that of the Western European tradition and canon.

The fame attributed to the Boom in general, and the work of Fuentes more specifically, spurred a tidal wave of writings and innovative thematic issues in Mexican literature. There was a growing attention to topics previously marginalized by most Mexican writers in the past, such as women and sexism, homosexuality, and gritty urban life. There was also a notable rise of female writers, including Elena Garro, Margarita Michelena, Guadalupe Dueñas, Amparo Dávila, Josefina Vicens, Inés Arredondo, Julieta Campos, Elena Poniatowska, and Margo Glantz. Subsequently, younger authors, like Carmen Boullosa, Laura Esquivel, and Silvia Molina, joined the growing list of writers who explored more forcefully themes related to women and their place in Mexican society.

Not surprisingly, a much more explicit political literature appeared that was trenchant in its criticism of the dominant one-party government and the official cultural nationalist discourse promoted by the state. This type of writing became known as Literatura de la Onda (The Wave's Literature) and included writers José Agustín and Gustavo Sainz. The writers of La Onda intended to discredit the conventional views of Mexico and its traditional attention to notions of identity by delving into the cultural fracturing of Mexican society, for example, its variety of subcultures, the incidence of drugs and crime, and the existence of alternative lifestyles.

In the 1970s, two distinct genres appeared, what Mexican critic Carlos Monsiváis (1938–2010) called Literatura del Arrabal or del Barrio (Neighborhood's Literature) and the *cronica* ("literary essay focused on everyday life"). Monsiváis argued that the Literatura del Arrabal focuses on forceful male archetypes (the macho male) in the context of the seamy underbelly of Mexican daily life and its marginalized population. Monsiváis pointed to the *cronica* essay's attention to the marginal voices of Mexican society as a means of illuminating the social and political problems of the country. In the latter genre, among the most celebrated examples is *La Noche de Tlatelolco* (The Night of Tlatelolco; published in English as *Massacre in Mexico*) by Elena Poniatowska, which narrates the events of 1968.

From the 1960s to the 1980s, poetry in Mexico underwent a clear change in its use of language as poets ventured away from rhyme toward a greater use of free verse. Poets also became more concerned with the readership of poetry, and they made efforts to make poetic verse more accessible to a broader public. The work of Jaime Sabines was especially popular. Similarly, the thematic material of poetry gave greater attention to the everyday lives and struggles of the breadth of Mexican society. Among the notable poets of the 20th century are Carlos Pellicer, José Gorostiza, Xavier Villaurrutia, Gilberto Owen, Salvador Novo, Jorge Cuesta, Renato Leduc, Efraín Huerta, Octavio Paz, Alí Chumacero, José Carlos Becerra, and José Emilio Pacheco.

In dramatic literature, the works of Vicente Leñero, Hugo Hiriart, and Emilio Carballido stand out for the range of topics they tackle and their diverse probing of the disenchantment with the prevailing order in Mexico in the fateful wake of 1968. In the 1990s, particularly with the unraveling of the dominant political order, noteworthy dramatic works turned to the question of the future direction of Mexico and the role of the writer in charting a new course for the country.

From the late 1980s to the present, Mexican literature has grown enormously, nurtured by the willingness of publishing houses to produce new works in diverse genres and support younger literary voices as well as the increased public demand for well-known authors. No one essay can capture the full range of works and authors that merit attention for their quality and innovative attributes. Still, canonical frames remain, with certain literary magazines in particular possessing much influence over the fame and fortunes of Mexican authors. *Letras Libres* is exemplary; edited by renowned intellectual and historian Enrique Krauze, the magazine holds a powerful place in Mexican letters, featuring the works of several of the country's literary luminaries in addition to writers of international repute, including Juan Villoro, Gabriel Zaid, David Huerta, and Mario Vargas Llosa. Few publications have the sway of *Letras Libres,* and it has received a measure of criticism for its rather exclusive, rarefied perspective on the quality and breadth of contemporary Mexican literature.

Since the 1950s, Mexican literature has shown enormous diversity and productivity, with thematic elements that have reflected a persistent and often explicit concern for the challenges of daily life in Mexico. In one generation, punctuated by the landmark events of 1968, Mexican writing basically redefined itself, no longer the purview of a small literary circle centered in Mexico City or a limited, elite audience found mainly in the nation's handful of metropolitan areas. Rather, writing in Mexico sustains a youthful quality, critical, restless, inquisitive, making it difficult to easily characterize given its complexity, richness, and variety.

Italia Boliver

See also Nationalism and National Identity; Popular Culture; Theater; Universidad Nacional Autónoma de México

Further Reading

Brewster, Claire. 2005. *Responding to Crisis in Contemporary Mexico: The Political Writings of Paz, Fuentes, Monsiváis, and Poniatowska.* Tucson: University of Arizona Press.

Foster, David William, ed. 1994. *Mexican Literature: A History.* Austin: University of Texas Press.

García, Cristina, ed. 2006. *Bordering Fires: The Vintage Book of Contemporary Mexican and Chicano/a Literature.* New York: Vintage Books.

van Delden, Maarten, and Yvon Grenier. 2009. *Gunshots at the Fiesta: Literature and Politics in Latin America.* Nashville, TN: Vanderbilt University Press.

López Portillo, José

José López Portillo was president of Mexico from 1976 to 1982. He is considered one of the most controversial Mexican presidents because of his extravagant personality, some major economic and political choices he made, the world economic context he had to deal with, and later for accusations of his participation in the repression of students' demonstrations. At the beginning of his presidency, Mexico had experienced one of the most successful periods of economic growth in its history. However, at the end of his term, the economy was in crisis due in part to international petroleum price fluctuations. The first political reforms toward democratic transition also took place during López Portillo's sexenio. A new electoral organism was created with relative independence from the government. The roots of these and economic democratic transitions can be found in the López Portillo administration.

Background and road to the presidency During the hegemony of the Partido Revolucionario Institucional (Institutional Revolutionary Party, PRI), the political mechanism that appointed Mexican presidents was known as *dedazo* ("finger-pointing"). A president at the end of his tenure would make a nonexplicit selection of his successor. It had become nonwritten tradition that the current Minister of the Interior would become the next president. José López Portillo was minister of the interior during the presidency of Luis Echeverría (1970–1976) and was considered the president's close friend. Public opinion held that López Portillo would be the next president.

As the only candidate in the race, López Portillo won the 1976 election. The traditional opposition party, the Partido Acción Nacional (National Action Party, PAN), had no candidates due to an internal struggle. The dying extreme left-wing Mexican Communist Party was considered illegal but still claimed to receive over a million votes for its candidate. The legitimacy of the election was questioned, producing social instability and exposing the PRI's authoritarianism. López Portillo needed to achieve stability by reforming the political regime.

Political reforms By the first year of López Portillo's administration, a first substantial political reform was undertaken, the Ley Federal de Organizaciones Políticas y Procedimientos Electorales (Federal Law for Political Organizations and Electoral Procedures, LOPPE). It was enforced in 1977. This law described and ordered a new electoral college, which was relatively more independent from the government. It allowed the registration of some organizations that were considered illegal, permitted coalitions, and opened television and radio time for opposition propaganda.

LOPPE also included a new formula for proportional representation, distributing 100 seats among the political parties according to the national election percentage of votes, in order to guarantee the presence of minor political forces. A new building for the Cámara de Diputados (Chamber of Deputies) was needed, because the number of representatives increased from 186 to 400. The current San Lázaro building was built as a result. LOPPE resulted in the growing representation of opposition parties in the first election after its promulgation.

Despite these reforms, the authoritarian mechanism and power alternation remained in place. The desolating economic panorama in 1982 changed the internal way in which the *dedazo* worked. A president with more experience in economics than politics was needed. The PRI's 1982 presidential candidate was the minister of finance, Miguel de la Madrid. This was a major shift in the ideology and selection of PRI candidates, who were no longer required to share most of the "revolutionary values."

Economic policy Just a few months before López Portillo took office, the Mexican peso suffered a strong devaluation due to excessive spending in the Echeverría administration. The government turned to the International Monetary Fund (IMF) for a huge loan. The IMF's conditions for granting the loan were low government expenditures and low public wages.

Despite the devaluation at the beginning of his term, López Portillo kept the exchange rate fixed with a peso that was overvalued against the dollar. Nonetheless, during the first three years, he maintained low public expenditures and public investments. The Mexican government was acting with caution in light of the international economic panorama.

Things changed after Mexico became the largest exporter of petroleum for a short period. Arab countries suspended their exports to the United States as a punishment for the Western world's support of Israel in the Yom Kippur War in 1973. At the same time, rich oil fields were found in southern Mexico. Since Mexico's internal oil market was controlled by the public enterprise Petróleos Mexicanos (PEMEX), the government quickly made use of the abundant resources. López Portillo's administration began taking loans from diverse international agencies in order to create public programs and expand the bureaucracy.

In his long list of remarkable speeches and quotes, López Portillo is remembered for saying that "Mexico used to administrate scarcity. Now with the booming of petroleum resources, we will administrate abundance." However, oil prices later fell lower than expected, and excessive public expenditure surpassed the petroleum surplus, increasing Mexican external debt. A devaluation was needed, but López Portillo believed that "a President who devaluates, devaluates himself." He finally devaluated the peso when it had an approximately 400 percent exchange rate. He declared suspension of payments on government debt and left his successor with an economic crisis that would require extreme measures to correct.

In his last State of the Nation Address, López Portillo blamed bankers for the devaluation due to a "lack of patriotism." Just before leaving office, he nationalized all banks. At the end of his speech, López Portillo cried in front of the national media and the Congress for failing the poor.

Foreign affairs   López Portillo also maintained a controversial foreign policy. Like his predecessor, he tried to get closer with revolutionary and socialist governments. He expressed sympathy for the governments of Nicaragua's Daniel Ortega and Cuba's Fidel Castro, resulting in negative reaction from the U.S. government. López Portillo responded with the organization of a North-South Summit in Cancún in 1981. The summit's aim was to promote dialogue among First World and Third World countries.

In 1981, López Portillo publicly received Pope John Paul II during the pontiff's first official visit to Mexico since diplomatic relations were broken with the Church in 1857. This act was criticized by many PRI sectors and left movements, which were historically strongly anticlerical.

The López Portillo administration reestablished diplomatic relations with Spain that had been broken since the Francisco Franco dictatorship.

Social policy and sectorial relations   Like that of his predecessors, López Portillo's populist policy boosted his popularity among unions and peasant organizations. His increasing of expenditures in public firms, expropriations, and social programs aimed at the working classes and indigenous people were celebrated and actually gave him high approval rates during his term as president.

Relationships with the opposition groups, both PAN and the leftist leaders, improved significantly due to López Portillo's political reforms. He also had a better relationship with the student movements than his two predecessors. Yet while his administration did not initiate any important acts of repression against these groups, he was still tied to a student massacre in 1971.

Juan Manuel Galarza and José Ignacio Lanzagorta

See also De la Madrid, Miguel; Echeverría Álvarez, Luis; Partido Revolucionario Institucional

Further Reading

Krauze, Enrique. 1997. *La presidencia imperial.* Mexico City: Tusquets.

Lustig, Nora. 1992. *Mexico: The Remaking of an Economy.* Washington, DC: Brookings Institution.

Lucha Libre

Lucha libre ("free wrestling"), which combines spectacle with the sport of wrestling, is hugely popular in Mexico. As an organized sport, it began with the founding of Empresa Mexicana de Lucha Libre (Mexican Company of Lucha Libre) in 1933. Presently, the Consejo Mundial de Lucha Libre (Worldwide Commission of Lucha Libre, CMLL) sets the rules for the sport.

In Mexico, *lucha libre* has led to large-scale businesses in which companies and promoters compete in the presentation and production of dramatic fights. As a sport, *lucha libre* is controversial. Detractors of Mexican wrestling question the authenticity of the matches, the integrity of the outcomes, and the skill of the sport. Still, to be a professional wrestler and obtain a license granted by the CMLL requires at least five years of tests and training. Unlike boxing, *lucha libre* allows all types of blows during a match. In fact, wrestlers are encouraged to use almost anything handy to defeat their opponents, such as chairs, pails, stools, tables, and so on, when necessary and available.

Lucha libre consists of hand-to-hand wrestling, and its goal is to make one's opponent surrender. The rule for achieving victory is winning two of three falls with no time limit. There are four types of fights: individual-to-individual, pairs, trios, and tag-team fighting (there is no limit in the number of wrestlers in tag-team fighting).

Large arenas have been built in order to accommodate the popularity of the sport. Among the most important are the Arena Revolución, the Arena México,

Lucha libre fighter Brazo de Plata, above, flies from the top rope as he prepares to flatten two rival fighters during a fight at the historic Arena Coliseo in Mexico City. (AP/Wide World Photos)

the Arena Coliseo, and the Juan de la Barreda Arena in Mexico City and the Arena Victoria and the Arena Coliseo in Guadalajara.

During the year several titles are disputed, each belonging to a different weight category: heavyweight, cruiserweight, light heavyweight, middleweight, welterweight. There are also title fights for tag teams, trios, *atómicos* ("four-on-four fighting"), women, and midgets (in Spanish popularly referred to as *minis*).

In *lucha libre* there are basically two types of wrestlers. The *rudos* ("tough ones" or "crude ones") are usually cast as the "bad guys." The *técnicos* ("technicians" or "scientists") are usually presented as the "good ones." These two types of wrestlers generally battle each other in every fight. The differences are also in terms of skill as the *rudo* is usually less agile than the *técnico* opponent.

As for their behavior in the ring, the *rudos* insult the public, break the rules, and use dodgy tricks to try to defeat the *técnico* wrestler. The *rudos* will use unfair techniques such as chairs and bottles to hurt their opponents. In contrast, the *técnico* wrestlers are the embodiment of the rules and are always very respectful of the audience and the referee of the match.

Wrestlers have the choice of changing their ring identity as long as the manager allows them to do so. However, *técnicos* are more likely to become *rudos* than the other way around. *Técnicos* tend to stay loyal to their fan base, which is largely composed of young children to whom the wrestlers become role models and idols.

Regardless of their good or bad guy personas, all wrestlers use a stage name and a costume that identifies them before the audience. A wrestler can represent a well-known character or social type like El Mestizo ("a person of mixed racial ancestry"), El Cafre ("a reckless driver"), and El Huichol ("an indigenous person"); or they can take on abstract ideas like Kahos ("Chaos") or Psicosis. Some wrestlers have taken bold names: there has even been a wrestler called PRI (for the Partido Revolucionario Institucional [Institutional Revolutionary Party]) and another that, after the rise of the Ejército Zapatista de Liberación Nacional (Zapatist Army for National Liberation, EZLN) in 1994, became El Zapatista (The Zapatist). In addition to their costume and name, there is a third optional element that allows the public to distinguish the wrestlers: their masks. The design and color of the mask must be coordinated with the rest of the wrestler's clothes and their name. Fighters are free to choose and change their appearance. A good example is the case of the famous wrestler Mil Máscaras (A Thousand Masks), who uses a different mask whenever he fights and whose only distinctive symbol is the letter M that can be found on top of every mask he wears. A wrestler is expected to act according to the character that he represents. For example, in the 1990s, the wrestler Caló (Slang) made moves in the ring similar to the dance steps of the rap group of the same name.

In the world of *lucha libre,* there have been wrestlers who have become legends, like El Santo (The Saint), undeniably the greatest star in the history of Mexican *lucha libre;* the Blue Demon; El Rayo de Jalisco (Lightening of Jalisco); and Tinieblas (Darkness). In contemporary Mexico, among the most famous wrestlers are Hijo del Perro Aguayo (Son of the Aguayo Dog) and Último Guerrero (Last Warrior). It should also be noted that among the immortals of *lucha libre* is female wrestler Martha Villalobos.

Lucha libre enjoys an enormous audience due to the sport's popularization in films of the 1940s and the onset of television in the early 1950s. The golden age of *lucha libre* cinema featured wrestlers like El Santo, Blue Demon, and Mil Máscaras, making them Mexican movie stars into the 1960s. Television ended the genre of *lucha libre* filmmaking, but the sport became a staple of the new medium in Mexico.

Since the foundation of the company of Asistencia, Asesoría y Administración (Assistance, Advisory, and Management, AAA) in 1992, *lucha libre* has spread from Mexico to Latin America. The sport has also gained more widespread popularity from being televised. In fact, in recent years, foreign wrestlers have been recruited, primarily from Japan and the United States.

The business of *lucha libre* has produced ancillary activities such as the making of toys, T-shirts, masks, key rings, posters, mugs, and so on, representative of the sport and those who participate. As a consequence, this form of wrestling has become an icon in art, design, and advertising in Mexico. Although the sport is generally perceived as belonging to the working class, its fame crosses all social boundaries, and it has been embraced as a unique expression of Mexican popular culture.

Citlali López Maldonado

See also Photography; Popular Culture; Television

Further Reading

Levi, Heather. 2008. *The World of* Lucha Libre*: Secrets, Revelations, and Mexican National Identity.* Durham, NC: Duke University Press.

Levi, Heather J. 2001. Masked Struggle: An Ethnography of Lucha Libre. PhD dissertation, New York University.

Möbius, Janina. 2007. *Y detrás de la máscara—el pueblo: Lucha libre, un espectáculo popular mexicano entre la tradición y la modernidad.* Mexico City: Universidad Nacional Autónoma de México, Instituto de Investigaciones Estéticas.

Monsiváis, Carlos, and Gabriel Rodríguez, text. Photographs by Lourdes Grobet. 2005. *Lucha Libre: Masked Superstars of Mexican Wrestling.* New York: D.A.P.; Mexico City: Trilce Ediciones.

M

Maquiladoras

Maquiladoras, initiated by the Border Industrialization Program (BIP) in 1965 and originally called in-bond plants, are sites of product assembly or manufacturing operations that exist in every major Mexican city along the U.S.-Mexican border. (The concept would later be extended to the interior of the country.) Many maquiladoras are foreign owned by multinational corporations that import raw materials into the Mexican plants where workers assemble the products. Maquiladoras often export their products out of Mexico. The proliferation of maquiladoras has drastically increased the industrialization and population of border cities, leading to hopes for a more modern Mexico as well as worries about the significant disparities between wealth and poverty and the environmental effects of such dramatic changes.

Upon the termination of the Bracero Program in 1964, about 200,000 unemployed workers returned to the Mexican side of the border seeking jobs. Thousands more unemployed individuals were already waiting in border cities with the hope of journeying to the United States as part of the Bracero Program. The unilateral termination of this program by the United States created an abyss for unemployed individuals. Unemployment hovered around 40 percent to 50 percent in many border towns during this era. The Mexican government, fearing violence and havoc, urgently sought to create new opportunities for employment. The government promoted the BIP to its citizens by arguing for the need for foreign investment, new technologies, an increase in Mexican workers' skills, and an increase in demand for Mexican products.

When the BIP began, maquiladoras were the only companies authorized for 100 percent foreign ownership without prior authorization. Mexico first attracted companies from the United States and later from other countries such as Canada and Japan by offering to finance infrastructure and guarantee cheap workers. The BIP allowed the duty-free importation of machinery, operational components, raw materials, and parts if the company importing the materials guaranteed the exportation of the finished products. In theory, this would keep foreign companies from competing with Mexican industries. Mexico's proximity, relatively stable political atmosphere, and somewhat familiar culture persuaded U.S. companies to relocate their international operations from Asia to the U.S.-Mexican border.

In the beginning of the maquiladora program, companies frequently assembled only parts of their products in Mexico. They then shipped their unfinished products across the border, where their sisters, or "twin" plants, finished the assembly process. By creating this system, companies were able to label their products as "Made in the U.S.A." For this reason, people also refer to the maquiladora industry as the "twin plant assembly" industry.

Changes in the international economic markets are the primary causes for the dramatic fluctuations in the number of maquiladora operations, employed individuals, and output. The industry moderately expanded from 1965 to about 1974, when Mexico's stable and hearty economy allowed for a slow but continuous increase in the minimum wage. In 1976, Mexico began its devaluation of the peso, which caused a rapid increase in the minimum wage, subsequently worrying transnational companies. The maquiladora industry initially shrank during the early 1980s. However, while more devaluations of the peso occurred in the 1980s, a matching increase in the minimum wage did not accompany the resulting inflation. The cheap cost of labor attracted more companies back to the border states and a dramatic growth in the maquiladora industry occurred. Later, maquiladora plants were permitted to move to the interior of the country, such as to Aguascalientes, Guadalajara, and Guanajuato, and to Yucatán.

Several laws and treaties dramatically affected the maquiladora operations. Mexico joined the General Agreement on Tariffs and Trade (GATT) in 1986, which curtailed labor union activities, limited protectionist tariffs, and reduced minimum wage increases, among other changes that made the Mexican border more attractive to foreign investors. The 1989 Maquiladora Decree decentralized the government agencies in charge of overseeing the maquiladora program, and it simplified the requirements for establishing and running a maquiladora. It reduced the customs paperwork and allowed companies to file most applications for licenses and other approvals at a central office. The 1994 North American Free Trade Agreement (NAFTA) also altered the functioning of maquiladoras. This agreement lowered tariff barriers on goods, which allowed increased direct foreign investment on the border and promoted trade among Canada, the United States, and Mexico. Many proponents of the agreement argued that the broader reduction of protectionist tariffs would encourage maquiladoras to relocate their operations further into the interior of Mexico and hence limit population growth on the border. These predictions overestimated the movement of plants away from the border, as the majority of companies kept their maquiladora operations close to the border, limiting transportation costs and facilitating cross-border living for upper-level management. The 1998 Decree for the Promotion and Operation of the Maquiladora Export Industry abolished the 1989 Maquiladora Decree and set forth new regulations to bring Mexico into compliance with NAFTA. The most recent major legislation on the maquiladoras was the Maquila 2001 rules. These rules increased the complexity of customs duties. They increased these duties for some maquiladoras, but it continued to exempt many maquiladoras from paying importation duties. The heyday of the maquiladoras began to ebb by the early 2000s. A major challenge to the industry in Mexico has been the rise of competing low-wage countries, most notably China but also Vietnam and Malaysia. Moreover, a recurring problem has been the swings in the U.S. economy, given that any downturn has a negative impact on the maquiladora industry and its workers. Furthermore, the violence of the illegal drug trade has also played havoc with the maquila plants along the border, providing yet another reason for companies to relocate to sites outside of Mexico and adding to the concern over unemployment and underemployment in the country.

While initially billed as a source of employment for the newly unemployed primarily male workers displaced by the discontinued Bracero Program, company hiring practices favored females. Since the 1980s, the proportion of women to men gradually shifted. While women still accounted for the majority of workers on the line, men also made up a large segment of these workers. Management also shifted its hiring practices from favoring single, young, childless, and inexperienced women to choosing older mothers. Theoretically, these mothers would be more dependent on their jobs, because their children relied on their salaries, and therefore they would be less likely to risk their jobs by limiting their production or by participating in prolabor activism. While this argument may seem reasonable, others contend that companies only shifted their ideologies about the preferred woman in order to continue paying workers low salaries.

Within the plants, management practices certain strategies, and the workers counter with their own inventive tactics. Maquiladora management seeks to divide workers by creating competition among labor areas of the plant as well as between individuals within their own sections. This works to hinder successful union formation, strikes, and other collective organization. Workers' effective responses include *tortugismo,* or the conscious slowing down of the production process, as well as strikes and the formation of outside networks of support that foster community among the workers and help to counteract the attempts by management to divide them.

Researchers have blamed the maquiladoras for a host of environmental and health problems. These include, but are not limited to, high blood lead levels in children, tuberculosis, asthma, hepatitis A, and birth defects. Most of these conditions actually result from the inadequate environmental infrastructure that includes a lack of potable water. However, scholars and environmentalists trace these problems back to the maquiladoras because of their intense drains on the available resources and their seemingly magnetic ability to attract too many migrants, which the border is unprepared to support.

The maquiladoras remain controversial. Since their start in 1965, the maquiladoras greatly affected trade beween the United States and Mexico, but the plants also impacted border cities and their workers as well as their environments. While the maquiladoras are profitable and contribute to the Mexican economy, the public, media, and social critics will continue to question an industry that thrives as a result of the gendered inequities in Mexican society.

Erin Graham

See also Aguascalientes; Baja California Norte; Chihuahua; Coahuila; Economy, U.S.-Mexican Border; Environment; Environmental Issues; Income; Jalisco; Labor Force and Labor Movements; North American Free Trade Agreement; Sonora; Tamaulipas; Yucatán

Further Reading

Fernández-Kelly, María Patricia. 1983. *For We Are Sold, I and My People: Women and Industry in Mexico's Frontier.* Albany: State University of New York Press.

Kopinak, Kathryn. 1996. *Desert Capitalism: Maquiladoras in North America's Western Industrial Corridor.* Tucson: University of Arizona Press.

Peña, Devon G. 1997. *The Terror of the Machine: Technology, Work, Gender, and Ecology on the U.S.-Mexican Border.* Austin: The Center for Mexican American Studies, The University of Texas at Austin.

Tiano, Susan. 1994. *Patriarchy on the Line: Labor, Gender, and Ideology in the Mexican Maquila Industry.* Philadelphia: Temple University Press.

Media Arts, New

In the 1990s, with the creation of the government-funded Centro Multimedia México (Multimedia Center, CMM), Mexico debuted as a site for institutionally supported production of digital arts and for the exploration of new media. The center was intended to be a fundamental part of the Centro Nacional de las Artes (National Center for the Arts, CNA), inaugurated in November 1994 by then-president Carlos Salinas de Gortari. The establishment of the Multimedia Center marked an effort to make Mexico a world leader in the relationship between technology and artistic production. It was a key event in the government's cultural policy to promote research, teaching, and production of new media arts.

Unfortunately, the political and economic turn of the last year of Salinas's presidency made for an inauspicious start for the CNA and its units, including the Multimedia Center. The onset of the cutting-edge activities of the center appeared to be at odds with the age-old grievances that surfaced in the political and economic crises of 1994 and the severe criticism of the federal government's spending priorities. In a context in which government critics decried the entrenched social inequities of Mexico, the center and its highly advanced technological facilities became a symbol of the tenacious disparities in Mexico.

In response to that initial stigma of its programs, a group of artists, researchers, and art critics came together to move the new center forward and to situate its work within the social conditions of the country. Led in this effort by its director, Andrea Di Castro, the center consistently faced sparse budgets and a lack of enthusiastic political support for a project associated with the discredited presidency of Salinas de Gortari. Frustrated by the precarious financial base of the center, Di Castro resigned as director in 2001 after a six-year struggle to sustain and promote the center's activities.

The center represented the fruition of many years of experimentation and pioneering exhibits by several artists in the 1980s. For example, heliographs, electrographs, fax art, and works obtained through the use of photocopiers or mimeographs constituted the first steps that were later consolidated as multimedia arts. The works of Felipe Ehrenberg, Arnulfo Aquino, Carlos Aguirre, and Mauricio Guerrero set early standards for the credibility of technological media as art. Two exhibits in particular were crucial to this process of advancing digital arts: *Electrosensitivity,* organized by the Universidad Autónoma Metropolitana (Metropolitan Autonomous University) in 1988, and *I Find Other Graphs,* organized in 1993 by the Academy of San Carlos at the Universidad Nacional Autónoma de México (National Autonomous University of Mexico, UNAM). Those exhibits built on the works of pioneers in the medium, such as Manuel Felguérez and Pola Weiss in the 1970s and 1980s. Later, with the expansion of personal computers and unrestricted access to the Internet, experimentation surged in the area of digital arts, cybernet, and virtual reality, bringing together skills in computer engineering and graphic design for the purpose of artistic creation.

Artist Guillermo Gómez-Peña, marginal to government-supported art circuits and private venues for exhibition and diffusion, blazed new forms of expression in his fusion of performance art, activism, critique, journalism, photography, and audio with new technologies. Based in the United States, Gómez-Peña founded the art collective *Our Pocha,* where various alternative multimedia projects emerged, such as *Temple of Confessions, Cybervato,* and *The Chica-Iranian Project.* These projects intended to explore the complexity of the sociocultural nexus between Mexico and the United States and entailed harsh criticism of racism, discrimination, and intolerance. The trajectory of Gómez-Peña's work in the 1990s became a reference point in the development and conceptualization of multimedia arts in Mexico.

Another example of the progressive incorporation of distinct media to create critical-interactive artworks is the work of Andrea Di Castro (1953–). Italian by birth, he has lived in Mexico since 1966, where he has enriched national artistic production by participating in the multimedia art scene with computerized animations, interactive CD-ROMs, and remote-transmission video performances. In 1990 and 1992, respectively, he participated in the first and second Biennials of Video in Mexico, highlighted by a series of talks about the relationship between art and new technologies. He formed part of the group of artists that solidified the production of the Multimedia Center of the CNA in its first years, co-organizing the Festival of Video and Electronic Art (VIDARTE) in 1999 in which he was recognized for his artistic endeavors in the field. Di Castro's career in the development of digital art was furthered when, in 2000, he created and directed the Cyberlounge of the Tamayo Museum, a space dedicated to the production, exhibition, and debate of multimedia art. The site at the Tamayo Museum has served as an important link in the network of institutions dedicated to advancing the field of art and new media in Mexico.

It was also in the year 2000 that the Laboratorio de Arte Alameda (Alameda Art Laboratory) was launched in Mexico City's historic center, after the space (originally a convent that subsequently housed an art gallery) underwent a major renovation to create the laboratory. Since its inception, the Laboratorio de Arte Alameda has been at the forefront of the field, organizing scores of digital and multimedia art exhibits, as well as a series of activities related to research, discussion, and diffusion of art and new technologies; in this effort, the leadership of Priamo Lozada has proven instrumental.

Since these early steps, other multimedia art venues have emerged in Mexico City that exhibit and promote initiatives related to digital art, such as the Museo Carrillo Gil, the Museo Universitario de Ciencias y Artes of the UNAM, Universum, and the Ex-Teresa Arte Actual, as well as the Centro Cultural de España and the Sala de Arte Público Siqueiros. In addition, the Festival Internacional de Artes Electrónicas (International Festival of Electronic Art and Video), which is celebrated every two years in the Multimedia Center of the CNA, has played a key role in the promotion of digital art of Mexico. Furthermore, the event has served as a crucial forum for the discussion of multimedia arts and as means for Mexican artists in the field to participate in the international circles dedicated to the digital arts, especially those in Latin America.

In the 1990s, the works of multimedia artists became incorporated into the established art-exhibition circuit, paralleling the creation of the Multimedia Center and the initial festivals and international competitions that prodded digital arts production. The majority of these Mexican multimedia artists had studied abroad for some time, but upon returning to Mexico they found that conditions were far from optimal. Nonetheless, they found a stimulating and receptive environment in which many artists' works responded to the problems that the country faced at that time. Among that initial generation of multimedia art, the works of Rafael Lozano-Hemmer, Arcángel Constantini, Fernando Llanos, Minerva Cuevas, and Fran Ilich were particularly important given the diversity of the issues raised by their projects and because of their exploration of technological innovation with social criticism. In these representative works, one work of Minerva Cuevas merits specific mention: *The Better Life Inc.* (2000), where the artist created a freewheeling, completely accessible Internet site depicting relationships between corporations and people.

Unosunosyunosceros.com (2000) by Arcángel Constantini is another site that has earned much attention as a laboratory that explores the social, economic, political, and cultural contradictions of present-day Mexico in the global context of the Internet. *Borderhack* (2001) by Fran Ilich was an initiative that brought together a group of artists, activists, and migrants concerned with conditions at the U.S.-Mexican border in order to reflect on the situations that migrants must endure to survive on the other side. *Video-mails* (2000) by Fernando Llanos was another notable project, a weekly e-mail publication, including his own digital video, sent to artists, curators, and critics with the goal of creating awareness in the artistic field about video art and its diffusion. *Alzado Vectorial* (1999) by Rafael Lozano-Hemmer was the first multimedia work of monumental character. Using his concept of relational architecture, Lozano-Hemmer organized a series of works involving large-scale interactive events capable of transforming buildings into artistic sites by using new technological interfaces. Other notable works created by Lozano-Hemmer include *33 preguntas por minuto* (2000), *Caguamas sinápticas* (2004), *Público subtitulado* (2005), and *Entrelazamiento* (2005). These shows of multimedia arts clearly indicate the maturation and acceptance of the digital arts medium, earning Lozano-Hemmer individual recognition, and equally important, recognition of this rich and growing field of artistic production.

Olivia Vidal López

See also Art Education; Art Exhibitions; Arts, Alternative Venues for; Photography; Visual Arts

Further Reading

Biesenbach, Klaus, pub. and curator. 2002. *Mexico City: An Exhibition about the Exchange Rates of Bodies and Values.* Exhibition catalog. New York: P.S.1 Contemporary Art Center.

Gallo, Rubén. 2004, August. *New Tendencies in Mexican Art: The 1990s.* New York: Palgrave Macmillan.

Made in Mexico. 2004. Boston: Institute of Contemporary Art.

Mraz, John. 2009. *Looking for Mexico: Modern Visual Culture and National Identity.* Durham, NC: Duke University Press.

Mexican Ecologist Green Party

See Partido Verde Ecologista de México

Mexican Petroleum

See Petróleos Mexicanos

México, State of

The official coat of arms of the Estado de México. (Corel)

The state of México (often abbreviated to Edomex from Estado de México in Spanish) is in the center of the country of Mexico. The state of México has an area of about 8,687 square miles, which represents 1.1 percent of Mexican territory. It is bounded to the north by Hidalgo and Querétaro, to the east by Tlaxcala and Puebla, to the south by Morelos and Guerrero, and to the west by Michoacán. The history and development of the state of México are tied intimately to those of Mexico City. The modern boundaries of the state were set in 1869, when Toluca became the capital city. The enormous archaeological site and ancient city of Teotihuacán or "place of the gods," which contains some of the largest pyramidal structures built in the pre-Columbian Americas, is located in the state of México. In 2005, its total population was estimated at just over 14 million, making it the most populous state in Mexico.

The state of México is crossed by three parallel volcanic chains. There are mountains in the west, the Monte Alto and Las Cruces mountains in the center of the state, and the Sierra Nevada in the east. The northern region consists of flatlands and hills; in the south, there are mountains, canyons, and ravines; in the east, there are mountains and volcanoes; in the west, there are plains, hills, and mountains; and in the central area, there are extensive broad valleys surrounded by hills. One of the largest volcanoes is Iztaccíhuatl (17,343 feet). The state of México's rivers include the Lerma, the Tula, the Moctezuma, and the Pánuco. Some areas of the state, such as the valley of Cuautitlán-Texcoco, have no water resources.

In the eastern part of the state, the mountains of the Sierra Nevada are covered with pine, oak, white cedar, and fir trees. Plants native to the valleys are cactus, nopal (similar to prickly pear), copal trees (a type of tree with heavy, thick resin), and gourds. Native animals include coati (a raccoonlike animal) and deer. There are many bird species native to the state, including the sparrow hawk. The state of México and its southern neighbor, Michoacán, are winter homes to hundreds of thousands of migrating monarch butterflies, which return annually.

México State was part of a broader area that gave rise to several urban cultures before the colonial period. Important population centers included Teotihuacán, Tula, Chalco, and Texcoco, and many areas had come under Aztec domination on the eve of the Spanish conquest. Spaniards arrived in central Mexico in 1519 and soon captured the Aztec capital (which became Mexico City). With help from native allies, the area surrounding the city was subdued. Hernán Cortés parceled out lands and native laborers to the conquerors, including himself.

The colonial economy of México State was based on agriculture and cattle ranching. The large and growing market of Mexico City provided consistent demand for

The skyline of downtown of Mexico City with poor suburban barrios on the mountain slopes in the background. (Dreamshot | Dreamstime.com)

crops produced with the help of native labor. Silver mining also developed in the area, with mines at Zacualpán, Sultepec, and Temascaltepec utilizing native labor. The revolt of Miguel Hidalgo and José María Morelos, which began México's struggle for independence in 1810, attracted some of the region's natives, whose lives were increasingly affected by labor and tribute demands. There were several insurgent victories here, including the brief capture of Toluca.

In 1824, statehood was granted to a large entity that included today's México State, Hidalgo, Morelos, the Federal District, and much of Guerrero. Mexico City was initially the capital, and the new state contained the most significant population center in the new country. As the 19th century progressed, México State assumed its modern shape. Mexico City was separated and Toluca chosen as the permanent capital. Guerrero was carved out in 1849, and in 1869 Hidalgo and Morelos were established.

Despite the autocratic nature of its political system, the Porfiriato brought remarkable progress to México State. Mining and industry expanded with the help of foreign investment, and the railroad enhanced the region's links with the Federal District and other areas of the country. Governor José Vicente Villada helped foster these developments while also maintaining a degree of popular support through construction of new schools and declaration of laws that benefited the working class. But Villada and other state leaders also witnessed increasing opposition to the Porfirio Díaz regime and its model of development, which did not benefit all sectors of society.

In 1909, Andrés Molina Enríquez, a teacher from México State, wrote a pointed critique of Mexico's social problems, including peonage and land concentration. Molina was among those who supported Francisco I. Madero's rebellion against Díaz in 1910–1911. Molina, however, was blocked in his bid for the governor's post, and he was captured and imprisoned. Several of his followers, upset with Madero's lack of attention to land reform, joined the movement of Morelos rebel Emiliano Zapata. The state's Zapatista movement, led by Genovevo de la O and Francisco Pacheco, grew in importance, and after Madero's death, it challenged Venustiano Carranza's Constitutionalist movement for control of the state. Briefly in 1915, Mexico's Convention government (with which Zapata sided) dominated, and Governor Gustavo Baz embraced Zapata's Plan of Ayala, which called for sweeping agrarian reform. Carranza's Constitutionalists soon occupied Toluca, however, and hopes for radical reform diminished.

After 1940, as Mexico's leaders shifted attention from revolutionary reform to development and economic modernization, México State (along with the Federal District) experienced an industrial transformation. Private investment in electricity, steel, textiles, construction, and tourism all aided in this change. During the late 1950s and early 1960s, Governor Gustavo Baz welcomed the establishment of several automotive plants (including General Motors and Ford). Baz also promoted the creation of industrial zones in the Toluca Valley, Texcoco, and Chalco. México State's impressive economic growth did not affect agriculture, which attracted little investment and remained technologically backward. Additionally, the economic boom did not benefit all areas of the state. The south in particular remained rural, agricultural, and underdeveloped.

Urbanization accompanied the industrial boom, and during the last three decades of the 20th century, México State witnessed a steady and overwhelming growth in its population. People poured into the state to fill the jobs created by industry, and many more spilled in from the congested Federal District. Just as Mexico's capital city found it increasingly difficult to provide housing and services to its inhabitants, México State also struggled to accommodate the necessities of its residents. The dynamic growth of both areas also brought environmental problems (particularly air pollution and the depletion of water resources) and a steady decline in living conditions for many. When Mexico began experiencing an economic crisis during the 1980s, rising crime rates were added to the picture. Nonetheless, the dominant party, the Partido Revolucionario Institucional (Institutional Revolutionary Party, PRI), was able to contain the political dissatisfaction that arose through the 1990s, despite the economic doldrums of that decade. In an area populated disproportionately by those tied to the PRI, the political leaders of the state of Mexico (or Edomex as it is popularly referred to) managed to divert large amounts of resources to its principal towns as a means to dampen discontent. Thus, the PRI found the means to sustain support in Edomex as opposed to the party's travails in many other parts of the country. In the 2005 gubernatorial election, the PRI candidate won but with only 47 percent of the vote. Nonetheless, it was an important victory, given the challenge posed by the left-of-center party that had taken the crucial mayoral race of Mexico City next door. And the PRI's winning of the governorship of Edomex was also significant in light of the population of the state and its consequent political clout in congressional representation for the former ruling party of the country. Six years later the PRI gubernatorial candidate achieved a convincing victory with 63 percent of the vote, providing a decisive confirmation of the political comeback of the old dominant party in the context of the impending 2012 presidential contest. Indeed, the current configuration of the congressional delegation from Edomex has 50 members from the PRI, while the two major opposing parties together have but 12 seats. The future of México State, like that of the Federal District, will largely depend on how its leaders manage the multiple challenges that face the most densely populated area of the country and its highly politicized environment.

Suzanne B. Pasztor

See also Mexico City; Partido de la Revolución Democrática; Politics and Political Parties; Urbanization

Further Reading

Jarquín, O., Teresa María, and Carlos Herrejón Peredo. 1995. *Breve historia del estado de México.* Mexico City: El Colegio de México.

Portal del Gobierno del Estado de México. http://www.edomex.gob.mx.

Valdivia-Machuca, Arnulfo. 2005. *State and Business Groups in Mexico: The Role of Informal Institutions in the Process of Industrialization, 1936–1984.* New York: Routledge.

Mexico City

Mexico City occupies about two-thirds of a political entity called the Distrito Federal (Federal District, DF), which has a status that is comparable to that of any state. In the popular mind, the city *is* the Distrito Federal. Mexicans generally do not refer to the city by name but talk instead of the "DF" or, more confusingly, of "México." But the truth is that the DF is an area that also has agriculture and forests, and metropolitan Mexico City (whatever the official political border may indicate) is not only in the DF, but also spills over into the state of México. In fact, the DF is almost completely surrounded by the state of México; only one other state, Morelos, shares a border with it, to the south. The adjective *chilangos* is often used, sometimes pejoratively, to refer to people from the DF.

The DF as such came into being in the 19th century. When the republic was first established, in 1824, a state of México was created, with Mexico City as its capital; about five months later, the decision was made to make Mexico City (then

Skyline of the financial center of Mexico City. On the right is Torre Mayor, the highest sky-scraper in Latin America; below it is Museo Rufino Tamayo in Chapultepec Park. Historic downtown is in the distance in the middle. (Dreamshot | Dreamstime.com)

still of modest size) part of a new and independent entity, the Distrito Federal. Officially, the DF now covers 1,490 square kilometers (approximately 581 square miles), about 10 times as much as its U.S. equivalent, the District of Columbia; this equates to 0.1 percent of the country. The DF is divided not into administrative municipalities, as are the states, but into *delegaciones* ("delegations"), of which there are 16. Thirty-four people represent the DF in the National Congress. The senior executive of the DF is its mayor, who used to be a presidential appointee but has been democratically elected since 1997; the election is timed to coincide with presidential elections. About two-thirds of the members of the legislative as-sembly of the DF represent specific electoral districts; the rest are there as a result of proportional representation.

To say how many people inhabit the DF it is not to say how many live in Mexico City and its sprawling suburbs—that is, the metropolitan area—into which it has been estimated that 1,000 new people enter and settle each day. The official total population of the DF, according to the 2010 government census, was just over 8.6 million; 90 percent of the inhabitants of the DF are Catholic, and roughly four percent are Protestant or evangelical. The relatively high densities in the two neighboring states reflect the geographic spread of the Mexico City Metropolitan Area, one of the world's most heavily populated conurbations, with something in the neighborhood of 20 million people.

Among its many institutions of higher education, Mexico City has the largest university in the Americas: the Universidad Nacional Autónoma de México (National Autonomous University of Mexico, UNAM), founded in 1551 and now attended by about 270,000 students.

Mexico City is the cultural capital of the country and the location of its main print and electronic media. In many ways, it can claim to be those things for the whole of Spanish America as well. It is a magnet for refugees from other Hispanic countries and for people from the provinces who come in search of job opportunities and a better life; as a result, a great many of its present-day inhabitants were born elsewhere. The traditional concentration of power in this place, dating as far back as the time of the Aztecs, has caused a similar concentration of administrative agencies, industry, commerce, and finance; of course, the same can be said of most capital cities, but in Mexico the phenomenon is extremely pronounced.

Mexico City sits at about 2,100 meters (7,000 feet), in a wide valley surrounded by mountains. The DF's highest point is at the Cerro La Cruz del Marqués in the south (Ajusco), which is just short of 4,000 meters (13,200 feet); there are several volcanoes that rise to 3,000 meters (10,000 feet) or more.

The climate is generally quite benign: cool or chilly nights and comfortably warm days, with very moderate rainfall. In the northwestern part of the DF the average annual temperature is 16.7 degrees Centigrade (62 degrees Fahrenheit) and the average annual rainfall is 584 millimeters (23 inches). In the mountains to the southwest and south, the figures are 11.4 degrees Centigrade (53 degrees Fahrenheit) and 1,129 millimeters (45 inches). Most rain falls during the summer months. The prevailing winds are from the north or northwest.

In flat parts of the DF, most of the rivers have been canalized or made to run underground. A few surface rivers remain, such as the Tacubaya, the Remedios, and the Magdalena. There is only one natural lake, Xochimilco, which is partially fed by recycled water. The major dams are Ansaldo and Canutillo. Mexico City's water basin has been artificially linked to others to guard against possible floods.

Because of the concentration of people, vehicular emissions, and industry, and because air is trapped in the Anáhuac Valley where the city sits, Mexico City has become one of the world's most polluted—the air is harmful to breathe about 80 percent of the time. Vehicles are registered to circulate either on odd or even days of the month in an effort to control their numbers, and recent governments have been taking measures to improve air quality by controlling pollutants. Parts of the DF have been made into protected natural areas.

There are some agricultural areas in the southern part of the DF, and some oaks, pines, and firs in the mountains; otherwise vegetation is to be found only in parks and gardens, and likewise the fauna. Wildlife found in nonurban areas includes coyotes, pumas, squirrels, foxes, rabbits, rattlesnakes, frogs, and birds such as falcons, eagles, hummingbirds, and ducks.

Cultural groups and languages   Although Mexico City was once the site of the Aztec capital, with many thousands of Indians, and a magnet for indigenous people from other parts of the country, it is frequently the case that its indigenous peoples have become integrated with the Hispanic majority. The 2005 census stated that 118,424 people (1.5 percent of the population) over the age of five spoke an indigenous language. The dominant language was that of the Aztecs, Náhuatl (with 30,371 speakers); the next most widely spoken, with figures ranging between 9,000 and 12,000, were Otomí, Mixtec, Zapotec, and Mazatec. Nine percent of those who said they were speakers of an indigenous language did not identify the language spoke.

Economy   Industrial activity in the Distrito Federal is far too extensive to describe here in any detail. In economic terms, the DF is Mexico's largest contributor in both the industrial and service sectors, but the smallest in agriculture. Most agriculture is concentrated in the south; 13 percent of the district is cultivated with oats for forage and corn, spinach, green beans, and nopales for human consumption. Another 5 percent is pastureland, and forests of pine, oak, eucalyptus, fir, and ash cover 19 percent of the district.

Overall, the DF accounts for approximately 20 percent of Mexico's gross domestic product. Mexico City has one of the world's largest urban economies. About a third of Mexicans countrywide live in poverty, but only about 15 percent of the inhabitants of Mexico City do; the city's per capita income is among the highest in Latin America. In recent decades, manufacturing industries have spread out increasingly into the state of México, partly as a result of government incentives designed to combat pollution.

Arts   No other Latin American city can rival Mexico City in terms of cultural variety and tradition. The Aztecs valued the arts, music, dance, and poetry; Tenochtitlán-Mexico City has always been a place of performance. Moreover, Mexico City was an artistic powerhouse in the colonial era, known for its poetry, theater, music, and art. Every imaginable type of music can be found in modern Mexico City, from organ-grinders to mariachis, jazz groups to rock bands, church choirs to symphony orchestras. Mexico City is the home of the National Conservatory, the National Symphony Orchestra, the famed Ballet Folklórico, and many other dance companies. It has a theater infrastructure that no other Latin American country can match; only a few cities in the world (such as London, New York, and Toronto) have more theaters.

Mexico has the most important cinema industry in the Hispanic world—one that has offered Spanish speakers an alternative to the dominance of Hollywood fare and produced a good number of films of real quality. The Instituto Mexicano de Cinematografía (National Film Institute, IMCINE) is headquartered in Mexico City. The major international publishing conglomerates of the Hispanic world all have offices there, as well, and Mexico's own imprints figure prominently.

Given its political and cultural importance, Mexico City has attracted countless artists and intellectuals from all over the country and farther afield. Furthermore, it has become home to many creative people seeking a refuge from political pressures elsewhere; for example, many people from the southern cone of Latin America fled to Mexico during the dictatorships of the late 20th century. Long before that, Mexico City had benefited from an influx of artists from Europe and the United States—filmmaker Sergei Eisenstein, for example, and avant-garde figures such as surrealist André Breton, composer Aaron Copland, and author D. H. Lawrence. Some of these people came because Mexico was fashionably "primitive." Others, such as Spaniards opposed to the dictator Francisco Franco, came because they could not stay in their own countries in the 1930s and 1940s. Many such foreigners put down deep roots in Mexico.

The list of distinguished artistic figures associated with Mexico City is very long, even if strictly limited to people born in the DF. For example, Carlos de Sigüenza y Góngora (1645–1700) was an official astronomer, mathematician, cartographer, and writer who produced one of the key creative texts of his time, *Los Infortunios de Alonso Ramírez*. José Joaquín Fernández de Lizardi (1776–1827) was a journalist, social critic, and writer; the founder of the influential newspaper *El Pensador Mexicano*; and a champion of independence. He also wrote what is generally regarded as Latin America's first novel: *El Periquillo Sarniento*.

Vicente Riva Palacio (1832–1896) fought against the U.S. and French invasions and served as a politician and diplomat and is also remembered as a journalist and creative writer. Angela Peralta (1845–1883) acquired the nickname "The Mexican Nightingale." She was a soprano who sang grand opera internationally and also founded her own company. Juan de Dios Peza (1852–1910) was another politician and diplomat who doubled as a writer, especially of popular poetry; he was a professor at the National Conservatory of Music as well.

Antonio Caso (1883–1946), a lawyer, writer, and philosopher, was one of a small group of leading thinkers in the first half of the 20th century. He was a member of the Academy of the Language and cofounder of the influential Ateneo de la Juventud. Alfonso Caso (1896–1970) was an archaeologist, politician, and writer who occupied a number of high-level national positions, such as the directorships of the Museum of Anthropology, the National Indian Institute, and UNAM. He was also a vital force behind the excavations at Monte Albán, in Oaxaca.

Jaime Torres Bodet (1902–1974) became very influential in education during the time of José Vasconcelos. He also served as a government minister and diplomat and won the National Prize for Literature. Salvador Novo (1904–1974) was one of Mexico's leading modern dramatists, a cofounder of Teatro Ulises, and a writer in other genres as well. He, too, won the National Prize for Literature.

Carlos Monsiváis (1938–2010) has been one of the country's most acerbic journalists and cultural commentators. The painter Frida Kahlo (1907–1954) was born in Coyoacán, where there is now a museum in her name. The wife of muralist

Diego Rivera, she was also active in the circle of intellectuals and artists that opposed the dictatorship in Spain.

Others on the long list of creative artists born in Mexico City include the poet, essayist, and Nobel laureate Octavio Paz (1914–1998); Rodolfo Usigli (1905–1979), probably Mexico's most famous dramatist; Arturo Ripstein (1943–), a leading film director; actor Mario Moreno, alias "Cantinflas" (1911–1993); and Carlos Chávez (1899–1978), the most famous Mexican composer of classical music.

Social customs   There are countless exhibitions, contests, and commercial events in the Distrito Federal. Every feast or saint's day has its celebrants in a district such as this. Some festivities are associated with particular communities; examples include Holy Week in Iztapalpa and Villa Milpa Alta; Santa Cruz and the Day of Builders, Engineers, and Architects in Santa Cruz Acalpixca, Xochiltepec, Xochimilco, and Villa Milpa Alta; the Feast of the Assumption in Tepepan, Xochimilco, and Milpa Alta (a major occasion also for the cathedral); the commemoration of the cry for independence, marked by a celebration and military processions in the Zócalo; and a similar commemoration of the start of the Revolution.

One festivity that has a very special meaning for Mexico in general and the DF in particular is December 12's Feast of the Virgin of Guadalupe. The story is that the Virgin Mary appeared to a Christian Indian laborer, Juan Diego, in 1531 at Tepeyac, addressing him in the Aztec language and telling him of her wish to have a shrine there. She gave Diego some roses to carry to the bishop, wrapped in a cloak made of maguey fibers, and when Diego opened the cloak in front of the bishop, the roses had miraculously been replaced by a mestiza image of the Virgin. The shrine was duly set up, and eventually a basilica to accommodate 20,000 people was constructed close by. Tepeyac, which was a sacred place even in Aztec times, has become a place of pilgrimage to rival Rome, receiving an average of 10 million visitors a year. The dark-skinned Virgen de Guadalupe is seen as making Mexicans legitimate; Catholic authorities have deemed her the patron saint of the city, the country, and indeed of Latin America.

One Mexico City square, the Plaza Garibaldi, is famed for the mariachi bands and other regional ensembles that congregate in it. There are many places such as the Zócalo (officially the Plaza de la Constitución) where troupes perform indigenous music and dances, though the authenticity of these is in some doubt. Entertainers—for example, clowns—are commonplace in public squares and parks, which are also crowded with vendors of balloons and stalls selling drinks and snacks. Open-air markets are an Indian tradition that survives in the Zócalo and many other places.

The range of sporting activities is wide, but soccer is the most popular. Mexico City has twice hosted the World Cup; its Aztec Stadium has room for 126,000 fans. The DF has two first-division soccer teams: América and Cruz Azul. Baseball is also quite popular, as is *lucha libre,* Mexico's form of all-in wrestling.

Noteworthy places   The center of Mexico City is the Zócalo, which has the long and imposing National Palace along one side. Construction of the palace was begun by Cortés, who set it on the site of Moctezuma's palace. For a long time, it was the palace of the viceroys. The present building dates from the late 17th century, except for one floor that was added in 1926. It is now a government building. Inside the palace are some of Diego Rivera's most famous murals, tracing the course of Mexican history. Others, by Rivera and other leading muralists, can be seen in the Secretaría de Educación, not far away.

The other dominant building on the Zócalo is the massive and heavy cathedral, whose interior cracks show that there have been problems with subsidence and earthquakes. Work on building the cathedral was started in the late 16th century and continued intermittently for three hundred years thereafter; unsurprisingly, the overall effect is a mixture of the baroque and the neoclassical. There are 14 domes and 14 chapels in its cluttered interior. Beside the cathedral sits the Sagrario Chapel, which has paintings by Cristóbal de Villalpando. The Iglesia de San Francisco is an 18th-century church that sits on the site of Mexico City's first convent, which was built in 1524; what was intended as a Catholic church has served variously as a barracks, a circus, a theater, and a Methodist church. It is also the place where a mid-19th-century conspiracy was hatched.

In 1978, telephone workers digging not far from the Zócalo came across a massive stone disk representing the Aztec goddess of the moon; they had unearthed the site of the Templo Mayor, the main Aztec temple. Archaeological excavations revealed the remains of several buried pyramids, a carved frieze of skulls, and about 3,000 artifacts that have since been housed in an adjacent museum.

Also in the historic center of Mexico City is the Plaza de Santo Domingo, with its church built of porous volcanic rock. It has a long gallery along one side of the square where people used to be burned at the stake by the Inquisition, whose headquarters are just opposite. Cuauhtémoc once had a palace there.

The Casa de los Azulejos (Tiled House) dates from the 17th century; it sports a tiled facade, iron grillwork, a mural by José Clemente Orozco, and a patio in the Moorish style. It is now occupied by Sanborn's, a department store. Banamex, one of the country's main banks, has taken over the baroque building that Emperor Iturbide made his residence. Under Mexico's second and much later emperor, Maximilian, the Paseo de la Reforma was built to link the palace with the Castillo de Chapultepec. This castle stands high in what were once the wooded hunting grounds of the Aztecs and the location of Nezahualcóyotl's palace. The castle was the site of a definitive battle between the Mexicas and the Spaniards. Later it became a cadet school famous for the cadets' self-sacrifice in the concluding battle of the Mexican-American War. Nowadays it is home to the valuable Museo de Historia (History Museum). Also in the expansive Bosque de Chapultepec (Chapultepec Forest) are two more major museums. The Museo Nacional de Antropología (National Museum of Anthropology), quite apart from its incomparable collection of Mesoamerican items, has a very attractive and simple design, the work of Mexican architect Pedro Ramírez Vázquez. The Museo Rufino Tamayo de Arte Contemporáneo is the premier Mexican museum of modern art. The Bosque de Chapultepec also houses the presidential palace, called Los Pinos. The Bosque still has *ahuehuete* trees that survive from the time of the Aztecs, and it is still very beautiful in parts, even though busy roads cut through it. The Bosque has become the main recreational area of central Mexico City, with a zoo, an amusement park, and a children's museum.

The other main park in the central area is the Alameda Central, once a market area for the Aztecs. The Alameda is a more formal park and much more modest area in front of the Palacio de Bellas Artes, which was built during the Porfiriato (in 1904) as an opera house; it is a ponderously impressive marble structure, the work of an Italian architect who also designed the surprisingly extravagant main post office. Bellas Artes has an art deco facade with pre-Hispanic motifs, and inside it has a Tiffany stained-glass representation of the major volcanoes, plus murals by Rivera, Orozco, David Alfaro Siqueiros, and Rufino Tamayo. There is also a concert hall where the Ballet Folklórico performs regularly.

During the 19th century, the Paseo de la Reforma was lined with trees and the residences of Mexico City's elite, but nowadays it has many office buildings and expensive hotels. The Torre Mayor, Latin America's tallest office building, is one of them. One of the most famous of the Paseo's many statues, built at the end of the porfiriato, is El Angel de la Independencia, a column with a victorious angel on top and a mausoleum beneath it housing the remains of heroes of independence. One intriguing inclusion is an Anglo-Irishman, William Lamport, who became Guillén Lombardo de Guzmán. He was denounced by a neighbor, who discovered that he was planning to declare independence from Spain, make himself ruler, and free the slaves and the natives, whereupon the Inquisition judged him a heretic, with predictable consequences. The Paseo leads through some of Mexico City's most exclusive and fashionable areas, such as Las Lomas, Polanco, and the Zona Rosa.

The DF has more than 150 museums, with artistic and architectural interest in abundance. The Museo Nacional de Arte (National Museum of Art, MUNAL) has a collection that ranges from colonial times to the early 20th century; other art museums include the Museo José Luis Cuevas, the Museo San Carlos, and the Museo Franz Meyer. The nation's premier art school, the Academia de San Carlos, became today's Escuela Nacional de Artes Plásticas. San Angel and Coyoacán, which were once separate towns but have become quiet suburbs as the city has grown, are the sites of the Frida Kahlo Museum, the Ex-Convento del Carmen, the Museo de Arte Carrillo Gil, and the Casa Municipal, which was once the residence of Cortés where Cuauhtémoc was held prisoner. Xochimilco has another museum, the Museo Dolores Olmedo, with works from the Rivera-Kahlo private collection, while the Museo del Anahuacalli was built by Rivera himself to house their important collection of pre-Hispanic artifacts. Other places of note include the library building of UNAM, famous for its mosaic facade (done by another of the muralists, Juan O'Gorman), and Tepeyac, with its shrine and basilicas dedicated to the Virgen de Guadalupe.

Xochimilco is the only place that still has part of the lake area settled by the Mexicas. There is a maze of islets and waterways—floating gardens—where people now spend their leisure time being paddled around and serenaded by mariachis. Xochimilco is also known for its flowers and its *tianguis* ("open air markets"). The Parque Nacional Desierto de los Leones takes its name not from lions but from a family named Leóna that once owned the land. This 2,000-hectare (5,000-acre) mountain park includes a ruined monastery.

Other archaeological sites apart from the Templo Mayor are Tlatelolco, Cuicuilco, the Cerro de la Estrella, Mixcoac, and Cuailama.

The social and cultural centrality of Mexico City is also found in its multiplicity of educational institutions and their importance in the making of the country's political leadership. The university student population of the city has always been the largest in the nation, and more so with growth of the city after World War II. The city's students have predictably played a key role in national politics as a consequence. Similarly, the elite of Mexico are concentrated in the metropolitan area of the city, which multiplies exponentially its prominence.

Not surprisingly, Mexico City has been and continues to be the fundamental political center of the country. No other metropolitan area rivals the electoral primacy and symbolism of Mexico City. Furthermore, Mexico City possesses enormous economic power in terms of the making of policy and in the production of goods and services. In short, the political economy of the nation gravitates around its capital, and it has been that way since at least colonial times. As a consequence, the city has been by far the most significant battleground for competing political and economic interests and views.

In 1968 Mexico City became the stage for the most dramatic moment in its modern history when the reigning party, the Partido Revolucionario Institucional (Institutional Revolutionary Party, PRI), faced a critical test of its dominance of the country's political system. Although the PRI survived the episode, its hold began to gradually weaken and reached crisis proportions by the mid-1990s. In this sense the mayorship of Mexico City became an enormously meaningful political prize with national symbolic significance. As the PRI's power ebbed with the 1997 midterm elections, its decline was reaffirmed decisively when the left-of-center opposition candidate won the mayoral race in 1997, as his victory marked a crucial loss for the former dominant party. Fueled in large measure by its well-educated youth and by disaffection among the generation of the events of 1968, the PRI has been unable to recover its primacy over Mexico City. Since 1997 there have been two other mayoral races, and each one has been won by the left-leaning Partido de la Revolución Democrática (Democratic Revolutionary Party, PRD). However, with the recent divisions within the PRD, its strength has lessened, casting doubt on its ability to continue its hold over Mexico City politics. Under these circumstances, the 2012 presidential contest will represent a decisive moment for Mexico City and the country's political economy.

Peter Standish

See also Archaeological Sites; Environment; Environmental Issues; Partido de la Revolución Democrática; Politics and Political Parties; Tourism; Transportation; Urban Culture; Urbanization

Further Reading

Brewster, Claire, and Keith Brewster. 2010. *Representing the Nation: Sport and Spectacle in Post-Revolutionary Mexico.* London: Routledge.

Caistor, Nick. 2000. *Mexico City: A Literary and Cultural Companion.* New York: Interlink Books.

Eibenshutz Hartman, Roberto, ed. 2010. *La zona metropolitana del Valle de Mexico: Retos de la megalopolis.* Mexico City: Universidad Autonoma Metropolitana.

Kandell, Jonathan. 1988. *La Capital: Biography of Mexico City.* New York: Random House.

Ramirez, Carlos. 2009. *El regreso del PRI (y de Carlos Salinas de Gortari).* Mexico City: Planeta.

Michoacán

The official coat of arms of Michoacán. (Corel)

Michoacán is one of the 31 constituent states of Mexico. It borders the states of Colima and Jalisco to the west, Guanajuato and Querétaro to the north, México to the east, Guerrero to the southeast, and the Pacific Ocean to the south. Michoacán has an area of 23,114 square miles. It is the 16th largest state in Mexico, taking up 3 percent of the national territory. In a 2005 census, the population was at over 3.9 million people. The state is very similar to the southern Mexican states of Guerrero and Oaxaca, and its capital is the city of Morelia (previously known as Valladolid), located between two main cities in the country of Mexico, Mexico City and Guadalajara.

Michoacán has a varied terrain, including valleys, highlands, and coastal lowlands. The state is home to several large lakes, including Lake Pátzcuaro. It also houses Latin America's largest steel factory and contains one of Mexico's most important Pacific ports, which is named after Lázaro Cárdenas, a native son. Michoacán's coastal regions are home to a wide variety of animals including snapper, bass, bream, skipjack, shark, turtle, crawfish, alligator, and birds such as herons, gulls, and pelicans. In the mountains and highland regions, wild turkey are found in abundance, as well as quail, coot, mourning dove, eagle, owl, jaguar, deer, and opossum.

An economy based on mining and the production of sugar, indigo, cotton, and other crops emerged, and the city of Valladolid (today's Morelia) became Michoacán's political and economic hub. By the 17th century, Valladolid was a prosperous area, and many wealthy mine owners and landowners resided in the city. Their wealth helped produce the art and architecture that continue to draw visitors to today's capital city. Valladolid was also a center of the Roman Catholic Church, with which the economic elite had strong ties. Many of Michoacán's native peoples were drawn into the colonial economy as a labor force for the haciendas ("plantations") and mines. Indian lands, meanwhile, came under attack as Spaniards sought to build larger estates. By the late colonial period, Indian discontent over labor demands and land disputes encouraged rebellion against colonial rule.

Michoacán has always played a central role in Mexico's history. It produced the main leaders of the independence movement, and during the revolutionary period of the early 20th century, Lázaro Cárdenas carried out sweeping reforms, which anticipated his efforts at the national level. In the latter part of the 20th century, Michoacán struggled to create a viable economy, and it became a center of opposition to the Partido Revolucionario Institucional (Institutional Revolutionary Party, PRI).

An area of great cultural diversity, Michoacán hosted several native groups in the centuries before Spanish contact. Among the most important were the Purépecha or Tarascan peoples, who arrived in the 12th century. The Tarascans extended their influence throughout much of the state, establishing an empire with urban centers at Pátzcuaro and Tzintzuntzán. This empire was a rival of the Mexica-Aztec kingdom, which unsuccessfully sought the help of the Tarascans in resisting Spanish conquest.

Initial contact between the Spaniards and Tarascans was peaceful, though many Indians fled from Spanish control. Missionaries arrived in the 1530s to begin the work of converting Michoacán's native peoples. Vasco de Quiroga led these efforts, and he was named Bishop of Michoacán in 1536. Quiroga gained a reputation as a defender and champion of the Indians. He established a college in Pátzcuaro that was devoted to the study and preservation of native languages, and he encouraged Indians to develop the artisanal skills that earned Pátzcuaro its reputation as a center of native crafts (a reputation that has persisted).

Indian unrest helped produce recruits for the anti-Spanish revolt of Miguel Hidalgo and José María Morelos, both of whom were natives of Michoacán. In this early phase of Mexico's independence movement, many mestizos (people of Spanish and Indian ancestry), also joined the Hidalgo-Morelos insurgency. Valladolid remained a center of support for the Spanish Crown, however. In 1821, Agustín de Iturbide, another native son, occupied the city and imposed independence on

A fountain in front of an old church in Morelia, the capital city of Michoacán, Mexico. (Stephan Scherhag | Dreamstime.com)

its reluctant elites. Iturbide became the country's first leader, though his Mexican Empire lasted only briefly. Michoacán gained statehood in 1824. Valladolid was designated the capital, and its name was soon changed to Morelia, in honor of José María Morelos.

Under the national regime of President Porfirio Díaz (1876–1911), Michoacán enjoyed greater stability and prosperity. Foreign investment helped build the state's railway lines and expand industrial production, particularly in mining and wood products. Foreigners also invested in land, bringing mechanized agriculture to some areas of the state. This latter development, aided by national laws that encouraged land concentration, occurred at the expense of the state's campesinos ("peasants"), who became increasingly restive on the eve of the Revolution of 1910.

Several outstanding figures provided leadership in Michoacán during the revolution. Salvador Escalante was among the first to support Francisco Madero's 1910–1911 revolt against Díaz, and his forces captured Morelia in 1911. After Madero's death, Gertrudis Sánchez led the local rebellion against Victoriano Huerta, who was responsible for Madero's demise. Sánchez joined Venustiano Carranza's Constitutionalist movement and consequently captured Morelia in 1914 and briefly served as the state's governor. In 1920, after the death of Carranza, Francisco Múgica became governor. An opposition journalist during the Díaz years, Múgica had supported the revolts of both Madero and Carranza, and he served as a representative to the congress that drafted Mexico's Constitution of 1917. Múgica was a dedicated reformer, and during his term as governor, he began the process of land distribution. Múgica also established a friendship with Lázaro Cárdenas, who assumed the governorship in 1928. Cárdenas continued Múgica's work, organizing urban workers and campesinos, carrying out land reform, and reining in the power of the Roman Catholic Church. With his reputation as a social reformer well established, Cárdenas moved into national politics, serving as Mexico's president from 1934 to 1940. As a national leader, Cárdenas included the like-minded Múgica in his cabinet.

The land reform that was championed by Múgica and Cárdenas was also encouraged by Primo Tapia de la Cruz. A member of the Tarascan community of Naranja, Tapia spent time working in the United States, where he was exposed to the radicalism of the International Workers of the World (IWW). Tapia also allied himself with the Partido Liberal Mexicano (Mexican Liberal Party, PLM), which sought significant social reform and was a leading critic of the Díaz regime on the eve of the Revolution of 1910. When he returned to Michoacán in 1921, Tapia became the state's main agrarian leader, helping to organize campesinos and resisting the attempts of the Mexican government to co-opt them. Tapia became increasingly dissatisfied with the pace and nature of agrarian reform, and he led others in seizing lands in the Naranja region. On the order of President Plutarco Elías Calles, Tapia was captured, tortured, and shot in 1926.

After the era of reform that characterized the 1920s and 1930s, Michoacán, like many areas of Mexico, turned its attention to economic modernization. Under a series of governors, social reform was deemphasized in favor of development. Irrigation and the application of science and technology to agriculture helped Michoacán become an important producer of fruits and vegetables for U.S. markets. Cattle ranching expanded, as did the state's fishing industry. Forestry also remained important, and in 1973 the Mexican government established Productos Forestales de Michoacán to promote the wood products industry. Although such developments did expand the state's economy, Michoacán never fully industrialized, and it remained dependent on outside markets for its agriculture and forestry products. The growth of the agroexport sector was also accompanied by a resurgence of land concentration. Ultimately, Michoacán failed to produce the jobs needed for a growing population. By the late 20th century, Michoacán's people were migrating to the United States in increasing numbers in search of work and better opportunities. The state remains one of the most important sources of Mexican migration to the United States, and its remittances have become a major source of income for tens of thousands of households in the rural areas of Michoacán. The dissatisfaction with governmental policies has not only led to migration but has also fueled political opposition to the federal government long dominated by one party.

Contemporary Michoacán is known for its defiance of the PRI, the party that dominated Mexico for most of the 20th century. Particularly in the last two decades of the century, the state became a center of opposition. In 1987, Cuauh-témoc Cárdenas (son of the former president) withdrew from the PRI to protest its selection of Carlos Salinas de Gortari as Mexico's next president. In 1988, Cárdenas unsuccessfully challenged Salinas in an election riddled with fraud, though he gained the support of voters in Michoacán. One year later, Cárdenas helped establish the Partido de la Revolución Democrática (Democratic Revolutionary Party, PRD), which became Mexico's main left-of-center party. The PRD proved especially strong in Cárdenas's home state, and the PRI's efforts to suppress it led to political violence. Rigged municipal elections in 1989, for example, encouraged PRD sympathizers to occupy government buildings. Soldiers and tanks were sent to dislodge the protestors, several of whom were arrested and killed. The 1992 governor's election was also volatile, with the PRD defying the questionable election results that favored the PRI and installing their own candidate, Cristóbal Arías, as the leader of a rival government. Since then, the PRD has dominated the state's political structure through the mid-2000s; in 2007 the PRD candidate won the gubernatorial race. Nonetheless, the power of the PRD has waned compared to the past. The divisions within the national leadership of the left-leaning party have undermined the strength of the PRD in Michaocan. Moreover, the performance of the current governor has been less than expected, even among stalwart supporters of the PRD. As a result, the right-of-center Partido Acción Nacional (National Action Party, PAN) has made inroads among the state's electorate, and the PRI has also regained lost ground. In the 2007 mayoral elections, PRI candidates were victorious in 49 contests, while the PRD won in 41 races and PAN took 18 of the posts. In short, the PRD is in trouble in the state most identified with the left-of-center party, given the importance of Cuauhte-moc Cárdenas to the party's origins. Indeed, the November 2011 state elections will prove to be a critical test for the PRD on the eve of the 2012 presidential campaign.

The problems of the PRD in Michoacán are also tied to the power and influence of the illegal drug trade. One of the most-feared drug cartels has emerged in the state, La Familia Michoacana (the Michoacán Family). The reach of the drug organization has penetrated deep into the state's small rural towns and has also spread into the largest city, Morelia, as well as other key urban areas of Micho-acán. Politicians have been implicated in the development of the activities of the drug cartel. The attendant violence of the drug trade has escalated, as La Michoa-cana Familia has had to fend off rival drug gangs in addition to the federal troops and local police agencies intent on destroying the organization. (Michoacán is the home state of President Felipe Calderón, 2006–2012.) In December 2010 the head of La Michoacana Familia was killed in a shootout with law enforcement authorities, but the organization as of this writing has been able to weather the loss of its principal leader. For the state's political parties, and most importantly for the PRD, the powerful presence of La Michoacana Familia has contributed to an uncertain future for Michoacán. Migration continues to reflect the persistence of socioeconomic inequities and the growing sense of insecurity generated by drug trade–related violence. The outcomes of the 2012 presidential election will no doubt hold decisive implications for Michoacán.

Suzanne B. Pasztor

See also Agriculture; Drug Trade and Trafficking; Immigration and Emigration; Partido de la Revolución Democrática; Peasantry

Further Reading

Florescano, Enrique, ed. 1989. *Historia General de Michoacán,* 4 vols. Morelia, Michoacán: Instituto Michoacána de Cultura.

Friedrich, Paul. 1970. *Agrarian Revolt in a Mexican Village.* Englewood Cliffs, NJ: Prentice Hall.

Gobierno del Estado de Michoacán. http://www.michoacan.gob.mx.

Grayson, George W. 2007. "Showdown for the Democratic Revolutionary Party in Michoacán." *CSIS Hemisphere Focus* 15(3) (June 20). www.csis.org.

Ramirez Sevilla, Luis. 1997. *Dibujo de sol con nubes: Una aproximacion a los limites y potencialidades del PRD en un municipio michoacano.* Zamora, Michoacán: El Colegio de Michoacán.

Suarez, Luis. 2003. *Cuauhtemoc Cárdenas: Politica, familia, proyecto y compromise, tres generaciones, un mismo destino.* Mexico: Grijalbo.

Mining

Mining is an industry deeply rooted in Mexican history. From pre-Hispanic times to the middle of the 20th century, it was the preeminent industry in the country, as well as the major source of tax revenue for the Mexican government. As recently as 1939, mining contributed 39 percent of the country's total exports and 28 percent of its tax revenue. However, the industry has experienced a gradual decline, at least in relative terms. From 1980 to 2005, its relative size in the economy, not including oil and natural gas, went down from 2.5 percent to 1.3 percent of the country's gross domestic product. Nevertheless, it did experience modest growth in value added over the period (65 percent in real terms; 2.2 percent per year).

More recently, performance has been mixed. After lackluster results for almost a decade, the sector experienced rapid growth in both 2004 and 2005 (7.2 percent and 6.9 percent, respectively), driven by high international prices in most major mineral commodities where Mexico is a significant producer (silver, zinc, cadmium, copper, etc.). Most mining and metallurgical activity is concentrated in nine states of northern and central Mexico (Sonora, Zacatecas, Chihuahua, Durango, Guanajuato, San Luis Potosí, Coahuila, Nuevo León, and Baja California Sur), although there are some important production areas farther south (e.g., Michoacán). Production is concentrated in a relatively narrow range of products, such as precious metals (gold, silver), nonferrous metals (lead, copper, and zinc), and steel-related substances (coal, iron, and manganese).

Legal framework   The legal and regulatory framework for mining in Mexico starts with article 27 of the Constitution, which establishes underground resources as the property of the nation and creates a state monopoly for the exploitation of hydrocarbons. Private firms are allowed in mining under the terms of the Mining Law, last reformed in 1992. That reform eliminated most restrictions on foreign ownership of Mexican mining companies, although it still gave some leeway to the regulatory authorities (Economy Ministry, National Foreign Investment Commission, etc.).

Business   Mining in Mexico is a highly concentrated industry, with a relatively small number of significant players. Some of the most important companies in the sector include: Grupo México, Industrias Peñoles, Minera Autlán, Altos Hornos de México (AHMSA), and Villacero.

Labor   Employment in the sector has also declined in the long term. Although the number of laborers involved in mining has picked up slightly over the years, it went down to 286,000 workers in 2000 and 248,000 in 2003, bouncing back to 257,000 in 2004. Similarly, investment in the sector has been fluctuating, from $795 million in 2000 to $348 million in 2003, increasing to $585 million in 2004.

Mining is also a highly unionized sector. The Mexican Miners and Metalworkers' Union claims over 250,000 workers as members. The union is one of the oldest in Mexico: its origins precede the Mexican Revolution of 1910–1917. Nevertheless, until recently, it was seen as a relatively nonmilitant organization and even as a model of cooperative labor-management relations.

In the late 1980s, during the privatization of the state-owned copper mining complex, the union obtained a 5 percent share of the privatized assets. That windfall (ultimately worth $55 million and paid to the union in 2004), along with the passing of the leadership from longtime secretary-general Napoleón Gómez Sada to his son, Napoleón Gómez Urrutia, determined the turn of the miners' union toward confrontational tactics. In recent years, there has been a rash of strikes and other forms of activism as companies seek to contain labor costs.

Government   Several public agencies are in charge of regulating the mining and metallurgical industry. Among them is the Mining Coordination Unit within the Ministry of the Economy. The unit is in charge of overall mining policy, including the concession of mining rights. Moreover, mining is also heavily regulated by the Ministry of the Environment, as well as by local environmental agencies. The authority in charge of both labor relations and occupational safety is the Ministry of Labor.

Juan Manuel Galarza and José Ignacio Lanzagorta

See also Foreign Direct Investment; Foreign Trade; Global Market and Multinational Corporations; North American Free Trade Agreement

Further Reading

El sector minero en México; diagnóstico, prospectiva y estrategia. 2004. Mexico City: Centro de Estudios de Competitividad.

Monetary System

In 1925, the Banco de México (Bank of Mexico) became the central bank of the country, and since then it has provided oversight to the Mexican monetary system and implemented monetary policies. A primary responsibility of the Bank of Mexico is managing the nation's exchange rate, that is, the value of the basic unit of currency, the Mexican peso (the U.S. dollar is used as the reference point for the value of the Mexican peso). Generally speaking, there are two types of exchange policies (often referred to as exchange regimes). One is a floating exchange system, where the peso is allowed to fluctuate in value compared to the U.S. dollar. For example, if the peso loses too much value, the central bank may buy dollars on the international currency markets to boost the value of the peso. In contrast, a fixed currency exchange policy means that the central bank attempts to maintain a certain value of the peso based on the U.S. dollar (or what is called a pegged value). The central bank must maintain large enough reserves of U.S. dollars, for instance, to maintain a set ratio of value between the peso and the U.S. dollar.

During the period 1976–1994, the Banco de México adopted several types of managed float regimes, in which the central bank intervened in the foreign exchange market in order to avoid abrupt fluctuations of the exchange rate. During those years, the bank conducted its monetary policy by simply defending the level of the exchange rate. At the same time, the federal government moved toward an expansive fiscal policy (tax rate reductions) with the intent of attracting more capital into the country. As a result, the value of the peso rose relative to the U.S. dollar.

Even though the maneuverability of the central bank was limited in terms of monetary policy, the Banco de México took several actions to promote economic development in the aftermath of the disastrous economic problems of the late 1970s and early 1980s. From 1983 to 1988, the Mexican government created a trust to protect companies from abrupt devaluations of the exchange rate. In addition, a law was passed that limited the amount of domestic financing that the

Mexican pesos. (Ferenz | Dreamstime.com)

central bank could provide to the financial system. Unfortunately, these policies led to a steep rise in inflation, reaching 159 percent by December of 1987 and provoking a devaluation of the peso. In order to stem the resulting rate of inflation, the government worked out an agreement with banks and the private sector, based largely on price controls on fundamental staples, products, and services.

In 1993, one of the most important changes in monetary regulation took place with the approval of the Banco de México Law, which intended to secure the purchasing power of the Mexican peso. Equally important, the new law prevented political control of the country's central bank. Under the law's provisions, five members of the bank's board of governors are selected by the president of Mexico in staggered terms of six years and eight years for deputy governors. The selection of the governors would have to meet the approval of the Mexican Senate. Consequently, no single Mexican president would have full control of the board of governors of the bank. Given the long history of political dominance exercised by one party, the Partido Revolucionario Institucional (Institutional Revolutionary Party, PRI), this latter provision of the new law was hailed as a crucial step toward the independence of the financial system from the influence of one political party and its leaders.

These changes in the governance of the Banco de México, however, came too late to avoid the cumulative impacts of previous policies under the stress of political events in 1994. In that year, a crisis that discredited the political system came with an armed rebellion in the southern state of Chiapas and the assassination of the dominant's party's presidential candidate. The value of the peso plunged, foreign investments fled the country, and Mexicans pulled their money out of Mexican banks to convert them to dollars. The reserves of the central bank reached critical levels, dropping from 25 billion U.S. dollars to about 6 billion U.S. dollars. Unable to sustain a fixed exchange rate, in December of 1994 the central bank was forced to adopt a floating exchange regime, as the peso lost enormous value in a short span of time. The financial assets of many individuals and companies evaporated as the peso's worth plummeted relative to the U.S. dollar. Inflation immediately set in and reached 52 percent within weeks of the crisis.

With the adoption of a floating exchange rate, the dollar-denominated domestic debt ballooned and pushed Mexico's financial system toward insolvency. In response, the Banco de México strove to recover the stock of international reserves to regain credibility among foreign investors and stabilize the dropping value of the peso. In addition, the central bank worked with governmental authorities to assist debtors to avoid the collapse of the private sector and undercut the spike in unemployment and underemployment. To stem inflation, the Banco de México instituted several measures, working with commercial banks to develop mechanisms to establish a monetary target (e.g., the deposits available to commercial banks) and an overnight interest rate (interest rate target) as means of restricting money supply.

Under this monetary target regime, which emphasized high interest rates, inflation was dampened. The policy proved to be effective as inflation gradually went down, the value of the peso recovered, and capital eventually came back to Mexico. By December of 2007, inflation was below 4 percent, and confidence in the Mexican financial system had been largely restored. Most importantly, with huge reserves of sound foreign currencies, the credibility of Mexico's central bank rose substantially within the international financial system. The dependence of Mexico's economy on the United States, however, influences the value of the peso and Mexican monetary policy. The U.S. recession of 2007–2010 lessened the value of the dollar and with it the value of the Mexican peso. On the other hand, European debt problems have contributed to fluctuations in the value of the euro and its relationship to the dollar and, by extension, to the peso. In this sense, Mexico's monetary policy has become ever more sensitive to economic trends and events elsewhere in the world.

Rodrigo Cano

See also Debt, Foreign; Foreign Direct Investment; Foreign Trade; North American Free Trade Agreement; Politics and Political Parties

Further Reading

Weintraub, Sidney. 2000. *Financial Decision-Making in Mexico: To Bet a Nation.* Pittsburgh: University of Pittsburgh Press.

Morelos

The official coat of arms of Morelos. (Corel)

Morelos is a south-central Mexican state sharing borders with the Distrito Federal (Federal District; Mexico City), Puebla, Guerrero, and México State. Cuernavaca is the capital. With an area of approximately 1,908 square miles, it is the second smallest of Mexico's states. In 2005, it had a total population of over 1.6 million.

In many ways, Morelos's history has been characterized by struggles over land and water. Beginning in the colonial period, land concentration occurred at the expense of the state's campesinos ("peasants" or "rural workers") and indigenous villages. Popular rebellion became a response to the steady growth of large estates, and in the early 20th century, many peasants took up arms in the Mexican Revolution, where Morelos native Emiliano Zapata was among the most important leaders.

Several native languages, including Náhuatl, Mixtec, Zapotec, and Otomí, are still spoken in Morelos, indicating the region's large indigenous population and its rich and varied pre-Columbian history. In the centuries before the Spaniards arrived, Morelos developed in conjunction with southeastern Mexico and central Mexico, evincing a pre-Columbian heritage that spans the eras of the Olmec and the Aztec. Morelos was also home to the ceremonial center of Xochicalco, which was a center of the Toltec culture and perhaps an ancient Maya site as well. The Spanish Conquest of Morelos began in 1521, and in 1523 Hernán Cortés captured Cuernavaca, where he established his residence. Cortés claimed much of Morelos's land as his own, and he established the first sugar mill of New Spain in Tlaltenango. Franciscan, Dominican, and Augustinian missionaries followed, introducing the Roman Catholic faith to many of Morelos's native peoples.

After Cortés, Morelos became home to several large sugar haciendas ("plantations"), which were worked by Indians and black slaves. Sugarcane became the main economic enterprise of colonial Morelos, and the sugar haciendas grew steadily. This expansion increased local competition for land and water, and it especially pressured native villages and their communal lands. Popular discontent resulting from the expansion of the sugar economy provided support for the rebellions of Miguel Hidalgo and José María Morelos in the early 19th century. Indeed, Morelos captured Cuernevaca in 1812 and also installed himself in Cuautla, a town to the east of Cuernavaca. In 1821, Agustín de Iturbide occupied Cuernavaca in the name of an independent Mexico before proceeding to Mexico City to become the new country's first leader.

Morelos did not immediately achieve statehood after Mexican independence. Instead, it became a part of México State and remained so until 1869, when Benito Juárez created the state of Morelos. Located in central Mexico and in close

A neighborhood in the valley of Cumbayá in Cuernavaca, the capital city of Morelos, Mexico. (Elena Elisseeva | Dreamstime.com)

proximity to Mexico City, Morelos directly experienced the political struggles of the 19th century. During the Mexican-American War (1846–1848), American troops occupied Cuernavaca, and during the War of Reform (1858–1861) Mexico's liberal and conservative factions vied for control of the capital city. During the 1860s, Cuernavaca was controlled by the French, who invaded the country and established an empire (1862–1867).

Morelos's sugar industry remained at the heart of the state's economy, and several laws passed during the second half of the 19th century facilitated the continued growth of the region's haciendas. Modernization was aided by the arrival of the railroad and by the introduction of steam-powered equipment. By the early 20th century, Morelos was among the world's largest producers of sugar. As during the colonial period, however, such expansion occurred at the expense of Indian villages and their communal lands. The man who eventually provided a voice for these traditional village communities was Emiliano Zapata.

Born to a campesino family in the village of Anenecuilco, Zapata became a local leader in the struggle to protect land and water from encroachment by the state's wealthy *hacendados* ("hacienda owners"). He responded to Francisco Madero's call for rebellion against President Porfirio Díaz in 1910–1911, and he gathered an army that succeeded in capturing Cuautla. Zapata's victory helped force Díaz from power and bring Madero into the presidency. Zapata, who insisted on land reform as the central component of the Mexican Revolution, did not remain allied to Madero for long; however, Madero supported the *hacendados* of Morelos, who installed Ambrosio Figueroa (a landowner from the neighboring state of Guerrero) as governor in 1911.

Zapata responded to the imposition of Figueroa and to Madero's failure to carry out meaningful reforms by breaking with the central government. By the end of 1911, he had issued his Plan of Ayala, which demanded the return of lands taken by hacienda owners and asserted the people's right to choose their leaders. Zapata's movement attracted a large following in Morelos, and it spread beyond the state. It continued to grow after Madero's overthrow and death in 1913. Attempts by the central government to suppress the Zapatista rebellion brought heavy fighting to Morelos and resulted in the destruction of many of the state's haciendas, as well as the collapse of the sugar industry. Morelos also suffered a precipitous decline in its population through death and emigration.

From 1914 to 1916 the Zapatistas controlled Morelos, and they were allied with the so-called Convention government against Venustiano Carranza's Constitutionalist movement. Under Genovevo de la O and Lorenzo Vázquez, Morelos' state government divided the state's sugar haciendas and redistributed land. The revolutionary gains of Zapata's local regime were short-lived, however. In 1916, Constitutionalist general Pablo González began an offensive that, by 1919, left Carranza in control of Morelos. In the same year, Zapata was ambushed and killed. His movement waned, though many of his followers continued to wage guerrilla warfare.

In 1920, the surviving leaders of Zapata's rebellion, including Gildardo Magaña (who assumed leadership of the movement after Zapata's death), adhered to the Plan of Agua Prieta, which overthrew Carranza and aided Alvaro Obregón in his ascension to the presidency. In Morelos, José G. Parres, a medic in Zapata's army, assumed control of a new state government. Parres called on the people of Morelos to submit claims for land, and the state was among the first to see land distributed to campesinos. Some 200,000 hectares of land had been distributed in Morelos by 1929. But the agrarian reform of the 1920s was designed as much to placate the peasants as it was to make them beholden to the central government and a new group of local political leaders. Indeed, Zapata's earlier land reforms were nullified, and land redistribution was carefully controlled and manipulated by the leaders of Mexico's national government. While some peasants received *ejidos* (plots of land granted by the government to be cultivated communally), villages like Anenecuilco, which claimed historic rights to land, did not see those lands returned.

During the 1930s President Lázaro Cárdenas distributed an additional 70,000 hectares in Morelos, as he brought campesinos into a national organization, the Confederación Nacional Campesina (National Peasant Confederation, CNC). Meanwhile, the state's haciendas, which survived the Mexican Revolution in diminished form, turned to commercial agriculture. Lacking the capital to participate in the new market-based economy, many peasants became indebted and beholden to those who could provide them with machinery and access to markets beyond the state.

The politicization of Mexico's land reform program, and the increasingly heavy hand of the national government, pushed some of Morelos's campesinos to rebel again. In 1935 and 1938 Zapatista veteran Enrique Rodríguez led an uprising against the intrusion of the Mexican government, and in the 1940s, Rubén Jaramillo, who had also joined Zapata's army, took up arms to protest the continued exploitation of the peasants. Although Jaramillo's efforts to organize the state's campesinos earned him death threats and the animosity of wealthy landowners, he remained active. He formed the Partido Agrario Obrero Morelense (Agrarian and Workers' Party of Morelos, PAOM), and during the 1950s he became a local representative of the CNC. Ultimately, however, Jaramillo supported land invasions as the only real way in which peasants could gain land. In 1962, Jaramillo was assassinated, most likely on orders from the central government.

The last decades of the 20th century saw the continued growth of commercial agriculture in Morelos, as well as the intensification of agriculture through the use of new machinery, chemical fertilizers, and insecticides. Access to capital and outside markets became crucial to the state's farmers, and peasants were left farther behind. Many responded by emigrating to the United States or to Mexico City. Industry and tourism also became part of Morelos's economy. Cuernavaca in particular became a major tourist destination, and a modern highway linking Cuernavaca to Mexico City helped make the state's capital a popular weekend spot for Mexico City residents. While the energy of Zapata's revolutionary movement seemed to have faded by the end of the 20th century, the ideals of that movement still exist. Peasants continued to raise their voices, as in 1996 when a group from Tepoztlán began a march to Mexico City to protest plans for a real estate development that included a golf course, an industrial park, and a resort. Police confronted the caravan and shot and killed one of the protestors. The public outcry over this event caused the suspension of the development project. Despite its proximity to Mexico City, Morelos retains its own local political and economic identity. As a consequence, when the dominance of the ruling party weakened in the 1990s, much of the electorate of Morelos deserted the PRI and went over to the right-of-center party, Partido Acción Nacional (National Action Party, PAN). In the 2006 gubernatorial race, the PAN candidate came away with the victory. On the other hand, five of the six seats in Congress from Morelos are in the hands of the PRI. The 2012 presidential election will provide an important test for the future of politics in Morelos.

Suzanne B. Pasztor

See also Agriculture; Mexico City; Peasantry

Further Reading

Brunk, Samuel. 1995. *Emiliano Zapata: Revolution and Betrayal in Mexico.* Albuquerque: University of New Mexico Press.

Camargo Gonzalez, Ignacio. 2010. *Actores de la politica: Un estudio de la lealtad y las activitudes de cambio de partido en tres municipios de Mexico a principios del siglo XXI.* Chihuahua: Universidad Autonoma de Chihuahua.

Gobierno del Estado de Morelos. http://www.morelos.gob.mx.

Padilla, Tanalis. 2008. *Rural Resistance in the Land of Zapata: The Jaramillista Movement and the Myth of Pax Priista.* Durham, NC: Duke University Press.

Warman, Arturo. 1980. *We Come to Object: The Peasants of Morelos and the National State.* Translated by Stephen K. Ault. Baltimore: Johns Hopkins University Press.

Womack, John. 1968. *Zapata and the Mexican Revolution.* New York: Random House.

Multinational Corporations

See Global Market and Multinational Corporations

Musical Groups and Artists

Popular artists   Popular Mexican music since the 1990s has shown a strong tendency toward romantic ballads and vernacular music. This genre enjoys a huge market nourished by its promotion by the powerful television and radio industries of the country. A large proportion of Mexico's population is relatively young, providing an additional fan base for the genre. Mexican popular music encompasses several specific forms that have been collectively grouped together under one term. Some of these forms have a long history, such as *ranchero* ("country music"), but the recent popularity of Spanish-language rock music, for example, indicates a gradual shift toward more urbanized musical forms.

Among the notable artists of the contemporary era are Juan Gabriel, Armando Manzanero, and Marco Antonio Solís ("el Buki"). Many more names could be mentioned, but these three are very prominent and have been recognized by numerous musical organizations.

However, perhaps the most popular contemporary performer is the Mexican artist known as Luis Miguel. His albums have achieved recognition in Mexico, the United States, and Europe. His live performances have earned him worldwide fame. Luis Miguel set an attendance record in Mexico City's Auditorio Nacional when he sold out 30 consecutive concerts in 1992.

Vernacular Mexican music artists represent a distinctive form. Vicente "Don Chente" Fernández for four decades set the standard for this type of music. He has sold more than 40 million records worldwide and his son, Alejandro Fernández ("el Potrillo"), has followed in his footsteps in the same genre. Another legendary figure of this form is Antonio Aguilar ("El Charro de México") (who died in 2007). His son José ("Pepe Aguilar") is considered the heir of Mexican traditional music. Among female singers of this genre are Lucero, Ana Gabriel, and Paquita la del Barrio, who merits special note for her intense performances and strong anti-machista lyrics that have earned her particular popularity with female audiences. The majority of the artists who perform vernacular music wear a costume known as the *charro* ("traditional horseman/cowboy") outfit.

Music and other media   Television and radio have played a decisive role in the development and promotion of popular music in Mexico. Links among the radio, television, and recording industries greatly facilitate the creation and marketing of musical artists. These connections have also proven useful in the diffusion of Mexican musical artists to Spanish-speaking audiences in Latin America, the United States, and Spain.

Mexican singing superstar Luis Miguel performs in celebration of Mexican Independence Day, 2010. Miguel is the recipient of four Latin Grammy Awards. (AP/Wide World Photos)

The musical variety show *Siempre en Domingo* (*Always on Sunday*) was by far the most important platform for the launching of Mexican musical artists from 1969 to 1998. The show was tremendously popular in all of Latin America and with Spanish-speaking audiences in the United States, as well as in Spain and with Spanish-speaking communities in Asia. The main force behind *Siempre en Domingo* was Raúl Velasco, who hosted the show from its beginning. Velasco became a godfather of sorts to a bevy of Mexican contemporary musical artists, such as Luis Miguel, Alejandra Guzmán, Pedro Fernández, Thalía, Paulina Rubio, Alejandro Fernández, and Lucero, just to mention a few. Raúl Velasco was also instrumental in introducing several non-Mexican popular artists through his show, like Ricky Martin (Puerto Rico), Enrique Iglesias (Spain), and Shakira (Colombia). Indeed, Velasco kicked off the career of dozens of singers and musical groups, and it became a ritual on the show for Velasco to playfully kick a new artist onto the stage for their first televised performance. Although the show ended with the retirement of Raúl Velasco in 1998, the legacy of *Siempre en Domingo* continues with the numerous Mexican artists who can trace the origins of their careers to the now legendary program.

In 1993, following the model of *Siempre en Domingo,* Televisa created Telehit and the international video music chain MTV Latinoamerica debuted. Both featured young musical talent catering to the Mexican teen audience and their taste for local and international rock, electronic and "pop" artists. Specialized channels for Norteña (Northern) music were also created, such as Televisa's Bandamax (1996) and VideoRola (1998).

Yet another key source of Mexican popular artists is the country's televised soap operas, where leading characters have doubled as singing stars. Notable examples are Verónica Castro, Lucía Méndez, Daniela Romo, Laura León, Mariana Garza, Aracely Arámbula, Ninel Conde, Lorena Herrera, and Maribel Guardia. Mexican telenovelas ("soap operas") have also groomed musical artists for the young teen market. Perhaps the most representative example of this process is the story of the group RBD. The group originally appeared on the highly watched telenovela *Rebelde* (*Rebel* or *Rebellious*) in 2004. Through exposure on the show, RBD forged its independent and very successful career, and the group's popularity persists into the present. Other young stars who have benefited from their appearances on telenovelas include Angélica Rivera, Biby Gaytán, Erik Rubín, and Eduardo Capetillo.

The introduction of reality television programming such as *La Academia* (*The Academy*) (2002–2007) also generated top-selling Mexican pop singers. Two of the most popular are Yahir and Yuridia.

Pop artists and groups   There are also artists and musical groups whose careers have developed largely independent of mainstream commercial television.

Among the most notorious of these singers is the Gloria Trevi. The provocative singer revolutionized Mexican pop-rock music with her ragged clothing style, suggestive lyrics, and spectacular live shows. Her debut album, *¿Qué hago aquí?* (*What Do I Do Here?*, 1989), was the highest selling recording of that year in Mexico; the follow-up album *Tu Ángel de la Guarda* (*Your Guardian Angel,* 1991) sold 2,800,000 copies worldwide, breaking sales records for the time. In 1991, she starred in her first movie, *Pelo Suelto* (*Hair Down*) based on her famous single by the same title; the movie broke box office records for that time. In 1993, *Zapatos Viejos* (*Old Shoes*) surpassed her former box office record, earning 17 million pesos. Gloria Trevi's career began to fade in 1995, but her style of performance and lyrics paved the way for a wave of female popular music stars, including Fey and Edith Márquez. Male solo pop artists, such as Flavio Cesar and Eduardo Capetillo, also produced hits.

So-called boy bands also became a popular trend, led by the group Magneto and later joined by more recent groups like Mercurio and Ragazzi. The "boy band" phenomena contributed to the rise of pop-dance and dance-rap groups like Caló and Onda Vaselina (later named OV7, the group that produced the male star Kalimba).

At the onset of the 21st century, a new generation highly influenced by foreign musical trends has emerged. Mexican popular music has been marked by a cycle of emerging new young stars, who often fade in popularity to be replaced by another group of singers and his or her fans.

Norteña or grupera music artists and groups   Norteña music, whose origins are found in northern Mexico and among the Mexican population of South Texas, has gained enormous popularity throughout Mexico. Its prominence nationally is due to several factors, most importantly, the number of immigrants to the United States that have returned as fans of the genre. The migration of rural people to the cities is another important reason for its popularity, as is the genre's exposure on radio and television. The common use of Norteña music in the large dance halls of urban Mexico has also contributed to its popularization, especially among low-income workers.

Los Tigres del Norte (The Tigers of the North) are by far the most significant band, and their lyrics and musical arrangements are among the very best of the genre. They have few rivals, though Ramón Ayala has also become an iconic figure of Norteña music. The popularity of Norteña music has led to a boom of groups and singers too many to list here. Unfortunately, the music's lyrics have recently been associated with drug trafficking, what has become known as "narco corridos." The violent murders of some well-known Norteño singers have been linked to narco-traffickers and their thugs.

Rock and alternative artists and groups   The launching of the "rock en tu idioma" marketing campaign heralded a resurgence of rock music in Mexico from the 1990s to the present. Commonly referred to as *rock en Español* (Spanish rock) this trail was blazed in the 1980s by groups like Caifanes and Maldita Vecindad (The Damned Neighborhood). The *rock en Español* era spawned two of Mexico's most internationally renowned rock bands, Café Tacuba and Maná. Café Tacuba has been particularly innovative, incorporating other musical styles such as hip-hop, electronic, and folk forms into their recordings. Their eclecticism and originality have received critical worldwide acclaim. Several other groups should be mentioned; among the most eminent are El Tri and Molotov. The rock genre encourages experimentation and the mixing of different styles and instrumentation, which generated a host of commercially successful groups and singers (male and female). It is important to note that Mexican *rockeros* ("rockers") now come from different parts of the country other than Mexico City, whose groups and singers early on dominated the Mexican rock scene. The diversity and internationalization of Mexico's urban culture suggests that rock music in particular will witness a continuing popularity, and increasing creativity and innovation.

Lina María Vargas

See also Folklore Culture; Folk Music; Popular Culture; Telenovelas; Television

Further Reading

Nettl, Bruno, and Ruth Stone, advisory eds., James Porter and Timothy Rice, founding eds. 1997. *The Garland Encyclopedia of World Music Online.* Alexandria, VA: Alexander Street Press. http://glnd.alexanderstreet.com/.

Riggio, Annette. 1982. The Popular Music Industry in Mexico: Producers, Products, Promoters and Implications for Mexican Culture. MA thesis, University of Texas at Austin.

Stevenson, Robert Murrell. 1952. *Music in Mexico, a Historical Survey.* New York: Crowell.

N

National Action Party

See Partido Acción Nacional

National Autonomous University of Mexico

See Universidad Nacional Autónoma de México

Nationalism and National Identity

The concepts of nationalism and national identity have been intrinsically linked in the discussion of Mexican culture since the era of the Mexican Revolution of 1910–1924. Following the end of the violent phase of the revolution, the Mexican government made nationalism fundamental to the ideology of the new order. Devastated by a decade of civil strife and fractured by political rivalries generated by the revolution, Mexico, under its new leaders, faced the challenge of building a sense of national unity. As a consequence, the promotion and construction of a nationalist discourse became central to the postrevolutionary government.

Thus, for decades, the ideas of nationalism and national identity have been associated with the ideology of the government and, more specifically, with the political structures of the long rule of one party in Mexico—the Partido Revolucionario Institucional (Institutional Revolutionary Party, PRI)—from 1929 until the end of the 20th century. As a result, nationalism became the official discourse of a one-party authoritarian state, a dialogue based on the celebration of *mexicanidad,* that is, on Mexicanness as defined by the government and its institutions. In this effort the government tolerated little dissent or criticism, blurring the distinction between official culture and that of everyday Mexican life, or popular culture. Under government tutelage, for nearly 50 years Mexico's plastic arts, literature, philosophy, films, music, and dance bore the marks of this official cultural policy in which culture became to a large extent a political tool of the one-party state. By the 1980s, however, the use of nationalism as an instrument of state power had waned, and the credibility of the dominant party eroded in the face of political and economic crises. Challenges arose to the official discourse on nationalism and national identity. As the power of the PRI collapsed by the end of the 1990s, the onset of a new political era has produced a continuing discussion over the meaning of nationalism and national identity in the context of globalization and the cultural differences evident in contemporary Mexican life.

The official nationalism of the postrevolution (1920–1940)   The economic and political development of Mexico in the 19th century was at best uneven, as much of the population identified primarily with their region and social group rather than with being Mexican. Thus, the postrevolutionary government understandably pushed nationalism and national unity as a means of consolidating its power, emphasizing an ideology based on the inclusion of all Mexicans into the new order. For example, the expansion of public education was accompanied by a decidedly secular discourse (such as in the revised texts on Mexican history) that was intended to promote national reconciliation of the different sectors of Mexican society, marked particularly by the valorization of the poor (populism) and the social incorporation of indigenous groups in the country (the idealization of the Indian, or *indigenismo*)—two groups largely neglected by the previous regime. The consequent populist discourse of the postrevolutionary government was most dramatically expressed in the muralist art movement, with its romanticized view of the working classes and indigenous people as the essence of Mexicanness, or what became commonly referred to as the popular classes. This official rhetoric was translated into a government-sanctioned promotion of the concept of *mestizaje,* that is, the mixing of European, Indian, and African peoples into one integrated society that epitomized the coming together of the Mexican people. This view led to the construction of an imagery in the 1920s and 1930s that allegedly represented the authentic culture of the people. These constructions basically created stereotypic and romanticized characterizations of being Mexican that were reproduced in various forms, from literature and paintings to posters and glorified cinematic heroes. During this period, this populist nationalism pervaded the government's ideological project and paralleled the reconstruction of the economy.

Nationalism in the era of national unification (1940–1960)   In the context of World War II and its aftermath, an evident shift took place in the discussion over national identity. The economic policies of the dominant party (renamed the PRI in 1946) moved toward the rapid industrialization of the country based on ideas of national development and progress, that is, to make Mexico a modern nation. As expressed most blatantly in the works of the government-supported film industry, the official populist, nationalist ideology continued, but it became increasingly clear that much of the urban poor and indigenous peoples of Mexico were largely excluded from the benefits of the state's programs for economic development. Modernity had failed to be egalitarian. This dilemma sparked a new round of debate among Mexican intellectuals over the meaning of national identity—that is, Mexicanness (or *lo mexicano*)—that often implicitly, and at times explicitly, challenged the official populist, nationalist rhetoric of the one-party state. These intellectuals, such as Leopoldo Zea, Luis Villoro, and Emilio Uranga, were subjected to criticism as reactionaries, elitists, and unpatriotic ingrates; most were based in the country's leading institutions of higher education that were funded by the government, adding to the awkward, ambiguous role of intellectuals in a political context whereby one party essentially controlled the educational system. The official nationalist discourse persisted, but it became obvious by the early 1960s that the effectiveness of the government's rhetoric was bankrupt, especially among the country's hard-pressed and financially strapped middle classes.

Nationalism and the society of consumption (1960–1980)   The government's repression of major strikes by teachers and industrial workers in 1958 and 1959 signaled an erosion of the support for the one-party state. At the same time, a growing portion of Mexican society became increasingly frustrated by the disparities between their conditions as opposed to those found next door in the United States. By the 1960s, the penetration of American influence was evident in the more urbanized parts of Mexico, but access to that style of life remained beyond the means of most Mexicans, including its restive middle classes. The lack of a democratic political system, the cultural gaps between Mexico and the United States, and the limited avenues of mobility (especially for women) were among the grievances shared by a large number of Mexicans and were issues that sapped the legitimacy and acceptance of the government's populist ideology.

These grievances crystallized in the student movement of 1968 and created a crisis for the state's nationalist ideology with enduring consequences. Through a combination of violent repression, intimidation, strategic concessions, and selective reforms, the one-party regime of the PRI maintained its political hold, but its ability to use populist nationalism as a means of ideological credibility would never be the same. The crisis of 1968 clearly led to a move away from the nationalist discourse of the past and the broad, contentious discussion over national identity in which no consensus was reached; the debate marked an obvious turn that could not be contained or managed by the one-party government and its allies, such as the privatized television and film industries.

Nationalism during the crisis (1980–1994)   The profound economic crisis of the 1980s shattered official nationalist rhetoric, as the credibility of the one-party state crumbled in the face of the economic disarray precipitated by its policies. The celebratory nationalist slogans of the past, such as *Como Mexico no hay dos* (There is no place like Mexico), and its associated images of an idealized, unified society were subjected to withering criticism and cynical ridicule. Although elements of patriotism and national pride remained, the official, institutional character of nationalist discourse gave way to everyday forms of cultural expression as essential aspects of Mexicanness; rather, *lo mexicano* was to be found in popular forms of entertainment, such as *lucha libre* (wrestling), sporting events (especially soccer), and related cultural arenas, far removed from government-sanctioned and government-promoted policies, programs, and institutions. In this light, Mexican-ness was best witnessed through the chaotic, improvised, and cathartic actions in the everyday frustrating lives of ordinary Mexican people. State-supported venues for the expression of national identity were suspect; indeed, intellectuals argued that the very concept of national identity was based on myth, invention, and misrepresentation, or entirely an ideological construct of the state created for its own purposes.

Thus, in the 1980s there was a diversification of the notion of national identity and its unitary character. Instead, a fragmented view of Mexican society ensued as the distrust of government intensified and, with it, a pervasive skepticism toward the state's nationalist rhetoric. Instead, more and more Mexicans turned inward toward a sense of identity rooted in local spaces, such as neighborhoods or small social groups. Moreover, given the urbanization of Mexican society, the everyday language of the poor of Mexico's cities—a majority of Mexicans are poor—became a prism for understanding the nation and its people. For example, the word *naco* and its connotative change became emblematic of this process (*naco* is a corruption of the term *totonaca,* derived from the name of a specific indigenous group). In the 1960s *naco* had a negative connotation, referring pejoratively to indigenous peoples who had recently arrived in the city. Since such newcomers came from a rural and traditional world, they found it difficult to adapt to the city, to speak fluent Spanish, and to easily manage the transition away from rural life. Over time, the meaning of *naco* was transformed to evoke the hybrid, uneven, and incomplete integration of people to urban life. This process led to a view, found in much of Mexican literature and art at that time, of a new identity that was referred to as neo-Mexicanism, an inversion of the official nationalist rhetoric of the past.

The criticism of the nationalist discourse of the past was in part a reaction to the lack of openness in the educational system and to the influence wielded by the government's overpowering cultural institutions. Nationalist sentiment could still be mobilized, such as toward the United States and its perceived dominance of Mexico; for critics of the one-party regime, however, demonstrations of nationalism did not justify the lack of a critical view of the inequities that characterized much of the everyday realities of most Mexicans. The 1990s would witness a radical change in the discussion of nationalism and national identity.

Nationalism and the national identity in the era of globalization (1994–2008)

By the 1990s, the country faced a new socioeconomic order with the introduction of free market policies intended to attract foreign investment, privatize the Mexican economy, and democratize the workings of government. Equally important, processes of globalization challenged the views of the past on the alleged singularity of Mexican culture. A growing number of intellectuals argued that multiculturalism—that is, the melding of local and global influences—best captured the realities of everyday Mexican life. The impact of the mass media, the diffusion of commercial consumption, and the celebration of capitalist principles had made Mexico a part of a universal language—a language symbolized by the signing of the North American Free Trade Agreement (NAFTA)—all marked a historic departure from past policies of economic development.

In a repudiation of this shift, the indigenous-based revolt against the government by the Ejército Zapatista de Liberación Nacional (Zapatista Army for National Freedom, EZLN) made clear the social fissures and economic disparities that still prevailed in the country and most dramatically in terms of the wretched conditions of Mexico's rural indigenous communities. To its credit, the EZLN exposed the hypocrisy of the official idealization of Mexico's indigenous past, a central element of nationalist discourse, by showing the harsh realities that confronted the nation's indigenous people. In this sense, the rebellion by the EZLN provoked a rethinking of Mexican identity and a realization of the multicultural diversity of Mexican life. As a consequence, there was a renewed interest in the local, regional, and cultural diversity generated by the intersections with global influences that clearly was at odds with the official nationalist rhetoric of the past of a homogenous Mexico. For example, given the extent and impact of immigration, there was keen interest in immigrant communities, that is, how immigration had changed the socioeconomic realities of towns and villages transformed by remittances, by the circulation of goods and people between Mexico and the United States, and by the emergence of distinct lifestyles due to the multiple cultural effects of immigration.

Nonetheless, much of the old nationalist discourse continues, despite the end of the one-party dominance of the PRI. The presidential electoral victories of the Partido Acción Nacional (National Action Party, PAN) of Vicente Fox (2000–2006) and Felipe Calderón (2006–2012) have failed to completely displace the nationalist perspective of the past. The nationalist discourse is still evident in the country's major cultural institutions, such as the Instituto Nacional de Bellas Artes (National Institute of Fine Arts, INBA), which continue to promote the singularity of Mexicanness (*mexicanidad, lo mexicano*) through iconic exhibits and shows, such as nationalistic tributes to such artists as Frida Kahlo and Diego Rivera. In this sense, the official nationalism of the past continues to operate in the workings of government-supported institutional cultural policies. On the other hand, the private sector has shown a willingness to depart from the nationalist trappings of an earlier era and to acknowledge the diversity of contemporary Mexican life. The notion of a collective single national identity still resonates with much of the Mexican population, a testament to the effectiveness of the official rhetoric of the past, including the idealization of the unique character of Mexico (commonly referred to as *guadalupanismo,* a reference to the Virgen de Guadalupe as a nationalist icon). Still, it is evident that the hold of the old stereotypes of Mexican national identity has weakened irrevocably. The search for a new understanding of Mexico and its identity indicates the passing of the idea of a unified concept of *mexicanidad*.

Acacia Maldonado

See also Archaeological Sites; Art and the Private Sector; Art Education; Art Exhibitions; Cultural Policies; Culture and the Government; El Museo Nacional de Antropología; Folklore Culture; Indigenous Culture; Indigenous Peoples; Painting; Partido Acción Nacional; Partido Revolucionario Institucional; Politics and Political Parties; Popular Culture; Religion; Soccer

Further Reading

Bejár, Raúl, and Héctor Rosales, eds. 1999. *La identidad nacional Mexicana como problema político y cultural.* México, DF: Siglo Veintiuno Editores: Universidad Nacional Autónoma de México, Centro de Investigaciones Interdisciplinarias en Humanidades.

Chorba, Carrie C. 2007. *Mexico, from Mestizo to Multicultural: National Identity and Recent Representations of the Conquest.* Nashville: Vanderbilt University Press.

Moreno, Julio. 2003. *Yankee Don't Go Home: Mexican Nationalism, American Business Culture, and the Shaping of Modern Mexico, 1920–1950.* Chapel Hill: University of North Carolina Press.

Mraz, John. 2009. *Looking for Mexico: Modern Visual Culture and National Identity.* Durham, NC: Duke University Press.

National Museum of Anthropology

See El Museo Nacional de Antropología

Nayarit

The official coat of arms of Nayarit. (Corel)

Located in western Mexico along the Pacific coast, Nayarit includes several small islands in the Pacific Ocean and has as its capital the city of Tepic. Nayarit covers 10,390 square miles, making it one of the smaller states of Mexico with a corresponding number of residents. Most of the state's population is concentrated in the fertile Tepic Valley, although the coastal area (including the port of San Blas) experienced a revival during the latter part of the 20th century, aided by the fishing industry and tourism. For centuries, Nayarit's sierras have been home to native groups, and the Huichol, Cora, and Tepehuan languages are still spoken. The Huichol Indians in particular have preserved their traditions, and they are now a tourist attraction, drawing visitors to their communities and marketing their crafts throughout Mexico.

Nayarit's terrain is broken up by the western ends of the Sierra Madre Occidental mountains. Its highest mountains are: San Juan, Sanguangüey, El Ceboruco, Cumbre de Pajaritos, and Picachos. Nayarit has two volcanoes, Ceboruco and Sangangüey. In the northeast are broad, tropical plains watered by the Río Grande de Santiago, a continuation of the Lerma River. The main state rivers are the Río Grande de Santiago, San Pedro, Acaponeta, Ameca, and Las Cañas. The last two also form natural boundaries with the states of Jalisco and Sinaloa, respectively. Nayarit also has several lagoons such as the Santa María del Oro, San Pedro Lagunillas, and Agua Brava. Nayarit contains hundreds of miles of rain forest in the sierra. The climate in the valley and coastal regions is typically warm; however, there are cooler temperatures in the mountain regions. There are mangrove forests along the coast, with guava trees found also in the state. Pine and oak trees grow in the mountainous regions. Its wildlife includes jaguars, mountain lions, wild bears, deer, caimans, armadillos, small wildcats, and many more species. Unfortunately most of the rain forest has been exploited, especially around the region of Santa María del Oro. The conservation and protection of the rain forest and wildlife of Nayarit is an issue of crucial importance.

Francisco Cortés, nephew of the Spanish conqueror Hernán Cortés, was the first European to pass through Nayarit, which became a part of the province of Nueva Galicia. Although initial contacts between the Spaniards and the native peoples of Nayarit were peaceful, the subsequent conquest of Nueva Galicia by Nuño de Guzmán brought repression and eventually encouraged a massive indigenous uprising known as the Mixtón War (1541–1542). Though the Spaniards managed to contain the uprising, many natives took refuge in the sierras of Nayarit, where they continued their resistance to Spanish control until the early 18th century. Franciscan and Jesuit missionaries also aided in the pacification of native peoples, and their efforts helped keep peace in the sierras during the late colonial period.

The rich soil of the Tepic Valley encouraged the development of haciendas during the colonial period, and Nayarit also produced some gold and silver. The local economy received a boost during the second half of the 18th century when San Blas was established as a military base, serving in the defense of the Californias, which were threatened by the English in Canada and the Russians in Alaska. San Blas and Tepic were connected by road to Guadalajara (the capital of Nueva Galicia and later of the state of Jalisco), and goods flowing to and from the port city helped create a regional economy that encouraged development in the Tepic region.

The Guadalajara–Tepic–San Blas axis grew in importance during the early 19th century, aided by the temporary closure of Mexico's main Pacific port of Acapulco, owing to the disruptions of the struggle for independence. For a time, San Blas became Mexico's most important western port, linking Tepic and Guadalajara to an extensive global trade. Tepic itself attracted foreign merchants from England, Spain, Germany, France, and the United States, and foreign investment aided the

Picturesque beach in Sayulita, Nayarit, Mexico. (Otto Dusbaba | Dreamstime.com)

growth of agriculture and industry. The sugar and tobacco industries, which remain an important part of Nayarit's economy, began in this way.

Politically, the 19th century was a volatile one for Nayarit. Despite growing sentiment for autonomy, the area remained under the jurisdiction first of the state of Jalisco and later of the federal government. (Nayarit did not become a state until 1917.) Civil unrest plagued Nayarit as wealthy members of the Barrón and Castaños families pegged their rivalry to Mexico's broader struggle between liberals and conservatives (the main political factions during the 19th century). Meanwhile, banditry and rebellion developed in the sierras as expanding sugar haciendas displaced older communities. From this popular struggle emerged Manuel Lozada, himself a victim of the encroaching hacienda system. Lozada became a regional leader and he made allies of sierra Indians, including the Coras and Huicholes. Until his death in 1873, Lozada fought for the return of lands that had been taken from Nayarit's native peoples since the colonial period. Other agrarian leaders continued Lozada's struggle, but the trend was toward more loss of land, particularly during the reign of Mexico's dictator Porfirio Díaz, who ruled the country from 1876 to 1911.

During the Porfirian era, Nayarit maintained a healthy agrarian economy (producing sugar, tobacco, cotton, and coffee), although the late arrival of the railroad (1912) limited the development of mining and industry. As was typical in Mexico during this period, wealth and power became increasingly concentrated in the hands of a small, elite group. A Spanish family named Aguirre came to control over half of Nayarit's wealth, and some seven families monopolized most of the state's land, mines, and industry.

In the early phase of the Mexican Revolution, Tepic was occupied by General Martín Espinosa. Espinosa arrived from neighboring Sinaloa to claim the area for Francisco Madero, whose movement succeeded in deposing Porfirio Díaz in 1911. Espinosa continued the revolutionary struggle in Nayarit after Madero's assassination in 1913, and the city of Tepic changed hands several times as the revolution splintered into factions. Although Nayarit finally gained statehood in 1917 as a result of the new constitution that emerged from the Mexican Revolution of 1910, it continued to be plagued by unrest and economic dislocation. Thirty-two governors attempted to pacify the state between 1918 and 1934, and many politicians and labor and agrarian activists were killed.

The popular struggle for land reform that had gained momentum in the 19th century under Manuel Lozada's leadership was effectively blocked by a series of governors assisted by large landowners, including the Aguirre clan. Not until the middle of the 1930s were the immense holdings of the Aguirres and other elites dismantled, creating *ejidos* (communal plots) for many inhabitants of Nayarit. The state's economy, however, was slow to recover from the disruptions of the revolution. Despite growth during the late colonial period and early 19th century, Tepic remained a fairly provincial city and San Blas declined as a port.

The revival and modern growth of Tepic and Nayarit depended on new transportation systems developed during the 20th century. The first of these was a railroad line, completed in 1928, that linked Tepic to Guadalajara and to the port of Mazatlán. The second was a highway linking the same cities (and extending to Nogales, on the U.S.-Mexican border) and completed by midcentury. These transportation networks helped to integrate Nayarit and create more effective links with the rest of Mexico. They also encouraged an impressive increase in Tepic's population and aided in the revival and further growth of Nayarit's agricultural sector, which continues to export its products internationally. By the end of the 20th century, San Blas and Nayarit's coastal area had also experienced a revival, helped by the growth of the fishing industry and tourism. Bahia de las Banderas, an area to the south of San Blas, was built as a tourist area with funding from the United States, Canada, and Japan.

As the 21st century began, Nayarit was increasingly seen as a tourist destination. Other sectors of the state's economy were beginning to mirror modern realities. In response to the global market and the exigencies of free trade, Nayarit added the production of specialty crops such as mango and watermelon to its list of agricultural export goods. The fishing industry, also largely geared toward export, faced the challenges of overexploitation and water pollution. Politically, Nayarit had achieved a remarkable stability, compared to that of its past. In 1999, Antonio Echevarría Domínguez was elected as Nayarit's first non–Partido Revolucionario Institucional (Institutional Revolutionary Party, PRI) governor, thus helping to erode the political monopoly held by PRI since its establishment in 1929. Nonetheless, the grip of the PRI over the state's politics returned in its 2005 gubernatorial victory, which the party renewed in the 2011 elections. To most observers, the resurgence of the PRI has much to do with the perceived failures of the consecutive presidential administrations of Vicente Fox (2000–2006) and Felipe Calderón (2006–2012), both of whom belong to PAN. A major factor in that regard has been the inability of the Calderón administration to stem the tide of illegal drug trade–related violence in the country, including Nayarit. In 2009 there were 37 homicides in the small state, but in 2010 the number of murders soared to 377, most of which were related to drug cartel killings. The tourist industry, a key source of revenues for the state, suffered as a consequence, leading to an increase in underemployment and unemployment as well as declining monies from the state's once-dynamic economic sector. In the 2011 gubernatorial elections, the PRI garnered 49 percent of the vote, while the PAN candidate received 33 percent of the ballots. In this context, it is likely that the PRI will maintain its political preponderance, but it will have to contend with an electorate that will expect an effective suppression of drug cartels' activities in the state and a renewal of economic stability and growth, particularly for its tourist industry.

Suzanne B. Pasztor

See also Drug Trade and Trafficking; Tourism

Further Reading

Archibold, Randal C. 2010. "Gunmen Kill 15 in Mexico; Gang Link Seen." *New York Times,* October 10, A10.

Castellón Fonseca, Francisco Javier, ed. 1998. *Nayarit al final del milenio.* Tepic, Nayarit: Universidad Autónoma de Nayarit.

Meyer, Jean. 1997. *Breve historia de Nayarit.* México, DF: Fondo de Cultura Económica.

Nayarit. http://www.nayarit.gob.mx.

New Media Arts

See Media Arts, New

North American Free Trade Agreement

On January 1, 1994, after ratification by the legislatures of Canada, the United States, and Mexico, the North American Free Trade Agreement (NAFTA) took effect. Since then, it has bound these three countries together in an ambitious experiment in regional economic integration. The successful negotiation of NAFTA has undoubtedly been the most important political and economic decision of the past 50 years for Mexico. Indeed, Mexico was taking a step forward in its path toward perpetuating the neoliberal economic reforms initiated by President Carlos Salinas, after several protectionist decades under ISI (import substitution industrialization). NAFTA was to be the instrument that would integrate the Mexican economy with other North American economies by setting rules and procedures that regulate the commercial relationships between these countries.

U.S. President George H.W. Bush attends the North American Free Trade Agreement (NAFTA) initialing ceremony in October 1992. (George Bush Library)

The main purpose of the agreement was to open up borders and ease trade restrictions with the goal of regional commercial integration. Opportunities for investment would be increased, the circulation of goods and services would be eased, and loyal competition would be promoted. NAFTA was the first trade agreement involving developed and developing countries and it therefore generated great expectations. Mexico was expected to be more efficient in its productive processes, hence more competitive, generating more wealth and job opportunities for its population. In fact, Mexico has actually shed its stereotypical image of an emerging market suffering from trade deficits and recurring financial crises. From a political perspective, NAFTA meant setting aside many of the national prejudices that Mexican elites and society held regarding the United States. The agreement also meant accepting that Mexico had a real relationship with the United States, leaving aside mistrust and hostility to focus on shared goals and values and embracing cooperation.

The ratification of NAFTA gave continuity to the economic policies implemented by previous administrations in Mexico and granted certainty and predictability to the economic policies implemented by the Mexican government, a sine qua non for attracting foreign investment. Furthermore, NAFTA has increased the level of trade in Mexico. But NAFTA has also generated a good amount of controversy. It has been harshly criticized and highly praised by analysts of the three member countries, and debates about NAFTA have varied sharply within these countries. One of the most symbolic demonstrations against NAFTA was the uprising of the Ejército Zapatista de Liberación Nacional (EZLN) in Chiapas on January 1, 1994, the day when NAFTA was officially in effect.

In 2008, the liberalization of goods ended with the removal of the last remaining trade restriction on a handful of agricultural commodities such as U.S. exports to Mexico of corn, dry edible beans, nonfat dry milk, and high fructose corn syrup and Mexican exports to the United States of sugar and certain horticultural products. Angry masses of farmers demonstrated in late January in Mexico City and even U.S. presidential Democrat candidates Barack Obama and Hillary Clinton talked about opting out of NAFTA if it were not renegotiated. All these events were a response to the unpopularity of NAFTA in a bad economic environment both for the United States and Mexico. The question is: Can NAFTA really be blamed for slower growth and unemployment?

With respect to the ways in which Mexico has dealt with NAFTA, the benefits to the Mexican economy from NAFTA are described first, followed by the difficulties to the Mexican economic and political horizon. This analysis will facilitate the understanding of the challenges Mexico has to face and the reforms it might implement in order to take as much advantage as possible from the North American integration.

As economic interactions began developing, leaving aside protectionist and closed trade rules in vogue during the Great Depression and World War II, one of the main concerns of the economists of that time was to propose an adequate model of development for the Third World countries. Mexico, as many other Latin American and African countries, adopted the import substitution industrialization (ISI) model. Under this model, Mexico maintained high tariffs on imports so as to promote domestic production, which worked for about 40 years. When Europe began recovering from World War II, the American-led key economic organizations—the General Agreement on Tariffs and Trade (GATT), the World Bank, and the International Monetary Fund (IMF), all founded during the late 1940s and 1950s—started to play an important role in the economic transactions of the Western and developed countries. The ISI model first worked spontaneously; afterward, in the 1970s, it relied on high oil prices and on the availability of money in the financial markets. The IMF was eager to lend money to the developing countries, believing it would be highly profitable.

In the late 1970s and the early 1980s, the international environment changed. The debt crisis pointed out all the flaws of the ISI model and the need for developing countries to find a viable model of development. Therefore, since the early 1980s, Latin American policy makers have embraced the concept of market liberalization. An export-oriented industrialization policy, along with deregulation and liberalization, came to be seen as imperative for developing countries trying to restructure their production systems and to enter the globalizing marketplace.

The process of reducing state participation in the Mexican economy began in the 1980s with the sale of parastatal companies. The opening of Mexico's markets and trade liberalization can both be traced to Mexico's adhesion to the GATT in 1986. However, Mexico's efforts to gain access to the global economic stage go back even further, to the country's unilateral tariff reductions initiated in 1982. Thus, when NAFTA negotiations began in 1989–1990, the Mexican economy was already relatively open. President Carlos Salinas, when trying to achieve a North American agreement, wanted to make clear to the international community that Mexico would not reverse its integration process to the world economy. The purpose was to attract investment in a time of slow growth at the international level.

Once NAFTA was ratified in 1994, Mexico was perceived as a country that would eventually be part of the developed countries. However, different political and economic events reflected another reality. The uprising of the EZLN and the deep economic crisis of that same year proved the world wrong. NAFTA, even though it limited the resources the government had to palliate the crisis, also proved to be useful. The U.S. government, led by the Clinton administration, could not afford to allow the Mexican economy to sink.

In terms of volume of trade and investment, NAFTA's results are much more favorable than both supporters and detractors had predicted at the beginning of the 1990s. Convergence was indeed experienced in these areas. Exports increased 15.1 percent of Mexico's gross domestic product (GDP), rising from 16.8 percent to 31.9 percent, and trade grew 26.8 percent of total Mexican GDP, from 38.2 percent to 70 percent from 1994 to 2007. Mexico has become the third-largest trading partner of the United States, behind Canada and China. Last year, Mexico sent abroad nearly $250 billion of merchandise, 4.8 times more exports than in 1993. Moreover, the fact that exports to the U.S. and Canadian markets have increased their shares means that imports from those markets have decreased their shares proportionately. Mexico has also increased its participation in U.S. imports from 6.9 percent in 1993 to 10.8 percent in 2007. It transformed a $3 billion trade deficit with the United States in 1993 into an approximate $50 billion surplus in 2006. Also because of NAFTA, Mexico has come to be viewed as a relatively attractive target for foreign investment. Indeed, Mexico has attracted some $223 billion of foreign investment in 13 years. Changes in the laws that regulate foreign investment, property rights, trade, and privatization have consolidated the increase in investment inflows. However, the key has been the credibility that NAFTA provides.

At first look, these indicators suggest that NAFTA has achieved its objectives. It should also be considered that rising economic numbers have coincided with macroeconomic stability and less poverty. Indeed, macroeconomic stability shows in the convergence of inflation rates of both the United States and Mexico and in the significant reduction of interest rates in Mexico. In fact, the inflation rate for Mexico decreased from 35 percent in 1995 to around 3 percent in 2006, reaching the same level as U.S. inflation. Food poverty has been reduced by 7.4 percent, from 21.2 percent to 13.8 percent; capacity poverty by 9.3 percent, from 30.0 percent to 20.7 percent; and finally, assets poverty has decreased 9.8 percent, from 52.4 percent to 42.6 percent. (According to the Mexican Secretariat of Social Development, food poverty is the inability to pay for food baskets; capacity poverty is the inability to provide for food, education, and health; and assets poverty is the inability to provide for food, education, health, dress, dwelling, energy, and transportation.)

However, even if those benefits seem to be apparent, inconsistent results have arisen. On January 1, 2008, the last trade barriers and tariffs were eliminated between the United States, Canada, and Mexico. The farmer demonstration on January 31, demanding that NAFTA be renegotiated, was more the reflection of Mexico's incomplete economic transformation than a direct critique of NAFTA itself. With full implementation, the last remaining trade restriction on a handful of agricultural commodities—such as U.S. exports to Mexico of corn, dry edible beans, nonfat dry milk, and high fructose corn syrup and Mexican exports to the United States of sugar and certain horticultural products—were removed. All these sensitive farm products had been given a special 15-year protection, so that farmers would have time to prepare for competition. Mexico does not seem to be ready to face agricultural competition; for example, it consumes much more corn than it produces. Although NAFTA has expanded business in Mexico and benefited its middle class, it has done poorly in terms of agricultural farmers' life conditions.

Given the heterogeneity of Mexico's economic sectors, NAFTA's performance in achieving its objectives in Mexico is uneven. Indeed, although the manufacturing sector registered higher levels of job creation (an increase of 500,000 from 1994 to 2002), it did not contribute to the development of Mexican industry or the domestic market as a whole. Analysis of NAFTA by the Confederación Patronal de la República Mexicana (Mexican Employers' Association, COPARMEX) clearly shows that exporting enterprises and maquiladoras represent an important source of job creation; they pay salaries 40 percent higher than nonexporting enterprises. The agricultural sector has suffered the most, with a net loss of 1.3 million jobs from 1994 to 2002. The rising levels of Mexican exports, foreign investment inflows to Mexico, and the burgeoning maquiladora sector together helped create roughly 1.5 million jobs during the first 10 years of NAFTA implementation. However, the employment situation remains precarious in several economic sectors. One indication of the lack of employment options is the continuing out-migration of Mexican workers to the United States.

Moreover, the World Bank stated that the Mexican economic growth has not been sufficient to level the per capita income of the Mexican economy with its NAFTA partners. Mexico's growth during the NAFTA period has been mixed. In 1994 the Mexican economy grew by 4.5 percent. Only a year later the economy suffered the effects of the peso crisis and GDP fell by 6.2 percent. During Salinas's administration (1988–1994), the GDP average annual growth was 3.91 percent; during Zedillo's administration (1994–2000), 3.39 percent; and under Fox's administration (2000–2006), only 2.32 percent. These poor economic results stress the fact that Mexico needs to rethink its production model framed by NAFTA. Clearly, NAFTA should be understood as only one element in Mexico's model of economic integration. It does not account for every improvement or flaw in the Mexican economy, nor is it able to solve every Mexican problem. One of the principal problems of Mexico under NAFTA is the technology gap between U.S.

and Mexican firms. It remains so wide that innovative processes are essentially imported. Thus, Mexico has yet to exploit the access to foreign technology that NAFTA provides. Foreign technology has not been disseminated to Mexican firms, and Mexico continues to be a technology follower. This phenomenon shows in all sectors but is especially true for the agricultural sector. Mexico has to improve its productivity in that area in order to profit as much as possible from NAFTA. Even though the agroalimentary and fishing trades in 2006 amounted to 2.6 times the volume traded in 1994, there are poor productive agricultural areas that must be boosted. Agroalimentary exports still represent a small share of total Mexican exports and are concentrated in a few sectors, especially the maquiladora sector. There is no evidence that NAFTA has had a negative impact on corn production or other sensitive products. Indeed, since the liberalization of some sensitive products in 2003, the production of those goods has increased. Poor wages and unemployment accounted for angry farmers in recent demonstrations, and the performance of nonexporting economic sectors has been underprivileged and inconsistent.

The economic benefits Mexico received from NAFTA are evident in its macroeconomic indicators. First, Mexican exports have dramatically increased, allowing for better performance than in the late 1980s. Second, Mexico has been able, through NAFTA, to attract foreign investment. Third, poverty has been reduced and macroeconomic stability has been observed despite the dependence of the Mexican economy on the U.S. economy brought about by NAFTA.

However, the asymmetry across the Mexican industrial sectors seems to be more evident since NAFTA was signed. Thus, the Mexican government has the important task of supporting those sectors that are not competitive and productive enough by improving infrastructure, its fiscal system, and its legal framework. Special emphasis should be put to the agroalimentary sector to turn it into a comparative advantage instead of the present burden it represents for the Mexican economy. NAFTA would be a much more efficient instrument for Mexico if the country adapted fully to the changes it has brought economically, socially, and politically. In order to do so, leaders in Mexico have to think of different and new productive strategies, because the old strategies are not compatible with this new economic context.

Christelle Pages Patron

See also Debt, Foreign; Ejército Zapatista de Liberación Nacional and the Indigenous Movement; Foreign Trade; Salinas de Gortari, Carlos

Further Reading

Carlsen, Laura. 2007. "TLCAN: Inequidad e inmigración." *Programa de las Américas,* November 20, http://www.ircamericas.org/esp/4747.

Castañeda, Jorge C. 2004. "NAFTA at 10: A Plus or a Minus?" *Current History* 103(670): 51–55, http://ejournals.ebsco.com/direct.asp?ArticleID=6RYT97WVNVBDHEH5TV2F.

COPARMEX. http://www.coparmex.org.mx/upload/bibVirtualDocs/TLCAN%202008-LDLC.pdf.

Fernández, Arturo. 2000. Presentation of *TLCAN ¿Socios Naturales? Cinco años del tratado de libre comercio de América del Norte,* coord. Beatriz Leycegui and Rafael Fernández de Castro, 7–10. México, DF: ITAM.

Ordorica Mariscal, Ana Paula. 2001. *El TLCAN: Una herramienta de desarrollo para México.* México, DF: Tesis ITAM.

Valdés Ugalde, José Luis. 2002. "NAFTA and Mexico: A Sectoral Analysis." In *NAFTA in the New Millennium,* edited by Edward Chambers and Peter Smith, 61–82. La Jolla: Center for U.S.-Mexican Studies, University of California.

Nuevo León

The official coat of arms of Nuevo León. (Corel)

The state of Nuevo León is among the most important in Mexico for the strength of its economy and its political clout. Since the late 19th century, this state has often been described as the Pittsburgh of the country for its distinctive industrial history and its continuing importance as a manufacturing center. The state is the home base of several of Mexico's most successful and powerful corporations, among them one of the world's largest cement-making companies, CEMEX, as well as one of Latin America's biggest beverage firms, FEMSA. Indeed, the state has been historically associated with the influence and economic prowess of its business class. As a result, Nuevo León also holds national political significance, as the state has generally been a bastion of conservatism. Indeed, Mexico's contemporary right-of-center party, the Partido Acción Nacional (National Action Party, PAN), had its roots in the Nuevo León capital city of Monterrey in 1939. Thus, for its economic and political importance, Nuevo León represents a pivotal state in modern Mexico. By far, much of the past and present of Nuevo León is dominated by Monterrey, which arguably ranks only second to Mexico City in significance to the modern history of the country.

Nuevo León is located in the northeastern corner of Mexico, flanked on the east by the state of Tamaulipas, on the west by Coahuila, and with San Luis Potosí to the south. A short strip of nine miles of the state borders Texas. As of 2010 Nuevo León ranks eighth in population in Mexico, though about 80 percent of the people in the state reside in the metropolitan area of the capital, Monterrey.

The state is generally dry and much of its territory is semidesert, especially its northern tier, while the southern portion of the state is semiarid; the Sierra Madre Oriental mountain range runs down the spine of the state. Temperatures during the long summer can be extremely hot, and during the winter months it can be very cold. Rainfall is scarce throughout the state, and its rivers tend to be dry or nearly so for much of the year. As a consequence, agriculture represents a meager component of the state's economy. There is a narrow slice of land that is conducive to growing fruits (particularly oranges) and vegetables in and around the town of Montemorelos. Flora and fauna correspond to the climate and topography of the state. Mountains in Nuevo León support deer, black bears, and pumas, and desert and semidesert plants abound. Despite less-than-optimal natural resources, such as easy access to waterways, Nuevo León became one of Mexico's premier economic centers by the end of the 19th century.

The proximity of Nuevo León to the United States has figured decisively in its economic development since at least the mid-19th century. During the American Civil War, the Confederacy shipped its cotton through south Texas into Nuevo León and then on to European markets as a means to evade the Union economic blockade of the South. Monterrey's merchants garnered large profits from the cotton trade, which greatly contributed to the expansion of a regional trade network involving Nuevo León and south Texas, going back to earlier in the century; that trade network continued after the conclusion of the American Civil War in 1865. Moreover, the entrepreneurship of Nuevo León's businessmen proved to be crucial to the rise of Monterrey as an industrial center. By the early 1900s, the city boasted Latin America's first steel plant, a large brewery, a glass and bottling plant, a packaging factory, and related industries. Various companies were founded in the late 19th century that formed the cornerstone of a closely-knit group of interests that provided the foundation for a powerful group of businessmen that became known as the Grupo Monterrey, whose influence and economic clout would reach national proportions by the 1920s. The main businesses were relatively unscathed by the violence of the Mexican Revolution (the period between 1910 and 1920). Thus, once stability was achieved the major enterprises of Monterrey resumed production with little trouble, protected in many respects by the nationalist economic policies of the new Mexican postrevolutionary government. But the 1930s brought troubles associated with the Great Depression, and equally important, with the progressive, populist, prolabor policies of the presidency of Lázaro Cárdenas. Those troubles, however, subsided with the end of Cárdenas's term in office and the onset of World War II, when Nuevo León's businessmen took ample advantage of the wartime economy to boost their interests and profits. Nuevo León generally prospered through the 1950s, spearheaded by the expansive businesses of Monterrey. During the crisis of the early 1980s, however, the vaunted firms of the state underwent a serious setback, punctuated by the near collapse of one of Nuevo León's largest companies at that time, the ALFA Corporation.

For decades, the politics of Nuevo León have revolved around the state's rather conservative business class and its relationship to the political party that dominated Mexico from the late 1920s through the 1990s: the Partido Revolucionario Institucional (Institutional Revolutionary Party, PRI). The relationship has been uneven, at times tense and fractious, but not without periods of an uneasy collaboration.

The origins of that inconsistent political relationship can be traced to a historic confrontation in 1936 between the major businessmen of Nuevo León and the Cárdenas administration. That conflict contributed importantly to the formation of an oppositional conservative, probusiness party that became known as the Partido Acción Nacional (National Action Party, PAN). Eventually, PAN was able to make significant political gains by the 1980s, setting the stage for a surge in that party's power with the unraveling of the dominant PRI by the early 1990s. In 2000, the PRI lost the presidency to PAN after holding the presidential chair since the PRI's founding in 1929. In PAN's gradual rise to power, the Grupo Monterrey played a critical supportive role. Nonetheless, despite its frequent criticism of the PRI, the major businessmen of the state maintained a cooperative though brittle relationship with the PRI-dominated federal government. Tensions particularly took place in the 1970s, but relations were patched up when the federal government, controlled by the PRI, rescued the financially beleaguered companies of Nuevo León in the midst of the 1980s economic crisis. More importantly, during the 1980s, Mexico's president moved toward a more probusiness stance that was continued by his successor, Carlos Salinas de Gortari (1988–1994). Relations soured, however, by the mid-1990s and much of the business community of Nuevo León supported the winning bid of the PAN candidate in the 2000 presidential election.

Since the end of the PRI's dominance in the late 1990s, politics in the state have teetered between PAN and the PRI. In 1997, the governor's race went to PAN, yet in 2003 the contest for the gubernatorial chair was won by the resurgent PRI, as the former dominant national party benefited from the inept leadership of the previous PAN governor. In the 2009 gubernatorial elections, the PRI candidate was again victorious; the falling popularity of President Felipe Calderón, a *panista,* had added to the electoral problems of his party's campaign for the governorship of Nuevo León. In spite of the PRI's very recent success, Nuevo León remains a fairly conservative state, as the PRI governors in the last two terms (2003–2009 and 2009–2015) have maintained a fairly collaborative relationship with the state's private sector. In 2010, of the state's 12 federal deputies (members of the Mexican Congress), seven belonged to PAN, and five belonged to the PRI; the right-of-center party held two of the three senatorial seats. As an indication of the conservative electoral tenor of the state, the left-of-center party, the PRD, continues to be a marginal political presence in Nuevo León. In brief, the political climate of the state has a moderate, probusiness bent, which has made it relatively easy for the business class to maintain its influence over the political process.

The economy of the state revolves around four major activities based in the capital of Nuevo León, as more than 80 percent of the state's gross domestic product (GDP) is produced by companies in the metropolitan area of Monterrey. Manufacturing represents about a third of Nuevo León's GDP and is the state's leading economic sector, closely followed by the state's services economy (about 25 percent), and trade sector (20 percent). Financial and transport sectors compose about 15 percent and 11 percent, respectively, of the state's economy. In contrast, agriculture produces only about 2 percent of Nuevo León's economic production. Nuevo León's strong industrial sector is spearheaded by some of the Mexico's most prominent corporations, such as CEMEX, one of the world's leading cement-making companies. Given the proximity of the United States, the strength of the state's manufacturing sector has been bolstered for three decades by the number of assembly plants (maquiladoras) that have been built in Nuevo León since the 1960s; that type of manufacturing activity has been further accelerated by the impact of the North American Free Trade Agreement of 1993. At this writing, there are over 150 assembly plants in the vicinity of Monterrey, and they employ nearly 20,000 workers (most of them female).

Part of the Parque Fundidora (old steel mill) at Monterrey, Nuevo León, Mexico. (Enrique Gomez | Dreamstime.com)

A key artery in the U.S.-Mexico trade runs through Nuevo León's capital from central Mexico to the border portal of Nuevo Laredo in the state of Tamaulipas (across from Laredo, Texas). As a consequence, Monterrey is a major stop and distribution center for the commercial traffic between the two countries, which has contributed to the importance of the transport and services sectors of Nuevo León's economy. On the other hand, like all of Mexican states dependent in large part on foreign markets, especially that north of the border, any recessionary dip in the United States has a negative economic impact (Mexico sends 80–90 percent of its exports to the United States). The U.S. recession that began in 2007 dampened business activity related to the production of goods destined for North American markets—and Nuevo León was no exception. Furthermore, Nuevo León is among those states in Mexico that are particularly sensitive to increasing international competition, especially the trend of U.S. companies to relocate their production facilities to lower-wage countries, such as China, and/or mergers between companies in the state with larger foreign conglomerates. For instance, the brewery Cervecería Cuauhtémoc, one of Nuevo León's most storied companies, was sold to the Heineken Corporation of Holland in 2010.

The social structure of the state reflects its economic profile. The state has a robust upper class, an extensive and significant middle class, and a very large working class; consistent with the economic structure of the state and the demography of Nuevo León, the overwhelming majority of the economically active population is located in the Monterrey metropolitan area. As a result, it is estimated that the per capita income in Nuevo León is among the highest in Mexico, exceeding by more than 80 percent the national average for the country. On the other hand, the numerous assembly plants employ thousands of low-wage workers that attract many migrants from the region's rural areas. It is estimated that about a third of those who live in extreme poverty in Nuevo León are found in the state's rural areas; the extreme poverty rate is about 7 percent in Monterrey. In this context, there are a large number of underemployed and unemployed people who eke out a living in the informal sector of the state, particularly in the Monterrey area. Poverty and poor housing mark the lives of most of the rural migrants in the state who have moved to the capital, and their conditions stand in sharp contrast to those who are employed by the major firms of the state and whose incomes by Mexican standards are among the best in the country.

Due to its economic structure, Nuevo León possesses a relatively higher level of education compared to most other Mexican states. There are three major institutions of higher education in the state, the largest of which is the publicly funded Universidad Autónoma de Nuevo León. The most prestigious is the private Instituto Tecnológico y de Estudios Superiores de Monterrey, popularly referred to as Tec de Monterrey, which is modeled on the Massachusetts Institute of Technology (MIT) in the United States. There is also the private Universidad de Monterrey. The schools of higher education in Nuevo León are among the best equipped in the country, with up-to-date technology and computer facilities. The well-regarded Tec de Monterrey has developed a number of satellite campuses in various parts of the country, most of which are oriented toward the preparation of professionals and to augment professional education. The influence of the Tec has widened as a consequence, and it has become a highly visible national educational institution.

The social and cultural life of the state is dominated by Monterrey. The city boasts a number of cultural institutions, including museums of contemporary art, history, anthropology, and history, as well as cultural centers for music and dance, a major theater for musical, dance, and dramatic performances, and an IMAX dome. The universities of the city also contribute to the lively cultural life of the area. Moreover, the city has an array of sports teams, including professional soccer and baseball teams. With its relatively large and rather affluent, sophisticated population, the nightlife of Monterrey teems with dance clubs, excellent restaurants, a host of popular music venues of diverse genres, lounges, and coffeehouses. In short, Monterrey represents the cultural limelight of the state.

Unfortunately, the social life of the state has been marred recently by an increase in violence associated with the illegal drug trade. The competition among the Mexican drug cartels for the drug route via the south Texas border has made the zone between Monterrey and Laredo in particular a key battleground among rival drug gangs. In addition, the extensive business infrastructure of Monterrey has made the city an important venue for the money laundering of drug trade profits. As a result of its position within the drug trade, Monterrey has become a site of an unprecedented number of shootings, kidnappings, and similar forms of violence. Drug trafficking–related crime organizations have spread into other illegal activities, such as property theft and robberies, which have had an unsettling social impact and have tarnished the former image of the state as having a low rate of crime and violence. In 2010, law enforcement agencies in the state recorded 650 murders, most of which were attributable to drug trade–related violence.

Nevertheless, Nuevo León continues to be one of Mexico's most important states both politically and economically. Its stature as an industrial and financial powerhouse remains largely intact and its entrepreneurial character persists as a distinguishing aspect of the state.

Alex M. Saragoza

See also Drug Trade and Trafficking; Foreign Trade; Income; Maquiladoras; North American Free Trade Agreement; Transportation

Further Reading

Alarcon, Gustavo, and Victor Maldonado. 2009. *La industrializacion de Nuevo León: Retrovision y perspectiva.* Monterrey: Universidad Autonoma de Nuevo León.

Cerda Perez, Patricia Liliana. 2009. *Violencia y ciudad.* Monterrey: Universidad Autonoma de Nuevo León.

de los Angeles Pozas, Maria. 1993. *Industrial Restructuring in Mexico: Corporate Adaptation, Technological Innovation, and Changing Patterns of Industrial Relations in Monterrey.* San Diego: Center for U.S.-Mexican Studies, University of California, San Diego.

Nuevo León Official State Website. http://www.nl.gob.mx.

Snodgrass, Michael. 2003. *Deference and Defiance in Monterrey: Workers, Paternalism and Revolution in Mexico, 1890–1950.* Cambridge: Cambridge University Press.

O

Oaxaca

The official coat of arms of Oaxaca. (Corel)

The Mexican state of Oaxaca is located in the southeast of Mexico, on the Pacific side of the Isthmus of Tehuantepec, and is adjacent to the states of Chiapas to the east, Puebla to the northwest, Veracruz to the north, and Guerrero to the west. The state is among the largest in Mexico, ranking fifth in size, though 10th or so in population. Oaxaca contains a wide range of climates and geographic features, from the coastal plains along its shore facing the Pacific Ocean to its jagged mountains and the high plateau of its interior, as well as a wide, fertile, and well-watered valley that runs through the central corridor of the state.

Oaxaca shares distinctive characteristics with the southern region of Mexico, notably, a large proportion of indigenous peoples, high rates of poverty, low levels of schooling, a substantial rural population, a social structure composed of scores of small towns and villages, and a cultural character clearly influenced by the region's Indian groups. More so than its neighboring states, however, Oaxaca has increasing out-migration to the United States, as the poor socioeconomic conditions of the state have induced Oaxacans to migrate in increasing numbers since the 1970s. Initially, working-age males became a key source of the migrant farm-labor cycle of Mexico, especially with the agricultural development of northern states like Sonora, Sinaloa, and Baja California Norte in the 1950s and 1960s. The proximity of those farming areas to the United States eventually attracted the attention of agricultural labor employers across the border, who subsequently recruited Mexican migrant workers to assist in the harvesting of various field crops in the southern junction of Arizona and California, such as the Imperial and Coachella valleys (with water derived from the Colorado and Gila rivers that made possible irrigation projects in that area). Of that labor force, many of them came from Oaxaca, and thereby began the making of a migratory flow from Oaxaca to the agricultural areas first of southern California, then into the San Joaquín Valley, gradually spreading to the coastal valleys of California, the upper Sacramento Valley, and eventually to Oregon and Washington. For some older Oaxacan men, this migrant farm-labor trek recalled their participation in the U.S.-Mexico guest worker agreement of 1942–1964 (the so-called Bracero Program). Particularly after the 1980s, remittances to Oaxaca

The coastal town of Escondito in Oaxaca, Mexico. (Michael Levy | Dreamstime.com)

from migrants in the United States have represented an important source of income to the state and its residents.

The economy of the state is highly diversified, including various types of agricultural production, commercial fishing, tourism, and a broad services sector generated by the importance of the city of Oaxaca on the main transportation artery between the central and southern reaches of the country, as well as the city's governmental functions and tourist attractions.

Oaxaca's farmers produce beans, sugar cane, mangoes, and melons in those parts of the state conducive to the growing of those crops. Large-scale agave cultivation also takes place in Oaxaca for the making of the region's characteristic alcoholic drink, *mezcal*. Of greater importance, the richest source of agricultural income comes from the state's production of its highly regarded shade coffee. Unfortunately, a major proportion of the farming population does not share equitably in the state's agricultural bounty. Small landholders are dwarfed by the much larger landowners and their resources, forcing many of the region's peasant farmers to sell, rent, or lease their lands—a key factor in the migratory flow to the United States. Cooperatives have emerged in an effort to improve the conditions of small farmers, but the results have been uneven at best. The retreat of the federal government from agrarian reform since the early 1990s has exacerbated the problems facing Oaxaca's peasant farmers, as well as the adverse impacts of competition from imported farm products facilitated by the North American Free Trade Agreement. In recent years, concentration of landownership has increased in Oaxaca as small farmers have sold out to large agribusiness firms.

For decades, tourism has contributed significantly to the state's economy. Cultural tourism has flourished in the city of Oaxaca since the development of the most prominent archaeological sites nearby, those of Monte Albán and Mitla; both were made World Heritage sites by UNESCO in 1987. In addition, the city's Spanish colonial architectural sights have also been a magnet for travelers. Furthermore, since the 1980s, there have been efforts to develop beach tourism on the state's Pacific coast, specifically in and around Huatulco. To date, the area has been much less successful than anticipated by government tourism planners, as other tourist spots along the Pacific, such as Puerto Vallarta and Los Cabos, have outshined Huatulco. However, the federal government, in conjunction with the state of Oaxaca, have moved recently to ease tourist traffic between the beach resort and the very popular cultural tourist sites of the interior by the construction of a new multilane highway to replace the former, dangerously narrow roadway; with the new thoroughfare, travel time between the two tourist areas will be cut nearly in half, allowing for a tourist circuit that will, it is hoped, enliven Huatulco's tourist traffic and supplement the tourist itineraries of those visitors to the city of Oaxaca.

The state also possesses a substantive services sector, fueled by the city of Oaxaca's tourist industry, the governmental services as the state's capital, and its importance as a transportation hub for the southern region of the country. Restaurants, hotels, transportation services, and retail trades comprise a major portion of the economy of the state, concentrated in the city of Oaxaca.

Since the 1970s, remittances, as noted earlier, have been an important adjunct to the state's economy, particularly for the Mixteca, the high plateau of the state from which a large proportion of immigrants originate.

Yet, in the midst of the state's diverse economy, the rate of poverty is among the very worst in Mexico. The poorest are found mainly in the rural areas of the state, marked by a significant proportion of indigenous peoples. For decades, scores of villages remained relatively isolated, erratically connected by bad roads and unreliable means of transportation, and where subsistence farming prevailed. The remoteness of these villages contributed to the maintenance of indigenous cultural forms, but the social cost of that relative isolation was high: a lack of educational facilities, a dearth of basic health services, high rates of infant mortality, malnutrition, and scant if any access to electricity, sanitation, and potable water systems. Huge social disparities, evident since colonial times, continued into the 20th century. The social reforms generated by the Mexican Revolution of 1910 and the subsequent prevailing political order failed to have a transformative impact on the social and economic structures of the state. Vast socioeconomic differences became entrenched with few alternatives for the state's poor, especially for those of indigenous, rural backgrounds, other than to migrate to larger cities and take low-wage jobs, or to head to the United States.

In this light, the reformist left-of-center party, the Partido de la Revolución Democrática (Democratic Revolutionary Party, PRD), found fertile soil among the voters of Oaxaca, when the party launched organizing efforts in the early 1990s. For example, seven of Oaxaca's 11 congressional seats belong to the PRD in 2011. In contrast, the conservative Partido Acción Nacional (National Action Party, PAN) has had a much more difficult time displacing the old dominant Partido Revolucionario Institucional (Institutional Revolutionary Party, PRI) that controlled the political system from the 1930s to the 1990s. Since that party's near collapse in 2000, the PRI has regained much of its lost ground in Oaxaca, winning the governorship in 2004, and holding up to three senatorial seats. Indeed, a coalition of

PAN and PRD was necessary to thwart the return of the PRI's dominance in the state in the 2010 gubernatorial elections. The PRD's divisions at the national level had sapped its previous strength locally in Oaxaca, and PAN has long been a relatively weak presence in the state. But the PRI governor opened the door for the coalition's electoral success in 2010 when he mishandled a major outbreak of protests in 2006 by using harsh methods to deal with protesters. Nonetheless, the political future of the state remains unsettled, made more so by the social divisions that characterize Oaxaca, including the level of poverty that disproportionately affects the state's Indian population.

The large presence of indigenous groups in Oaxaca—about half of its residents—has lent a distinctive and rich quality to the cultural life of the state, despite the material impoverishment that characterizes most of the Indian communities of Oaxaca. In its folk crafts, homespun textiles, traditional attire, cuisine, and cultural festivals, the state's Indian heritage remains vibrant and a major tourist attraction, however diluted by the effects of its commercialization. More specifically, various indigenous groups contribute to the region's Indian cultures, notably those of the Zapotecs and Mixtecs. Two major cultural events in particular—in spite of the impact of tourism—signify the indigenous elements of Oaxaca: the Guelaguetza, which is held every year in the stadium of the capital and features thousands of participants, and Día de los Muertos (Day of the Dead, which corresponds to Halloween in the United States), in which throughout the region families pay their respects to their ancestors in rituals of Indian origin.

In a more contemporary vein, Oaxaca is a thriving arts center of international acclaim, founded primarily by legendary painter Rufino Tamayo and later reinforced by Francisco Toledo, among other artists of repute. The state's capital also boasts a number of excellent museums and galleries.

For all its cultural richness and economic assets, Oaxaca faces ambiguous prospects. Three key aspects of the state's economy present challenges. First, the shade-tree coffee industry must deal with increasing competition from within and outside of Mexico, a problem compounded by mounting deforestation and soil erosion. Second, the tourist industry is profoundly dependent on international visitors; during the worldwide recession of 2008–2011, travel to Oaxaca declined, with evident adverse impacts on the local economy. And as noted earlier, Huatulco has failed to meet expectations; the new highway offers at best a modest boost to the tourist traffic to the beach resort. The recession in the United States during 2008–2011 has also led to a decline in remittances, as Oaxacan immigrants have had to face a dwindling job market for their services.

Third, the political situation of the state is equally unclear at this writing. Tensions soared in 2006, leading to a protracted struggle in the streets of the capital between contending groups involving, among others, the political arm of the powerful teachers' union and the PRI governor, who had been narrowly elected in 2004. The teachers' strike ignited other grievances in which rival political groups had a hand.

Violence ensued and severely disrupted tourism to Oaxaca as the protests stretched from June until December, encompassing the Guelaguetza and Día de los Muertos celebrations. The bitterness of that conflict led to a coalition between the PRD and PAN to oust the PRI from the governorship in the 2010 elections. For the PRD the stakes were especially high, given the party's internecine troubles at the national level that threatened its loss of support in Oaxaca. For PAN, the advantages of a coalitional victory against the PRI were several: gaining ground in a state where the party has had a weak presence, increasing its political visibility as an alternative to the PRI and to the divided PRD, and providing a foothold in southern Mexico where the party has fared poorly as it heads toward the 2012 presidential election.

Meanwhile, for the poor of Oaxaca, improvements in their condition have been slow to take effect, as the economic prospects of the nation appear anemic in the near future. For those groups dependent on agriculture, tourism, and remittances, the future remains equally clouded.

Alex M. Saragoza

See also Archaeological Sites; Drug Trade and Trafficking; Immigration and Emigration; Indigenous Peoples; North American Free Trade Agreement; Painting; Politics and Political Parties; Tourism

Further Reading

Esteva, Gustavo. 2008. *Cuando hasta las piedras se levantaron: Oaxaca, Mexico 2006.* Buenos Aires: Editorial Antropofagia.

Holo, Selma. 2004. *Oaxaca at the Crossroads: Managing Memory, Negotiating Change.* Washington, DC: Smithsonian Books.

Oaxaca Official State Website. http://www.oaxaca.gob.mx.

Stephens, Lynn. 2007. *Transborder Lives: Indigenous Oaxacans in Mexico, California and Oregon.* Durham, NC: Duke University Press.

Opera

Opera—*El espectáculo sin límites* ("the show with no boundaries")—is where orchestral music, ballet, scenographic design, choreography, costumes, and most of all, voice live together; without voice, there is no show.

Historical context   During the past century, this art went through one of its most intense dramas. By the end of World War II, Europe had a desolated scenario that had a repercussion on the spirit of its artists. Especially for opera, things were somber. Theaters such as the Scala in Milan, Italy, and Covent Garden of England were destroyed; companies separated and everything was improvised; most essential elements were scarce. Consequently, the opera world circuit changed its geographical orbit, installing itself on the American continent. The Palacio de Bellas Artes (Fine Arts Palace) in Mexico City became a mandatory stop on the corridor between the Teatro Colón (Columbus Theater) of Buenos Aires, Argentina, and New York's Metropolitan in the United States.

The golden era   In 1941 the Ópera de México was founded, giving birth to a new period of Mexican lyric art, with short annual seasons but with guest artists and spectacular productions. However, this company was not able to endure the changes in production costs and singers' fees. It would be with the Ópera Nacional that the golden era of this art form begins in Mexico. Just as with the postwar times, several opera stars saw their European work drastically reduced. Under the direction of Antonio Caraza Campos and the talent of Carlos Díaz Du-Pond, Ópera Nacional recruited renowned international singers, such as the Italian tenors Giuseppe Di Stéfano and Gianni Poggi, the Czechoslovakian Kurt Baum, baritones Enzo Mascherini from Italy and the New Yorker Leonard Warren, the mezzo-soprano Giuletta Simionato, and basses Cesare Siepi from Italy and the Greek Nicola Moscana. There is no doubt that this was the best Mexican operatic time, distinguished by the presence of the diva and ultimate soprano in the world, María Callas. It is worth highlighting that Mexican singers shared the stage with stars who only appeared in Bellas Artes, allowing them to perform at a prestigious level; such are the cases of sopranos Oralia Domínguez, Evangelina Magaña, Verdad Luz Guajardo, Rosa Rimoch, and Irma González. Among the male voices, José Sosa, Roberto Silva, and Humberto Pazos excel. With the presence of these singers, the taste for Italian opera was renewed; since Mexico's independence, Mexican social spirit had identified itself with the Italian nationalistic profile. There were sporadic Mexican works that were presented for the first time during that period. Such was the case of *La mulata de Córdoba,* the only opera of José Pablo Moncayo, written upon request of Carlos Chávez in 1948. In 1957, Luis Mendoza López presented *Eréndira* in Xalapa, Veracruz, with repetitions in Guadalajara and Guanajuato, and in 1959 in the Jorge Negrete theater of Mexico City, with the appearance of tenor Plácido Domingo in a brief section of it.

With the disappearance of the Ópera Nacional in 1952, opera in Mexico took uncertain paths again. In the meantime, the National Institute of Fine Arts Company, headed by Carlos Chávez, was consolidating little by little. They began doing more theater, an initiative supported by Salvador Novo, and presented Mexican artists and productions. Opera did not benefit by this action. The Instituto Nacional de Bellas Artes (National Institute of Fine Arts, INBA) officially began its operatic activities in 1948 with a season of the Fine Arts Opera Company.

The dark opera   With the presidency of Adolfo Ruíz Cortines, cultural activities stopped being a priority. A reverse period came about with the growing unionism positioned by the Partido Revolucionario Institucional (Institutional Revolutionary Party, PRI), whose leaders, to a large degree, were only looking to occupy a public office position or gain personal privileges unconditionally subject to the instructions of the government. Doors to corruption were opened. All of this took place within a time when the development of the national economy put Mexico on the threshold of an era that neglected Mexican operatic activity.

Few Mexican operas were premiered during that time; among them were: *El último sueño* by José F. Vásquez, with Plácido Domingo in 1961; *El romance de doña Balada* by the pianist and composer Alicia Urreta, which premiered in 1974 in the Cultural Center El Ágora; and the premiere of *Encuentro en el ocaso,* by Daniel Catán in 1980, at the Theater of Mexico City, former the Esperanza Iris theater. After the 1980s, it is worth mentioning Eduardo Mata, Mexican orchestra composer and director, who attempted to recover the lyric art's quality and vision in Mexico when directing the National Symphony Orchestra. Although the musicians themselves and the audience wanted him to continue in charge, INBA's bureaucracy prevailed and he moved to Dallas, Texas.

The platinum era   At the beginning of the 1990s, the landscape changed favorably. The transitional work was the premiere of *Aura* in the Palacio de Bellas Artes (Fine Arts Palace) in 1989, by Mexican composer Mario Lavista; this work, based on the novel by Carlos Fuentes, was very successful and it was presented in Monterrey, Nuevo León, during that same year. In 1991, Gerardo KIeinburg was appointed director of the National Opera Company; with his sensitivity and vision, and in conjunction with the National Culture and Arts Council of the INBA, he addressed the genre from a contemporary and multidisciplinary perspective. Without the presence of important international stars, as there were in the 1950s, with the exception of the presentations of tenor Luciano Pavarotti already in his last years, Mexico became the cradle of the most important opera singers worldwide.

It is worth mentioning that during the golden era feminine voices stood out, although nowadays tenors are mainly those with greater projection. Among them, mention can be made of Francisco Araiza at the beginning of the 1980s; then Ramón Vargas, Alfredo Portilla, Rolando Villazón, Fernando de la Mora, Jorge López Yáñez, and Rafael Rojas came to play; among the baritones, mention should be made of Carlos Almaguer, Genaro Sulvarán, Jorge Lagunes, and basses such as Rosendo Flores, all of them extraordinarily gifted. Sopranos Lourdes Ambriz and Encarnación Vázquez and tenor Jesús Suaste are other essential singers of those times. *Florencia en el Amazonas* by Daniel Catán, *El pequeño príncipe* by Federico Ibarra, and *The Visitors,* the only opera by Carlos Chávez, premiered in 1999 and illustrate the prestige of operatic creation. The multidisciplinary nature of them is reflected in the works of artists such as the scenography designer and illuminator Alejandro Luna; directors such as Juan Ibáñez, Benjamín Cann, and Sergio Vela; and in the works for the *Salomé* opera by painter Rafael Cauduro and filmmaker Arturo Ripstein. Major restitutions of operas were made, such as

Electra, by Strauss; *La Favorita,* by Donizetti; *Turandot,* by Puccini; *Nabocco,* by Verdi; *Cosi fan tutte,* by Mozart; *Tristán e Isolda,* by Wagner, with a new perspective for traditional repertoire.

Undoubtedly, there is still a lot to do. Composers such as Ángel Vargas indicated that making opera in Mexico is an aggressive and spiny road. However, we can say that, for now, the conjunction of talents and all of the above-mentioned elements serve as a safe index on the degree of progress of musical and operatic culture in Mexico, and that they give a ray of light whose warmth is shaping a new beginning in the Mexican lyric scenario.

Aarón Polo López

See also Classical Music; Dance; Theater

Further Reading

"Breve Visión de la Ópera en México." *AprendeTV.* http://aprendetv.sep.gob.mx/micro sitios/opera/opera.htm.

México. 2004. México, DF: Consejo Nacional para la Cultura y las Artes/Instituto Nacional de Bellas Artes.

Sosa, Octavio. 2004. *70 años de Opera en el Palacio de Bellas Artes. Investigación documental, hemerográfica, iconográfica, fichas bibliográficas y textos adicionales.* Mexico City: Consejo Nacional para la Cultura y las Artes, INBA.

Tello, Aurelio, coord. 2010. *La música en México: Panorama del siglo XX.* México, DF: Fondo de Cultura Económica, Consejo Nacional para la Cultura y las Artes.

P

Painting

Background   Modern Mexican painting builds on two distinctive currents, one that focuses inwardly toward the national and another that looks outward toward the world. With the end of the Mexican Revolution in 1910, artists engaged in the task of developing a style that incorporated European elements, such as cubism and expressionism, consistent with the nationalist and populist ideology of the revolution. The outcomes of this artistic process were exemplified in images that became iconic, such as the use of pre-Hispanic pictorial language, of heroic peasants and workers associated with the revolution, and of popular culture—that is, an art of the people and for the people. Nowhere was this better seen than in the works of three internationally renowned Mexican muralists: José Clemente Orozco, Diego Rivera, and David Alfaro Siqueiros. Particularly as a result of the widespread recognition given to postrevolutionary mural painting, a style emerged that became identified as uniquely Mexican: the Escuela Mexicana de Pintura (Mexican School of Painting). Nationalistic in character, colorful, laced with allusions to the past, dramatic, and exuberant, the style exercised a dominant hold on the representation of *mexicanidad,* or the essence of being Mexican, for nearly half a century.

Influenced by the German artist Mathias Goeritz in the mid-1950s, a group of young painters challenged the Mexican nationalist school of painting, led by José Luis Cuevas. Inspired by Goeritz's abstract artistry, in 1957 Cuevas published a manifesto against the nationalist style, entitled *La cortina de Nopal* (The Cactus Curtain, an allusion to the Iron Curtain associated with the Berlin Wall and Soviet censorship). In his manifesto, Cuevas opposed the rigidity of the forms that had developed in Mexico—forms that were choking creativity, innovation, and experimentation, and inhibiting an openness to international trends and fresh artistic ideas. The impact of Cuevas's declaration had a shattering impact, marking a rupture in the nationalist tradition that became known as *la ruptura* in Mexican art history. Two styles distinguished this dissident artistic movement; one tended toward a figurative, expressionist approach, while the second had an abstract quality, emphasizing geometrics, graphic and editorial design, as well as gestural and organic painting. The movement headed by Cuevas, the *generación de la ruptura* (generation of the rupture), eventually penetrated The Cactus Curtain and displaced to a large extent the dominance of the nationalist school over Mexico's

Mexican painter Diego Rivera seated in front of his mural-in-progress depicting American "class struggle," 1933. The mural, *Man at the Crossroads,* created in New York's Rockefeller Center, was eventually destroyed because Rivera refused to remove the portrait of Vladimir Lenin he had included in the painting. (Library of Congress)

major artistic institutions and venues for exhibition. Through the 1980s, the two approaches basically coexisted; other types of painting generally failed to elicit recognition, especially from the government's main sources for arts funding.

Contemporary painting in Mexico Diversity of styles characterizes painting in Mexico today, as no one artistic approach exercises the influence of the two previously dominant schools of art, that of the postrevolutionary era or that of the generation of the rupture. Rather, a series of movements in painting have achieved national as well as international prominence. For example, in the 1980s the work of Francisco Toledo, whose style reflected the influence of Rufino Tamayo, commanded international fame. Working largely in his native state of Oaxaca, Tamayo had attracted a group of younger followers who coalesced around Tamayo, and then Toledo, and collectively became known as the Oaxacan school of Mexican painting. Using a figurative approach, the so-called Oaxacan style was often embellished with pre-Hispanic and indigenous motifs, and was marked by elements of mysticism and magic in addition to experimentation on the application of paint to canvas. With Toledo as its leading figure, the Oaxacan group also included well-known artists Sergio Hernández, Rodolfo Nieto, and Maximino Javier.

In 1985, Neomexicanismo (neo-Mexicanism) emerged, based largely on the international appreciation and commercialization of the figure of Frida Kalho and an idyllic vision of postrevolutionary Mexico. The painters associated with this movement, such as Enrique Guzmán, incorporated Mexican motifs while supplementing the nationalist style with forms of exaggeration and the use of representations of the body of the artists themselves. In the works of painters such as Nahum B. Zenil and Julio Galán, self-allusion distinguished their work, painting their own bodies onto Mexican scenographies in an apparent satire of the national style. Neo-Mexican painting reflected a highly personal quality, where the naked body became a form of expression of social criticism in which the main figures are the artists themselves. The artistic relationship of body and gender, pioneered in the 1970s by Mónica Mayer and Maris Bustamente, was renewed, especially in the works of Monica Castillo and Carla Rippey.

Into the 1990s, a pictorial movement acquired prominence known as *neofigurativismo* (neofiguratism) led by artists Santiago Carbonell, Rafael Cauduro, Alejandro Colunga, and Arturo Rivera; the style, however, held different themes, from the hyperrealism of Canduro to the more existentialist and violent topics found in the works by Rivera.

Since the decade of the 1990s, Mexican painting has been displaced in the international arena by works with a more interdisciplinary and conceptual nature. Within Mexico, various styles continue to be practiced as a number of painters—such as Gustavo Aceves, Alberto Castro Leñero, Luis Argudín, Roberto Cortazar, Gabriel Macotela, Magali Lara, and Carmen Parra—have commanded national attention using different approaches.

With its uncertainty and tumult at the beginning of the new century, Mexico has found it difficult to find firm political and economic footing. The political and economic volatility of the first decade or so have contributed, it seems, to the lack of coherence in the arts in Mexico. Diversity remains the distinguishing characteristic of the present artistic scene. In this context, with his depictions of urban poverty and inequality, Daniel Lezama has earned particularly high praise from critics, though his paintings are marked by graphic representations of violence, nudity, and misery. As rising talents on the Mexican art scene, Lezama has been joined by Germán Venegas, Javier Manrique, Estrella Carmona, Víctor Rodríguez, Ray Smith, Marianela de la Hoz, Rocío Caballero, Fernando Guevara, Claudia Gallegos, Javier Guadarrama, Adriana Raggi, Patricia Soriano, Juanita Pérez, Roberto Parodi, Pablo Rulfo, Ignacio Salazar, and Rocío Maldonado. As a whole, these painters do not necessarily represent a specific style nor do they share consistent thematic concerns; rather, they suggest the stylistic fragmentation of painting in Mexico as the country grapples with its societal challenges.

Luis Vargas Santiago

See also Art and the Private Sector; Art Criticism; Art Education; Art Exhibitions; Art Market; Arts, Alternative Venues for; Culture and the Government; Nationalism and National Identity; Oaxaca; Politics and Political Parties

Further Reading

DuPont, Diana C. 2007. *Tamayo: A Modern Icon Reinterpreted.* Santa Barbara, CA: Santa Barbara Museum of Art in association with Editorial Turner de Mexico.

Eckmann, Teresa, curator. 2010. *Neo-Mexicanism: A New Figuration: Mexican Art of the 1980s: Rocío Maldonado: Nature Human Nature: Javier de la Garza: Climate Change.* Exhibition of Latin American Art. http://www.latinamericanart.com/en/art-events/neo-mexicanism-a-new-figuration-mexican-art-of-the-1980s.html. San Antonio: University of Texas at San Antonio.

Gallo, Rubén. 2004. *New Tendencies in Mexican Art: The 1990s.* London: Palgrave Macmillan.

Goldman, Shifra M. 1991. *Women in Mexican Art.* Catalog. Los Angeles, CA: Iturralde Gallery, 1991.

Goldman, Shifra M. 1995. *Contemporary Mexican Painting in a Time of Change.* Rev. ed. Albuquerque: University of New Mexico Press.

Rochfort, Desmond. 1998. *The Mexican Muralists: Orozco, Rivera, Siqueiros.* San Francisco: Chronicle Books.

Sullivan, Edward J., curator. 1990. *Aspects of Contemporary Mexican Painting.* Exhibition organized by the Americas Society. New York: Americas Society.

Partido Acción Nacional

Founded in 1939 by Manuel Gómez Morín, the Partido Acción Nacional (National Action Party, PAN) is generally considered a right-of-center party and was the first genuine opposition party to develop in Mexico. Traditionally, the party advocated free enterprise, supported socially conservative values, and promoted the principles of minimal government intervention in the economy. PAN, which emerged as a conservative reaction against the nationalizations and land confiscations of President Lázaro Cárdenas (1934–1940), began as an organized opposition to the party in power (then known as the PNR, the predecessor to what became the PRI). Over time, especially since the 1960s, the party has moved toward the center of the political spectrum and away from the rightist stance of its origins. Since the mid-1980s, PAN's economic programs have been very similar to those of the PRI. Thus, in an effort to distance itself from the hegemonic party in power, in the 1990s PAN stressed the need for democratization and eradication of government corruption and pushed for more liberal electoral reforms.

Traditionally, PAN's support came from the Catholic Church, the business sector, and the wealthiest and most urbanized regions of the north and center of the country, particularly in Mexico City, Jalisco, Nuevo León, and Puebla y Sonora. Since the 1980s, PAN had significant electoral victories in the northern part of the country. During the Salinas administration, PAN won the governorships and congressional majorities in Baja California Norte and Chihuahua.

PAN presented a candidate in every presidential election since 1946 with the exception of 1976, consolidating itself as the main opposition political force in the country. After a historic election in 2000, the PAN candidate won the presidency of Mexico, defeating the party that had held the office since 1929. Six years later PAN repeated its victory and once again claimed the country's highest public office. The party's success at the national level has been paralleled by its increasing power in the Mexican Congress, where its representatives hold pluralities in both the Chamber of Deputies and the Senate as of the 2006 elections (206 of the 500 seats in the lower house and 52 of the 128 senatorial positions). Nonetheless, the party has yet to achieve an absolute majority, forcing PAN to negotiate with its rivals for the passage of legislation and related governmental tasks (most often with the PRI); this has also tended to be the case at state and local levels of governance. PAN benefited from the decline and internecine problems of the once-dominant PRI, particularly after the 1970s. Once in charge of the presidency, however, PAN has learned that governing the country can be an enormous challenge with uncertain political consequences for the long-term prospects of the party.

Origins of PAN: Liberalism and Christianity   Manuel Gómez Morín, a former rector of the Universidad Nacional Autónoma de México (National Autonomous University of Mexico, UNAM), is generally credited as the founder of the party. Trained as a lawyer, Gómez Morín was involved in the organization and operations of the Mexican central bank system following the Mexican Revolution. An advocate of free enterprise and Christian values, he and other like-minded intellectuals and businessmen represented the original core of PAN. The leadership of the party, however, refused to become formally a Christian Democratic political organization. Much of the impetus for the formation of the party was a reaction to government policies in the 1930s, especially the anticlerical stance and prolabor actions of then-president Lázaro Cárdenas (1934–1940). The initial base of support for PAN was among the urban middle classes and businessmen, particularly in the northern tier of the country. From 1939 until 1949, Gómez Morín headed PAN, but in these initial years of the party, its candidates made little headway against the dominant PNR and later the PRM (forerunners to the PRI).

Electoral evolution during PRI's hegemony   Immediately following its foundation, PAN faced the question of the 1940 presidential elections. Without an official endorsement, much of the new party's supporters apparently gave their votes to the unsuccessful oppositional candidacy of Juan Andrew Almazán. PAN's first electoral victory took place in 1946, when it won a congressional seat, and that minor success would be followed a year later with the winning of a mayoral race in the state of Michoacán. Those initial electoral victories led to other successes, but they were few, rather unimportant, and mainly in the central and northern parts of the country. In 1952 the party fielded its first presidential candidate, Efraín González Luna, with abysmal results. Finally, a hopeful signal for the future emerged from the 1970 presidential contest—following the political debacle of 1968—when the PAN candidate received nearly 13 percent of the vote despite a rigged electoral process.

Nonetheless, PAN began to gain a foothold in local and state politics, especially in the country's northern states, where the party has traditionally possessed its greatest strength. In spite of the PRI's blatant use of electoral fraud, PAN activists nonetheless disputed contests, notably over the governorship of Baja California Norte in 1957; army troops had to be called in to quell the protests by angry voters who were convinced that the PAN candidate had actually won the race. The events in Baja California Norte reflected the gradual building of support by PAN in response to growing dissatisfaction toward the ruling party, especially among businessmen and the urban middle class. Key to PAN's growth was the participation of women in the party's organizational structure. Not surprisingly, it was the first party to nominate a woman as a gubernatorial candidate in 1962 (in Aguascalientes); two years later, a PAN female member was elected to a congressional seat in the state of Chihuahua. Other women of PAN would stand for office in the years subsequent to those early victories.

By the 1960s, however, the party faced questions over its future direction. For example, one wing of the party argued for a more secular ideology that also took into account the obvious social and economic disparities in the country. Another faction of the party was interested in joining the Christian Democratic movement that combined a conservative social and cultural outlook with a concern for economic policies aimed at lessening poverty and class inequalities. This split and its consequent debates within the party led to an open breach over the nomination for the presidential campaign of 1976. The resultant conflict led to PAN's failure to offer a candidate for the presidential contest of that year. Nevertheless, the party's leadership overcame its internal differences by the time of the 1982 presidential election and fielded a candidate. More importantly, after the 1976 elections, the PRI-dominated Congress passed a modest electoral reform that permitted an expansion of congressional seats based on proportional representation for oppositional parties. As a consequence, PAN increased its political voice at the federal level.

PAN and the democratic transition   In the decisive 1988 presidential election, PAN took advantage of the political fallout from the highly disputed victory of Carlos Salinas de Gortari of the PRI. On several issues, PAN and the PRI converged toward the support of market-oriented economic reforms, such as the privatization of the Mexican economy. On the other hand, PAN benefited from the electoral reforms that followed the fraud-tainted outcome of the 1988 election. Equally important, PAN was emboldened by the magnitude of opposition to the PRI. Led by PAN's charismatic leader Manuel Clouthier, the center-right party energized voters seeking an alternative to the PRI yet unwilling to cast their ballots for the leftist co-alition that emerged from the 1988 presidential contest, the PRD. Despite a major setback in 1989 when Clouthier died in a mysterious auto accident, PAN made significant political headway, particularly in local electoral contests. In the same year of Clouthier's death, PAN scored an important victory of significant symbolic value: the governorship of a Mexican state, the first time that the PRI had tasted defeat in a gubernatorial election since its founding in 1929.

The creation of an independent Instituto Federal Electoral (Federal Electoral Institute, IFE) in 1990 boosted the political prospects of PAN as well as the electoral rules under the new Código Federal de Instituciones y Procedimientos Electorales (Federal Code for Electoral Procedures and Institutions, COFIPE). These reforms made the electoral process much more transparent and honest. Although PAN's candidate, Diego Fernández de Ceballos, lost again in the 1994 presidential contest, the political tide was turning away from the old dominant party. In the wake of those electoral changes of the early 1990s, the gains for PAN multiplied, as the party won a series of local elections, including governorships in 1991 (Guanajuato), 1992 (Chihuahua), and 1995 (Jalisco).

The surge in support for PAN led to a crucial showing in the 1997 midterm elections. In that pivotal election, PAN won 121 seats in the Chamber of Deputies. As a result, the PRI lost its absolute congressional majority for the first time in over six decades. Consistent with PAN's success in congressional races, the party also won two governorships (Querétaro and Nuevo León) in 1997; a year later, PAN claimed an additional gubernatorial victory in Aguascalientes and another in 1999 in the state of Nayarit. As the dominant party unraveled, PAN drew a large portion of disaffected voters, while the left-of-center coalition struggled to galvanize its constituency.

For the 2000 presidential election, PAN presented an attractive, unconventional candidate, Vicente Fox. Tall, folksy, and unpretentious, the ex-business executive smashed the 71-year hold of the PRI over the presidency. Fox led PAN to a decisive victory, capturing almost 46 percent of the vote to that of the losing PRI candidate of 36 percent; the left-of-center PRD contestant was a distant third at 17 percent of ballots cast. Fox's success also meant that PAN achieved a plurality in the Chamber of Deputies, winning 221 seats to the PRI's 211 of the 500 positions available. Only in the Senate did the former dominant party maintain its plurality, holding 60 seats to PAN's 51. Clearly PAN had become the main alternative for voters tired of the corruption and policy failures associated with the PRI's seven decades of political dominance of the country.

The rise and eventual triumph of Vicente Fox, however, generated tensions within the party that revealed simmering internal differences. The old guard of PAN, closely tied to the conservative origins of the party, resented somewhat the upstart businessman who had only recently joined the party (1988), received the financial support of wealthy corporate executives (the so-called Amigos de Fox, similar to a PAC in U.S. terms), and had a relatively skimpy electoral record (a one-term congressman, 1988–1991, and a one-term governor, 1995–2000). Worse for several loyalists of PAN, Fox reached outside the established leadership circle of the party for political consultation and support, alienating in the process key figures of his own party (among those was Diego Fernández de Cevallos, the PAN presidential candidate of 1994 and a senator of high standing within the party). Once in office, the split widened between Fox and congressional leaders of his own party, contributing to an impasse between the two branches of government over the president's legislative initiatives. As a result, PAN's Vicente Fox frequently appeared ineffective, disappointing the expectations of his party's supporters.

PAN as government   In order to advance his policy agenda, Vicente Fox found it difficult to negotiate the diverse political and ideological currents in Congress without a majority. Alliances with congressional leaders, including those from PAN, proved to be elusive, fragile, and often short-lived. As a consequence, Fox's legislative initiatives often went nowhere, including his ill-fated effort for fiscal reform. Fox entered office under enormous public optimism and hope, given the historic turn in the political history of the country away from the old dominant party. But the euphoria of his historic victory soon dissipated. The new president failed to meet anticipated results with negative consequences for the standing of his party. Worse, the hoped-for prosperity under PAN leadership failed to materialize, as the Mexican economy slowed and stalled. To be fair, the dependence of the Mexican economy on that of the United States contributed to the problems facing Fox. The post-9/11 years put Mexico on the back burner for the U.S. policy makers, in sharp contrast to the beginning of the Fox administration. U.S. president George W. Bush (2000–2008) had earlier promised a close relationship with Mexico, and the prospects for relations between the two countries appeared bright—but much of that situation changed with 9/11. The gradual downward slide of the U.S. economy inevitably spelled trouble for Mexico and, as it turned out, added to the problems confronting Vicente Fox and his party. Just a few years into the first PAN presidency, the approval ratings for Vicente Fox plummeted, as the high expectations of basic political change crumbled among the Mexican electorate.

Disappointed by the first three years of a PAN-led government, Mexican voters expressed their disappointment in the 2003 midterm elections. The outcomes represented a major setback for the party of Vicente Fox. While the opposing two parties made gains in their congressional representation, PAN lost seats, unable to build on its victory of the 2000 elections. PAN's delegation in the Chamber of Deputies, for instance, went from 221 seats down to 149. To make matters worse, the PRI made a remarkable recovery, regaining its plurality by winning 224 seats out of 500, and the left-leaning PRD added to its presence in the lower house, boosting its membership from 68 to 97 seats. Much of the blame for the poor showing of PAN was pinned on Vicente Fox. (The election was marked by a high degree of voter abstention.) PAN looked toward the 2006 elections with understandable trepidation.

In a bitterly contested campaign, PAN's Felipe Calderón won the presidential race of 2006 by an extremely thin margin over the leftist PRD candidate; the PRI's standard-bearer ran a distant third that led to his party's dismal performance in federal contests. PAN regained its plurality in Congress by adding over 50 seats for a delegation of 206 members, as opposed to the 127 and 106 seats, respectively, for the party's two major rivals in the Chamber of Deputies. In the 128-member Senate, PAN maintained its position of 52 positions (the PRI's Senate delegation sank to 35 members from its previous 60 seats).

Felipe Calderón had been a longtime member of the party and seemed to enjoy the staunch support of party regulars; he was able to attract a sufficient number of young urban voters, much of the middle class, and drew rural voters who in the past tended to cast their ballots for the PRI in particular. Still, the 2006 elections continued to show that the strength of PAN remained in the northern tier of states and in the country's leading urban metropolitan areas. The south of Mexico, with its more rural, agrarian-based population, offered much less support for PAN. More importantly, at the subnational level—that is, in terms of party representation in state legislatures and in gubernatorial posts—PAN found it much more challenging to dislodge the two competing parties.

To what extent PAN will be able to extend its political reach throughout the country looms as a crucial question for the party. Much will depend on the perceived success of President Felipe Calderón, as well as the performance of local and state leaders of PAN's opposition. Clearly, the terrible campaign by the PRI's presidential candidate dragged down his party's showing in the 2006 election, which benefited PAN among many voters. Nonetheless, the PRI's ability to recover and regain support in municipal and state electoral contests since 2000 suggests that the ex-dominant party remains a formidable adversary in the future for PAN.

In terms of the left-leaning PRD, PAN faces a party at a crossroads in the wake of its losing the presidency by such a thin margin. The postelection antics by the leftist party candidate generated serious splits within his own party, which does not augur well for the left-leaning party at the national level. Yet, again, at the local level of government, the party on the Left has done well, increasing its representation in the Chamber of Deputies, for example, in the electoral rounds of 2000, 2003, and 2006. Thus, for the near future PAN will likely face an invigorated PRI and a resolute though brittle PRD. In its contest with its two major rivals, a key challenge for PAN will be its ability to continue to attract and to keep younger urban voters in its ranks and to build support in the southern region of the country.

Juan Manuel Galarza and José Ignacio Lanzagorta

See also Calderón Hinojosa, Felipe; Election, Presidential, 2000; Election, Presidential, 2006; Electoral Institutions; Fox Quesada, Vicente; Partido de la Revolución Democrática; Partido Revolucionario Institucional; Politics and Political Parties

Further Reading

Magaloni, Beatriz, and Alejandro Moreno. 2000. "Catching All Souls, Religion and Ideology in the PAN." *Working Papers in Political Science.* México, DF: Instituto Tecnológico Autónomo de México (ITAM).

Middlebrook, Kevin, ed. 2001. *Party Politics and the Struggle for Democratization in Mexico.* La Jolla, CA: Center for U.S.-Mexican Studies.

Serrano, Mónica, and Neil Harvey, eds. 1994. *Party Politics in an "Uncommon Democracy" Political Parties and Elections in Mexico.* London: Institute of Latin American Studies.

Partido de la Revolución Democrática

Formed in the immediate aftermath of the 1988 election, the Partido de la Revolución Democrática (Democratic Revolution Party, PRD) is considered the major leftist party in Mexico. After the 2006 elections, where the PRD presidential candidate lost by narrow margins, the left-leaning party won 127 seats in the Chamber of Deputies, making it the second-most important delegation; its congressional victories marked the third straight electoral round where the representation of the PRD had increased in the lower house. Moreover, PRD members accounted for 31 of the 128 contested seats in the Mexican Senate (previously, the party had only 17 members in the upper house). In addition, after the 2006 electoral contests, PRD governors headed five states, including the Federal District. The party's extremely strong showing in the 2006 elections, however, was followed by internal strife involving two factions. One group was associated with Andrés Manuel López Obrador, the charismatic candidate of the party for the 2006 presidential race. Charging electoral fraud, the PRD candidate and former mayor of Mexico City refused to recognize the outcome of the election. The actions of his supporters after the election (such as the blocking of major thoroughfares in traffic-congested Mexico City), served to erode the popularity of López Obrador, and by extension, that of the PRD. Calling for the end of postelection protests, critics within the party called for a responsible left and disavowed the unwillingness of López Obrador and his loyalists to accept the results of the election. An open split ensued, as the party faces an uncertain future at the national level. Nonetheless, at local levels of government, the party has shown its capacity to draw voters to a progressive political agenda, such as support for social programs, reconsideration of neoliberal policies, government intervention in the economy, and related positions. The PRD has a relatively brief and complicated history, which accounts in several ways for its contemporary situation.

The Left before the PRD Before the PRD, the political left in Mexico was splintered into various factions, most visibly the Communist Party, but other leftist groups have existed in the country since the Mexican Revolution. In ideological terms, the dominant party, the Partido Revolucionario Institucional (Institutional Revolutionary Party, PRI), promoted welfare state ideas, such as a strong government presence in the economy, public enterprises, social welfare programs, economic protectionist policies, and government-controlled public education. These ideas were especially important during the presidency of Lázaro Cárdenas (1934–1940), and his administration accommodated leftist measures, such as land distribution schemes for the peasantry and prounion policies. The ideological splits involving communists, Trotskyites, anarchists, liberal democrats, socialists, and other leftist-leaning organizations made for a weak, divided movement that failed to develop a large, disciplined public support. World War II and the subsequent Cold War political environment served to undermine the emergence of a well-organized leftist movement. The dominant party, the PRI, also worked to suppress a vibrant left movement, although various socialist and radical groupings existed and struggled to survive, inspired by the Cuban Revolution of 1959 and anticolonial struggles in Africa, and elsewhere. These small leftist organizations were animated by the discontent of the 1960s toward the dominant regime and joined student-based groups with leftist leanings. In this regard, the events leading to the pivotal student protests of 1968 and their aftermath radicalized many young people in particular. Workers dissatisfied with the government's retreat from the reformist, prolabor stance of the 1930s also contributed to an increasing critique of the dominant party. Furthermore, the apparent collusion between the PRI and the private sector added to the growth of antigovernment sentiment that led to the proliferation of anticapitalist and reformist political currents in the 1970s.

The 1976 presidential elections produced the first important coalition of leftist organizations. Economic problems plagued the previous administration, and the resurgence of discontent toward the PRI fueled an attempt to unite the Left in Mexico. Spearheaded by the Mexican Communist Party, various leftist groups joined in supporting the candidacy of labor activist Valentín Campa for the presidency. PRI-controlled electoral officials declared Campa's presidential bid illegal, and the votes cast for him were discarded; allegedly Campa received about a million votes. The PRI candidate won handily, but the tainted process brought such criticism and public outcry that the incoming administration of José López Portillo (1976–1982) was forced to make various political concessions, including the legal recognition of the Mexican Communist Party. Taking advantage of its ability to operate openly, and building on the impetus of the Campa campaign, the Mexican Communist Party incorporated left-leaning groups into its organization. As a result, the party was reconfigured and became the Partido Socialista Unificado de México (Mexican Socialist Unified Party, PSUM). Although the new leftist party failed to attract much public support for its presidential candidate in the 1982 election, the formation of the PSUM signified an important step for the Mexican Left, as it brought together various like-minded factions under one organization (later it would be renamed the Mexican Socialist Party, or PMS).

The 1988 election and PRD's foundation   The policies of PRI president Miguel de la Madrid (1982–1988) generated a split within the dominant party, as the economic situation of Mexico deteriorated during his administration. Evident signs of public dissatisfaction toward the government flared and spread. As a result, criticism of de la Madrid's neoliberal policies proliferated within the president's own party. As the 1988 presidential nomination process neared, dissidents within the PRI coalesced around a group of prominent members that included Cuauhtémoc Cárdenas (son of ex-president Lázaro Cárdenas), Porfirio Muñoz Ledo (ex-president of the PRI), Ifigenia Martínez, and Andrés Manuel López Obrador. When Cárdenas failed to win the presidential nomination of the PRI, he left the party to run an independent campaign for the presidency as the candidate of the hastily organized Frente Democrático Nacional (National Democratic Front, FDN). This split within the PRI was a protest over the party's choice of Salinas, a free market reformer, as the PRI's presidential nominee and the economic reforms implemented since the mid-1980s. Thus, since its beginnings, the FDN (later the PRD) opposed the neoliberal changes that promoted trade and foreign investment to boost the Mexican economy introduced by the PRI during de la Madrid's administration and promoted economic nationalism and social welfare programs.

As the son of Mexico's most popular president, Cárdenas had name recognition and a reformist platform that attracted voters disaffected by the dominant party and its market-oriented policies. Cárdenas clearly represented a potent alternative to both of the major parties, the PRI and PAN. Veterans of the 1968 student movement, young people coming of political age during hard economic times, and older men and women with fond memories of Lázaro Cárdenas were among those who gravitated toward the National Democratic Front and its candidate. For the PMS, the Cárdenas campaign raised a major question. The Socialist Party initially proposed its own candidate, the charismatic Heberto Castillo, but it quickly became obvious that Cárdenas was a much more popular figure and had the best chance of defeating the PRI candidate. Castillo subsequently withdrew his candidacy and threw his support to Cárdenas.

The 1988 presidential election became the most controversial in 20th-century Mexican history. As the campaign neared its conclusion, polls indicated a very close two-man race between Cárdenas and his PRI adversary; the PAN candidate lagged in third place. On the day of the election, the process for the counting of ballots failed to operate properly, according to PRI-appointed electoral officials. When the results were finally announced, the PRI candidate, Carlos Salinas de Gortari, was declared the winner. Cárdenas's supporters, as well as those of the PAN candidate, charged widespread electoral fraud, but the opposition eventually conceded and accepted Salinas's disputed victory.

In the aftermath of the 1988 campaign, however, the Left in Mexico faced the awkward relationship between the PMS and the organization put together by Cárdenas for the presidential race. The FDN leadership opted to admit PRI dissidents into its ranks and to use the legal charter of the party to reconfigure itself as the Party of the Democratic Revolution, or PRD. In effect, former PRI members, most notably Cuauhtémoc Cárdenas, had become part of the official political left. To the dismay of some longtime leftists, Cárdenas quickly assumed leadership of the newly organized party. Moreover, Cárdenas's cabal of ex-PRI dissidents, such as Muñoz Ledo, immediately took a highly visible role in the PRD, sparking resentment among many loyalists of the traditional left. Although the PRD held a good part of the former communist and socialist groups' ranks, the new leftist party was controlled and led by former PRI members. In other words, the newly formed PRD was composed of a fragile alliance of factions united largely by their common opposition to the dominant party rather than a shared ideology. These factions, or tribes as they were subsequently called, created an enduring and significant tension within the left-of-center party. Equally important, the new party confronted the daunting task of building a national party structure. The outcome of the 1988 campaign indicated less a vote for a leftist ideology and more a vote against the PRI.

Early history   Two stories comprise the early history of the PRD; one involves national politics and efforts to win the presidency, while the other is about the construction of the party at the local level in order to run candidates for municipal, state, and congressional offices. The PRD's quest to win the presidency and its consequences has drawn the most attention. From 1988 through 2000, Cuauhtémoc Cárdenas was the titular head of the PRD at the national level, as he ran as its presidential candidate in 1994 and again in 2000. Cárdenas's near victory in the 1988 presidential contest initially gave him enormous credibility within the PRD and command of the party. In 1994, as Mexico reeled from political and economic troubles, the PRD initially had high hopes to claim a presidential victory and to deal a mortal blow to the long dominance of the PRI. Nonetheless, in a basically honest election, Cárdenas lost by a surprisingly large margin. He placed third in the race, with just 17 percent of the total ballots, while the PRI candidate received about 48 percent of the vote. Three years later, Cárdenas made a political comeback by winning the mayoral contest of the country's most populous metropolis, Mexico City. The crucial victory allowed Cárdenas to regain political viability within the party, though he stepped down as the formal head of the PRD. More importantly, Mexico City became a bastion of support for the PRD, giving Cárdenas decisive political leverage as the 2000 presidential race loomed on the horizon.

The presidential hopes of Cárdenas and the PRD were buoyed by the erosion of support for the PRI in the midterm elections of 1997, as the dominant party lost its absolute majority in Congress. Forced to negotiate with smaller parties to advance its legislative agenda, the PRI tended to work with PAN and to resist cooperation with PRD legislators. Still, the presidency seemed a feasible goal for the PRD, given the application of electoral reforms for the next contest for the country's highest office. Moreover, a PRD candidate won the race for the governorship of the state of Zacatecas in 1998, and that victory was followed by two more gubernatorial victories in 1999 in Tlaxcala and Baja California Sur, all of which added to the presidential aspirations of the left-leaning party.

The 2000 presidential election, however, turned out to be disastrous for the PRD. Cárdenas once again carried the banner for his party, but once more he was a dispiriting third-place finisher. Moreover, the representation of the party in Congress decreased, as Cárdenas's poor showing dragged down the PRD in general. Worse for the former PRI governor, his former supporter, Porfirio Muñoz Ledo—after his own abortive presidential bid—crossed over to endorse the winning PAN candidate. The Cárdenas-led period of the PRD had clearly ended, and the party had to look elsewhere for a national leader.

After the 2000 election   Andrés Manuel López Obrador became the most prominent PRD politician in the wake of the 2000 elections, when he won the Mexico City mayoral race of that year. As formal head of the PRD in the previous three years, he had managed to consolidate sufficient support among the different factions of the party, despite his earlier association with the PRI and Cárdenas. As mayor, López Obrador (or AMLO, as he was referred to in the press) pushed a strong reformist agenda that focused on the poor and working classes of Mexico City, while he consistently used his office to criticize the neoliberal policies of President Vicente Fox of PAN. (Federal government officials and conservative pundits on more than one occasion also attempted to discredit the political stature of the leftist mayor.) The popularity of AMLO soared as well as his national political visibility, as the leftist mayor adroitly used the media to promote his agenda and to demean that of PAN's presidency. Meanwhile, the various contending currents within his own party wrestled for leadership of the party. Two rival camps emerged within the PRD: one that supported a moderate position allowing for cooperation and negotiation with the opposition, and another that promoted an activist, populist, and staunchly antineoliberal stance. In this backdrop, López Obrador, fueled by his popularity in Mexico City, won the presidential nomination of the PRD for the 2006 election.

According to most polls, AMLO was in the lead for nearly the entire campaign. But a last-minute push by the PAN candidate (aided by a massive wave of negative television spots against López Obrador) apparently induced sufficient numbers of independent voters to cast their ballots for PAN's Felipe Calderón. The unsuccessfull race run by the PRI candidate also worked in Calderón's favor. The leftist candidate and his supporters were stunned by their defeat and immediately charged electoral fraud as the reason for their loss; questioning the integrity of the electoral commission, the PRD took the matter to the Federal Electoral Court. After a review of the PRD's charges, the Electoral Court confirmed the victory of the PAN candidate. Incensed supporters of AMLO protested for weeks, while López Obrador staged rallies as the real and legitimate president of the country, but to no avail. In fact, public sympathy for the party waned as a result of the disruptive demonstrations of López Obrador's more radical supporters in Mexico City.

The deflating presidential loss of AMLO widened the rifts within his own party, as the moderate tribe of the PRD moved to distance itself from their erstwhile leader. On the other hand, López Obrador's loyalists worked to maintain their control of the party and its populist agenda. The rivalry quickly became a bitter contest, fanning the resentments of past factional competitions over the selection of a national leader. Some pundits even predicted a breakup of the leftist party. In late 2008, after months of highly public wrangling and internal disputes in the election of a new PRD president, the Electoral Court ruled that the moderate wing of the party had won the contest. The overt split cast an ominous shadow over the PRD and its prospects for the 2009 midterm elections, though the losing side pledged to stay within the party.

At the subnational level, the PRD suggested a different story than the political drama that unfolded in Mexico City. The results of the 2006 election showed a vibrant, robust party that had penetrated much of the country. AMLO's candidacy attracted double the percentage of total voters (35 percent) than had supported Cárdenas's run six years earlier (17 percent). Of major significance, the PRD made substantial gains in its representation both in the Chamber of Deputies and in the Senate with the 2006 election; results also showed that the party had drawn major support from voters in traditionally PRI strongholds, such as southern Mexico. In addition, PRD candidates had made impressive gains in municipal offices, gubernatorial races, and state legislatures; the PRD was no longer a political reflection of one or two states and a handful of major cities. Clearly, the erosion of support for the PRI in the 2006 presidential election had benefited its opponents, including the PRD.

Nevertheless, the PRD faces the challenge of a resurgent PRI, whose long period of dominance has facilitated its ability to maintain a party structure throughout the country. In addition, the PRD must contend with a PAN that has large resources, such as the support of much of the private sector. While its two rivals have a much longer history of development, the PRD is still constructing a national party apparatus. On the other hand, the PRD's main opposition carry heavy political liabilities. The PRI is saddled with its entrenched association with corruption and electoral chicanery, while PAN is frequently perceived as the party of the wealthy people of Mexico in a country where much of the population is poor. And the electoral reforms after 2006 may also serve the interests of the leftist party, such as equitable access to television for political spots.

The PRD has maintained its position as the third political force in Mexico. Even though the PRD has maintained control over Mexico City since 1997, the party only has electoral presence in central and southern Mexico; in northern Mexico its voting averages are very low. The results of the latest elections indicate the incapacity of the leftist party to increase its presence in subnational electoral contests, that is, in races for municipal office, gubernatorial posts, and congressional seats. The factional splits within the party and the video scandals (in which notable party members were taped receiving cash funds) have had negative effects, reflected in the 2009 midterm election results. In the 2006 legislative elections, the PRD won 127 seats (out of 500) in the Chamber of Deputies and 31 seats in the Senate. After the 2009 election, the PRD decreased its presence in the Chamber of Deputies almost by half, obtaining only 72 seats. The PRD will likely find it difficult to thrive and to expand its political reach in the absence of a consensual set of goals and strategies and an ideological common ground within the party.

Juan Manuel Galarza and José Ignacio Lanzagorta

See also Electoral Institutions; Partido Revolucionario Institucional; Politics and Political Parties

Further Reading

Bruhn, Kathleen. 1997. "The Seven Month Itch? Neoliberal Politics, Popular Movements, and the Left in Mexico." In *The New Politics of Inequality in Latin America: Rethinking Participation and Representation,* edited by Douglas A. Chalmers, Carlos M. Vilas, Katherine Hite, Scott B. Martin, Kerianne Piester, and Monique Segarra. New York: Oxford University Press.

Bruhn, Kathleen. 1997. *Taking on Goliath: The Emergence of a New Left Party and the Struggle for Democracy in Mexico.* University Park: Pennsylvania State University Press.

Partido del Trabajo

Mexico's Partido del Trabajo (Labor), or PT as it is generally referred to, is a relatively new and small left-wing political party. For the 2006–2009 congressional cycle, the PT commanded 14 seats (out of 500). Founded in 1990 by Alberto Anaya, the party is associated with a radical communist ideology, though it has moved recently toward a more moderate democratic socialist position.

Anaya, a Marxist economist from the Universidad Nacional Autónoma de México (National Autonomous University of Mexico, UNAM), played a leading role in the 1980's radical social movement known as Tierra y Libertad (land and liberty); he was jailed for six years for his alleged subversive activities. Two years after his release in 1988, he founded the PT. Political rumors have suggested that his party was in fact created clandestinely by the PRI to siphon off support from the main leftist-oriented party, the PRD, that emerged from the 1988 presidential election.

The PT participated in the 1991 congressional elections, but it failed to receive the 2 percent of the national vote necessary to maintain its legal charter as a political party. In order to survive as a distinct political organization, the PT formed a coalition with the much larger PRD in the 1994 presidential electoral contest. As a result, the PT earned more than 4 percent of the national vote and achieved 10 seats in the Chamber of Deputies. In an alliance again with the PRD in the 2000 elections, the Labor Party won one Senate seat and seven seats in the Chamber of Deputies. For the 2003 midterm elections, the PT ran as an independent party and its slate of candidates for Congress received 2.4 percent of the national vote, which made for six seats in the 500-member Chamber of Deputies. In the context of the huge popularity for the PRD presidential candidate in the 2006 presidential contest, the PT became an ally of the much larger reformist party and received 12 seats in the Chamber of Deputies and three positions in the Mexican Senate of 128 members.

However, in races for local offices, the PT has shown a willingness to form coalitions with the ex-dominant party, the PRI. By 2008, the Mexican Labor Party held 38 state legislative seats.

Nonetheless, the PT has sustained its leftist tilt at the national level. After the highly disputed 2006 presidential election, the PT participated in a political coalition known as the Frente Amplio Progresista (Broad Progressive Front, FAP), which opposed the legislative agenda of new president Felipe Calderón. Much of the FAP's attention has focused on its opposition toward any effort to privatize the government-controlled oil industry, PEMEX. The government's ownership of the major source of foreign earnings has been at the center of heated discussions over neoliberal policies in Mexico. Conservatives lament the inefficiency of the oil industry and argue for selling the public enterprise in order to boost production, to introduce new technology, and to lessen government costs. Neoliberal critics charge that PEMEX must remain the property of the Mexican people. The debate over the privatization of PEMEX has been used by FAP as a means of sustaining the political visibility of the issues raised by the PRD candidate for the presidency of 2006, Andrés López Obrador. The leftist candidate has vehemently denounced any discussion that smacks of the privatization of PEMEX.

The future prospects of the PT will likely depend on the outcome of the internal differences within the much larger party on the Left, the PRD. The PT has a core following that, when combined with other minor leftist groups, may enable the Mexican Labor Party to survive as a distinct political organization. In 2007, the Mexican Congress passed new electoral rules that may endanger the ability of small political parties to survive. For example, access to the media for political parties will be distributed in proportion to the votes cast for each party. Thus, small parties will receive much less air time for campaigns, as opposed to the three major parties; this provision will make it more difficult for small parties to expand their membership. Regardless, it is unlikely that the PT will attain more than a minor role in Mexican politics.

Juan Manuel Galarza and José Ignacio Lanzagorta

See also Partido de la Revolución Democrática; Politics and Political Parties

Further Reading

Partido del Trabajo. www.partidodeltrabajo.org.mx.

Partido Revolucionario Institucional

The Partido Revolucionario Institucional (Institutional Revolutionary Party, PRI) was founded in 1929; at that time the predecessor of the present-day PRI was named the Partido Nacional Revolucionario (National Revolutionary Party, PNR). Until the 2000 election, the PRI had held the presidency of Mexico, allowing for a stable transition of power from one administration to the next for 71 years. In the context of Latin American politics, Mexico was virtually unique in its political stability, unlike many other countries of the region that suffered through military coups and periods of intensive political violence through much of the 20th century. However, the PRI fostered an authoritarian regime from the presidency down to the municipal level. Fraud and political corruption marked the electoral process and permitted the PRI to dominate the political life of the country. Thus, government at all levels was essentially an extension of the party.

Government revenues, therefore, were often used in effect for political purposes. With key enterprises under government authority, such as the oil industry and utilities, the party used revenues from those monopolies to enhance its power, to reward its loyalists, and to influence diverse interest groups, from businessmen and labor organizations to peasants and large farmers. Cronyism was rampant in the operations of government, where PRI leaders, for example, used publicly funded payrolls to hire friends, to exploit government projects to give contracts to favored companies, and to grant licenses to businessmen supportive of the PRI. The tentacles of the party also penetrated the cultural life of Mexico. The government's role in the oversight and funding of cultural institutions gave the PRI enormous reach into the intellectual life of the country. Moreover, newsprint was under government control, forcing most publications, such as newspapers and magazines, to follow the political mandates established by the party. Cognizant of the need to renew their broadcasting licenses from government agencies, radio and television operators generally stayed within the political parameters set by the PRI.

As a result, over time the PRI built an extensive political machine of tremendous power. Elections generally had predictable results and were a facade for a highly centralized, undemocratic regime. Or, as author Mario Vargas Llosa put it at one point, Mexico exemplified the perfect dictatorship. Thus, the democratization of Mexico since the 1990s is to a large extent the story of the PRI's decline as the dominant political force in the country. Nonetheless, the aging party sustains a hold in many parts of the nation, especially at the local and state levels of government and in the composition of the Mexican Congress. A large proportion of Mexico's governors continue to be members of the PRI, and the party's representatives remain a major presence in most state legislatures. Though a weakened giant, the party refuses to quietly wither away and remains a viable political organization of considerable clout and influence.

Origins: The Mexican Revolution and the Maximato The origins of the party date back to the 1920s. Though the violence associated with the Mexican Revolution subsided

The logo of Mexico's Partido Revolucionario Institucional (PRI) (The Revolutionary Institutional Party). (Courtesy of the Partido Revolucionario Institucional)

after 1917, political instability wracked the postrevolutionary years. A pivotal political crisis occurred with the assassination of president-elect and revolutionary hero Álvaro Obregón in 1928. The outgoing president, Plutarco Elías Calles (1924–1928), wanted to avoid another round of conflict over the presidency in the aftermath of the death of the Obregón. But Calles also understood that he could not take the reins of the presidency again without provoking an armed response from political rivals. In order to ensure a peaceful transition of power, Calles organized a political party as a means of creating a process for the designation of a presidential candidate and containing the political competition of revolutionary factions. As a result, the Partido Nacional Revolucionario (National Revolutionary Party, PNR) was formed in 1929, an unusual confederation of local political and military bosses, labor unions, peasant organizations, and regional political groups. With Calles in control of the new party, a series of interim presidents was appointed and outright conflict was averted over the presidency. For the next six years or so, Calles held political sway in the country through his manipulation of the PNR and his rule known as the Maximato (that is, Calles was the Maximum Chief). The PNR was consolidated during this period, with Calles presiding over the different interest groups and political bosses that vied for influence within the government. Thus, the PNR became a mechanism for negotiating who would be candidates for public office, from the local level and governorships to congressional seats and the presidency itself. Through this process, the PNR provided the means for competing constituencies to work out the distribution of political power so as to avoid disagreements that might lead to instability or open violence.

The PRM: Cárdenas and the breaking of the Maximato Calles's control of the party ended during the presidency of Lázaro Cárdenas (1936–1940). Though handpicked by Calles, Cárdenas came to the conclusion that the concentration of power within the party risked an eventual reaction from those groups and interests who felt excluded from access to the political process. Cárdenas skillfully maneuvered to break Calles's hold over the party, and in a historic showdown, Calles was forced into exile and several of his associates were arrested.

In 1938, Cárdenas reorganized the party and renamed it the Partido de la Revolución Mexicana (PRM, Party of the Mexican Revolution) and began the foundations of the present-day PRI. Cárdenas incorporated organized labor into the party; most unions in effect became extensions of the federal government through the formation of the Confederación de Trabajadores de México (Confederation of Mexican Labor, CTM). Similarly, large numbers of peasants and small farmers were the basis for the formation of the Confederación Nacional Campesina (National Peasant Confederation, CNC). Cárdenas reunited the labor and peasant organizations, and through the incorporation of the CTM and CNC to the party, he gave the PRM an organization by sectors: labor, agrarian, popular, and military. Many businessmen also found it politically prudent to join the bureaucracy dedicated to the promotion of Mexican enterprise that had been established in 1917, the National Confederation of Chambers of Commerce. Under Cárdenas, this organization became a means for the private sector to express its views, for instance, on labor-related matters such as the setting of minimum wage levels.

Furthermore, under Cárdenas tens of thousands of acres of land were distributed to landless peasants, and workers enjoyed an unprecedented measure of support from government. As a consequence, a large segment of workers and peasants became strong and loyal supporters of the party and of Cárdenas more specifically. To enforce his reforms, on more than one occasion Cárdenas authorized the confiscation of land from those who opposed his agrarian policies; dissident businessmen also felt pressured to go along with government policies or face possible retaliation from government agencies involved in the enforcement of private sector regulations. With its ability to command vast numbers of voters, the party expanded its influence under Cárdenas from the national level down to the selection of governorships, congressional representatives, judicial appointments, and even municipal offices. For example, given that the federal government was in charge of public education, the teachers' union became a crucial source of votes for the party as well as a means of political influence wherever a public school was located. The support of the teachers' union earned its members various rewards in terms of wages, benefits, and job security from the government that in turn cemented the tie between the party and a union with huge numbers of members.

The popularity of Cárdenas personally among many peasants and workers added to the strength of the PRM and to the credibility, for instance, of the CTM and CNC. In short, Cárdenas built an effective and powerful political apparatus that spanned diverse sectors of society. To fund these reforms, Cárdenas used the monies generated by government revenues and monopolies, such as over utilities, ports, and railroads. In this regard, the nationalization of the oil industry in 1938 and the formation of PEMEX proved to be a continuous and decisive source of funds for the federal government, and by extension, for the party.

This is not to say that Cárdenas and his party went unopposed. Dissident movements surfaced against the government of Cárdenas and against the growing dominance of the PRM. Government-imposed and secularized curricula in public schools met resistance, for example, in those parts of Mexico still highly influenced by the Catholic Church. Most importantly, in 1939, the National Action Party appeared to contest the party built by Cárdenas. Still, the political machine created by Cárdenas became an effective force that founded the dominance of the PRI in the decades that followed Cárdenas's tenure in office.

The Mexican miracle and PRI's authoritarianism   Cárdenas was succeeded by Manuel Ávila Camacho (1940–1946); he was the first president subject to the change in the Mexican Constitution where presidents serve a six-year term without the possibility of reelection. In 1946 President Camacho abolished the military sector within the organization and renamed the party the Partido Revolucionario Institucional. Political peace and economic stability followed, consolidating the PRI's hegemonic postion in the Mexican political system.

Ávila Camacho's administration enjoyed the benefits generated by Mexico's ability to contribute raw materials, such as oil-related products, to the Allied effort during World War II. The wartime economic boom served to tighten the connections between the United States and Mexico, while also stimulating a period of relative prosperity in the country that continued into the postwar years. Government revenues increased, to the advantage of the now-dominant party, whose members filled public offices from top to bottom and who used their positions to dispense favors to their constituents, and usually for themselves. From 1940 to 1970, gross domestic product (GDP) increased sixfold and the population only doubled, while the peso-dollar parity was maintained, allowing an economic largesse that served to strengthen the power of the dominant party.

During the last year of his term in 1946, Manuel Ávila Camacho dissolved the PRM and founded the Institutional Revolutionary Party, the namesake of the current PRI. The centralization of political influence in Mexico marked the formation of the PRI, with the president as titular head of the party as well as the chief executive of government. Through the federal government's control or partial ownership of key economic enterprises, notably energy production and distribution, the party possessed the financial means to exercise its influence.

The PRI provided upward mobility for the middle class through the political bureaucracy or through businesses in the protected national industry and integrated workers and peasants into the political system through the distribution of political patronage from the top down to members of organized labor and the agrarian movement. Public service employees also became a source of electoral support, as party loyalists rose to leadership positions in workers' organizations tied to government agencies across a wide range of occupations, from elementary school teachers and university administrators to museum directors and painters employed by federally funded public works projects. Thus, government social services employees, among other state-funded labor forces (such as the oil workers union of PEMEX) were incorporated into the political machinery of the dominant party. Through this hierarchical political pyramid, the PRI in the 1940s and 1950s reached the zenith of its power: Governors of all of the states, mayors of major cities, the overwhelming majority of congressmen, and most judges at all levels of the judiciary owed their allegiance to the PRI. With the president at the apex of this political edifice, government and party were largely indistinguishable. Elections were held, legislation submitted, and judicial decisions made usually with predictable results from the local to the national level. During his term in office the president had nearly unchecked power, including the ability to select his successor (known in Mexico as the *dedazo,* "to point out with his finger"). Although the party's presidential candidate was formally nominated at the national assembly, in practice the assembly served only to ratify the candidate handpicked by the president.

In this context, competing political groups found it extremely difficult to mount a viable opposition or they were declared illegal by PRI-controlled electoral officials. With the mass media overseen by government censors and regulators, sources of information and analysis basically kept within the boundaries set by the party's government officials. Failure to do so held any number of retaliatory actions, such as government agencies withdrawing paid announcements, the loss or suspension of a broadcasting license, a cutback in newsprint, or companies unexpectedly canceling their promotional advertisements. (Only a few valiant journalists and writers dared to criticize the dominant party or the government.) In short, the party's influence over the media gave the PRI a huge political advantage against its critics and opposition. During the PRI's monopoly of public office in Mexico, there were few incentives to seek political alternatives outside the party's structure, and corruption at all levels characterized this coalition of networks, as the PRI has been commonly described. From illegal landholdings and manipulation of public-sector enterprises to bribery, nepotism, and illegal use of public money, official corruption reached unprecedented levels during the 1960s and 1970s, particularly with oil revenues.

By the 1960s, however, the PRI machine began to show signs of weakness. The inequities and inefficiency of the party's workings sowed the seeds of rising discontent that culminated in large-scale, student-led protests at a critical moment: the 1968 summer Olympic Games in Mexico City. Spearheaded by students at the two main public universities—the Universidad Nacional Autónoma de México

(National Autonomous University of Mexico, UNAM) and the Instituto Politéc-nico Nacional (National Polytechnic Institute, IPN)—large crowds demonstrated their growing frustrations over the increasing economic and social disparities in Mexico over housing, employment, education, and health. The government's will-ingness to spend enormous amounts of resources on the Olympics angered ordi-nary Mexicans with limited prospects for economic mobility and social amenities. For most of Mexico's dissatisfied population, there was an obvious culprit—the dominant party and its control of government. The attempt to violently suppress the protests on the eve of the opening Olympic ceremonies only served to discredit further the government and the party. Furthermore, the foreign press generally criticized the brutal actions of Mexican federal authorities to quash the protests. Most importantly, the events of 1968 clearly exposed the authoritarian, undemo-cratic nature of the political system of the PRI. The severity of the crisis passed, but 1968 represented a turning point in the history of the party—it would never recover its former power or prestige.

The slow democratic transition   The 1970s represented a transition toward the gradual unraveling of the PRI and its dominance over politics in Mexico. Under the successive terms of two PRI presidents, Mexico underwent a period of wrenching economic troubles that sapped the strength of the PRI and generated damaging tensions within the party. Luis Echeverría (1970–1976) and his succes-sor, José López Portillo (1976–1982), each contributed to the worsening crisis that engulfed the country following their 12 years in office. Under their steward-ship of the country, Mexico accumulated an enormous deficit due to ill-guided policies, mismanagement, and unforeseen events, particularly the ups-and-downs of oil prices. The latter keyed a cycle of borrowing based on anticipated oil ex-port revenues and a subsequent crash of oil prices that added to mountainous debt, terrible inflation, and ruinous monetary devaluations; then more borrow-ing took place from international banks and financial institutions to cover previ-ous losses, adding to the enormous debt of the country. With each downturn, the erosion of support for the party accelerated. Investment fled, wealthy Mexicans moved their capital to foreign accounts, and eventually large financial institutions began to transfer their assets overseas. In a desperate measure to stem the flow of capital going out of the country, in 1982 José López Portillo nationalized the banking industry just before he left office. The stunning act by the president of Mexico turned much of the private sector once and for all against the government and the party. Ravaged by the results of failed economic policies, much of the middle class had also lost its confidence in the party. Moreover, the support for the presidential campaign of the leftist Valentín Campa in 1976 against López Portillo manifested the obvious restiveness among large segments of the working class against the PRI. The seemingly invincible party faced a critical loss of its legitimacy before the Mexican public, despite the modest electoral reform passed during the López Portillo administration that allowed 100 seats in Congress to be allocated proportionally to opposing parties.

The corruption and the severe financial crisis left after the administration of López Portillo had a significant impact on the PRI's internal politics and undermined the party's public support. Internally, an emerging generation of technocrats, with increasing influence in the government, began to distance themselves from the PRI's traditional populist and nationalist agenda and adopted neoliberal, probusiness, and free market economic policies.

López Portillo chose Miguel de la Madrid, his chief of budget and programming, to be his successor. As the presidential candidate of the PRI in 1982, Miguel de la Madrid led a new current into the party that pushed for privatization, for a market-based approach to the economy, for less protectionism and more free trade. Yet such policies also meant major cutbacks in social spending, higher costs of living, reductions in government payrolls, competitive pressures on Mexican companies, and higher unemployment. When a devastating earthquake hit Mexico in 1985 (badly damaging parts of Mexico City), de la Madrid's slow response to the crisis discredited his administration among a public already resentful toward the PRI and its leadership. In the midterm elections that followed in 1986, voters in large numbers expressed their impatience with the failing policies of the PRI-controlled government by casting ballots against the party's candidates.

The evident loss of public support for the party led a faction within the PRI to challenge the views of de la Madrid and his followers as the 1988 presidential election neared. In a bitterly disputed nomination process, the dissident group was defeated and subsequently left the party to form an oppositional coalition to challenge the PRI's nominee, Carlos Salinas de Gortari. Amid charges of massive electoral fraud, the PRI candidate won the election of 1988, but the party was clearly on the defensive against its rivals on the Left and on the Right. The vaunted PRI machine noticeably faltered, when, for the first time since the consolidation of single-party rule, the PRI lost a governor's race in 1989, opposition leaders were elected in the Senate, and the party lost more than one-third of the seats in the Chamber of Deputies to the two main opposition forces, the PAN and the group led by Cárdenas. President Salinas attempted to improve the PRI's public image without changing its authoritarian and clientelist practices, seeking to avoid further rupture within the party. Salinas allowed some electoral reforms and moved against those elements of the party and organized labor associated with corruption, mainly union leaders. Salinas's manipulation of state resources through popular programs such a Pronasol, political measures, and economic recovery resulted in a better position for the PRI in the midterm elections of 1991. However, a political and economic crisis characterized the last year of Salinas's presidency. During 1994, the Ejército Zapatista de Liberación Nacional (EZLN) rose up against the antidemocratic government and its neoliberal policies, particularly NAFTA; the PRI's presidential candidate, Luis Donaldo Colosio, was assassinated; the party's secretary-general, Francisco Ruiz Massieu, was also assassinated; and an economic crisis seemed inevitable by the end of Salinas' term.

With the political and economic crisis of 1994 in the background, the PRI candidate for the presidency in that year, Ernesto Zedillo, was able to squeak out a victory. Nonetheless, it was a Pyrrhic victory, marred by an internal struggle within the party after the initial presidential candidate for the PRI was assassinated. In spite of winning the presidency, the party's decline appeared unmistakable. The competing political parties made telling gains in congressional representation, governorships, and municipal offices. Under immense political pressures for electoral reform, Congress passed a series of measures that were implemented for the 1997 midterm elections. The results proved devastating for the PRI: for the first time since 1929, the party lost in majority in Congress.

The outcome of the 1997 elections set the stage for the PRI's historic loss of the presidency in the 2000 elections. Prior to the 2000 presidential election, the PRI held its first primaries to elect the party's presidential candidate. The primary candidates were Francisco Labastida, Roberto Madrazo, Manuel Bartlett, and Humberto Roque. The differences among the primary candidates and their campaigns against one another further weakened the PRI. In the presidential election of 2000 the PRI's candidate Francisco Labastida was defeated by Vicente Fox. It was to be the first presidential electoral loss of the PRI since its founding.

Riddled with internal dissension after its electoral reversals of 1997 and 2000, the PRI became an opposition party. Without the means to easily fund its activities from governmental coffers, to use state workers as a source of voting leverage, to exercise its influence over the private sector as before, or to control federal legislation, the PRI after 2000 had to contend with a decidedly democratic political process for the first time. In the 2006 elections, the party failed again to regain the presidency, as its candidate came in a disappointing third in the wake of a deeply divisive internal nomination process. Although the national leadership of the party appeared disunited, the depth and longevity of the PRI machine at the state and local levels allowed the party to hold on to a number of governorships and congressional seats, particularly in its traditional strongholds in the more rural areas of the country.

Yet the prospects for the party are at best mixed, as much of the younger, urban electorate continues to be skeptical of the PRI, given its authoritarian past. On the other hand, the PAN presidential victors in 2000 and 2006 have found it difficult to meet expectations in the midst of the economic slowdowns that marked their periods in office.

The PRI's performance in the 2006 presidential election was a direct outcome of the party's internal disputes and the ongoing restructuring as an opposition party. In 2005, Roberto Madrazo, president of the PRI, left his post and nominated himself as the party's candidate in the presidential elections. However, a group formed by

PRI governors and former state governors called "Todos Unidos Contra Madrazo" (Everybody United against Madrazo) opposed Madrazo's candidacy and postulated Arturo Montiel as its candidate. Montiel later withdrew from the race, but the PRI's candidate did not have enough support, and the party came in third in the presidential election.

As the PRI looks to the future, it remains a formidable political presence at the subnational level, giving the party the capacity to wield meaningful clout in Congress and to use its political resources to negotiate with its rivals. For example, PRI members represented the largest voting bloc in the Mexican Congress among the three major parties after the 2003 federal elections (224 seats out of 500). On the other hand, after the 2006 elections, where its presidential candidate performed dismally, the representation of the party in Congress fell drastically to only 121 deputies out of 500 seats; and its presence in the Mexican Senate also declined, from 60 seats in 2000 to 39 senators after the 2006 campaigns.

Clearly, the 2006 elections reflected a party internally divided over its future leadership and direction at the national level. In local races, however, remnants of the PRI machine proved resilient and have permitted the party to recover somewhat from the disaster of the 2006 federal elections. For example, PRI candidates ran strongly in state and municipal contests in the 2007 elections, winning a substantial number of mayoral and state legislative seats.

In the 2009 midterm elections, the PRI regained control of the Mexican Congress for the first time since the 2000 elections, in which the opposing party, PAN, won the presidential seat. With 241 seats in the Chamber of Deputies, the PRI has plural majority. In the opposition, the PRI has exploited the lapses of its competition to maintain the party's viability, but its days as the overwhelming political force in the country have ended irrevocably.

Juan Manuel Galarza and José Ignacio Lanzagorta

See also Debt, Foreign; Election, Presidential, 2000; Election, Presidential, 2006; Electoral Institutions; López Portillo, José; Partido Acción Nacional; Partido de la Revolución Democrática; Petróleos Mexicanos; Politics and Political Parties; Salinas de Gortari, Carlos

Further Reading

Hellman, Judith Adler. 1997. "Continuity and Change in the Mexican Political System: New Ways of Knowing a New Reality." *European Review of Latin American and Caribbean Studies* 63.

Mexico Transforming. 2000. Pacific Council on International Policy, University of Southern California.

Middlebrook, Kevin J. 1995. *The Paradox of Revolution: Labor, the State and Authoritarianism in Mexico.* Baltimore: Johns Hopkins University Press.

Molinar Horcasitas, Juan. 1992. *El tiempo de la legitimidad.* México, DF: Cal y Arena.

Molinar Horcasitas, Juan, Kevin Middlebrook, and Maria Lorena Cook, eds. 1995. *The Politics of Economic Restructuring in Mexico.* San Diego: University of California Press.

Partido Verde Ecologista de México

The Partido Verde Ecologista de México (Mexican Ecologist Green Party, PVEM) represents one of the most viable of the minor political parties in Mexico. Its significance lies primarily in its ability to lend its support to the large major parties in close votes for legislative measures. The ideological position of the party therefore has been inconsistent. The party originally cast its support for the dissident presidential candidacy of Cuauhtémoc Cárdenas in 1988, but for the 2000 presidential contest, the PVEM allied with PAN's Vicente Fox. Three years later, the Green Party began an alliance with the PRI, which continued through the 2006 presidential elections. The party's congressional delegates have cast votes for legislation along various points on the political spectrum, from right to left. In recent years, the PVEM has tended to be identified as a center-right party, often using its congressional votes in support of PAN or the PRI. After the 2006 elections, when it supported the PRI candidate, the PVEM had 17 members in the Chamber of Deputies and five senators.

Founded in 1986 as the Mexican Green Party, the PVEM was initially associated with the political left in Mexico, given its support for Cuauhtémoc Cárdenas for president in the election of 1988. The PVEM, however, lost its legal charter when it failed to receive at least 2 percent of the national vote in the midterm elections of 1991, a stipulation under Mexican electoral law. The party's founder, Jorge González Torres, was forced to renew the PVEM's registration in order to compete in the 1994 electoral round. Running as an alternative to the major parties, the PVEM was able to build a small but sufficient following to sustain its political presence. By the 1997 midterm elections, the Mexican Green Party received nearly 4 percent of the national vote, although its platform strayed away from a strictly environmental line. (Major international environmental organizations, such as Greenpeace, have generally distanced themselves from Mexico's Green Party.)

For the 2000 presidential election, the PVEM gave its support to the winning candidacy of PAN's Vicente Fox. The alliance quickly disintegrated, as Fox basically ignored the Green Party's support; his choice for the cabinet seat on the environment was not granted to a PVEM member. The short-lived relationship with PAN ended with the 2003 midterm elections, when the PVEM allied itself with PRI. The coalition with the former dominant party allowed the Green Party to run candidates in numerous local contests for mayoral offices, state legislative posts, and congressional seats.

The PVEM has a checkered history, which has proven to be a political liability. The Green Party began essentially as a closed political organization, dominated by relatives of the party's founder, Jorge González Torres. Internal tensions have surfaced within the party as a consequence, including an evident rift over the alliance with the PRI presidential candidate for the 2006 election. (The PVEM had originally proposed its own candidate, but he withdrew from the race, presumably under pressure from the González Torres family.) Moreover, PVEM elected officials have been accused of corruption, tarnishing the party's stature among Mexican voters. For example, in 2004 a videotape showed a meeting involving an illegal land-use deal near the beach resort of Cancún that apparently implicated a PVEM mayor.

The Green Party has failed to demonstrate a capacity to expand its ranks, and its recent record of political opportunism will likely stunt its ability to draw large numbers of new members. The party's significance will persist so long as the major parties need votes to pass meaningful federal legislation. In such situations, the PVEM's congressional delegates may be in a position to decide close votes among the competing major parties. The political prospects for the Mexican Green Party, however, do not appear to be robust. The PVEM is more likely to remain a minor if not diminishing political force in the country.

Juan Manuel Galarza and José Ignacio Lanzagorta

See also Partido Acción Nacional; Partido de la Revolución Democrática; Partido Revolucionario Institucional; Politics and Political Parties

Further Reading

Partido Verde Ecologista de México. www.pvem.org.mx.

Peasantry

The peasantry in Mexico has historically been the most impoverished sector in a country whose society and economy have been traditionally tied to agriculture. The belief in Mexico that land produces wealth is contradicted by the fact that most of the country's land is not conducive to extensive farming, as much of the terrain is mountainous and dry, with very few river systems that make irrigation easy and accessible for agricultural production. For much of its history, farming in Mexico was conducted on small plots of land worked by a huge number of peasants. In contemporary Mexico, about 26 percent of the population is employed in agricultural production, but the agriculture sector accounts for only 9 percent of the nation's gross domestic product.

Several inequalities also prevail in the agricultural industry organization. The states in the north have a more organized and technical production. In this sector, northern agroindustry implemented production modeled after the successful use of technology in other countries. In the central states of the country, agricultural production does not have the same technological development as the northern states. The highest levels of poverty are found in the southern states. Ironically, southern Mexico is more humid and conducive to agriculture. However, its farmers are the poorest in the country and are subject to authoritarian forms of organization.

Moreover, since the colonial era, the peasantry has been a marginalized sector. Throughout Mexican history, some experimental changes have been attempted, but none of them with real success. The social and political consequences of rural underdevelopment—most importantly, the impoverished peasantry and its exclusion from a market economy—have become an anchor for the country's economic growth. The problems for peasantry are not just lack of investment; they also involve Mexican history and social complexity. Nearly 100 percent of the indigenous population is rural; colonial figures, a sort of feudal landlord called a cacique, prevail over and subject the peasantry in a servile scheme. Agricultural modernization in Mexico implies fighting and modernizing old colonial structures and local power reserves.

Despite the land restrictions, many economists and sociologists claim that the problems of Mexican agriculture are largely social. They are the result not of nature but of failed public policies and a lack of real interest in developing farm industry. After the Mexican Revolution and under the Partido Revolucionario Institucional (Institutional Revolutionary Party, PRI) regime (1929–2000), the government extended its control over all aspects of the countryside in an effort to create a socialist system of agriculture. This resulted in the destruction of market incentives, pervasive underdevelopment, squandered resources, endemic poverty, and corruption.

Before NAFTA (that is, before 1994, and before 2008 for substantial agricultural products), the free market had never been allowed to operate in Mexico's agricultural sector. The landed classes and the government derived great power from their control over the countryside—a power they historically have been reluctant to give up.

The origins of an impoverished peasantry   In Mexico during the Spanish colonial era, land distribution was highly unequal. For nearly four centuries, much of the peasanty did not own land and instead, worked on large estates called haciendas, controlled by a small group of landowners whose holdings were concentrated in those areas favorable to agriculture: close to markets, sufficient rainfall, fertile soil, and terrain conducive to ranching and/or farming. The peasantry on these estates lived in perpetual indebtedness to the landowners through debt peonage. On the other hand, in many parts of Mexico subsistence farming prevailed, particularly in the more remote parts of the country; this pattern continued through the late 19th century.

In 1857, President Benito Juárez expropriated all lands belonging to the Catholic Church and started a privatization policy. However, this did not serve the peasantry, since the privatization was still done under the old scheme of land distribution. Beginning in 1876, the country was dominated by the dictator Porfirio Díaz, who followed an export model of development that favored the concentration of lands in the hands of a few rich owners. This policy led to the creation of large landholders as well as the expansion of existing haciendas into enormous tracts of land, also called latifundios, where the peons remained the major source of labor. Furthermore, the lands of many small landholders were forcibly taken by those well-connected to Díaz, especially in those areas conducive to the growing of highly lucrative agricultural products such as sugar and coffee.

The Mexican Revolution   This exploitative system and the peasants' demands for land were among the most important causes of the Mexican Revolution. In 1910, Porfirio Díaz was overthrown by a group of revolutionary leaders, and among the most important was Emiliano Zapata. The movement headed by Zapata originated in the state of Morelos, famed for its sugar-producing lands. Under Díaz, large tracts of land had been illegally confiscated from small landholders by sugar planters favored by the dictator's regime. Zapata's revolt called for the restitution of illegally taken lands and for an equitable redistribution of land.

In 1915, Emiliano Zapata pushed for an Agrarian Reform Bill through the Mexican Congress, which set the style of Mexico's agricultural policy for the rest of the century. The most important feature of this legislation was the government commitment to redistribute land to peasants by expropriating lands. Although other revolutionary forces would not agree with this project, the only way to pacify Mexican society was with the incorporation of these demands. The strength of the Zapatista movement led to a key provision in the charter of the Mexican Revolution, when Article 27 was written into the new Mexican Constitution of 1917. Article 27 of the Mexican Constitution conferred on each citizen a right to own land and obligated the government to provide it. This provision also gave the government the right to confiscate unused or underutilized lands and distribute them to Mexicans who petitioned the government for land. Inspired by the concept of communally held village land that went back to precolonial times, the new revolutionary government established the *ejido*. These were agricultural units collectively held by its members, or *ejidotarios*; the scheme provided landless peasants with the means to resume farming through a communal concept of land management, but ownership of the land remained in the hands of the state.

The *ejido* and the PRI   The postrevolutionary governments, however, failed to resolve the problem of the inequitable distribution of land.

The government divided land into plots that were cultivated individually or collectively, but they were operated communally by the people of the *ejido*. Landownership, however, remained in the hands of the state. Unfortunately, the *ejido* system too often became a tool of political manipulation whereby the dominant political party used its means of patronage to cultivate electoral support.

For 20 years following the revolution, fallow land once under the control of vast estates was cultivated as peasants worked the newly formed *ejidos*. Between 1940 and 1960 agricultural production in Mexico grew at an average rate of 4.6 percent, compared with 2.7 percent for all of Latin America. The principal cause of this growth, however, was not an increase in the efficiency of production, but the introduction of new technology, such as new harvesting and irrigation equipment and high-yield, pest-resistant crops. Also, new lands were brought under the plow as *ejido* farms were created and as private landowners cultivated formerly fallow land, hoping thereby to avoid its confiscation.

Expropriations, however, continued, and an ever-increasing percentage of land was brought under the *ejido* system. By 1988, half of Mexico's arable land was controlled by the government through the *ejido* system.

Much of the PRI's stability and success dwelled on its ability to build a corporative government. Through an extensive bureaucratic apparatus that included the unions of several state-owned enterprises (electricity, oil, trains, and telecommunications, among others), the PRI had support from virtually every economic sector. The peasantry was not an exception. The agrarian reform applied by the PRI was evidently popular for the peasantry; as in an industry union, the PRI encouraged the formation of peasant organizations tributary to the party.

In 1938, under President Lázaro Cárdenas's administration, the Confederación Nacional Campesina (Peasant National Confederation, CNC) was created. At its constituent meeting, 300 delegates attended, representing some 3 million peasants. In its early years, the CNC was the only organization representing the rural sector. Currently, the CNC shares space with a growing number of organizations, particularly after the PRI's loss of the presidency in 2000. The CNC had a presence in almost every Mexican municipality. Since the government distributed agricultural benefits through this organization, its leaders had become powerful among the peasantry, and the CNC served as political machinery for the PRI to win elections. Actually, it is said that it still wields an important power capable enough to maintain the PRI at the head of most municipalities and some state governments.

In order to deal with other peasant organizations, the PRI founded the Confederación Revolucionaria de Obreros y Campesinos (Revolutionary Workers and Peasants Confederation, CROC). The CROC gathers unions and local peasant organizations that are all directly affiliated to the PRI. While the CNC remains as a more independent organization, it is actually the PRI's agricultural political arm. During the era of PRI dominance, the CROC also received directly from the government a system of benefits that empowered most of its leaders.

The current problems of the peasantry and NAFTA   The growth of Mexican agriculture in the 20th century, however, brought major problems. The main problem was that, due to the government's protection, the *ejido* farms did not have any market incentives as did the private ones. Thus, the *ejido* system worked against the emergence of modern, efficient farms and led instead to the creation of very small farms of less than 12 acres. The peasants were practically dedicated to subsistence farming, and these small farms became substantially isolated from the national and international economies.

Under Mexican law, the peasants grouped in an *ejido* could neither sell nor rent the property. Title remained in the hands of the government. As a result, farmers had little incentive to invest in and improve the land they worked. The lack of capital and market incentives hampered modernization. Government control over all aspects of the agricultural system steadily increased, from the regulation of prices to the establishment of monopolies over purchase and supply. In effect, the *ejidos* became simple extensions of the economic and social planning bureaucracies in Mexico City. By the end of the century, rural Mexican wages were one-third that of the average Mexican worker. The enormous resources of the countryside went largely untapped and remained securely bound by government control. Under these circumstances, migration from the countryside to urban areas and/or to the United States accelerated after World War II and continued to mount through the rest of the century.

Also, the Mexican population grew significantly throughout the 20th century. Between 1915 and 1938, the government distributed 18.5 million acres to the peasants, but this represented only 6 percent of Mexico's farmland at that time, and it met most of the demands for land. However, by 1940 Mexico's population had grown to 20 million. From 1938 to 1943, the government confiscated and distributed an additional 44.5 million acres as the growing rural population demanded more land. Thirty years later, the population had increased to 51 million, creating tremendous pressures for further land confiscations and redistributions. President Luis Echeverría (1970–1976) expropriated 30 million acres from private farmers during his term, but only half of that was redistributed to peasants. The rest either remained in the government's hands or was distributed to wealthy Mexicans with political connections. By the time Echeverría left office, *ejido* lands had jumped from one fourth to almost one half of total agricultural lands. The next Mexican president, José López Portillo, seized 40 million additional acres, 16.5 million of which he made into *ejidos*.

When President Salinas took office in 1988, he inherited an agricultural system in crisis. Despite efforts by the government to distribute land, the promises of the revolution to the peasants had not been fulfilled. Rural Mexico was now poorer than ever. Dramatic steps were needed to turn around a system that constrained Mexico's agricultural production and compelled increasing food imports. As a first step, after a year in office, Salinas began limited reforms of the *ejido* system, like setting up 79 pilot projects to legalize *ejido* land rentals and also to attract capital from the private sector. The leftist and nationalist parties resisted the reforms, claiming that Salinas violated the Mexican Constitution and undermined the Mexican Revolution's achievements in the countryside. Despite that, in his 1991 State of the Nation address, Salinas stated that land distribution was finally over. In February 1992, the Mexican Congress adopted Salinas's free market reform package for the Mexican countryside. Salinas proposed to drastically reduce the government's role in agriculture, establish private property rights, and integrate the agricultural sector into the larger market economy, thus bringing it into the 20th century.

Also, the Salinas administration signed NAFTA, challenging the agricultural industry not only of Mexico but also of the United States and Canada. From the earliest negotiation, agriculture was a controversial topic within NAFTA. Agriculture was the only section that was not negotiated trilaterally; instead, three separate agreements were signed between each pair of parties. The Canada-U.S. agreement contains significant restrictions and tariff quotas on agricultural products (mainly sugar, dairy, and poultry products). However, due to the technological and facility inequalities between both countries, the Mexico-U.S. pact allows for a wider liberalization within a framework of phase-out periods. By the beginning of 2008, both countries had been forced to remove tariffs and quotas for all agricultural products.

NAFTA has been strongly criticized by peasant organizations and some scholars. They claim—particularly in the case of corn—that NAFTA, far from improving the Mexican economy, contributes to the impoverishment of the corn farmers.

Felipe Calderón's administration (2006–2012) also has reformed the agricultural industry. Through its Ministry of Agriculture, Calderón changed the way in which the government benefits are distributed to the farmers. The previous PRI governments distributed them through the CNC and CROC. Now, the government delivers a benefit or incentive to individual peasants, promoting competition. This, and the beginning of the agricultural phase of NAFTA, has encouraged protests demanding a renegotiation of NAFTA.

The peasantry nowadays faces another transition period. After a century of governmental protection, communal forms of organization, and uneven investments, peasants are now subject to free market rules and international competition. The persistence of migration from rural Mexico testifies to the failure of the Mexican revolution, and the PRI in particular, to fulfill its promise to the country's peasant farmers.

Juan Manuel Galarza and José Ignacio Lanzagorta

See also Agriculture; Corruption; Immigration and Emigration; Income; Indigenous Peoples; North American Free Trade Agreement; Partido Revolucionario Institucional; Salinas de Gortari, Carlos; Social Structures, Class, and Ethnic Relations

Further Reading

Pastor, Manuel, and Carol Wise. 1994, summer. "The Political Economy of North American Free Trade: The Origins and Sustainability of Mexico's Free Trade Policy." *International Organization* 48(3): 459–489.

Torres, Hernandez, Jose Luis, and Adolfo Orive. 2010. *Poder popular: Construccion de ciudadania y comunidad.* Mexico City: Juan Pablos.

Treviso, Dolores. 2011. *Rural Protest and the Making of Democracy in Mexico, 1968–2000.* University Park: Pennyslvania State University Press.

Petróleos Mexicanos

Petróleos Mexicanos (Mexican Petroleum, PEMEX) was a government agency established in 1938 to deal with the properties of foreign-owned oil companies that were expropriated by decree of President Lázaro Cárdenas in March 1938. The foreign-owned oil companies had been at odds with a series of presidential administrations since the outbreak of the Mexican Revolution in 1910, especially over issues of control of subsoil resources and taxation.

By 1938 the Mexican government had already experimented with a series of state organizations involved with the oil industry. In the early 1920s the government established the Control de Administración del Petróleo Nacional (Administrative Control for National Petroleum), which explored and drilled on oil lands belonging to the government. In 1925 the government set up the Administración Nacional del Petróleo (National Petroleum Administration), which engaged in both production and refining activities. In 1934 Petróleos de México (Mexican Petroleum, or Petromex) came into existence as a mixed-capital venture. By law, the Mexican government controlled at least 40 percent of the stock in the company. Any remaining stock could be purchased by private interests, but there was a specific ban on ownership of Petromex stock by foreigners. Petromex functioned as a fully integrated oil company, although on a much smaller scale than the foreign-owned oil companies with which it competed. In early 1937 yet another agency was created, the Administración General del Petróleo Nacional (General Administration of National Petroleum). This new agency was completely government controlled and engaged in exploration, production, and refining activities.

In the immediate aftermath of the expropriation of March 1938, Cárdenas established the Consejo de Administración del Petróleo (Board of Petroleum Administration) to administer temporarily the assets of the foreign-owned oil companies. The board was composed of two representatives from the Ministry of the Treasury, two from the Ministry of National Economy, and three from the oil workers' union. In July 1938 two more government agencies began operations: the Distribuidora de Petróleos Nacionales (Distributor of National Petroleum) and Petróleos Mexicanos (Mexican Petroleum, PEMEX). The Distribuidora handled the marketing of oil products while PEMEX took over the administrative functions previously exercised by the Board of Petroleum Administration. This division of responsibilities proved awkward, and in August 1940 President Cárdenas abolished the Distribuidora, turning over its responsibilities to PEMEX. PEMEX now exercised an effective monopoly on the Mexican oil industry. PEMEX itself was managed by a council of nine persons, five appointed by the president and four by the oil workers' union. The president also appointed the top official at PEMEX, the general director.

The world in which PEMEX had to compete was a complex and rapidly changing one. While the Mexican government promised to compensate the foreign-owned oil companies for their assets, the companies and the government became

involved in a lengthy dispute over the value of the properties involved. The companies took legal action against Mexican efforts to market oil products overseas. Foreigners had dominated the managerial and technical positions in the companies, so
there were few Mexicans prepared to take over operations of the companies. The
companies were able to protect their oil tankers, so PEMEX immediately encountered major problems with transporting its oil. PEMEX found it difficult to obtain
the supplies and the equipment it needed to operate, and lacked the credit and the
capital required to maintain and expand operations. The beginning of World War
II in Europe in September 1939 created a great demand for Mexican oil but also
caused major dislocations in the international oil market. There were also management problems with the powerful oil workers' union, the Sindicato de Trabajadores Petroleros de la República Mexicana (Union of Petroleum Workers of the
Mexican Republic, STPRM).

From its inception, PEMEX was expected to do more than simply manage the
Mexican oil industry. PEMEX was supposed to be an important source of government revenue, a role that varied depending on the price of oil. PEMEX was also to
be an important source of employment; in its first 18 months of operation, PEMEX
increased its employees by almost 50 percent and by more than 250 percent between 1938 and 1958. In addition, PEMEX was to support and promote the social
and economic goals established as national policy by the government and the official party. Finally, PEMEX was also to serve as a powerful symbol of Mexico's
economic nationalism.

During most of the 1940s, PEMEX struggled to fulfill its multiple responsibilities. Problems of labor and capital continued. Primary emphasis was on meeting
domestic demand for oil products; there was no significant effort to restore Mexico
to its former position of major oil exporter. PEMEX helped to promote the development policy being pursued in the postwar years by providing energy at subsidized
rates. PEMEX lacked the capital to engage in major new efforts at exploration, so
it had to depend on more intensive exploitation of existing fields; this approach
often reduced the total amount of oil that could be recovered from a field. PEMEX
also struggled with the organizational problems of trying to integrate fully from
exploration to distribution in order to compete with the large, multinational oil
corporations. In the early postwar years, private capital—including foreign—could
participate in exploration, drilling, and development of wells under contract with
PEMEX. In 1958 new legislation restricted private companies to service contracts
with PEMEX; the law specifically prohibited PEMEX from entering into contracts
that called for payment in the form of a percentage of production. This latter restriction was particularly discouraging to private investors. PEMEX did expand
its distribution capacity through the construction of new refineries and pipelines.

A major problem confronting PEMEX management was its lack of control over
many fundamental business decisions. Government officials—not PEMEX officials—set wages for workers in the industry and the prices that PEMEX charged

for its products. The oil workers' union, the STPRM, enjoyed privileges that cut into management's decision-making powers. The STPRM—not PEMEX management—controlled the hiring of workers. The union also had the right to participate in contracts PEMEX entered into with private companies; the STPRM was able to form cooperatives that received preferential treatment in the awarding of PEMEX contracts. A PEMEX job was considered so desirable that corrupt union officials regularly sold jobs to those seeking employment.

PEMEX was also in the forefront of the development of the petrochemical industry in Mexico. Legislation passed in 1958 that gave PEMEX exclusive control over the production of what were classified as basic petrochemicals. Private companies could produce secondary petrochemicals, with the restriction that such companies could not be more than 40 percent foreign-owned. In 1960 the government released a list of 16 specific products that were classified as basic; in 1967 the list of basic chemicals was expanded to 45. In 1971 legislation established the Mexican Petrochemical Commission to help determine whether petrochemical products should be classified as basic or secondary. While having a monopoly on basic petrochemicals, PEMEX also produced—and subsidized for the domestic market—secondary petrochemicals. By 1970 there were 217 petrochemical plants in Mexico, of which 41 belonged to PEMEX.

During the 1960s and the early 1970s, PEMEX experienced a steady increase in production, especially in the area of natural gas. Hydrocarbon consumption, however—driven by a growing population and rapid industrialization—was increasing at a much faster rate than production. PEMEX was unable to achieve its goal of hydrocarbon self-sufficiency and was forced to increase its importation of crude oil. In the late 1960s and early 1970s, PEMEX had to stop exporting crude oil for the first time in its history. In 1965 the government set up the Instituto Mexicano del Petróleo (Mexican Petroleum Institute, IMP) to promote the technical expertise of PEMEX. This scientific assistance was especially important as PEMEX found it necessary to engage in much more deep drilling and to become more actively involved in offshore drilling. The financial position of PEMEX deteriorated badly as extraction costs increased, oil prices declined, and the prices for PEMEX products domestically were frozen.

Despite the bleak financial and economic picture, PEMEX was on the verge of a major change in its fortunes. This change was a product of two forces—one beyond the control of PEMEX, the other directly connected with its activities. The factor beyond the control of PEMEX was the dramatic improvement in oil prices beginning with the Arab oil embargo of 1973 and continuing throughout the decade. The factor directly connected to PEMEX was the discovery of major new oil reserves in southeastern Mexico, both on land and offshore. The reserves would permit Mexico to return to the position of a major exporter of oil. Mexico was not a member of the Organization of Petroleum Exporting Countries (OPEC) because it had not been a major exporter of oil at the time the organization was founded.

Mexico was able to benefit from the price increases provoked by OPEC's manipulation of production but was not subject to the kind of criticism increasingly leveled at OPEC by the industrial countries. In fact, Mexico was even able to charge slightly more for its oil than the OPEC countries because of its greater proximity to major consumers, especially the United States.

It was the government—not PEMEX—that would decide how to deal with this new oil bonanza. The administration of President José López Portillo established maximum limits on daily production, overseas sales, and sales to any one country (meaning the United States). This was supposed to ensure the digestible exploitation of the oil wealth PEMEX would produce. PEMEX found itself indirectly subsidizing a number of consumer products, beyond its traditional direct subsidizing of energy. On the surface PEMEX's financial performance was spectacular; by 1983 PEMEX accounted for approximately 13 percent of Mexico's gross domestic product and almost 50 percent of government tax revenues. The downside was that the government was spending the additional revenue even faster than PEMEX could generate it and was borrowing heavily as well to maintain public spending. PEMEX's share of the Mexican government's foreign debt was also increasing dramatically, rising from approximately 10 percent in 1970 to almost 30 percent in 1981. Corruption connected with PEMEX also achieved new dimensions as the oil boom unfolded.

The decline in oil prices beginning in the early 1980s brought economic hard times to Mexico and greater attention to the role played by PEMEX in the economy. The near economic and financial collapse forced the government to adopt an austerity program that soon phased in the introduction of major economic and financial reforms. Critics attacked PEMEX for its inefficiency, mismanagement, and corruption. One of the first targets for reform was the powerful oil workers' union, the STPRM. A presidential decree in 1984 restricted the subcontracting activities of the STPRM with PEMEX. The STPRM publicly voiced its disenchantment with the newly implemented economic reforms and opposed the official candidate for the presidency in 1988, Carlos Salinas de Gortari. When Salinas assumed the presidency, he retaliated by arresting 35 of the top union leaders. The president made it clear that the new union leaders would be expected to support the government's economic policies or face similar treatment.

With labor subdued, President Salinas was able to undertake a major reorganization of PEMEX. PEMEX was divided into units responsible for exploration and production, refining, natural gas and basic petrochemicals, secondary petrochemicals, and international operations. New accounting and tax procedures were introduced to better determine profitability and efficiency. Employment at PEMEX dropped rapidly from 210,000 in 1987 to approximately 106,000 in 1993. These reforms were aimed at making PEMEX function more like the multinational oil companies with which it competed. Almost a decade later in late 2001, PEMEX's general director, Raúl Muñoz Leos, indicated that the reorganization of PEMEX in the early 1990s had not produced any substantial improvements in operations. Muñoz Leos also predicted that Mexico would soon be importing more gas, refined oil products, and petrochemicals if PEMEX was not allowed to increase its spending on exploration and production.

One of the reforms implemented in the 1980s and 1990s was privatization, the selling off of government enterprises to the private sector. With major government enterprises such as the national telephone system being sold off, many wondered whether privatization would be extended to PEMEX. The petrochemical activities of PEMEX were soon affected. The number of basic petrochemicals—those reserved exclusively to PEMEX for production—peaked in 1986 at 70. Thereafter, the list of basic petrochemicals contracted rapidly; by 1992 it was down to only eight. PEMEX also began to sell off some its secondary petrochemical activities to private companies. The administration of President Salinas was also actively pushing for implementation of the North American Free Trade Agreement (NAFTA), designed to improve the flow of capital and trade among the countries of Mexico, Canada, and the United States. Salinas hoped that NAFTA would lead to a significant increase in foreign investment in Mexico. NAFTA posed the issue of the role of PEMEX in a freer business environment. Because of the symbolic importance of PEMEX in national life, even the reform-minded Salinas was not willing to make major changes in the role played by PEMEX in the Mexican oil industry. When NAFTA went into effect in January 1994, it provided easier access for U.S. and Canadian companies to the petrochemical sector, to provision of oil goods and services, and to PEMEX contracts. The dominant role played by PEMEX, however, was left intact.

In recent years PEMEX has come under increasing criticism for its environmental practices. In its efforts to expand operations rapidly, PEMEX often ignored the environmental consequences of its actions. Farmers in southeastern states charged that PEMEX activities so polluted their lands that they could no longer be cultivated. Expansion of PEMEX operations offshore brought the possibility of water pollution to add to pollution of soil and air. The pollution charges were often followed by claims that PEMEX was slow to pay for or refused to pay for environmental claims. The debate over NAFTA heightened concerns about the environment, focusing more unfavorable attention on PEMEX. PEMEX officials maintained that they were tightening pollution controls; the most notable example of this new policy was the closing in 1991 of PEMEX's major refinery in Mexico City, a notorious polluter in the Distrito Federal (Federal District, DF). PEMEX also claimed to have accelerated payment of compensation for pollution but also made it clear that it would pay only when environmental damage could be clearly linked to PEMEX.

Despite its uneven environmental record, the government-run oil company remains a potent if not sacred symbol of Mexican nationalism. As a result, efforts to reform PEMEX have led to heated debates between those pushing for privatization as opposed to those who demand that the company continue to be run as a publicly owned corporation. Underlying this debate has been the uses of the monies generated by PEMEX, as it has provided the bulk of federal revenues that for seven decades were controlled by the dominant PRI. The federal government has exploited those funds to sustain governmental operations and programs, siphoning a huge proportion of the monies earned by PEMEX and lessening the resources for the company to install new equipment, apply new technologies, and boost production.

Regardless of the outcomes of those debates, PEMEX faces a very difficult situation. First, productivity of its oil fields declined by about 25 percent between 2004 and 2009. The sharp fall in production forced the Mexican Congress to pass some reforms in 2008. Most observers welcomed the measures, although they were considered insufficient to stave off the evident shortcomings of the management of PEMEX. (High prices for oil in recent years have cushioned the financial consequences of the fall in productivity.) The 2008 reforms permitted PEMEX to use private subcontractors, reduce the amount of the monies taken by the federal government, include professional experts on its management board, and conduct private audits of the oil company's books. Second, PEMEX has become a political football that will inevitably enmesh the company in the decisive 2012 presidential election. Given the revenues generated by PEMEX for the winning party of the 2012 elections, the country's oil company will be under constant political scrutiny. Third, PEMEX must find new sources of oil, but the options are enormously costly (such as deepwater drilling), will take years to bear fruit (if any), and will challenge the firm's technological expertise. Fourth, the international energy markets are subject to volatile changes, but PEMEX's political and productivity constraints will give it less maneuverability and flexibility in adjusting nimbly to the global oil market environment. PEMEX has survived a world war, huge price fluctuations, charges of corruption, debt crises, and peso devaluations to endure for much of the Mexican public as a symbol of Mexico's hopes for economic development and independence. But those hopes have dimmed in recent years, and the prospects for this icon of Mexican nationalism are at best tenuous.

Don M. Coerver

See also Corruption; Environmental Issues; Foreign Direct Investment; Foreign Policy; Foreign Trade; Government; Politics and Political Parties

Further Reading

Brown, Jonathan C., and Alan Knight, eds. 1992. *The Mexican Petroleum Industry in the Twentieth Century.* Austin: University of Texas Press.

Colmenares Cesar, Francisco, Fabio Barbosa Cano, and Nicolas Dominguez Vergara. 2008. *PEMEX: presente y futuro.* Mexico City: Plaza y Valdes.

Mancke, Richard B. 1979. *Mexican Oil and Natural Gas: Political, Strategic, and Economic Implications.* New York: Praeger.

Moroney, John R., and Flory Dieck-Assad. 2005. *Energy and Sustainable Development in Mexico.* College Station: Texas A&M University Press.

Rippy, Merrill. 1972. *Oil and the Mexican Revolution.* Leiden, Netherlands: E. J. Brill.

Shields, David. 2006. *Pemex: Problems and Policy Options.* Berkeley: Center for Latin American Studies.

Photography

The variety of photographic proposals disseminated and distributed throughout contemporary Mexico by the world of art indicates a clear opening of artistic institutions to the mechanical reproduction media. From documentary proposals, where photography acts as a mechanism of social memory, to esthetic proposals, where it acts as an image of formal and conceptual constructions, photography travels throughout the country as a heterogeneous means to create and understand Mexican society.

This acceptance of new ways of using photography, promoted in research, cataloging, restorations, publications, and expositions, is the result of an active process of negotiations initiated in the 1970s. Photography has always had a variety of uses: as historical documents, as a resource to build both public and private identities, as a legal means, as pornography, and so forth. From 1921 to 1969, image reproduction—known outside the country as Mexican photography—was dominated by an indigenous style whose main driving force was the documentation and recreation of indigenous people and peasants, distinguished by its use of black and white proposals, where the typical elements of the media (framing, brightness, and tone quality) were grouped together with the graphic inventiveness of the shot (discursive meaning, emotional touch, and humanistic quality) to build a characteristic discourse of the dominant photography in American publications, galleries, and museums.

The Manuel Álvarez Bravo case is paradigmatic to describe such style. Supported by the Museum of Modern Art (MoMA) of New York, his work was distributed in the publications and expositions in those decades. During the 1940s, MoMA built a style that would praise humanistic documentalism, which based its premises on the foregoing elements as the fundamental values of photography and created a trend of a straight photography that slips out from the mix of other discourses such as literature, painting, and sculpture to make its quest come true in an autonomy of photographic language. Directors of this museum's photography department, such as Beaumont Newhall and John Szarkowski, disseminated these perspectives of technical images, creating a canon.

This canon, along with the construction of a postrevolutionary nationalism promoted by the Partido Revolucionario Institucional (Institutional Revolutionary Party, PRI) that dominated the governmental power in Mexico for seven decades, created a Mexican photography style based on a preconception of what was considered Mexican: taking pictures of individuals who are least privileged by the

Museum goers look at photographs by Mexican photographer Manuel Álvarez Bravo at the Museum of Modern Art in New York, 1997. (AP/Wide World Photos)

system, such as indigenous people and peasants, in order to present them as noble and dignified individuals. Bending figures, seen from behind, wearing a serape and a sombrero, with no time or face, are objects of contemplation that are plentiful in the photography of Mariana Yampolsky, Graciela Iturbide, Lola Álvarez Bravo, Juan Rulfo, and Manuel Álvarez Bravo himself.

In the 1970s, this humanistic documentalism is subverted within the production and distribution system of photography to give way to an abundantly heterogeneous photographic production. The 1968 student movement and its dramatic outcome— a violent repression ordered by the government of Gustavo Díaz Ordaz—resulted in a strong experimental movement within the cultural arena where the artistic groups took center stage. Students and graduates from the faculties of arts from around the capital got together to create an urban, conceptual, and social art that forgot the canonic forms such as painting and sculpture, and focused on the hybridization of the media, having the performance, the happenings, and the facilities as their main driving forces. Such languages demanded, due to their ephemeral nature, a documentation supported in video and photography. Hence, photography was combined with other media and played a fundamental role in the artistic construction of that time.

Along with this movement, photography started achieving a privileged position in cultural government institutions, such as academic, museum-related, and educational initiatives. In 1969, Lázaro Blanco, a photographer, founded the Mexican photography workshop Casa del Lago at the Universidad Nacional Autónoma de México (National Autonomous University of Mexico, UNAM). This workshop became a strong driving force for young photographers and was a space for the dissemination of their works. In 1973, the first exclusive gallery opened to show photographic productions in that same university space. Carlos Jurado consolidated in 1975 the Talleres de Artes Plásticas (Plastic Arts Workshops) at the Universidad Veracruzana in Xalapa, capital of the state of Veracruz, and founded, years later, the first Latin American bachelor's degree program in photography. His curriculum was based on media, alternative printing, and shooting, using such tools as the stenopeic cameras and bichromed rubber. He built an antimerchandising and self-sufficient trend that contrasted with the visual production in the country. His influence in the capital can be seen in the works of Ruben Cárdenas and Javier Hinojosa.

In 1975 the Active School of Photography opened its doors, a clear counterweight to governmental artistic education concentrated in the National School of Fine Arts "La Esmeralda" of the Instituto Nacional de Bellas Artes (National Institute of Fine Arts, INBA) and the Escuela Nacional de Artes Plásticas (National School of Plastic Arts, ENAP; formerly the Academy of San Carlos) of the UNAM. The Active School of Photography continues to generate a large number of professionals whose images even today create standards and trends. In 1976, the group Independent Photographers based their work on photographic experimentation and on exploring other places for the distribution of the images, such as streets and neighborhoods. That same year, other groups engaged in this exploration with the media and its distribution, such as the Photographers Collective and the Light Workshop. The state, through the Instituto Nacional de Antropología e Historia (National Institute of Anthropology and History, INAH), acquired the Casasola Archive Foundation.

The Casasola Archive Foundation had one of the most extensive and significant collections of photographic art in the country, and they were the basis for the foundation of the National Photographic Library in the city of Pachuca, Hidalgo, a center of documentation and research on photography and one of the most important centers in Latin America. A year after this archive was opened, in 1975, the Consejo Mexicano de Fotografía (Mexican Photography Council, CMF) was founded based on the initiative of a group of photographers led by Pedro Meyer, supporting the vision of a Latin American photography whose premise was based on works committed to documenting Third World suffering. This council created an esthetic and ethical slogan through the debates held in the colloquiums and in the Latin American photography encounters (1978, 1981, 1984, 1992, 1993a and 1996), as well as in the biennial photographic shows held in the country after 1980.

Alejandro Castellanos, one of the most influential photographic critics in the country, divides the consolidation process of contemporary photographic production into two stages: from 1977 to 1989 and from 1989 to 2001. The first stage is defined by the birth of the CMF, which revalues the figure of the photographer as an author, and hence revalues the artistic potential of the media. During that time, there was great support from Mexico City's institutions to projects by a limited group of specialists who only considered certain pictures as art; this group strived to support those photographic productions that had the possibility of entering into the market, education, galleries, and all means of production, distribution, and reproduction in the world of art (schools, specialized magazines, museums, galleries, and so forth). As told by historian Raquel Tibol, this process began at the Graphic Biennial in 1977 when, due to the high volume of photographic works, the juries decided that photography required its own space.

This event, along with other factors, gave way to the construction of the CMF and the managing of the colloquiums and Latin American encounters mentioned earlier. These events encouraged cultural, academic, and artistic circles to question the nature of the media and defend the possibility of considering photographic images as art. The strength of the CMF led to a success in this battle, but under the premise that artistic photography would be expressed in its own biennial. The first Photography Biennial was held in 1980 and set the standard and trend of what would be distributed as artistic productions and, to a large extent, what would be distributed throughout the country as contemporary photography, dominated by a rhetoric of social complaint, parting, as Laura González Flores said, from an ethics of commitment that exalts an identity of Latin American photography.

In 1989, the sesquicentennial anniversary of the announcement of the invention of the daguerreotype was commemorated and, with this, a festival in the city of Xalapa opened the space for the dissemination and research of photography nationwide. This gave birth to the Festival Internacional Junio (International June Festival of Photography) promoted by the Fotoapertura group. In that same year, photographer Víctor Flores Olea, head of the National Council for Culture and Arts, carried out the project "150 Years of Photography in Mexico," organized by Manuel Álvarez Bravo and Pablo Ortiz Monasterio. Expositions were organized showing the different uses of photography in Mexican culture, specifically with the exposition curated by Mariana Yampolsky and Francisco Reyes Palma at the Museum of Modern Art, where the conservatorship revealed the different roles played by photography in social imaginary.

The second stage mentioned by Castellanos comprises the period from 1989 to 2001, where the relationship among the dominating, residual, and emerging elements in the field of photography is compiled. A broader and more open network for the dissemination and production of the media was created; in 1994, the Image Center was founded and spread out the revaluation of picture as an aesthetic object from its own purism. That same year, the first Photojournalism Biennial was held. The figure of straight photography promoted by the United States spread out, having as its direct predecessor the artistic group movements of the 1970s. Those visual artists ventured into the field of photography in order to use it as another element in their discursive construction repertoire, a production that was defined as built photography. Its primary protagonists were Gerardo Suter, Eugenia Vargas, Lourdes Grobet, Lourdes Almeida, León Rafael Pardo, Eduardo Enríquez Rocha, Carlos Somonte, Jan Hendrix, Laura Cohen, and Alfredo de Stéfano, among others. Such photography presents the crossing of media, styles, and techniques; the technical image is closely related to the written word, body language, conceptual art, painting, and sculpture.

In this way, the last decade of the 20th century had a polymorphous structure as its basis, where the private industry and nongovernmental organizations provided a counterweight to the cultural governmental institutions. Further means of distribution such as the Internet were discovered, which democratized the use of the media in such a way that it affected the authorship of the art itself, since any image or any text could be reproduced and distributed. Such production had been seen as artistic since the 1990s, if we take the Biennials as an example, which proposed the same democratization that we now have through the Internet. The Biennial of Photography of 2004 and 2007, for example, represent clusters of proposals and images immersed in several alternative perception games. We obviously have trends, rhetoric, repetition, and more. Submersion in the variety of images is so nourishing that, even for those spectators who have not been in contact with the world of art, it represents a good experience of otherness, enabling different ways of looking at ourselves, of building and understanding ourselves. The proposals often go from pornography to very sophisticated images of intellectual insight. Realities that go beyond what is Mexican are portrayed as microentities; such is the case of Edgar Rolando Martínez Ramírez who, with his *Retratos de familia,* won the 11th Biennial in 2004, or theoretical questioning of the ontology of the media (Ximena Berecochea and her project *Caperucita Roja,* 2003). There is something for everyone.

This democracy—if not about roles, at least about the construction of images—gives another glimpse of the abundant variety of images in daily culture; when contextualizing them in an exposition or catalog, they provide a different way by which we relate to them, sometimes imaginatively, sometimes indifferently, sometimes emotionally, and many times reflexively. We are faced with a panorama of images that goes from those that anyone could have taken to technically complex and intellectually dense images. The Image Center created the Fotoseptiembre Festival and decentralized national production, granting a space for creation and for multiple reflections on the image. If the Biennial of Photography is a thermometer for the creation of national photography that decides and regulates the production of artistic photography by disseminating the work of a few, the selected ones, then Fotoseptiembre is an inclusive event, since it fosters the opening of forums for photography and helps in promoting certain show spaces that were neglected before, where unknown artists mingle with famous artists.

An illustrative example of the foregoing panorama of contemporary photography in Mexico is the exposition "45 Contemporary Mexican Photographers" (curated by Pedro Meyer and Francisco Mata, and sponsored by the Pedro Meyer Foundation), since it shows precisely the assorted photographic productions considered as artistic; documentary discourses, narrative discourses, and conceptual discourses are mixed together to provide a critical sampling of Mexican photography that is, in Laura González Flores's words, a heterogeneous and complex media, with multiple performances in the temporary and the social.

From an intimate, markedly voyeuristic proposal of Ana Casas Broda to a socially critical proposal in Jerónimo Arteaga's documentary line, the exposition (which can be seen at www.zonerero.com) goes beyond a narrative linearity founded by Pedro Meyer. The exposition is a collage of Mexican photographic production and provides new possibilities of understanding and analysis. For many years, it has expanded the distribution possibilities of a large number of works. Works such as those of Agustin Jimenez, Luz Aurora Latapí, Luis Márquez, Kati Horna, among others, are displayed. Publications of the 1930s include the *Semanario Moderno* (Modern Weekly) magazine (1934–1939), whose visual production was engaged in an erotic photomontage stands out, as do the photo-stories of the late 1960s and early 1970s, and the works of photojournalists in *Unomasuno* (1977) and *La Jornada* (1984) newspapers, which marked paths of photographic images outside the modern style of "the Mexican." Little by little, these works enrichen and expand the abundance of iconic national production.

Josué Martínez Rodríguez

See also Art and the Private Sector; Art Criticism; Art Education; Art Exhibitions; Art Market; Arts, Alternative Venues for; Culture and the Government; *Lucha Libre;* Nationalism and National Identity

Further Reading

Debroise, Olivier. 2001. *Mexican Suite: A History of Photography in Mexico,* translated and revised by Stella de Sá Rego. Austin: University of Texas Press.

Debroise, Olivier, et al. 2006. *La era de la discrepancia: Arte y cultura visual en México, 1968–1997 (The Age of Discrepancies: Art and Visual Culture in Mexico, 1968–1997),* edited by Olivier Debroise, translated by Joëlle Rorive, Ricardo Vinós, and James Oles. México, DF: Universidad Nacional Autónoma de México, Turner.

González Flores, Laura. 2004. *Fotografía y Pintura, ¿dos medios diferentes?* Barcelona: Gustavo Gili.

Mraz, John. 2009. *Looking for Mexico: Modern Visual Culture and National Identity.* Durham, NC: Duke University Press.

Noble, Andrea. 2010. *Photography and Memory in Mexico: Icons of Revolution.* Manchester, UK: Manchester University Press.

Schwartz, Marcy E., and Mary Beth Tierney-Tello, eds. 2006. *Photography and Writing in Latin America: Double Exposures.* Albuquerque: University of New Mexico Press.

Segre, Erica. *Intersected Identities: Strategies of Visualisation in Nineteenth- and Twentieth-Century Mexican Culture.* New York: Berghahn Books, 2007.

Tejada, Roberto. 2009. *National Camera: Photography and Mexico's Image Environment.* Minneapolis: University of Minnesota Press.

Politics and Political Parties

The political system of Mexico is defined as a federal presidential representative democratic republic. Mexico has a congressional multiparty system, with the president as the head of the state and the government. The 1917 Mexican Constitution established a republican political system composed of three branches of government: the executive, the legislative, and the judiciary. The president is elected by direct vote every six years without the possibility of reelection. The Legislative branch is divided into two houses: the Chamber of the Deputies and the Senate of the Republic. The Chamber of the Deputies is comprised of 500 delegates, where 300 deputies are elected by direct vote in uninominal (electing a single member) districts; in addition there are 200 deputies who are selected on the basis of the proportion of the national vote received by each legally registered party in Mexico. In order to have legal status, a party must receive a minimum of 2 percent of the national vote in federal elections. All deputies are elected for a three-year period; deputies may be reelected, but they cannot serve consecutive terms. The Mexican Senate has 128 positions. Each of Mexico's 31 states and the Federal District has two seats that are based on direct vote. In addition, each state and the Federal District has a Senate seat allocated to the party that receives the second-highest vote. Moreover, 32 senatorial positions are assigned to parties in proportion to their percentage of the national vote.

At the state level, the political system reflects the federal government's three-branch structure, although the legislative branch is composed of a unicameral body for each state. State government follows the basic political principles at the federal level; for example, governors cannot be reelected. Each state establishes the rules for the election of state legislators, but those rules must conform to the principle of proportional representation of political parties. Similarly, each state determines the selection of their respective judiciary, and each state regulates the recognition of political parties for the election of state and municipal offices. State legislators cannot serve consecutive terms, but they can be reelected.

Local government is based on a municipal council and a mayor or municipal president. Each state determines the oversight rules for local governmental entities. Mayors and municipal council members cannot serve consecutive terms, but they can be reelected.

Political parties field candidates at each level of government in Mexico, including municipal offices (unlike the United States, where local offices are generally considered nonpartisan in nature). Mexico possesses essentially three major parties: the Partido Revolucionario Institucional (PRI), Partido de la Revolución Democrática (PRD), and Partido Acción Nacional (PAN). There are a number of smaller parties, and usually more at the state and municipal levels, given that each state has its own rules for the legal recognition of political parties. It is often the case that parties will form coalitions for electoral contests at all levels of government.

Development of the modern party system   From 1929 until the 1990s, Mexico was essentially a one-party political system, where the PRI (and its predecessors) dominated the political life of the country from the municipal level to the presidency. As a consequence, political power in Mexico became highly centralized in the hands of the federal executive, in which the democratic process deteriorated into an authoritarian form of government. The presidential election of 1988 represented a decisive turn in Mexican politics, as the PRI's control of the presidency was seriously challenged. In the wake of that pivotal election, the political power of the PRI gradually eroded, while public support for two rival parties—PAN and the PRD—expanded rapidly. In the 1997 midterm elections, the PRI lost its majority in Congress, which presaged the historic defeat of the candidate of the aging dominant party in the 2000 presidential election. Electoral reforms, especially after 1988, facilitated a dramatic increase in electoral partisan competition and in the democratization of the Mexican political system.

Of the three major parties, the contemporary PRI is considered centrist, supportive of neoliberal, market-oriented policies (as opposed to its original social welfare statist orientation). In contrast, the PRD is a party of the Left that has generally been critical of free market policies, while PAN is a procapitalist conservative party, including opposition to abortion and gay marriage. In recent years, the PRI and PAN have forged agreements on key issues at the federal level, to which the PRD has often been opposed. Each of the major parties has confronted internal tensions, particularly in terms of presidential politics. Although PAN has won two consecutive presidential contests, it has faced increasing public criticism and effective opposition from the leftist PRD and from a resurgent PRI, regarding congressional representation.

At the state and local levels of government, the political situation has become much more complicated since the PRI lost its political dominance. While PAN has maintained its regional source of strength in the northern part of the country, the PRD has made substantial gains in the southern reaches of Mexico, taking political terrain away from the PRI. Yet, the PRD has sustained much support from young, urban voters. Nonetheless, the refashioned PRI has made a comeback of sorts in local and gubernatorial races. And all of Mexico's parties must contend with a growing body of independent voters, whose party allegiances are fluid, making politics in Mexico much more volatile and much less predictable.

The Partido del Trabajo (Mexican Labor Party, PT) and the Partido Verde Ecologista de México (Mexican Ecologist Green Party, PVEM) represent the most viable minor political parties in Mexico. Both of these small parties have been opportunistic, taking advantage of the lack of any one party having an absolute congressional majority. At the local and state levels, a similar pattern of tactical moves has taken place depending on the situational politics involved for both of these minor parties. The PT and the PVEM have used coalitional politics to make advances in their respective agendas and in their representation at various levels of government, but they are likely to remain minor players in the overall political landscape of the country.

The flux in the Mexican political system has encouraged coalitional actions among the different parties along shifting, unstable lines. At the federal level, for example, the lack of any one party holding an absolute congressional majority since 1997 has led to changing alliances, interparty negotiations, and intraparty debates as each of the major parties has attempted to push its legislative agenda. To a large extent, the same pattern of politics has occurred in gubernatorial races, state legislative campaigns, and municipal electoral contests. In this context, minor parties and splinter groups from the major parties have emerged, complicating still further the politics of the country. For example, the so-called Convergence Party appeared in 2005, a social democratic political group that allied itself to the popular candidate of the PRD in the 2006 elections and earned several congressional seats. New Alliance is another small party, whose electoral base is the huge membership of the teachers' union and which has won a handful of congressional posts and some municipal contests.

The 2007 electoral reforms, which were implemented beginning with the 2009 midterm elections, suggest a complex political scenario for the near future. First, each party receives television time for its political spots based on its electoral performance; this tends to favor the three major parties. Second, the new laws restrict campaign spending and provide for public funding of political parties, but again on a proportional basis. These provisions work to the advantage of the three major parties. Third, the reforms reduce the time for parties to campaign, which, in light of the above, probably adds to the advantages of the three large parties. Not surprisingly, the three major parties cooperated in the making of the new electoral reform legislative package. Moreover, the Federal Electoral Institute (IFE), which oversees federal elections, has oversight over party primaries, which may be a crucial factor in factional disputes over a party's nomination process for the presidency. The nomination of the PRI candidate in 2006 generated much internal party division and contributed to that party's poor electoral showing; the PRD may face a similar dilemma, given the factionalism that exists within that party. With the end of the dominance of the PRI, Mexico continues to cope with a process of political reconfiguration and democratization, where the outcomes remain an open question.

Contemporary political competition   Since 1997, the politics of Mexico have become much more competitive on congressional representation. Although PAN has won back-to-back presidential races in 2000 and 2006, the party of the winning candidates failed to win a majority in Congress in midterm elections in 2003 and 2009. As a result, Vicente Fox (2000–2006) found it particularly difficult to push through his legislative initiatives; his successor, Felipe Calderón (2006–2012), has proven to be more adept in successfully negotiating the passage of key legislation with rival parties. For example, Calderón was able to get Congress to pass a fiscal reform package along with important changes to electoral laws. Still, presidential legislative initiatives are subject to the flux in congressional politics.

Juan Manuel Galarza and José Ignacio Lanzagorta

See also Calderón Hinojosa, Felipe; Electoral Institutions; Partido Acción Nacional; Partido de la Revolución Democrática; Partido del Trabajo; Partido Revolucionario Institucional; Partido Verde Ecologista de México

Further Reading

Camp, Roderic Ai. 2006. *Mexican Politics: The Democratic Consolidation.* New York: Oxford University Press.

Grayson, George. 2007. *Mexican Messiah: Andrés Manuel López Obrador.* University Park: Pennsylvania State University Press.

Hellman, Judith Adler. 1997. "Continuity and Change in the Mexican Political System: New Ways of Knowing a New Reality." *European Review of Latin American and Caribbean Studies* 63.

Mexico Transforming. 2000. Pacific Council on International Policy, University of Southern California.

Popular Culture

A highly complex topic such as Mexican popular culture must be understood and valued in this century as a set of scientific and politic operations, which initiated what is understood as popular, including folklore, cultural industries, and politic populism. Today, to speak about popular culture contradicts the diversity of cultural manifestations that arise from different focuses in different parts of the country, each possessing its own individual characteristics.

What is meant by popular culture? It deals with two sociohistoric concepts. On the one hand, it deals with the concept of culture as the production of phenomena that contribute to be understood, reproduced, or transformed in the social system through the representation or symbolic reelaboration of the materialistic structures, in other words, every institution devoted to the administration, renewal, and restructuring of the common sense. On the other hand, the concept of popular is regarded as everything that refers to traditional forms of productions, local manifestations associated with national and subordinate cultures—the popular assimilated to the primitive, and the premodern and subsidiary of the underprivileged.

Popular cultures arrived in the 21st century together with technological development, globalization, and the neoliberal system. As a result, handicrafts have been replaced by the audiovisual industry; media spectacles and transnational circuits have replaced local festivities. How are popular cultures presented nowadays? What is popular that is also traditional or mass-produced? García Canclini claims that popular cultures are a transition from the local-traditional to the massive-industrialized with multiple variations of handicrafts beginning with the circulation and consumption. He also says that we need to talk about popular cultures in order to understand the diverse production of the local and the massive inequality of the symbolic exchanges. The notion of popular used to refer to handmade products. However, in the past three decades, this notion has been replaced by the notion of popularity, which is linked to the industrialization of the culture and its mass diffusion. What is popular does not consist of what the town is or has in a given space. Instead, what is popular equals what is accessible, what people like, what deserves attention, or what is frequently used. Through time, this preference has been modified; it deals with the replacement of the oral by the written, and the written by the visual—the replacement of the local by the national and, today, by the global.

That which is popular today reflects a discourse that focuses less on what disappears than on what is transformed, on what elements mix together more than on what is left authentic. This can be illustrated, for example, at the San Ángel Bazaar in which a variety of expressions are mixed together: the popular, the mass-produced, the stands of regional candy next to paintings and stands of videos. The same happens in Mexico City's Zócalo, where the *concheros* dance next to the Templo Mayor and the stands of handicrafts. People observe the pastiche, which attracts different looks and opinions that may be opposing. Indigenous and mestizos, foreigners and tourists, are not surprised anymore at the sight of masks or plates used as decoration, *cazuelas* (pots) as flowerpots, and *sarapes* (blankets) as bedspreads.

In Mexico and Latin America, what is popular is not the same for the folklorists and anthropologists who work at museums, for communicators in the mass media, or for political sociologists who work for the state or for the parties and opposing movements. The popular has initiated countless discourses that are pluralized today. It is about popular cultures within the spectacle of diverse symbolic markets: bazaars, handicraft houses, museums, fairs and contests, celebrations and festivities—all embedded in the current problems of globalization and migration.

An example of what happens with artisanal products in today's globalized economical system is the work of the artisan Natividad González in Ocumicho, Michoacán. She recreated the events of September 11, 2001, in New York using ceramics. González includes a sophisticated and updated iconography in her artistic production. For example, there is a giant devil between the twin towers. In productions like this, it is impossible to distinguish between the traditional and the media-influenced popular culture or between the domestic and the global. Traditional products are influenced by the market, tourism, culture, industry, modern art forms, communication, and recreation.

In the 1980s, traditional handicrafts became known overseas and they mixed with cultures from other countries and continents. Indigenous designs, for example, were introduced to industrial production; that is, artisans incorporated the iconography of the mass media to their objects. For example, the Zapotecos from Teotitlán del Valle, Oaxaca, began to weave *sarapes* using Picasso's designs.

In current research about popular cultures, the social and cultural practices become more important. The object has become the subject of the action, the context where the popular is exhibited and spread: fairs, museums, national and regional contests, markets, urban stores, and art houses.

The National Museum of Popular Culture　The National Museum of Popular Culture is located on Hidalgo Avenue, Coyoacán. It was founded by Guillermo Bonfil Batalla and since its opening has been devoted to documenting, preserving, stimulating, spreading, and promoting the diverse manifestations of popular and indigenous cultures. During its first years, the museum included the context of popular products as an essential part of its discourse. Nowadays, the initial discourse of the museum has declined. However, it still displays temporary exhibits and organizes events according to the holidays of the traditional calendar. The museum develops didactic and artistic activities depending on the topic of the exhibitions; these include workshops, courses, seminars, concerts, and presentations given by publishing houses. The events and exhibitions include different cultural manifestations among which events like the *Expo-miel* or *Bienal Guadalupana* and themes such as migration in Mexico, death during childhood (*muerte niña*), or popular Mexican toys stand out.

A new Museum of Popular Art　An art deco building originally planned to serve the police and fire departments was refurbished to host the new Museo de Arte Popular (Museum of Popular Art, MAP). Antique and contemporary works of the main artisan expressions are exhibited in its five permanent exhibition rooms. These come from the 32 states in Mexico and are elaborated using a wide variety of techniques and materials, including pottery, basket weaving, paper, cardboard, wood, silver and gold, glass, textile, sculpture, metals, and tinplate. All these objects are decontextualized and displayed in a way that makes them appear more linked to a stereotype of art production than to a reflection upon such production. The MAP complements its public services with a documentation and research center. A museum shop offers a wide variety of popular handicrafts, from the most traditional to the latest trends, and from the finest and most select to small souvenirs.

The FONART and art production　The Fondo Nacional para el Fomento de las Artesanías (National Fund for the Promotion of Handicraft, FONART) was created in 1974 by the federal government as a public trust fund to promote the social and economic development of artisans in Mexico. Its goal is to contribute to the improvement of the lifestyle of the artisans and to the preservation of the values of their traditional cultures. The FONART attempts to link the creativity of the artisan to the final consumer. In order to do this, the FONART uses support programs and effective strategies of commercialization that ensure the positioning of high-quality artistic products nationally and internationally. In 2001, the FONART proposed a development plan that aimed to take advantage of the opportunities to export products as a result of the North American Free Trade Agreement and with the European Union. Thus, new stores were created in Cancún and Tlaquepaque, and in New York, New Mexico, Texas, Canada, Germany, and Spain. FONART has diverse support programs such as the purchase of handicrafts (the fund buys products directly from the artisans), the organization of contests where cash is offered as the prize, training and technical assistance to artisans in order to improve the quality of the production design based on the needs and requirements of the consumer, and financing of the artisan's production. In its role of shop and house, the FONART uses the Internet to broadcast the production of handicrafts, still with the political and anthropologic idealistic perspective of locating authenticity within a global market. Since the 1990s, the FONART has declined. Its goal was to have 25 exhibition and sale centers in the country, but now it only has three branches in the country. At the beginning of the 21st century, it was estimated there were 6 million artisans, out of which this organization supported less than 5 percent during the 1990s and not even 0.5 percent in the year 2001.

It was also during the 1990s when some Mexican handicrafts such as feather art declined. However, pottery retains its hold on first place in sales; textiles hold the second place, along with certain shellacs (*laca*), especially those from Olinalá, Guerrero, and silver work from Taxco, Guerrero. Generally speaking, due to the diversity, quantity, and quality of their handcraft products, the states of Chiapas, Guerrero, Oaxaca, and Puebla stand out in the current map of handicraft production in Mexico.

Fomento Cultural Banamex   Fomento Cultural Banamex was legally constituted in 1971 as an independent civil organization to professionally and systematically promote popular culture. Based in the Antiguo Palacio de Iturbide (Iturbide's Palace) located in Mexico City's Historical Center, it started operations in 1972. This organization has a popular art program that supports and promotes artisans and their work in important commercial fairs and popular art contests, nationally and internationally. The artisans enrolled in the program have received substantial acknowledgments, such as first place for Handicrafts of Latin America and the Caribbean Prize in 2002 given by the UNESCO. Fomento Cultural Banamex calls its support program to artisans the Great Masters of the Popular Mexican Art. In 1996, the organization began to compile what is now a wide collection of popular art. This collection has been displayed as an international cultural project in many cities in the United States, South America, and the Middle East. Also, it has opened branches in the most important museums and specialty shops in Mexico. Since this organization sponsors popular art, it sells art pieces in places such as North America and Europe. Private popular art collections such as that founded by Ruth Lechuga and museums and local culture houses exist in different states in the republic. They exhibit handicrafts as a genuine product of the Mexican culture without questioning their transformations and adaptations to a context where handicrafts are simply seen as merchandise.

Artes de México   The magazine *Artes de México,* founded by Miguel Salas Anzures in 1953, is an important means of promotion for popular cultures. Even though the magazine disappeared for eight years (1980–1988), it reappeared with new content and design. As the publishing house of Mexican cultures, *Artes de México* explores the new multiform, dynamic, and creative cultures from the perspective of the history of ideas and cultural studies. It is concerned about different phenomena, ranging from the painting of antique social rankings (*castas*) to the phenomenon of tequila. The varied topics of *Artes de México* provide the reader with a perspective of the current diversity of popular cultures and their artistic productions: altarpieces, Mexican shellac, *chaquira,* Huichol art, carnival masks, rituals and myths about corn, the pottery of Tlaquepaque, and much more.

Entertainment and devotion   Festivals and celebrations are cultural manifestations of great importance, exceptional for their special clothes, decorations, and typical food, and regarded as ways to symbolically create tension between what one owns and what one does not and the conflicts between traditions and modernity within a group. Today, many of these festivals and celebrations are decontextualized because they isolate elements in urban festivals, hotels, or conventions. This is the case of the *danza de los viejitos* (dance of the old men) from Michoacán and the *voladores de Papantla* (fliers of Papantla) from Veracruz. During the celebrations, cities and towns are full of music, happiness, and devotion. The celebration typically includes a set of activities to commemorate religious, social, or historic anniversaries.

In Mexico, popular festivities and celebrations have been established by the Catholic Church, civil authorities, and the community for the purpose of celebrating a notable event. These are exceptional occasions where people spend their savings on events such as weddings or processions. In almost all popular celebrations, an ecclesiastic ritual, mass, or collective blessing is accomplished. Often, these celebrations take place accompanied by dance, music, fireworks, fairs, bullfights, and *charreadas* (rodeos) so that the public is entertained. People take this occasion to sell, buy, or exchange regional products, ranging from food to decorative objects. The events celebrated nationwide are: Santa Semana (Holy Week, the week leading up to Easter), La Santa Cruz (Holy Cross) on May 3, Corpus Christi, La Navidad (Christmas), the Día de Reyes (Three Wise Men's Day, on January 6, when presents are traditionally offered), Saint Isidro Labrador (May 15), the Candelaria (February 2), and *el día de los muertos* (the day of the dead) (November 1–2). The latter, for example, is celebrated with humor, sugar skulls, *pan de muerto* (a special type of bread), and food. These elements are necessary in the traditional offering that also includes everything the dead person liked. Cemeteries are colorful and full of lights to guide the souls.

Pilgrimages, on the other hand, have a sacrificial aspect. At the same time, they constitute a way of leaving the place of birth for many days in order to travel by bus or on foot. One of the most important peregrinations in the country takes place every December 12 in the village of Guadalupe. Pilgrims from different parts of the country arrive at the *calzada de Guadalupe* to celebrate the Virgin. Another important peregrination takes place in Chalma on Miércoles de la Ceniza (Ash Wednesday) when people carry candles while groups of dancers pretending to be Moors and Christians perform in the atrium.

The great celebration of Oaxaca, the Guelaguetza, also called Monday of the Hill, is celebrated on July 16 to honor the Virgin of Carmen. The purpose is to thank her for her help, with an obligation to give something in return for that help. During the Guelaguetza, dancers from different parts of Oaxaca arrive in the capital. They come from the Mixteca (the high plateaus), the coast, the central valleys, and the region of the isthmus. Although it is organized by various governmental departments, this celebration is a meeting point of culture and state.

Some other celebrations such as celebrating a saint or carnival are exclusive to certain places. People organize dances, processions, parades, fairs, fireworks, and typical food for such holidays as the celebration of Niñopa in Xochimilco, Mexico City (February 2); the fair of San Marcos in Aguascalientes (April 25); the holiday of Saint Sebastian (January 20) and the celebration of the Atocha's child (February 28), both in Chiapa de Corzo, Chiapas; the holiday of the Virgin of the Ascension in Morelia, Michoacán (August 25); and the celebration of the Christ of Matehuala in San Luis Potosí (January 6). There are also the carpets made and decorated with flowers and sawdust in Huamantla, Tlaxcala (August 15); the holiday of the Morisma, Zacatecas (August 27); the *mojigangas* and dances in Alvarado and Tlacotalpan, Veracruz; the *vaquerías* in Yucatán; and the carnivals of Huejotzingo (Puebla), Cancún, Cozumel, and Chetumal (Quintana Roo), Mazatlán (Sinaloa), Villahermosa (Tabasco), and many others.

Other popular cultures In the megacity of Mexico City, other types of popular manifestations may be found, in addition to the holidays and celebrations already mentioned. In the first decade of the 21st century, these manifestations have been promoted by politic multicultural ideologies and by small groups to express their diversity. Some examples of these are the moving exhibitions in the subway stations of Pino Suárez, Hidalgo, or Centro Médico; cultural centers and small culture houses that are promoted in certain neighborhoods; public dances (salsa, merengue, *reggaeton, quebradita*); artistic disciplines; handcrafts; and events that constitute new forms of the popular every day. These are moving places and spaces that locate the popular in Mexico City. They encourage people to think and imagine strategic meeting points such as the Zócalo, which from the 1990s and even today is a popular space to meet, celebrate, and have fun. Thousands of people attend the plaza to enjoy open-air concerts, pose naked for a famous photographer in this historic scenario, queue to ice skate, or see a nomadic museum. Popular culture here is where politics, mass media, entertainment, and popularity mix together.

Cecilia Absalón

See also Cuisine; Cultural Policies; Culture and the Government; Folklore Culture; *Lucha Libre;* Musical Groups and Artists; Television; Urban Culture; Youth Culture

Further Reading

Beezley, William H., Cheryl English Martin, and William E. French, eds. 1994. *Rituals of Rule, Rituals of Resistance: Public Celebrations and Popular Culture in Mexico.* Wilmington, DE: SR Books.

García Canclini, Néstor. 1993. *Transforming Modernity: Mexico,* translated by Lidia Lozano. Austin: University of Texas Press.

Hayes, Joy Elizabeth. 2000. *Radio Nation: Communication, Popular Culture, and Nationalism in Mexico, 1920–1950.* Tucson: University of Arizona Press.

Hernandez, Daniel. 2011. *Down and Delirious in Mexico City: The Aztec Metropolis in the Twenty-First Century.* New York: Scribner.

Poverty

The International Monetary Fund (IMF), the United Nations, and various other government and nongovernment organizations have devised many different ways of measuring poverty, but a common factor is an attempt to identify and quantify certain minimum human needs; if a person fails to meet these needs, then he or she is defined as living in poverty. Also, a distinction is drawn between the poor or moderately poor who suffer considerable hardships but are able to feed themselves, and the extremely poor or indigent, who are unable to satisfy even their basic food needs. By any measure, Mexico has a large population of impoverished people, many of whom are living in extreme poverty. After the last economic downturn in 1995 and with a growing gross domestic product (GDP), the percentage of people living in poverty had begun to gradually decline, but the global financial crisis that began in 2007 caused the number of people living in poverty to increase once again.

The IMF estimates that Mexico's GDP was $875 billion in 2009, a decline from its peak of $1.09 trillion in 2008. (All figures are in U.S. dollars.) Mexico's purchasing power parity (ppp) per capita GDP was $13,609 in 2009, also a decline from its peak of $14,546 the previous year. After Mexico joined the North

A young girl walks past a garbage dump in Mexico City. In 2006, 18 percent of Mexicans lived below the official national poverty line. (iStockPhoto)

American Free Trade Agreement (NAFTA) in 1994, per capita GDP grew at an average rate of about 1.8 percent until 2007; however, this was still considerably less than the U.S. average of about 3.1 percent during the same period.

Although GDP and per capita GDP give a reasonable indication of the overall and average wealth of a nation, and correlate strongly with the percentage of people living in poverty, they are of limited use for determining the overall well-being of its people. Thus, since 1990 the United Nations Development Program (UNDP) has published the Human Development Index (HDI) that, in addition to per capita GDP, measures two other dimensions of human development: life expectancy and education (determined by literacy and school enrollment). A low HDI value is defined as being from 0.000 to 0.499, medium from 0.500 to 0.799, high from 0.800 to 0.899, and very high from 0.900 to 1.000. According to UNDP, in 2007 Mexico had a ppp per capita GDP of $14,104, an average life expectancy of 76, an adult literacy rate of 92.8 percent, and a school enrollment ratio of 80.2 percent. These dimensions are combined to give a high HDI value of 0.854, putting Mexico in 53rd place among the world's nations.

A variant of the Human Development Index is the Gender-Related Development Index (GDI). This is a separate measure for women, which is generally slightly lower than the HDI, despite the greater average life expectancy of women. According the UNDP, in 2009 Mexican women ranked 48th in the world with an overall GDI of 0.847, which is 99.2 percent of the national HDI of 0.854. The GDI is derived from an average life expectancy of 106.7 percent of that of men, 96.7 percent of the male literacy rate, and 96.9 percent of the male school enrollment ratio.

As well as these overall measures of well-being, UNDP has an index that specifically attempts to measure poverty, the Human Poverty Index (HPI-1). HPI-1 measures the failure to achieve benchmarks in four dimensions: life expectancy, literacy, access to clean water, and a healthy weight for young children. In Mexico, the probability of dying before the age of 40 is 5 percent, the adult (15 and above) illiteracy rate is 7.2 percent, the proportion of people who lack access to an improved water source is 5 percent, and 5 percent of children under the age of five are underweight for their age. When combined, these figures give an overall HPI-1 of 5.9 percent, placing Mexico 23rd among the 135 nations for which this figure has been calculated (a higher rank indicates less poverty).

In July 2010 the Oxford Poverty and Human Development Initiative (OPHI) and the UNDP released the results of the Multidimensional Poverty Index (MPI), which is a more comprehensive version of the UNDP's HPI-1. MPI comprises 10 indicators of deprivation in three dimensions: education (schooling, child enrollment), health (child mortality and nutrition), and living standard (electricity, sanitation, drinking water, a floor, cooking fuel, and assets). The MPI is both a measure of the number of people in a country who are poor and an indication of the intensity of their deprivation. The MPI figures for Mexico are based on the National Health and Nutrition Survey (ENSANUT) conducted by U.S. National Institute of Health in 2006. As a result of this survey, Mexico's MPI was estimated to be 0.015, with a 4.0 percent incidence of poverty, and an average intensity of 38.9 percent. This contrasts with the 2 percent of the population who were living on $1.25 a day or less (the Mexican government's definition of extreme poverty in rural areas), the 4 percent of the population who were living on $2.00 a day or less (the definition of extreme poverty in urban areas), and the 18 percent of the population who were below the official national poverty line in 2006.

Despite its high HPI-1 ranking, Mexico is a country of severe inequalities. Like many other Latin American countries, Mexico has an elite class of extremely wealthy people (including the world's richest man, telecommunications mogul Carlos Slim Helú) and also large numbers of poor and indigent people. Another metric, the Gini Index, is used to measure these inequalities. A Gini Index value of 0 represents a perfectly equitable social structure; a value of 100 is an absolutely inequitable society. Countries with the most equitable distributions of wealth have Gini Index values in the 25–30 range. The U.S. Central Intelligence Agency (CIA) rated Mexico as having a Gini Index of 48.2 in 2008, giving it the 28th most inequitable distribution of income in the world. The Economic Commission for Latin America and the Caribbean (ECLAC), one of the UN's five regional commissions, was even more pessimistic with a Gini Index value for Mexico of 51.5 in 2008.

Although there are various ways of defining poverty and of measuring the many types of deprivation and inequality, there is one point on which all analysts agree:

A higher proportion of poor people live in Mexico's rural areas than in the cities. Although the national MPI for Mexico is 0.015, the rural MPI is much higher at 0.045 (a higher number is worse in this scale) than the urban MPI of 0.007. According to ECLAC, in 2008 44.6 percent of people in rural areas were living below the poverty line, compared to the national average of 34.8 percent (no figures available for urban populations). In addition, 19.8 percent of people in rural areas were indigent, compared to the national average of 11.2 percent and the urban average of 6.4 percent. According to the World Bank, although only a quarter of Mexico's population resides in rural areas, more than 60 percent of the extremely poor and 46 percent of the moderately poor live in the countryside.

The origins of rural poverty stem from colonial times, when a large percentage of indigenous peoples were dispossessed of their lands by the Spanish authorities; much of the Indian population became low-wage laborers as a consequence. Independence from Spain in 1821 brought little relief to Mexico's working classes, and even less to the country's landless, mainly indigenous peasantry. There have been many attempts to redistribute land to landless peasants since the Mexican Revolution of 1910, particularly during the Cárdenas administration (1934–1940). Between 1917 and 1991 over half the land in Mexico was redistributed to the rural poor in collectively owned farms, or *ejidos*. However, most of these farms are small and generate few surpluses. (The cheap imported beans and corn that have flooded the market as a result of NAFTA have affected larger, commercial farms more than these subsistence farms.) Furthermore, poverty levels are higher in rural southern states, which have large populations of indigenous people and few cities. This is borne out by UNDP HDI values for individual states. The three southernmost states of Guerrero, Oaxaca, and Chiapas have the lowest HDI values in the country, while the highest HDI values are for Baja California Norte, Sonora, Chihuahua, and Nuevo León, all of which are in the north and border the United States.

Until the economic downturn that began in 2007, Mexico had made some progress in alleviating poverty. According to ECLAC, in 2002 39.4 percent of the population were living in poverty and 12.6 percent were indigent, while by 2006 these figures had declined to 31.7 percent and 8.7 percent, respectively. However, by 2008 the numbers of poor people were climbing upward again, with 34.8 percent of the population living in poverty and 11.2 percent indigent. The principal means of government intervention has been cash transfers through the Oportunidades and Procampo programs, which are mainly aimed at rural people. For example, the Oportunidades program provides grants that enable children primarily in rural poor families to attend school, eat nutritious food, and receive regular health checkups. Oportunidades focuses on the poorest southern states, and benefits over 5 million households, which represent almost a quarter of Mexico's population.

Rural people themselves have been actively attempting to leave agriculture and diversify into rural nonfarm activities such as construction and services. Many also migrate from rural areas to big cities, where there are more employment opportunities and better services; for the most part, this means that they are simply adding to the numbers of urban poor. For example, many young women end up working in assembly plants (popularly referred to as maquiladoras), the majority of which are located near the U.S. border, where the workers barely make a living wage. Many more poor people attempt to cross the border into the United States, from where, if they can establish themselves successfully, they can send remittances back to their families in Mexico. Remittances comprised 2.9 percent of Mexico's GDP in 2007.

The global financial crisis that started in 2007 has dealt a severe blow to Mexico's efforts to reduce poverty. Although redistribution of national wealth and income are essential to lifting people out of poverty, the country's economic slide has meant downward mobility, pushing people on the lowest rungs of the economic ladder back down into poverty and indigence. For example, according to ECLAC, from 2006 to 2008 some 5 million people were added to the ranks of Mexico's poor, and in 2009 the value of inward remittances dropped by 16 percent, or $3 billion. Furthermore, Mexico's economy is very dependent on the fortunes of its giant neighbor to the north; in 2008, Mexico's exports were 31 percent of its GDP, and over 80 percent of these exports went to the United States. Whenever a recession takes place in the United States, prospects for poor people in Mexico become more problematic.

Ian Wilson

See also Income; Land Distribution and Land Reform; Social Structures, Class, and Ethnic Relations

Further Reading

Moreno-Brid, Juan Carlos. 2009. *Development and Growth in the Mexican Economy: A Historical Perspective.* New York: Oxford University Press.

UNDP Human Development Index (HDI). 2009. *Rankings.* http://hdr.undp.org/en/statistics/.

Print Media

The print media in Mexico consists of two basic types of publications: newspapers and magazines. Within each category, however, there are different styles of publications: those of a serious variety with high journalistic standards and those that are of a popular tabloid nature. The description of the print media below refers primarily to newspapers that feature investigative reporting and information on domestic, international, and business affairs and to magazines that emphasize the discussion and analysis of current politics, economic questions, and/or social issues and the arts. It should be noted that some newspaper publishers produce both types of publications, where one publication is the flagship journalistic edition and the other is tabloid in style, focusing on sports coverage, sensationalist stories, and celebrity photos. For instance, the Mexico City daily *La Prensa* has its tabloid counterpart, *Esto*. Similarly, the very well-regarded Mexico City newspaper *Reforma* has a much racier broadsheet titled *Metro*. Overall, Mexico has well over 300 newspapers, with the larger cities and major metropolitan areas of the country publishing the bulk of them. They are of uneven quality. Generally speaking, small-town newspapers do not have the means to afford well-trained journalists, where most of the nonlocal coverage is based on articles distilled from news services. On the other hand, the larger cities are the most likely to have the most publications of questionable quality that feature sporting events, lurid stories, and grisly photos of murders, car crash victims, and the like.

The number of Mexican newspapers changes from one year to the next. Some newspapers fold due to financial reasons, while some are absorbed by other publishers. Moreover, given regional socioeconomic patterns, the newspapers and magazines in the southern portion of the country are few in number, tend to be of lower quality, have very limited circulation, and depend heavily on local advertisers. Also, resort areas with large numbers of international visitors, such as Puerto Vallarta, Los Cabos, and Cancún, usually have at least one publication (often in English or bilingual editions) that caters to foreign tourists and expatriates and contains stories from news services as well as articles on various local matters, from restaurant reviews to economic issues. Mexico City has an English-only broadsheet, the *News,* that is distributed in other parts of the country.

The focus below is on the publications of a national stature of the major metropolitan areas of the country, although virtually every state in Mexico possesses at least one reputable newspaper. Most of the established large-circulation newspapers offer online editions, although a relatively small proportion of the population has easy access to such portals. In several cases, those publications belong to a larger chain of newspapers owned by a conglomerate, usually based in Mexico City, as opposed to local ownership. For example, the publishing corporation Organización Editorial Mexicana (OEM) controls newspapers in various key cities such as Guadalajara, San Luis Potosí, Aguascalientes, Puebla, and Tuxtla Gutiérrez.

In the case of magazines, the description below reflects the dominance of the publications produced in Mexico City that have a national reach. However, it should be noted that most states possess locally produced magazines, and the major universities of the country also produce periodicals as well; the latter tend to be more academic in nature and reach a very limited audience.

The circulation and consumption of all print media in Mexico is constrained by several factors, notably the extent of income inequality, relatively low levels of education, competition from other sources of information such as the Internet, and public indifference. Furthermore, sales of the print media in Mexico continue to rely substantially on street vendors, as home delivery is available only to a very small segment of the population. Magazines also depend to a large extent on sales by street vendors, bookstores, and those commercial enterprises, such as grocery stores, that sell magazines. As a result, publishers face the difficult task of increasing their market for their publications and the constant pressure to expand advertising revenues. Virtually all of the major metropolitan newspapers have created online editions through their website portals in an effort to increase their market share and to generate revenues for their publications. Given the size of the relatively well-educated and more affluent population of Mexico City, the capital and its surrounding metropolitan area represent by far the largest market for the print media in the country and possess what are generally regarded as the best newspapers and magazines in the country, with very few exceptions. Outside of the country's major metropolitan areas, local newspapers are commonly of low quality, are highly dependent on local advertisers, and have very few reporters, relying primarily on wire services for copy.

The quality and integrity of the print media in Mexico are of recent vintage due to the level of censorship that marked Mexican journalism for much of the 20th century. From the early 1920s through the 1970s, Mexico was politically dominated by one party, the Partido Revolucionario Institucional (Institutional Revolutionary Party, PRI), whose tentacles reached from the federal government to the municipal level. The PRI broached little dissidence. As a result, publishers of newspapers and magazines avoided outright criticism of the government for fear of retaliation. During the long period of PRI political dominance, transparency was basically nonexistent. Occasionally a muckraking journalist or publication appeared, but PRI operatives usually found ways to muzzle them. In that period, the PRI-controlled government used various means to essentially censor publications. For instance, the production of newsprint was done by a government-owned enterprise. Thus, any publication that criticized the government was subject to losing access to paper to print its editions. In another form of censorship, government agencies often represented a major source of advertising revenue for magazines and newspapers; that is, a state government agency would pay for a full-page ad touting its tourist attractions. Thus, if a publication ran an article critical of the government, that publication would lose the state's advertising accounts. Similarly, if a major company had a large number of its contracts with government agencies, its advertisements were subject to the influence of PRI officials. Thus, as a concession to the PRI, a company would pull its advertisements from a publication that published an article critical of the party or its policies. And when PRI leaders deemed it necessary, the party found ways to intimidate journalists through beatings, threats, and the like. In addition, agents of the PRI would pay editors (and/or reporters) to publish pieces favorable to the government or for the alteration of an article so that it would be acceptable to government officials. And the government had its own news agency, Notimex, from which many newspapers dutifully published their stories.

Given this history, the concept of freedom of the press in practical terms was at best practiced infrequently. While there were many instances of courageous reporting, as a whole journalism in Mexico was generally considered to have very low standards and to be overly sensitive to governmental influence. A turning point in the relationship between the PRI-dominated government and the print media took place in 1976. In that year, Julio Scherer, editor of a major Mexico City newspaper, *Excélsior,* permitted the publication of articles highly critical of the government. Using its powerful influence, the PRI had the newspaper's ownership force Scherer to resign from his position. Several of the newspaper's reporters and columnists quit and, with Scherer, founded the leftist muckraking magazine *Proceso.* Public denunciations of the Scherer incident compelled the government to retreat from its hard-line position; soon thereafter, other publications appeared that signaled the break of the stranglehold of the PRI-dominated government on responsible journalism. Following the establishment of *Proceso,* the independent left-of-center newspaper *Uno Más Uno* (1977) quickly appeared, and subsequently *La Jornada* began its operations in 1984. Meanwhile, in Monterrey, Nuevo León, the young brash publisher of the newspaper *El Norte* had initiated since 1973 a move toward the development of sound journalistic practices. Indeed, for a time in 1973 the government withheld newsprint from *El Norte* for its critical pieces on state-run agencies and their supervisors.

Thus, the vise-like grip of the government over the print media had been successfully challenged, although *Proceso,* like its subsequent counterparts, struggled financially early on to stay afloat. Nonetheless, the momentum toward an independent press had clearly been established, and events in the 1980s facilitated the development of professional journalism. For example, the economic crisis of those years generated heated debate over the government's economic policies, contributing to the appearance of business-oriented publications, first *El Financiero* (1981) and later *El Economista* (1988). In addition, the massive earthquake of 1985 produced a great deal of criticism over the inept response and performance of federal agencies to the disaster, which led to critical investigative reporting that the state found difficult to control or to censor. In this context, the hotly contested election of 1988 stimulated still further public interest for independent news sources, given the allegations of voting fraud by the PRI-controlled electoral apparatus. The rise and spread of an independent press in that decade marked a fundamental shift in the quality of the print media in Mexico. The 1990s witnessed the rapid decline of the power of the PRI, which added to the impetus toward the improvement of journalism in Mexico. In this regard, the establishment of an independent press contributed importantly to the process of democratization in Mexico.

The media opening initiated by the Scherer incident also impacted the publication of magazines other than *Proceso.* Among the most important Mexico

City–based magazines that arose in that era included *Nexos* as well as the more literary *Letras Libres*; still later, other news-type magazines appeared, such as *Milenio.* The emergence of a more independent press took place in a highly politicized environment, and publications tended to take evident positions on the political spectrum. The magazine *Proceso* began as and remained a left-of-center progressive-minded magazine, along with newspapers such as *Uno Más Uno* and *La Jornada.* The business-oriented publications, such as *El Financiero,* usually took a conservative stance.

The debut in 1993 of the newspaper *Reforma* in Mexico City, published by the founder of *El Norte,* raised the journalistic bar, as the feisty *Reforma* featured hardnosed investigative journalism by well-trained reporters, which prodded Mexico City dailies, such as *El Universal,* to do the same. The shift in the quality and integrity of journalistic practices in Mexico City gradually spread to other parts of the country, at times led by the extension of Mexico City–based newspapers to other cities. For example, the publisher of *Reforma* established the newspapers *Mural* in Guadalajara and *Palabra* in Saltillo, to join their founding newspaper, *El Norte,* in Monterrey, Nuevo León. By far the most extensive newspaper publishing company in Mexico is the OEM, which was established in 1976 and based in Mexico City. The OEM publishes newspapers in more than 20 cities, led by its two Mexico City dailies, *La Prensa* and *El Sol de México.* Based on its flagship newspaper, *Milenio,* founded in 1974 in Monterrey, Grupo Multimedios publishes several newspapers in more than half a dozen cities including the capital as well as in Monterrey, Guadalajara, and Toluca, among others.

The most important national magazines are few in number. The leftist-oriented *Proceso,* published in Mexico City, has a relatively high visibility and a loyal following in those cities where it is distributed. Although *Proceso* emphasizes a muckraking approach that focuses on Mexican governmental misdeeds and deficiencies, it possesses sections on the arts, media, sports, and international affairs. Centrist in its political bent, *Nexos* magazine has a well-established reputation for the quality of its diverse content that encompasses a wide range, from literary essays to coverage of political and economic issues. Although it is distributed nationally, *Nexos*'s main market is the metropolitan area of Mexico City. The newsmagazine *Milenio* (named after its parent company's daily newspaper) covers mainly current affairs but other topics as well. Though of limited circulation, the magazine *Etcétera* focuses on investigative analysis of the media. Among business magazines, *Expansión* has a solid reputation and was acquired by Time, Inc., in 2005. Mexico's version of *National Geographic* is *México desconocido* and features articles on Mexican folk arts, geography, and archaeology usually with lavish color photographs.

The future of the print media faces a number of questions. Perhaps the most dramatic problem is the current level of violence against journalists by the illegal drug cartels. Reporters covering the illicit drug trade have been killed, beaten, kidnapped, and threatened by operatives of Mexican drug gangs. Between 2000 and 2010, more than 60 journalists were murdered by cartel gunmen. In 2008, the publisher of the well-respected *El Norte* newspaper of Monterrey, Nuevo León, Alejandro del Junco, moved his family to Texas after multiple threats against his family. As of this writing they remain in Texas still in fear for their safety while he commutes to continue running his newspaper. The lack of security for journalists in Mexico impacts the coverage of stories, the investigation of ties between crime organizations and the private sector over money laundering, and the linkages among corrupt police, the military, and government officials. Thus, the violence against reporters points to the larger issue of the role of a free press and transparency and democratization in Mexico.

Furthermore, like in most countries, Mexican publications confront a limited market, leading to intense competitive pressures among the country's newspapers and magazines. One reason is the Internet as an alternative source of information as well as the availability of radio and television programming that undermines the appeal of broadsheets for a large proportion of the Mexican population. To make matters worse, social structural factors also impede the growth of the print media. For instance, entrenched patterns of income inequality and educational inequity constrain the development of a robust audience for publications of high journalistic caliber. Although principal newspapers and reputable magazines have established websites to access their editions, the market for professional journalism continues to be hampered by the socioeconomic inequities that underlie Mexican society.

As a result, and consistent with a worldwide trend, there is an increasing concentration of ownership in the print media. The dominance of the journalistic market by a small number of publishers raises troubling questions over selective coverage and editorial perspective. Local newspapers find it very difficult to compete with print media conglomerates and yet maintain well-trained professional staff. The number of newspapers controlled in key markets by the OEM, for instance, tends to lessen the spectrum of opinion, reduce local coverage, and restrain the investigative capacity of Mexican journalism. Similarly, quality magazines confront enormous publishing costs relative to the size of the market for the writings of leading intellectuals, artists, poets, and novelists. Not surprisingly, only a handful of urban centers possess the means to sustain publications marked by the excellence of their content and editorial quality. In sum, despite the advances in the integrity of Mexican journalism, the print media in Mexico faces unsettled, difficult prospects.

Alex M. Saragoza

See also Drug Trade and Trafficking; Education; Income; Politics and Political Parties

Further Reading

Hughes, Sallie. 2006. *Newsrooms in Conflict: Journalism and the Democratization of Mexico.* Pittsburgh: University of Pittsburgh Press.

Lawson, Chappell. 2002. *Building the Fourth Estate: Democratization and the Rise of a Free Press in Mexico.* Berkeley: University of California Press.

Puebla

The official coat of arms of Puebla. (Corel)

Puebla is a central-eastern Mexican state with a capital city of the same name. Puebla's location between central Mexico and the Gulf Coast has made the region a participant in and witness to most of the major events of Mexico's past. The state has an area of 13,096 square miles and is divided into 217 municipalities. Historically one of Mexico's most populous areas (ranked fifth in 2005 with a population of 5,383,133), Puebla has also been an economic and cultural center. Puebla City attracts thousands of visitors each year, and *mole poblano,* one of Mexico's most distinctive dishes, was created here during Mexico's colonial era. By the end of the 20th century, Puebla had undergone a remarkable transformation from a rural to an urban state, and its capital city was Mexico's fourth-largest urban center.

The landscape is predominately mountainous. Wide valleys, such as the one where the capital is located, lie at high elevations. Among numerous volcanoes, Puebla's three highest are Citlaltépetl (also called Pico de Orizaba), which lies on the border with Veracruz and has an elevation of 18,700 feet; Popocatépetl, which lies about 30 miles west of the capital and has an elevation of 17,887 feet; and Malinche (also called Matlalcueyatl), which lies on the border with Tlaxcala and has an elevation of 14,636 feet. There are dozens of small rivers in Puebla. The Necaxa River flows for about 125 miles through Puebla and Veracruz to the Gulf of Mexico. It provides water for irrigation and hydroelectric power. Near the Veracruz border, the Necaxa Falls cascade over 540 feet. There are several reservoirs in the state. The mineral waters of the state's natural springs are believed to have healing properties. Puebla's fertile central valleys attracted a variety of peoples in the centuries before the Spanish conquest. Cholula, the site of a great pyramid, emerged as an important religious center. It was occupied by successive waves of people, including the Toltec-Chichimecs, and was eventually identified with the worship of Quetzalcóatl (the Feathered Serpent). Puebla's more rugged northern region, known as the Sierra Norte, was also home to several native groups, most notably the Totonacs and the Huastecs.

The arrival of Hernán Cortés and the Spaniards in central Mexico found the inhabitants of Puebla's central valleys in a state of political conflict and competition. Spanish conquest of the Puebla region began with the capture of Huejotzingo and Cholula, the latter city's seizure accompanied by a massacre of thousands of natives. The Spaniards coveted the rich agricultural lands of central Puebla, and they laid claim to those lands, insisting on indigenous labor to work their holdings. Franciscan, Dominican, Augustinian, and Jesuit missionaries all played a role in converting Puebla's natives and in establishing a strong presence for the Roman

The Popocatépetl and Iztaccihualtl volcanoes as seen from Cholula, Puebla, Mexico. (Albertoloyo | Dreamstime.com)

Catholic Church. In the Sierra Norte, conquest proceeded more slowly, and its native peoples resisted attempts at conversion and assimilation.

As created by the Spaniards, the province of Puebla (known as Puebla de los Angeles) stretched well beyond the current state boundaries, toward the Gulf Coast and the Pacific Ocean. The region became an important supplier of cattle and agricultural goods for central Mexico, and by the end of the colonial era, its southwestern corner had emerged as a prime sugar area. The city of Puebla (established in 1531) became an important textile center, supplying cotton goods for all of New Spain. Puebla City also gained fame as a cultural hub and was known for its architecture, literature, and music. The city's cathedral (the tallest in Mexico) is an outstanding example of colonial architecture. Finally, the capital came to be associated with the culinary arts. Mexico's famous *mole poblano,* a rich sauce combining chiles and dark chocolate, originated in one of the city's convents, which was given the task of creating a special dish to help welcome a royal official.

The revolt of Father Miguel Hidalgo that began Mexico's independence era brought insurgent activity to the Sierra Norte and to Puebla's southern zone. Rebel leaders in the province included Guadalupe Victoria, Vicente Guerrero, and José Francisco Osorno. In 1821, nearly a decade after Hidalgo's popular insurrection was crushed, Agustín de Iturbide (who became the first leader of independent Mexico) entered Puebla's capital and declared the region free of Spanish control. Puebla was granted statehood in 1824, and although it initially preserved its reach to the

Pacific Ocean and the Gulf Coast, during the 19th century, Puebla lost these outlets as other states were created and boundaries redrawn. Despite its loss of territory, however, Puebla remained one of Mexico's wealthiest and most populous areas.

The first 50 years of independence were politically difficult for Puebla. The capital city and its surrounding region were strategic prizes for Mexico's political factions and for foreign invaders. American troops occupied the city during the Mexican War, and although Ignacio Zaragoza led Mexican troops in the defeat of French forces on May 5, 1862 (an event celebrated today as Cinco de Mayo), the French later besieged and gained control of Puebla City. On both occasions, Puebla's government was relocated, and insurgents within the state harassed the foreign intruders. Mexico's War of Reform (1858–1861) also brought violence to the capital and elsewhere as liberals and conservatives clashed over the country's future direction. The latter part of the 19th century was a time of economic expansion for Puebla. Much of this expansion took place during the reign of Porfirio Díaz (1876–1911), which was characterized by its heavy emphasis on modernization and foreign investment. Railroad lines linking Puebla with Mexico City and the port of Veracruz were built, the state's textile industry grew, and coffee, sugar, and other agricultural products found new markets. By the turn of the century, Puebla was the fifth most important industrial state in Mexico, with foreign and Mexican capital providing the means for this expansion. Such growth did not bring equal prosperity, however. Owners of sugar haciendas in the southern part of the state, for example, augmented their holdings at the expense of small-scale and communal lands. Peasants became laborers on sugar plantations, and many became trapped by debt.

Among those who eventually emerged to challenge the dictatorship of Díaz and the behavior of his local cronies was Aquiles Serdán. A radical reformer, Serdán organized workers, students, and peasants in support of Francisco I. Madero, the hacendado (landowner) from Coahuila who campaigned against Díaz's reelection and who eventually called for his overthrow. Although Madero's rebellion attracted Pueblans from a variety of backgrounds, his presidency failed to consolidate this support. After Madero's overthrow and death, Puebla became a battleground for numerous revolutionary factions, and Puebla City a prize for Venustiano Carranza, Emiliano Zapata, and Pancho Villa. Although the partisans of Zapata gained a significant following and were active in Puebla until 1919, the tide was in favor of Carranza, who gained control of the state in 1915 and whose representatives held it until Carranza's own demise in 1920.

During the period of Carranza's control, a handful of governors, including Francisco Coss, Cesáreo Castro, and Alfonso Cabrera enacted limited agrarian reform while contending with the Zapatista threat and the state's restive workers. The 1920s and 1930s brought more significant gains for workers and peasants, particularly under Leonides Andrew Almazán, who organized workers and distributed nearly 210,000 hectares of land. From 1937 to 1941, Puebla was governed by

Maximino Ávila Camacho, whose brother Manuel became Mexico's president in 1940. Ávila Camacho focused on bringing stability to the state, and he worked with the national government to co-opt workers and peasants. He also smoothed relations with the Roman Catholic Church, which had come under attack during the revolutionary period. Finally, the governor worked closely with businessmen to promote Puebla's economic recovery and development.

Puebla achieved a degree of political stability by the 1940s (though the University of Puebla became a site of student unrest in the 1960s and 1970s), but it struggled to maintain a viable economy in the latter decades of the 20th century. As population increased and the economy stagnated, many chose to migrate to Mexico City and the United States. Beginning in the 1960s, the state and federal governments sought to bolster Puebla's economy by investing in the construction of industrial parks. Several new industries established themselves in the vicinity of the capital, including the Volkswagen automobile company and the Mexican steel manufacturer Hlysa. Industrial growth encouraged migration to the cities and helped transform Puebla into a highly urbanized state. Meanwhile, the Puebla countryside benefited from the Plan Puebla (announced in 1967), which brought a Green Revolution to the rural sector.

By the end of the 20th century, Puebla had managed to create a highly diversified economy. It had also maintained its reputation as a tourist attraction, and visitors were especially drawn to the pre-Columbian pyramid of Cholula and the historic center of Puebla City (which was jolted by a major earthquake in 1999). However, the economic gains were insufficient to stem the tide of out-migration, a sign that the state has been unable to generate the jobs and mobility necessary for a large portion of its population. Politically, the Partido Acción Nacional (National Action Party, PAN) has emerged as a strong opponent to the long-dominant Partido Revolucionario Institucional (Institutional Revolutionary Party, PRI). Nonetheless, a PRI candidate won the gubernatorial race in 2006, but his political blunders during his term cost his party dearly. In the 2010 elections, a PAN-led coalition, with support from the PRD and other splinter parties, was able to wrest away the governorship from the PRI. Furthermore, the unpopularity of the PRI governor also took a local toll, as the party's representation in the state legislature fell from 25 seats in 2007 to 18 following the 2010 electoral round. Meanwhile, the opposition garnered 21 seats, and the PRI also lost ground in mayoral contests, from 137 mayorships in 2004 to 106 after the 2010 elections. Still, the PRI holds most of the congressional seats from the state, and it is likely that the party's weak showing in 2010 had much to do with the PRI's gubernatorial stewardship in the previous term. The 2012 presidential election results will clarify whether the 2010 vote in Puebla represented a temporary setback for the PRI or whether it was in fact an indication of the PRI losing substantive support among the electorate of Puebla.

Suzanne B. Pasztor

See also Agriculture; Immigration and Emigration; Partido Revolucionario Institucional; Politics and Political Parties; Tourism

Further Reading

Furlong y Zacaula, Aurora, ed. 2010. *Crisis economica y desequilibrios sociales.* Puebla: Benemerita Universidad Autonoma de Puebla.

LaFrance, David G. 1989. *The Mexican Revolution in Puebla, 1908–1913: The Maderista Movement and the Failure of Liberal Reform.* Wilmington, DE: Scholarly Resources Books.

Lomelí Vanegas, Leonard. 2001. *Breve historia de Puebla.* México, DF: El Colegio de México.

Puebla Official State Website. http://www.puebla.gob.mx.

Smith, Robert. 2005. *Mexican New York: Transnational Lives of New Immigrants.* Berkeley: University of California Press.

Q

Querétaro

The official coat of arms of Querétaro. (Corel)

The state of Querétaro is one of the principal gateways to the most important city of the country, Mexico City, and into the valley in which the sprawling metropolis is located. Since colonial times, Querétaro has been a means of entry and exit from the center of the country and functions as a crossroads for the central and northeastern parts of Mexico. To this day, the main commercial artery northward from the central valley of Mexico—the Pan American Highway—traverses the state of Querétaro and its capital, Santiago de Querétaro (generally referred to as simply Querétaro). As a consequence, the state has had a historic and strategic role in the major conflicts of the country and remains a key state in the political economic panorama of Mexico.

The state of Querétaro is surrounded by various states: San Luis Potosí to the north; Michoacán and México to the southwest and southeast, respectively; Guanajuato to the west; and Hidalgo to the east. The topography of the state is marked by mountains and valleys, leading to several different microclimates. Querétaro is a small state, ranked 27th in size and 23rd in terms of the number of its residents, but it is among the most densely populated in the country. Thus, it holds an importance that far outweighs the dimensions of its territory or its census figures.

The economy of the state is anchored by its manufacturing sector, which employs about a fifth of the labor force. The state has attracted an inordinate amount of foreign investment since the 1990s, not only to the establishment of assembly plants (maquiladoras), but also to large-scale industry, such as the making of airplanes and machinery. Compared to other states, Querétaro boasts a high proportion of educated workers and professionals, which has attracted industrial investors as well as employers. The state's temperate climate, transportation facilities, and diverse attractions have added to its ability to draw interest from companies seeking to expand or begin production sites. As of 2009, nearly 200 plants were operating in the state, with over 40,000 employees.

The robust industrial sector of the economy has also been coupled with a dynamic services sector, generated to a great extent by Querétaro's function as a transportation hub for commercial traffic going both east-west as well as north-south. The latter connection became even more important with the North American

Historic Los Arcos aqueducts of the colonial city of Querétaro, Mexico. (Bryan Busovicki | Dreamstime.com)

Free Trade Agreement (NAFTA) in 1994, as Querétaro became a crucial trade link that takes goods from Mexico to the main entry point to the United States (and Canada) at Laredo, Texas; the route also passes through two key cities of economic importance, San Luis Potosí and Monterrey, Nuevo León. Similarly, imports from the United States and Canada often make their way south via Querétaro. Despite its economic advantages due to its location along this major commercial corridor, Querétaro is also therefore sensitive to the business cycles of the United States. As result, the economic recession of 2008–2011 in the United States slowed substantially the growth of the state, which had been among the highest during the four-year period before the financial crisis of its North American neighbor. The recovery of the American economy is of profound significance for the continuing prosperity of Querétaro.

The state attracts a substantial amount of tourism, particularly as a result of domestic travelers, which has also contributed to the state's services sector. A comfortable three-hour or so drive to the teeming metropolitan urban center of the country, Querétaro draws visitors for weekend excursions for those interested in hiking, biking, cultural tourism, or simply relaxation from the intense urban lifestyle of Mexico City and its environs. The state possesses three World Heritage sites, including the capital city's historic center, renowned for its colonial architecture; and there is also a recognized biosphere in a section of the state's Sierra Gorda mountain range.

Given its economic structure, the state of Querétaro has among the lowest indicators of poverty in the country. The prominence of a large middle sector and a relatively low level of unemployment lessens the overall numbers of low-income residents of the state. The poverty that does exist in the state disproportionately involves rural communities and the relatively small number of indigenous peoples in the state. Rates of immigration from the state are low in comparison with other states.

Society in Querétaro is characterized by a vibrant, comparatively well-educated, and energetic middle class, a large segment of small to medium-size businesses, and an entrepreneurial spirit that is complemented by a significant number of affluent professionals. Unlike several other Mexican states, Querétaro possesses a small agricultural sector, making for a highly urbanized social life. The state has numerous educational facilities, both academic and vocational, that contribute to the distinctive social character of Querétaro.

The social profile of the state has led to the strength of the right-of-center PAN. Particularly since the 1990s, politics in Querétaro has meant a battle between a surging PAN and the aging, formerly dominant party, the PRI. The left-of-center PRD has gained little traction in the state. The PRI won the gubernatorial election of 2006, but PAN has held most of the congressional and senate seats since the 2009 electoral campaign. The slide in the popularity of PAN since 2006 has had less of an effect in Querétaro, but the PRI has made inroads into the strength of its conservative rivals. Political corruption is considered to be low, as the state's business leaders, combined with its sizable middle class, have inhibited the level of corruption that plagues several other states in Mexico.

Given the power of PAN in the state, it is considered a barometer of the capacity of the right-of-center party to maintain its support in the face of sagging poll numbers, an economic downturn, and the seemingly ineffective efforts by President Felipe Calderón (2006–2012) against drug-related violence. Thus, the election of a PRI governor in 2009 in Querétaro casts a cloud over PAN's prospects for the 2012 presidential contest; the winning margin for the PRI candidate in the gubernatorial race (49 percent versus 43 percent) suggests that the declining stature of President Calderón's administration is having a negative impact on PAN. Given the divisiveness within the national party structure of the left-leaning PRD, the PRI appears to have made major gains in Querétaro at the expense of its political competition, especially against its most potent adversary, PAN.

The sensitivity of Querétaro to its economic ties to the United States exercises much influence for the political economy of the state, with apparent social implications. The results of the presidential elections of 2012 therefore hold decisive meanings for Mexico, none more important perhaps than for the state of Querétaro.

Alex M. Saragoza

See also Foreign Trade; Maquiladoras; North American Free Trade Agreement; Politics and Political Parties; Transportation

Further Reading

Carillo Pacheco, Marco Antonio. 2007. *La industria maquiladora de exportacion en Querétaro.* El Cotidiano, 22 (142), 32–39.

Federal Reserve Bank of Dallas, El Paso Branch. 2007. *Mexico Regulatory Change Redefines Maquiladora.* Dallas: Federal Reserve Bank of Dallas.

Henio Millan, Martagloria. 2010. *Cambio politico y democratico en Mexico.* Mexico City: Miguel Angel Porrua.

Querétaro Official State Website. http://www.Querétaro.gob.mx.

Serna Martinez, Alfonso. 2009. *Campo, ciudad y region en Queretaro, 1960–2000.* Mexico City: Plaza y Valdes.

Quintana Roo

The official coat of arms of Quintana Roo. (Corel)

The state of Quintana Roo faces the Caribbean Sea on the eastern side of the Yucatán Peninsula. On the mainland side, Quintana Roo is bordered by two Mexican states, to the north and northwest by Yucatán and Campeche, respectively. At its southern tip, a very small strip of Quintana Roo borders the country of Belize.

The climate of Quintana Roo is temperate most of the year. Like the rest of the peninsula, its land surface is largely composed of limestone with a thin layer of top soil, making intensive agricultural production difficult. Much of the state is covered by different flora with corresponding differences in fauna. Tropical forests (jungles), savannas, and mangrove forests compose the principal ecosystems, along with that of the long coastline of the state. Much of the coast of Quintana Roo is lined by white sand beaches, coral reefs, and lagoons, which have made the coastal strip of the state a major tourist destination. Due to its location facing the Caribbean, the state is subject to ferocious, destructive hurricanes and periods of intense rainfall. The state is home to the renowned Sian Ka'an Biosphere, among others, and interesting marine attractions, such as the underwater caves of Xel-ha, as well as archaeological wonders, such as Xcaret and Tulum. However, as a consequence of massive tourist development, the state has suffered much habitat loss, marine environmental damage, and degradation of the ecology of coastal areas.

Quintana Roo is basically divided into four geographic areas. The best known is the zone dominated by the hugely successful tourist complex of Cancún at the northern end of the state. The second zone of importance is in the southernmost part of the state, which is the site of the capital of Quintana Roo, Chetumal. The coastal strip in between Chetumal and Cancún comprises a third area, which has emerged as a distinct tourist destination, the so-called Maya Riviera. The interior of the narrow state represents the fourth section of the state; it is very sparsely populated, dotted with small settlements that are largely composed of the Mayan-speaking indigenous peoples of the state. In terms of land surface, Quintana Roo ranks 19th, but in spite of a sizable influx of newcomers since the 1970s, the population of the state still ranks only 26th in the nation.

Quintana Roo has a substantial indigenous population, composed of different Mayan-speaking subgroups. It is estimated that about a fourth of the state's population is of Mayan origin. Approximately 60 percent of the Mayan-speaking population is located in the central rural region of the state. A large portion of the Mayan-speaking population has moved to the resort areas of the state to seek employment. Due to poor schooling, most of them are employed in low-wage jobs as gardeners, kitchen help, handymen, restaurant servers, hotel maids, and similar occupations related to the services sector. Some of the Mayan peoples are essentially labor migrants, as they move back and forth between their villages and jobs related to the tourist sector; many others have settled permanently in the resort areas of the state, but usually in the poor neighborhoods on the outskirts of Cancún, for example, given their low-income status. The more urbanized Mayan peoples are commonly bilingual, while those who remain primarily in their rural hometowns are much less fluent in Spanish.

Since the 1970s, population growth in the state has surged due to in-migration as a consequence of the tourist boom initially stimulated by the building of the Cancún resort area. This influx of relatively well-educated migrants has provided the state with an expanding middle class and high-income earners, most of them tied to the tourist industry, and to a lesser extent, to government service. In this regard, the distribution of the population is essentially concentrated in two locations. About half of the state's population of 1.5 million resides in the metropolitan zone of Cancún, while Chetumal holds about a third of the population; the emergence of the Maya Riviera tourist zone in the 1990s has led to rapid social change in that area, especially in the vicinity of Playa del Carmen. As a result, Quintana Roo is highly stratified, with most of the Mayan-origin population marginalized both socially and economically. The middle and upper classes are most likely to be from in-migrant backgrounds, while the poor in the state are usually of Mayan origin or are native to the state.

The economy of Quintana Roo is overwhelmingly tied to tourism directly and indirectly. Some estimate that tourism represents nearly 90 percent of the gross domestic product (GDP) of the state. More importantly, since the 1990s, Cancún is the most lucrative of the tourist sites not only in the state but for the entire country. Cancún's tourist activities consistently account for over 20 percent of all revenues (and at times much more) produced by the Mexican tourist industry as a whole. Indeed, the construction and subsequent development of Cancún represented a

An aerial view of the resorts and beaches of Cancún, Quintana Roo, Mexico. (Atanas Bozhikov | Dreamstime.com)

transformative event in the history of Quintana Roo and within the framework of tourism in Mexico.

There are other economic activities in the state, such as forestry (the commercial exploitation of stands of mahogany and cedar wood) and some rubber production. But there is no question of the economic basis of Quintana Roo. The food processing industry and commercial fisheries in the state, for instance, are primarily oriented toward the markets generated by tourism. Similarly, the transportation and commerce of the state is tied essentially to meeting the needs of the tourist industry in one way or another. Tourism absorbs the vast majority of the labor force of the state. The city of Chetumal is the major exception, as the government holds the majority of employees in the capital city, yet even in the governmental sector, the revenue produced by the tourist economy funds most of the state's budget. Cancún's dominant role as a beachside resort complex reflects the general trends and problematic issues raised by the multiple types of tourism in Mexico and their implications.

With the enormous success of Cancún as its base since the 1970s, tourism in Quintana Roo has gone through different stages and types of development. These shifts have encompassed distinct segments of the travel market, from those who are drawn to very exclusive and expensive boutique hotels to youthful spring break visitors, who generally avoid high-end lodging or restaurants. Cultural tourism also became part of the tourist repertoire of Cancún, when tour operators began to offer trips to the archaeological sites near Cancún, notably Tulum and Chichén Itzá (the latter is actually located in the neighboring state of Yucatán). And, particularly since the late 1980s, Cancún has become an important site for Mexican domestic travelers, who compose another segment of the tourist market. (Domestic tourism generates about 75 percent of tourist revenues in the country, although Cancún attracts a much larger proportion of international visitors than most other tourist sites in Mexico.) Furthermore, in a bid to diversify its tourist attractions, Cancún's developers have also attempted to make the area more family friendly by offering a wider spectrum of activities, from jet skis and banana boats to theme parks, among other forms of family entertainment. By the first decade of the new century, Cancún was characterized by a jumble of types of tourism and touristic activities that held both benefits and liabilities for the long-term prospects for Cancún as a premier tourist site.

The initial impetus for the government's building of Cancún in the mid-1970s intended to attract high-budget international tourists whose interests were basically related to the beach tourism historically associated with the Caribbean. The original effort to make Cancún an exclusive resort area was a spectacular success. By the early 1980s, Cancún had become a highly visible and popular tourist site, studded with lavishly landscaped five-star hotels, designer golf courses, and chic restaurants. The rapid and huge influx of visitors into Cancún also contributed to the tourist development of the small island off the coast, Cozumel, which later spread to the tiny Isla Mujeres. The meteoric success of Cancún also meant a rush to take advantage of its phenomenal tourist attraction, but due to inept planning, corruption, and neoliberal policies, the original tourist focus of Cancún became blurred.

By 2000, the high-budget tourism began to move decidedly southward to a series of luxury hotels, such as those in the Playacar development, next to the seaport town of Playa del Carmen. That move provided competition to the original high-end hotels of Cancún. Soon, more hotels appeared south of Playa del Carmen that tended toward the very expensive end of the scale. Eventually, the tourist strip south of Playa del Carmen took on a distinct identity when it was officially described as the Maya Riviera and tour operators began to distinguish it from Cancún. Although Cancún receives the greatest number of visitors, the Maya Riviera for the moment has maintained its exclusive aura, allowing Cancún to be a destination for all types of tourist budgets.

In the attempt to be all things to all tourists, contemporary tourism in Cancún encompasses everything from inexpensive packages with low-cost lodging and a host of time share–type condominium complexes, as well as several of the original upscale brand hotels. Thus, the tourist industry in the state faces a fundamental decision: whether to permit Cancún to expand without much if any restriction, or whether to curb the growth of the resort in a particular direction for the future. Until the early 1990s, tourist planning was firmly in the hands of the federal government, which set policies and goals. Since then, the privatization of tourist development has led to less governmental oversight and management of projects, which has tended to worsen certain problems, such as runaway projects that often take years to finish, and lack of sufficient infrastructure, such as sanitation capacity; violations of environmental regulations and building codes; and high vacancy rates for periods of time due to overbuilding of hotel stock combined with the ups and downs of the travel market. For the coffers of the economy of Quintana Roo, however, the shifts in the structure of tourism in the state have seemed to be of secondary concern. For example, infrastructure for sanitation and waste management has lagged behind the accelerated growth of hotels, condominiums, golf courses, marinas, and hotel services. There is also clear evidence of the degradation of the coral reefs that parallel the coastline of Quintana Roo due to a number of tourist-related activities as well as the result of inadequate planning for the disposal of waste, rain run-off, and water treatment processes. In the poor neighborhoods away from the tourist hotel corridors, for instance, the continuing influx of labor migrants has led to persistent strains on the ability of governmental agencies to control the illegal building of shanty encampments without access to proper sewage facilities. Thus, the demographic consequences of the tourist industry have raised a number of questions for the future of the fundamental foundation of the state's economy.

Quintana Roo was very sparsely populated at the onset of the Cancún boom in the mid-1970s. In fact, thousands of workers had to be brought in to build the original resort complex. The quick development of Cancún subsequently led to an in-migration of workers for the tourism-driven services sector, and also the unprecedented arrival of professionals, from engineers and architects to hotel managers and airport management personnel. The expansion of tourism also prompted the expansion of midlevel employees, such as executive assistants, hotel management staff, executive chefs, landscape architects, and the like. And there was a corresponding increase in the number of governmental employees, from well-paid agency heads to midlevel managers. As a result of this influx of middle- to upper-income labor migrants, the visibility of poverty among the working classes has been minimized by the aggregated figures for the state's labor force. Hence, in 2010 the Human Development Index (an indicator of socioeconomic conditions used by the United Nations) for Quintana Roo ranks among the top 10 in Mexico. However, economic disparities in the state are much more severe than suggested by the HDI.

The political stakes in Quintana Roo are extremely important, given the monies generated by the tourist industry. Since the onset of the tourist boom, the state government has been in the firm grasp of the Partido Revolucionario Institucional (Institutional Revolutionary Party, PRI). Although the party lost much of its power nationally by the late 1990s, in Quintana Roo the PRI has maintained its control of the state's local and state governments. As of 2010, the governorship remains in the hands of the resurgent PRI. Congressional representation is split among the PRI (two seats); the conservative PAN and the Partido Verde Ecologista de México (Mexican Ecologist Green Party, PVEM) have one seat each. It is generally believed that the PRI apparatus in the state uses tourist-generated monies for its system of patronage to various constituencies, and allegations of corruption have long been associated with the relationship between the state's PRI organization and the tourist industry. The strength of the PRI in the state has led to talks of an alliance between the left-leaning PRD and the conservative PAN party, as has taken place elsewhere in Mexico during the 2010 midterm elections; in response, the PRI has forged a pact with the Green Party organization, which has its main base of support in Cancún; the PRI won the gubernatorial race in 2010 against a PAN-led coalition that included the PRD.

The taint of political corruption remains on the PRI, however, and the party's alleged tacit collaboration with the illegal drug trade has served to sustain the unsavory image of the PRI in Quintana Roo. It has been alleged, for example, that the development of the Maya Riviera was to a large extent funded by the drug cartels, particularly when Mexican crime organizations began to take over the trade from the Colombian drug lords in the 1990s. Moreover, the allegations suggest that the marinas on the Maya Riviera, for instance, facilitate the entry of illegal drugs, such as cocaine from South America, on speedboats launched from larger vessels off the Yucatán coast. Regardless of the veracity of such claims, the PRI has been unable to shed entirely its corrupt image from the past. Furthermore, the persistence of violations of environmental regulations by tourist developments, for instance, leads to the perception that the government's lax oversight is due to bribery or similar methods orchestrated by PRI operatives within the state's regulatory agencies. The enormous revenues generated by the tourist industry make Quintana Roo a valuable political asset, and partisan frictions over the control of state government will constitute a major question for the future. On the other hand, the PRI has increased its electoral showing, such as in gubernatorial elections, from 41 percent of the vote in 2004 to nearly 53 percent in the 2010 electoral contest. In this regard the dismal polls for President Felipe Calderón (2006–2012) of PAN have been a detriment to his party's capacity to regain its strength in Quintana Roo.

The social and cultural life of the state reflects its economic geography and social stratification. The upscale hotels, restaurants, shopping malls, beach clubs, golf courses, and discos of the tourist zones represent one aspect, while the working classes participate in another world of entertainment and diversion. The rural, mostly indigenous population represents yet another dimension of the culture of the state. The middle classes, concentrated in Chetumal and Cancún, lie in between these social extremes. Cancún and Chetumal contain virtually all of the state's formal cultural amenities, such as theaters, museums, art galleries. In contrast, the lifestyle of the Mayan indigenous population, largely living in the countryside of the central region of the state, incorporates tradition along with modern elements, e.g., televisions, cell phones, and CD players. The relatively isolated, remote village life of the Maya of Quintana Roo, however, has also led to out-migration, particularly among youth, who seek relatively better incomes and an alternative social life. Elementary schools are generally poor in the interior, and better middle schools are clustered in the two main cities of the state; children in rural areas often have to rely on televised long-distance learning programs. Higher educational opportunities are limited, with the small number of institutions concentrated in Chetumal; the state public university, the Universidad Autónoma de Quintana Roo, has its main campus in Chetumal, but maintains a satellite center in Cancún.

The future of Quintana Roo hinges almost entirely on its tourist industry. For the near term, with Cancún and the Maya Riviera leading the way, the state will likely continue to enjoy its top spot in the revenues produced by both domestic and international travel in Mexico. Yet a number of troubling questions cast a shadow over the long-term prospects for Quintana Roo as Mexico's most important tourist destination. The resolution of those questions, such as those regarding unchecked tourist development, will invite partisan battles involving the captains of the travel industry, government, and the representatives of the major parties in the state.

Alex M. Saragoza

See also Archaeological Sites; Environment; Environmental Issues; Indigenous Peoples; Politics and Political Parties; Tourism; Yucatán

Further Reading

Castellanos, Maria Benet. 2010. *A Return to Servitude: Maya Migration and the Tourist Trade in Cancun*. Minneapolis: University of Minnesota Press.

Laguna Coral, Manuela. 2009. *Las desigualdades territoriales y el desarrollo del estado de Quintana Roo*. Mexico City: Plaza y Valdes.

Quintana Roo Official State Website. http://www.quintanaroo.gob.mx.

Torres, Rebecca, and Janet Momsen. 2005. "Planned Tourism Development in Quintana Roo, Mexico: Engine for Regional Development or Prescription for Inequitable Growth?" *Current Issues in Tourism* (July): 259–285.

R

Racism

The equality of all Mexican citizens has been the official ideology and policy of Mexico since its independence from Spain in 1821. (Note: The principle of equality was for males only; women were not granted full suffrage until 1953.) This principle has been upheld in all of the constitutions written since that time, including the Constitution of 1917, the current basic charter of Mexico. This legal tradition was a response to the social structure that developed during 300 years of Spanish colonial rule and its consequences. Under Spain, a socio-racial hierarchy emerged, the so-called *casta* system (not be confused with the caste system of India and other countries).

The *casta* system purported to define the social status of individuals based on their racial/ethnic background. In part, this was an extension of the concept of *pureza/limpieza de sangre* (purity/cleanliness of blood) that attended the wave of religious intolerance following the reconquest of Spain by Christians over the Muslims. Christian zealots, spurred by the Catholic Church and its tribunals (the Inquisition), sought to identify those who had intermarried with Muslims or Jews during the long period of Islamic occupation of the Iberian Peninsula (from about 700 until 1492, when the last Muslim bastion of Granada fell to Christian forces). This attitude carried over into the New World and influenced the views of colonial officials and that of the Catholic Church and the Inquisition. Initially, the Spanish colonial social hierarchy had five basic groupings; at the top were those born in Spain (so-called *peninsulares*); second in standing were those of Spanish parents but born in the New World (called *criollos*); in a third position were those of mixed Spanish and Indian descent, called *mestizos*; fourth in rank were indigenous peoples; and last were slaves (that is, those of African descent).

High rates of sexual unions (forced and consensual) between Spanish men and indigenous women raised the question of whether the progeny of those unions (called mestizos) were legitimate, and therefore considered Spanish. The arrival of African slaves with the Spanish colonial effort further complicated social relations, as slaves could not be considered citizens. Yet, sexual unions among African slaves, Spaniards, criollos, and mestizos, and combinations thereof, quickly made for a racial/ethnic complexity that challenged notions of *pureza/limpieza de sangre* and the ability of priests—through their control of birth certificates—to define social standing. Moreover, various posts within the colonial bureaucracy were open only to those of appropriate social background; favoritism toward those born in

Spain, for instance, was common in employment of high-ranking colonial bureaucratic posts and even in the assignment of priests to parishes. In this sense, lineage held economic advantages. As a means of sustaining the social superiority of Spanish ancestry, the *casta* system arose, which was in effect a social classification scheme based on lineage with as many as 16 different categories (combinations of racial/ethnic backgrounds and their nomenclature). The classification system, however, became unsustainable, as priests found it impossible to verify the genealogy of children or parents; and corrupt priests often succumbed to falsifying birth certificates in order to elevate one's social status, for a price.

Unlike what took place generally in the North American British colonies, Spanish colonialism incorporated indigenous peoples through their conversion to Christianity; renouncing Indian religion and the acceptance of Catholicism made native peoples legally and socially acceptable as Spanish subjects, in theory. The missionary impulse of the Spanish colonial Catholic Church inhibited the idea of indigenous peoples as members of sovereign nations who could not be citizens, as was the case in the United States (which led ultimately to the American policy of Indian reservations). African slaves, however, were inadmissible as Spanish subjects. But in contrast to the United States, Spanish colonialism did not establish a one-drop rule, wherein any evidence of African blood made the person black and therefore socially unacceptable in a binary (black/white) racial hierarchy. Furthermore, there were no formal antimiscegenation laws, unlike the United States. Nonetheless, the prejudice embedded in the *casta* system persisted, particularly toward those at or near the bottom of the *castas* (those most likely to be primarily of Indian or African descent).

Over time, as the *casta* system broke down, color became increasingly important as a social marker, on the assumption that one's complexion denoted an Indian or African background, or some sort of combination involving the lowest rungs of the socio-racial colonial hierarchy. Because of the relatively small number of African slaves introduced into Mexico (and with the abolition of slavery in 1829), the development of a separate, distinguishable African-origin population essentially did not take place (although, to this day, there are vestiges of Afro-mestizos in a few places in Mexico, such as in the states of Veracruz and Guerrero). After independence, institutional legalized forms of segregation (separate but equal principle, or Jim Crowism) based on race failed to materialize, as opposed to what occurred in the United States, for example, especially in the South. Still, the bias based on color remained, despite the rhetoric of equality after independence; to be dark-complexioned was not a social asset in the new nation of Mexico.

The existence of large numbers of indigenous peoples postindependence therefore sustained the racialized distinctions inherited from the colonial past. This social view was abetted by the fact that the vast majority of the Indian population for much of the 19th century resided in countless small, remote villages, largely disconnected from mainstream Mexican society. As a result, through much of the 19th century, indigenous peoples were able to maintain to a great extent their customs, their way of attire, and their mode of life—that is, to be Indian—in contrast to the urbanized cultural orientation of modern Mexican society. Especially for the Mexican elite, the Indians of Mexico were perceived as a drag on the nation's progress.

In the late 19th century, the notion of Indians as backward and inferior was reinforced by the racial ideologies of that era, such as social Darwinism and the "science" of eugenics. The two concepts basically fused among the Mexican elite, who were already predisposed to the notion that Indians were essentially, if not genetically, inferior; that sense of indigenous inferiority was also common among the middle and even within the working classes of Mexico. Social vernacular associated with whiteness/darkness also remained commonplace, such as *blanca/morena, rubio/prieto, guera/tisnada,* and so forth. Thus, to have a light-complexioned child was commonly considered to be more desirable, as opposed to a child who was too dark or looked like an *indio* (Indian). Nonetheless, with the exception of anti-Chinese legislation at the turn of the 20th century, antimiscegenation laws failed to take hold in Mexico during the period when social Darwinistic thinking became a widely accepted idea among most of the upper and middle classes of Mexico. This prejudice led to economic discrimination against the dark-skinned; worse, the reach of the educational system rarely made its way to those parts of Mexico still densely populated by indigenous peoples, which served to reinforce the perception that Indians were inherently inferior.

The Mexican Revolution of 1910 led to the writing of a new Mexican constitution in 1917, where the principle of equality for all Mexican citizens was once again restated. But social practice told another story. Despite the celebration of Mexico's indigenous past as a foundational aspect of postrevolutionary nationalism, the treatment and attitudes toward Indians in everyday life too often mirrored the country's colonial social heritage and violated the spirit if not the letter of the Constitution. The policies of the postrevolutionary order were paradoxical. Clear strides were made in improving educational access for the urban and rural poor, including areas with substantial indigenous populations, yet these reformist efforts were at best uneven and incomplete. The social gaps between indigenous peoples and the rest of Mexico continued, and the color prejudices of the past proved resilient and tenacious, in spite of the official cultural ideology of the postrevolutionary order.

In this history of racialized bias, class position could and often did mitigate the negative consequences of being too dark; as was often intimated in popular vernacular, "money whitens." That is, affluence lessened the social stigma of being *prieto/a.* Yet the means to wealth were generally subject to the constraints of racial attitudes in Mexico. Unfortunately, the stigma associated with skin color was popularized still further by the rise of mass communications.

The development of the mass media in the early 20th century sustained the persistence of color prejudice in Mexico, where this view was translated into the emergence of stereotypes regarding Indians, and more generally the dark-complexioned. This biased imagery made its way into silent film, vaudeville, and later, radio, sound film, and eventually television. Thus, it became common practice for female models and leading actresses, for instance, to be fair-skinned, and rarely, if ever, dark-complexioned. In this sense, the prejudice was often one of omission, or slighting of the dark-skinned. For example, it was common in Mexican films from the 1930s onward for the maids to be dark-skinned—rarely blondes—but the main star to be light-complexioned or white. Similarly, commercial advertisements rarely pictured dark women or men; and this biased imagery invariably would be repeated with the advent of television. Thus, while official policy touted the accomplishments of the country's indigenous past—as found in government-made posters promoting tourism—social bias against the dark-complexioned generally, and Indians more specifically, continued.

Mexico, it should be noted, avoided the ravages of institutional racism that were found in the United States, that is, the legalized practice of separate but equal. Yet Mexico rarely confronted the question of social prejudice toward dark-skinned Mexicans. One exception would be the film *Angelitos negros* (Little Black Angels, 1948), whose narrative acknowledged the African-origin remnants among Mexico's population specifically, but more importantly, the racism faced by the dark-skinned. The film was made more exceptional by the fact that one of the country's most popular stars—Pedro Infante—played the role of protector and defender of the black child born to a white mother, whose ancestry evidently included a relative of African or partial African origin.

The 500th anniversary in 1992 of the encounter between the Americas and the Old World—Columbus's "discovery" of the hemisphere—led to a heightening of a simmering debate over the meaning of Mexican national identity. Leading toward the recognition of Columbus's first voyage, two works published in 1987, one by Guillermo Bonfil Batalla, the other by Roger Bartra, raised a question that had been periodically a matter of intellectual discussion in Mexico since the early 20th century: What does it mean to be Mexican? By extension, the two books raised the issue of racial/ethnic differences in Mexico and their implications for any notion of Mexican national identity. In terms of social practice and popular culture, however, the debate failed to produce any remedial measures to lessen the obvious: the persistence of the social bias against those considered too dark.

As if to confirm the neglect of race as a social issue in Mexico, the official celebration of the Columbian anniversary led to a governmental program acknowledging the third root (*tercera raíz*) of Mexican identity: one indigenous, another European, and third, the African. Nonetheless, in film, in advertisements, in television programming, and in other ways, the bias of the past continues to exercise its influence in Mexican society.

Alex M. Saragoza

See also Chiapas; Ejército Zapatista de Liberación Nacional and the Indigenous Movement; Government; Indigenous Peoples; Nationalism and National Identity; Oaxaca; Peasantry; Popular Culture; Social Structures, Class, and Ethnic Relations; Yucatán

Further Reading

Bonfil Batalla, Guillermo. 1996. *Mexico Profundo: Reclaiming a Civilization.* Austin: University of Texas Press.

Urias Horcasitas, Beatriz. 2007. *Historias secretas del racismo en Mexico, 1920–1950.* Mexico City: Tusquets Editores.

Religion

Since the onset of Spanish colonialism in the 16th century, Catholicism has dominated religious practices in Mexico. The Census of 2010 found that about 87 percent of Mexicans consider themselves Catholics. Although various indigenous forms of religious expression persist, they are usually subsumed into Catholic rituals and ceremonies. As a consequence, in many parts of Mexico, religious practices possess syncretic forms, that is, a fusion of Catholic and indigenous customs. A telling example of Catholic syncretism is the observance of the Catholic Church's All Soul's Day, which in various parts of the country has incorporated pre-Columbian beliefs and rituals and has become known as Día de los Muertos (Day of the Dead, which corresponds to Halloween in the United States). In order to facilitate their evangelical efforts, Spanish missionaries early on understood the need to incorporate indigenous religious concepts and ceremonies into their teaching of Christianity. This process of proselytization produced what has often been referred to as folk Catholicism, which is especially apparent in rural areas with marked concentrations of Indian peoples. In general, this type of Catholicism is most evident in southern and central Mexico, but its vestiges can be found in other parts of Mexico as well. By far, the most dramatic and enduring example of Catholic syncretism is the veneration of the Virgin of Guadalupe, the patron saint of Mexico.

Catholicism was the official religion of Mexico until the Constitution of 1857 established the legal separation of church and state and the principle of religious freedom. In practice, the Catholic Church retained much of its secular influence, including its domination of the educational system. After the Mexican Revolution of 1910, the Constitution of 1917 reaffirmed the concept of the separation of church and state, but in effect, much of the social and cultural influence of the Catholic Church continued, albeit in violation of Mexican federal law. The attempt of the government to enforce the Mexican Constitution's mandates regarding the church led to an armed rebellion from 1926 to 1929—the so-called Cristero Rebellion—which acquired this term because the defenders of the Church would often shout "Que viva cristo rey" (Long live Christ the King) during the fighting with federal troops. A tacit accord eventually was reached between the Mexican federal government and the Catholic Church hierarchy, and the tensions between the state and the Catholic Church subsided after the 1930s.

A typical rendition of The Virgin of Guadalupe. Also known as Our Lady of Guadalupe, the image is based on a vision experienced by a Mexican Indian in 1531. Though the vision was clearly the Catholic Virgin Mary, her features were Mexican, her attire indigenous, and she carried objects of Aztec significance. Depicted in many ways since then, she legitimized religious and social equality for Indians, and helped consolidate disparate Spanish and indigenous beliefs into one unifying cultural icon. (Courtesy of Linda Lane)

Non-Catholic religions have existed in Mexico in spite of the dominance of Catholicism, including Judaism, Protestantism, Buddhism, Islam, among others.

Judaism has a long history in Mexico, which began with the arrival of Jews who had converted to Catholicism (*conversos*) as a means of avoiding persecution and the Inquisition in Spain that began in the early 16th century. Once the *conversos* settled in Mexico, many of them secretly reverted to practicing Jewish religious customs, given the presence of the Inquisition in Mexico. Since then there have been occasional influxes of Jews into Mexico, such as following the pogroms of Eastern Europe in the 1880s, those who fled Turkey after the end of the Ottoman Empire, and the best known, the sizable group of Jewish refugees from Nazi Germany and Eastern Europe who entered in the 1930s. The Census of 2010 indicated that there are about 50,000 Jews in Mexico, the overwhelming majority of whom reside in Mexico City.

Mormons (that is, members of the Church of Jesus Christ of Latter-day Saints) began their missionary work in Mexico in the 1870s and the first Mormon immigrants arrived in the country in 1885. According to the Mexican Census of 2010, over 200,000 people attend Mormon services regularly; Mormon officials claim that there are more than 1 million Mormons in Mexico.

Mennonites represent an early and distinct religious community in Mexico, presently numbering about 80,000, almost all of them located in the northern states of Chihuahua and Durango. Their migration to Mexico dates from the early 1920s, when President Álvaro Obregón provided the Mennonites with incentives of various sorts to settle in northern Mexico (among the reasons why he wanted to attract the Mennonites to Mexico was their cheese-making fame). Most Mennonites in Mexico continue to live in the north, principally in Chihuahua, though there has been some out-migration due to the drug-trade-related violence that has taken place in the state since 2004.

Beginning in the 1970s, Pentecostal Protestant groups began to emerge in growing numbers in Mexico. As of 2010, Protestants compose about 9 percent of the Mexican population, where the major sects include Jehovah's Witnesses and Seventh Day Adventists, but other groups also exist, such as Assembly of God congregations. The proliferation of these non-Catholic evangelical sects has also led to the construction of buildings for their religious observances. As a result, there are nearly 4,000 Protestant-based churches in Mexico—more than Catholic houses of worship (around 3,200).

Despite the historic association between indigenous groups with Catholicism in Mexico, Protestant groups—especially Pentecostal sects—have made the greatest inroads in those areas with large numbers of indigenous populations, particularly in the southern tier of the country. Scholars of religion offer various explanations for the surge in non-Catholic sects in Mexico, particularly in indigenous-populated areas of the country. Some experts argue that the psychological toll of modernization explains the turn against Catholicism, as Protestant groups offer an alternative to traditional ways in the face of secularizing, modernizing influences. On the other hand, some anthropologists suggest that indigenous peoples are drawn to evangelical, charismatic styles of worship because it resonates with their religious beliefs and forms of expression. Still other social scientists point to the impact of the market economy on traditional religious customs. For example, in many indigenous-based communities, the traditional system of the rich sharing their wealth with community members as a religiously sanctioned custom (called the *cargo* system) has waned. As a result, Protestantism offers a way to both hold onto wealth and to practice religion. Yet other scholars emphasize the loss of credibility of Catholicism because of its long-standing association with conservative, elite, political and economic groups in rural areas, pushing many people toward Protestant sects. More recently, Protestant sects have also spread into urban centers, nourished by the influx of migrants from the countryside where Protestant groups have established an influence.

According to the 2010 census, there are approximately a million members of the Jehovah's Witnesses in Mexico, and about half a million Seventh-day Adventists. The states with the highest percentage of Protestants (between 18 percent and 22 percent) are Chiapas, Tabasco, Campeche, and Quintana Roo, all of which are in southern Mexico and possess sizable numbers of indigenous peoples. Recent studies indicate a slowing of the growth of Protestant-based groups in Mexico, as early converts become older and the younger generation becomes more secularized.

There are very few Muslims (about 200,000), Orthodox Christians (around 25,000), and Buddhists (approximately 100,000) in Mexico. The Muslim population in Mexico is derived primarily from immigrants from Syria, Palestine, and Lebanon due to historical events, such as the Lebanon war of 1948, when thousands of Lebanese fled to Mexico as refugees.

While non-Catholic religious groups have grown in number, particularly Protestant sects, Catholicism continues to retain its grasp of the overwhelming majority of Mexicans who practice a religion. However, an increasing number of Mexicans do not believe in any type of religion, with 3 million claiming to be atheists in the 2010 census.

Anisha Hingorani

See also Catholicism

Further Reading

Cahan, Peter S. 2003. *All Religions Are Good in Tzintzuntzan: Evangelicals in Catholic Mexico.* Austin: University of Texas Press.

Camp, Roderic Ai. 1997. *Crossing Swords: Politics and Religion in Mexico.* New York: Oxford University Press.

Research

See Science and Research

Revolutionary Institutional Party

See Partido Revolucionario Institucional

S

Salinas de Gortari, Carlos

Carlos Salinas de Gortari, who served as the president of Mexico during 1988–1994, began his administration with a strong legitimacy problem, due to an accused electoral fraud in the 1988 election. During his term, major economic and political reforms were achieved, such as the incorporation of Mexico into the North American Free Trade Agreement (NAFTA); the privatization of financial institutions; the autonomy of the Central Bank; and the first steps in the opening of the electoral system. However, by the end of his term, the uprising of the Ejército Zapatista de Liberación Nacional (Zapatista Army for National Liberation, EZLN), the assassination of Partido Revolucionario Institucional (Institutional Revolutionary Party, PRI) candidate Luis Donaldo Colosio, and the explosion of the Mexican crisis in the first days of Ernesto Zedillo's administration undermined his political image and popularity. He was accused of stealing from the country and producing the economic crisis, and his family (his brother Raúl) was linked with millionaire corruption scandals and was under suspicion of an assassination.

Carlos Salinas was one of the last presidents under the 70-year PRI hegemony. After the 1970s' economic disasters, with irresponsible presidents, and into the 1980s, Mexico moved into a new generation in the history of the PRI, with presidents who were more aware of economic dynamics and modern policies. Their sympathy with neoliberal policies earned them the name of "technocrats." These presidents were Miguel de la Madrid, Carlos Salinas, and, the last of the PRI's hegemony presidents, Ernesto Zedillo.

Background and arrival to the presidency   The arrival of the technocrats and the lack of democratic practices in the party produced the split of left movements of the PRI by the late 1980s. Cuauhtémoc Cárdenas, PRI's dissident and son of President Lázaro Cárdenas (1936–1940), registered as an opposing candidate from a left-wing coalition called Frente Democrático Nacional (National Democratic Front). He soon became a popular figure and the first opposing candidate to seriously threaten the PRI. The Ministry of Interior, through its Federal Electoral Commission, was the institution in charge of the electoral process, and it installed a modern computing system to count the votes. However, the Minister of the Interior suspiciously declared a failure in the system the night of the election and later declared Carlos Salinas as the official winner, even though several national and international surveys showed Cárdenas as the winner. The social agitation could have been strong enough to collapse the political system, but Cárdenas finally accepted Salinas as president.

The Partido Acción Nacional (National Action Party, PAN) also condemned what they thought was electoral fraud and claimed itself victorious. Its candidate, Manuel Clouthier, started a symbolic alternative government, including a cabinet. His project came to an end with his unexpected death in a car accident. The accident was viewed with suspicion by many PAN supporters and international critics.

Salinas knew that he needed a strong empowerment act in order to gain legitimacy. After a few months of assuming the presidency, Salinas ordered the incarceration of Joaquín Hernández Galicia, alias the "Quina." He was the leader of the Petróleos Mexicanos (PEMEX) workers' union and popularly known for his corruption. This union was considered one of the biggest corporative structures of the PRI. Also, it was widely known that Quina was a friend of López Portillo and favored Cuauhtémoc Cárdenas's candidacy. The considerable unpopularity of Quina and what it implied in terms for breaking away from past presidents who supported corruption in PEMEX gave Salinas some needed popularity within his administration.

Economic policy Salinas continued with strong restrictive macroeconomic policies to stabilize the economic situation. By the end of his term, inflation had been reduced to 7.05 percent in 1994, the lowest figure in 22 years. However, because of unsustainable economic measures such as a strong credit deficit and uncontrollable balance of payments deficit and due to an overvalued peso, the economy collapsed a few weeks after the end of his term. Shortly after leaving office, the economic crash increased inflation to 51.48 percent. During his term, the peso depreciated nearly 70 percent. But by the last day of his term, the peso had depreciated far less than it had in the two previous terms. Nevertheless, Salinas managed to reduce the external debt from 45 percent of the gross domestic product to 22 percent.

The Salinas administration also continued the privatizations policy of his predecessor, Miguel de la Madrid. The corporative bureaucratic apparatus built during the "Mexican Miracle" era and its growth during the López Portillo administration were no longer sustainable in a state affected by a high public deficit. Salinas privatized large public agencies such as the telecommunications company, Teléfonos de México (Telmex).

Telmex was far from an efficient company. It was constantly being sued and receiving complaints due to its terrible service. Salinas sold Telmex in a public auction with the requirement that the main actionist should be Mexican. The company was sold to Carlos Slim, now a multimillionaire. At the beginning, Telmex received protection from the government as a monopolistic firm, which eventually transformed it into one of the strongest telecommunications firms in the world.

The other capital privatization that took place during the Salinas administration was the nationalization of financial institutions. Although the privatization started in the de la Madrid administration by selling 33 percent of stocks to private capital, the government still owned most of the social capital. The privatization was accomplished through constitutional reform to Articles 28 and 123 in 1990. Guillermo Ortiz, former minister of the treasury, was the main political operator of this maneuver. As in the case of Telmex, the privatization was done through public auctions.

Salinas also ended the agrarian policy of all Mexican governments since the Revolution. It used to be a legal right for every peasant to receive land if it was requested. Salinas stated that the current population number and the eroded land conditions made it impossible for the government to continue distribution. His declarations reached the core of the PRI's ideology and it generated a complicated debate. Nonetheless, the constitutional reforms needed to end the land division laws passed in 1991.

Salinas also began negotiations with the United States and Canada in 1990 to create a free trade agreement. By the end of his term in 1994, the North American Free Trade Agreement (NAFTA) had come into effect.

Social policy   Since the beginning of his term, Salinas ran a social program called *Solidaridad*. It consisted of achieving social justice through the focalized distribution of financial resources to marginalized families in Mexico. By the end of his term, $18 billion had been invested, of which 67 percent consisted of federal resources and the rest came from local governments and privates. Salinas created the Ministry of Social Development (Secretaría de Desarrollo Social, SEDESOL) for the management of all social programs. *Solidaridad* was criticized by many as another mechanism to obtain votes in elections. Despite that, the program has been continued by later administrations. Zedillo changed its name to *Progresa* ("Progress") and Fox changed it to *Oportunidades* ("Opportunities").

Foreign affairs   Besides NAFTA, Salinas maintained a relatively low international profile. As did Miguel de la Madrid, Salinas stayed away from Latin American affairs, and, generally speaking, from other major international events such as the fall of the USSR. However, an important change was implemented during his term. The Salinas administration restored the right to vote for the priests and the Vatican City sent a *nunciature* to Mexico.

Political reforms   During Salinas's term, Congress started a series of political reforms that ended in Zedillo's administration in order to generate an electoral system that was citizen controlled and independent of the Ministry of the Interior.

In the political reform of 1990, voter identification was introduced. The Federal Code for Electoral Institutions and Procedures, created in 1990, allowed the 1994 election to be the first election to have international observers.

EZLN, political instability, and economic crisis   The very first day of the enforcement of NAFTA (January 1, 1994), the beginning of the last year of the Salinas administration, the EZLN announced its takeover of the city of San Cristóbal de las Casas in the southern state of Chiapas. The rebellious army demanded social justice for a historical debt with the Mexican indigenous people and rejected NAFTA and the government market-oriented policies. Salinas sent the Mexican army to fight the Zapatistas for some days, but the international pressure in favor of the EZLN cause forced him to avoid the armed path and begin negotiations and dialogue with the insurrect groups. The EZLN insurrection brought public attention to the discontent of some social groups, such as the indigenous groups in Chiapas.

The political campaigns for the presidential election started with Luis Donaldo Colosio as the PRI's candidate. Despite his popularity, during a campaign stop in the city of Tijuana, Colosio was shot to death by Mario Aburto. However, it is still not known who ordered the assassination. Immediately after, the PRI named Ernesto Zedillo as the new candidate for the PRI. There were several suspects in Colosio's death, including President Salinas, because of the known differences he and Colosio held, particularly their vision of social and economic policy.

Notwithstanding the political instability of the first months of the year, Salinas still was more popular than he was at the beginning of his administration. The presidential election came, and Zedillo was named winner in a flawless vote.

In keeping with the PRI election-year tradition, Salinas launched a spending spree to finance popular projects (and thus obtain sympathy for his own party), which translated into a historically high deficit. This budget deficit was coupled with a current account deficit, fueled by excessive consumer spending due to the overvalued peso. In order to finance this deficit, the Salinas administration issued *tesobonos,* an attractive type of debt instrument that ensured payment in dollars instead of pesos. The unsustainable economic situation might also have been triggered by three important events that had shaken investor confidence in the stability of the country: the aforementioned Zapatista uprising, the assassination of Luis Donaldo Colosio, and the assassination of Francisco Ruiz Massieu, Salinas's former brother-in-law who was also the secretary general of the PRI and whose murder was never solved.

These events, together with the increasing current account deficit fostered by government spending, caused fear among Mexican and foreign *tesobono* investors, who sold the *tesobono* rapidly, thereby depleting the already low central bank reserves (which eventually hit a record low of $9 billion). The economically orthodox thing to do in order to maintain the fixed exchange rate functioning (at 3.3 pesos per dollar, within a variation band) would have been to sharply increase interest rates by allowing the monetary base to shrink, as dollars were being withdrawn from the reserves. But given the fact that it was an election year, which outcome might have changed as a result of a preelection-day economic downturn, the Central Bank decided to buy Mexican Treasury Securities in order to maintain the monetary base and thus prevent the interest rates from rising. This, in turn, caused an even more dramatic decline in the dollar reserves. These decisions aggravated the already delicate situation to a point where the crisis became inevitable and devaluation was only one of many necessary adjustments. Nonetheless, nothing was done during the last five months of Salinas's administration, even after the elections were held in July of that year. This was done in part to maintain Salinas's popularity, as he was seeking international support to become the head of the World Trade Organization.

When Zedillo took office, he announced the fixed rate range to increase 15 percent by stopping the unorthodox measures employed by the previous administration. This measure, however, was not enough, and even the government was unable to hold to this level and decided to let peso rates float. The devaluation measures made investors withdraw their investments immediately. The result was that the peso crashed under a floating regime from 4 pesos to the dollar (with the previous increase of 15 percent) to 7.2 pesos to the dollar in the span of one week.

Aftermath   After his presidential term, Salinas faced widespread criticism in Mexico. He was blamed for the collapse of the economy and the process of privatization of several government-run businesses (which had benefited a few of his friends). Moreover, he was blamed for allowing corruption, cronyism, and drug dealing. His unpopularity forced him to exile in Dublin, Ireland.

The rage grew after his brother Raúl went to jail, accused of masterminding the political assassination of Francisco Ruiz Massieu and of committing fraud while working for the government during Salinas's presidency. In 2004, Salinas's youngest brother, Enrique, was found dead inside his car.

Juan Manuel Galarza and José Ignacio Lanzagorta

See also Ejército Zapatista de Liberación Nacional and the Indigenous Movement; North American Free Trade Agreement; Partido Revolucionario Institucional; Zedillo Ponce de León, Ernesto

Further Reading

Centeno, Miguel. 1994. *Democracy within Reason: Mexico's Technocratic Revolution.* University Park: Pennsylvania State University Press.

Domínguez, Jorge I., ed. 1997. *Technopols: Freeing Politics and Markets in Latin America in the 1990s.* University Park: Pennsylvania State University Press.

Krauze, Enrique. 1997. *La presidencia imperial.* Mexico City: Tusquets.

San Luis Potosí

The official coat of arms of San Luis Potosí. (Corel)

The state of San Luis Potosí is located in central eastern Mexico and its capital city is the same name. Its central geographic location makes it a link between northern and southern Mexico, and it has served as a passage from the Gulf Coast to the interior. The population of the state according to the 2010 census was about 2.6 million people.

When the Spaniards arrived in the area, they encountered a variety of native peoples, including the Huastec and Chichimec groups. Particularly in the center and north, the Spaniards faced a long pacification campaign due to the resistance of the Chichimec tribes. That campaign lasted for most of the 16th century. The city of San Luis Potosí, which was located on the east side of the Sierra Madre Oriental, was officially established as a Spanish settlement in 1592, displacing native groups already settled there. The Spanish discovered mines in San Luis Potosí, and it soon became the hub of a rich silver region that also included Guanajuato, Querétaro, and Zacatecas. Mining helped make San Luis Potosí one of Mexico's wealthiest provinces during the colonial period. It also spurred the growth of cattle ranching and agriculture, and as a result, wealth became concentrated among the owners of the mines and haciendas. By the end of the colonial period, disputes over land and other resources were emerging, foreshadowing a problem that would persist into the 20th century.

Mexico's independence struggle did not bring significant destruction to San Luis Potosí. Although some who had been deprived of their lands during the colonial period joined the Miguel Hidalgo insurgency (which began in neighboring Guanajuato), their rebellion was quickly crushed with the help of wealthy mine owners and *hacendados* (hacienda owners). Once Mexico finally broke from Spain, the area achieved statehood. Despite the disruptions of the Mexican War of Independence, the city of San Luis Potosí maintained its position as an important economic center, and it served as an important link between central Mexico and the important port of Tampico, in the Gulf of Mexico.

Like many areas of Mexico, San Luis Potosí experienced impressive economic growth in the last three decades of the 19th century. Foreign investment, encouraged by the national policies of President Porfirio Díaz, spurred growth in mining, which came to be dominated by the American Smelting Company, owned by the Guggenheim family. At El Ébano, in the southeastern section of the state, foreign money helped initiate the exploitation of oil, adding a new and strategically important sector to its economy. Overseeing much of this economic boom and the accompanying growth of the state's infrastructure was Carlos Díez Gutiérrez, who governed with only one interruption from 1877 to 1898.

A square in downtown San Luis Potosí, Mexico. (Sunju1004 | Dreamstime.com)

By the early 20th century, the capital city was emerging as a center of liberal thought and opposition to the regime of Porfirio Díaz. Juan Sarabia, Camilo Arriaga, and Antonio Díaz Soto y Gama were among the prominent intellectuals who published opposition papers and organized a formal challenge to Mexico's dictatorial political system. In 1901, San Luis Potosí was the site of a national liberal convention that brought together opposition groups from other areas of Mexico. Arriaga, who hosted this convention, was arrested for his political activities and soon joined other exiles in San Antonio, Texas, in calling for the overthrow of Porfirio Díaz and the implementation of a program of significant social reform.

Not surprisingly, given these land and resource disputes, the growth of a viable workers' movement, and the efforts of intellectuals like Arriaga, San Luis Potosí was the center of a rebellion in 1910–1911 that finally deposed Porfirio Díaz. Miners, railroad workers, and landowners of modest means all joined the rebellion, as did native peoples and *campesinos* ("peasants"). This early phase of the Mexican Revolution of 1910 resulted in the emergence of an agrarian movement in southeastern San Luis Potosí. By 1912, Alberto Carrera Torres had emerged as a leader of this movement, along with the Cedillo brothers (Cleofas, Magdaleno, and Saturnino).

Beginning in 1919 and continuing through the 1920s, San Luis Potosí had two governors, both of whom focused on reforms that benefited workers and *campesinos*. Rafael Nieto and Aurelio Manrique encouraged the growth of the state's workers' movement, and they began the process of land reform. Nieto also distinguished himself by granting the vote to women in San Luis Potosí decades before national suffrage was granted to them. From 1927 to 1931, Saturnino Cedillo served a term as governor, continuing the distribution of land in his native state. Cedillo kept peace within his state, successfully muting the Cristero Rebellion of 1926–1929 and crushing other challenges to the postrevolutionary state. Cedillo also served two terms as Mexico's secretary of agriculture under presidents Pascual Ortiz Rubio and Lázaro Cárdenas. Ultimately, the Mexican government began to seek a political centralization that would not tolerate the kind of local autonomy that Cedillo represented. As a result, in 1938, Cárdenas, who was increasingly at odds with Cedillo, arrived in the capital of San Luis Potosí and ordered him to lay down his arms. Cedillo refused, and he began a rebellion that cost him his life. Thereafter, military generals governed the state, until 1943 when civilian Gonzálo N. Santos assumed the governorship.

Although the last decades of the 20th century were politically volatile, they were also characterized by economic growth and modernization. San Luis Potosí emerged as an important agricultural region, and during the 1970s and 1980s, the national government sponsored a large irrigation project that benefited the state's southeastern section. By the end of the 20th century, San Luis Potosí was exporting its agricultural goods, as well as its wood products. Like many Mexican states that practice intensive agriculture, San Luis Potosí has been forced to confront the negative consequences of this model of development, including erosion and deforestation. Steady growth in the population has contributed to the lack of sufficient jobs, in spite of the establishment of foreign-based assembly plants by General Motors and Cummins. As the new century dawned, many residents of San Luis Potosí were leaving Mexico for the United States, hoping for better economic opportunities. Nonetheless, the majority of the electorate of the state has maintained its allegiance to the old dominant party, the Partido Revolucionario Institucional (Institutional Revolutionary Party, PRI). In the gubernatorial contest of 2009, the PRI candidate won the race, an indication of the continuation of that party's strength in San Luis Potosí.

Suzanne B. Pasztor

See also Maquiladoras; North American Free Trade Agreement; Transportation

Further Reading

Ankerson, Dudley. 1984. *Agrarian Warlord: Saturnino Cedillo and the Mexican Revolution in San Luis Potosí.* DeKalb: Northern Illinois University Press.

Falcón, Romana. 1984. *Revolución y caciquismo: San Luis Potosí, 1910–1938.* Mexico City: El Colegio de Mexico,

Miasterrena Zubiran, Javier. 2007. *Mentira de progreso y democracia en el campo: Procesos de agroindustrializacion y poder en le municipio semiarido de Villa de Arista, S.L.P.* San Luis Potosi: El Colegio de San Luis.

Monroy, María Isabel, and Tomás Calvillo Una. 1997. *Breve historia de San Luis Potosí.* Mexico City: El Colegio de Mexico.

Rivera Gonzalez, Jose Guadalupe. 2010. *Globalizacion, procesos locales, territorios y cambio sociocultural en San Luis Potosi.* Mexico City: Miguel Angel Porrua.

San Luis Potosí Official State Website. http://www.slp.gob.mx.

Science and Research

Mexico possesses a long tradition of research in science and technology, going back to pre-Columbian times, when the Mayans and Aztecs, among other indigenous groups, formulated complex mathematical and astronomic concepts. This knowledge was also reflected in the architectural and engineering achievements of pre-Columbian societies. In contemporary Mexico, however, research in science and technology has been largely nourished by governmental resources. More than half of the total investment in scientific and technological research comes from public sources, although private industry, nonprofit organizations, foreign funds, and institutions of higher education also provide support for science-related activities. As a result, most researchers in these fields are found in small numbers at publicly funded institutions. Unfortunately, monies for such research remain relatively scarce, making it difficult for Mexican researchers to be at the forefront of scientific and technological advances.

Only one person of Mexican origin has been awarded a Nobel Prize in science, José Mario-Pasquel Molina-Henríquez, based on his pioneering work regarding the Antarctic ozone hole. Like most elite scientists in the country, Molina came from a wealthy family that afforded him an excellent education and the means for advanced training at foreign universities. Educated at the country's premier public university, Molina subsequently studied at the University of Freiburg and received his doctoral degree at the University of California, Berkeley, in 1972. His career path is similar to that of Mexico's leading scientists, who usually leave the country for their advanced studies and often find employment at foreign universities and/or research centers (or what scholars call "brain drain"). Superior salaries, state-of-the-art research facilities, and attractive working conditions frequently combine to lure the best scientists away from their native country, though there are always those who return to continue their careers in Mexico.

The Consejo Nacional de Ciencia y Tecnología (National Council of Science and Technology, CONACYT) is the primary institution responsible for the promotion of science and technology in the country, similar to the National Science Foundation in the United States. CONACYT, was created in 1970 by the federal government. The main objectives of the organization are: (1) to develop science and technology policy, (2) to increase the nation's scientific and technological capabilities, and (3) to conduct research that will have a positive impact on the society and economy of the country.

Generally speaking, Mexican students compete for the funds granted by CONACYT for postgraduate studies, commonly at foreign universities or research centers. Preference for such funding is given to students who are graduates from public universities; scholars from private educational institutions must usually seek support for their advanced research from foundations or fellowships from universities overseas.

CONACYT has oversight responsibility for public spending on science and technology activity; in recent years, expenditures for activities related to science have represented less than 1 percent of gross domestic product. Although the budget of CONACYT has grown impressively in the past few years, spending on scientific research and related activities remains a small portion of the national budget (the United States in contrast regularly spends more than 3 percent of its gross domestic product on research and development).

In 1970, the newly created CONACYT established the "urgent needs" that would guide the agency's priorities for science and technology. At that time, the foci of the organization were grouped around (1) health and nutrition, (2) natural resources, (3) education, (4) labor, (5) industrialization, (6) rural development, (7) community service, (8) housing, and (9) foreign commerce. In 2006, however, a different agenda was developed for CONACYT, defined as "strategic areas of knowledge": (1) information and communications, (2) biotechnology, (3) materials science, (4) design and manufacturing processes, and (5) urban and rural development and infrastructure.

The main sites of science and technology research in Mexico are public institutions, notably, the Universidad Nacional Autónoma de México (National Autonomous University of Mexico, UNAM), the Instituto Politécnico Nacional (National Polytechnic Institute, IPN) or at regional research centers, such as the Centro de Investigación Científica de Yucatán (Scientific Research Center of Yucatán, CICY). More than 90 percent of the funding managed by CONACYT is used to support research projects at public institutions. These sites for advanced research are concentrated in the country's three primary urban centers: Guadalajara, Jalisco (west); Monterrey, Nuevo León (north); and Mexico City (center).

Among the advances made in the past based on research done at Mexico are the development of the contraceptive pill, synthesized by Mexican chemist Luis E. Miramontes; the discovery of the chemical element vanadium by Andrés Manuel del Río; a primitive color television system by Guillermo González Camarena early in the 20th century, and the Large Millimeter Telescope developed by Mexican scientists of the Instituto Nacional de Astrofísica, Óptica y Electrónica (National Institute of Astrophysics, Optics and Electronics, INAOE) in collaboration with the University of Massachusetts at Amherst.

Careers in science in Mexico reflect an established but rather narrow path; few people in the country become research scientists, as employment opportunities and the means for advancement are limited. The usual pattern is for a student to be admitted to a science-related program at the National University or the Polytechnic Institute and there develop ties with key faculty and their research projects. Those connections facilitate the acquisition of research opportunities, internships, and, eventually, upon completion of an undergraduate degree, a scholarship for postgraduate study funded by CONACYT, most frequently at a foreign university. Graduation with an advanced degree from a foreign university generally means the choice of returning to Mexico or seeking a position in a foreign country, as noted above. For those students funded by CONACYT, there is a provision that requires scholarship recipients to repay their debt through some form of service to Mexico as stipulated by the agency.

Research scientists in Mexico often become professors at the country's leading universities and are expected to publish in international peer-reviewed journals and remain current in their specific fields of research. They usually become members of the Sistema Nacional de Investigadores (National System of Researchers, SNI). This national organization comprises three levels, with level III reserved for the most prestigious and recognized researchers (about 1,100 at the present time); there are about 7,500 scientists at this writing.

Luis M. Martínez Cervantes

See also Education; Universidad Nacional Autónoma de México

Further Reading

Gonzalez Brambilia, Claudia, Jose Lever, and Francisco Veloso. 2007. "Mexico's Innovation Cha-Cha." *Issues in Science and Technology* (Fall). www.issues.org/24.1/gonzalez-brambila.html.

Veloso, F., C. Gonzalez-Brambilia, and L. Reyes-Gonzalez. 2006. *Mexican Science in Global Context*. Pittsburgh: Carnegie Mellon University Press.

Sculpture

The politically charged events of 1968, particularly the killing of hundreds of protesters by government troops in Mexico City, culminated a growing rift within artistic circles in Mexico, including among those involved in the plastic arts, such as sculpture. For decades, official policies and institutions had promoted and supported nationalist themes related culture and national identity in artistic representation, or what became known as the Mexican school of art. Dissident works found it difficult to find venues and financial resources. By the 1960s, however, the dominant view of artistic production in Mexico was increasingly questioned and challenged. The violence at the plaza of Tlatelolco in October of 1968 discredited the prevailing political order, and with it, the grip by the government and its loyalists over art and its meaning in Mexico. As a consequence, a much more critical perspective emerged among Mexican artists, as reflected in their visual representation.

Gradually, this new view was accommodated by established cultural circles and displaced to a large extent the traditional approach to sculpture in the country and its artistic practitioners.

Mexican sculpture and design moved toward a much more abstract, interactive approach, inviting the spectator in effect to participate in the form, as opposed to the didactic nature of the traditional school of art. In this movement, the works of Enrique Carbajal González, better known as Sebastian, and Manuel de Jesús Hernández Suárez, better known as Hersua, were particularly important, as well as the collaboration of Mathias Goeritz with the architect Luis Barragán in the creation of the Torres de Satélite in Mexico City. Perhaps the landmark work of the new trend was the collaborative design and construction of the large walk-through sculpture at the University Cultural Center of the National Autonomous University of Mexico at the southern edge of Mexico City. The massive project integrated the volcanic rock upon which the center was built, creating a connection between nature and sculpture. Begun in 1979 and designed by leading figures of the new approach to sculpture—Helen Escovedo, Manuel Felguerez, Federico Silva, as well as Goeritz and Barragán—the "sculptural space" (as it was named) became a monument to the distinct style that had developed after 1968. In this effort, the role of Helen Escovedo was especially noteworthy for her use of natural and synthetic materials, experimental attitude, and both permanent and ephemeral installations.

Figuration art also registered important changes from the past, led by artists such as Reynaldo Velázquez and German Venegas. Using woodcarvings, both artists have explored themes at odds with the traditional nationalist school of art. Velázquez, for example, has focused on the male figure with flourishes of drama and eroticism to suggest a sensual, sensitive aura to his works. Venegas, on the other hand, has recovered pre-Hispanic and colonial plastic forms to turn them into eclectic pieces that fuse personal expression with myth, religious icons, and legends. More recently, the sculptor Javier Marin has attracted attention with his complex work with terra-cotta, ceramic, and clay. Meanwhile, the artist Eloy Tarcisio has reconfigured the iconic use of cactus (*nopales*), fruits, flowers, and popular symbols to suggest a neo-Mexican art that is nonetheless critical of the traditional nationalist artistic perspective.

Since the 1990s, conceptual art has made inroads into the works of the country's artists, spearheaded by the creations of the renowned Gabriel Orozco. In this movement, Orozco organized a series of pivotal discussions and debates about art that became known as the Friday Workshops, which included artists such as Abraham Cruz Villegas. Like Orozco, Villegas often uses everyday, common objects (i.e., readymade art) to provoke the spectator to reflect on the ordinary of the world, such as his use of boxing gloves, shoes, and speedballs to induce the viewer to contemplate the meanings of that popular sport in Mexico, or his deployment of scores of beer bottles of the brand Indio in an exposition at the Palace of Fine Arts. Like Cruz Villegas, artist Carlos Mier y Terán Benitz uses unconventional readymade items for his compositions, a giant spider made of black garbage bags, for instance, to prod viewers to confront everyday fears.

Although these novel forms of sculpture have received much recent attention, the more aesthetic mode of expression remains vibrant in Mexico through the use of traditional techniques and materials, such as wood, ceramic, and marble. Such work is represented by those of Gustavo Pérez, Leonor Anaya, Margariza Chazaro, Paloma Torres, and Elsa Navega, as well as that of Rafael Villar and Edna Payares.

With abstractionism, the new figuration art, the reappropriation of objects, and the use of new organic and synthetic materials, contemporary Mexican sculpture has established a new understanding of space and its relationship to the spectator. It is clear that the practice of sculpture has successfully overcome the hold of traditional nationalist forms in artistic production in Mexico.

Fernanda Álvarez Gil

See also Architecture; Art Education; Art Exhibitions; Art Market; Culture and the Government; Nationalism and National Identity; Painting; Visual Arts

Further Reading

Marin, Javier. 2009. *Seven Heads and Three Wigs,* translated by Ana Maria de la Ossa. New York: Nohra Haime Gallery.

Temkin, Ann, et al. 2009. *Gabriel Orozco.* New York: Museum of Modern Art.

Sinaloa

The official coat of arms of Sinaloa. (Corel)

The Mexican state of Sinaloa is located in the northwestern region of Mexico, its western edge facing the Sea of Cortez (Gulf of California), with an equally long valley between its mountainous eastern side. Sinaloa's territorial size and population ranks in the middle of Mexico's 31 states. To its south lies the state of Nayarit, to the east the state of Durango, and to the north it is bordered by Sonora and Chihuahua. The moisture from the Pacific Ocean provides rainfall for agricultural production, and as the interior mountains catch that moisture, it creates the headwaters for three major rivers and several tributaries that generally run east to west and supply the coastal plains below with water for farming irrigation.

The geographic features of Sinaloa allow for a wide range of climates, from the cold heights of its mountains to the humid, hot coastal areas. The temperate climate of the state's coastal plains allows a long growing season for vegetables and fruits (much of which is exported to the United States in the winter). The population of the state is concentrated in the strip along the coast, where three cities hold more than half of the state's residents: the port city of Mazatlán, Ahome, and the capital, Culiacán.

The economy of Sinaloa has three pillars: agriculture, tourism, and, although an illegal resource, the drug trade. Agricultural production has been central to the state's economy, and more so after the federal government invested in building irrigation works in the 1940s and 1950s to improve farming productivity. That period was also instrumental to the increase of exports due to wartime demand, and subsequently, the burgeoning population of the American southwest. Tomatoes—fresh and for processing into paste, sauces, and catsup—are particularly important as an export crop, but many other vegetables (e.g., broccoli, green beans, asparagus, peppers) for both domestic and foreign markets are grown in Sinaloa's long coastal valley. The North American Free Trade Agreement (NAFTA) of 1993 expanded the amount agricultural exports to the United States and Canada. Livestock are also raised for dairy production as well as for meat products. Fisheries along the coast, especially in and around Mazatlán, also produce seafood products, such as fresh and canned shrimp, for domestic and foreign consumption.

Tourism has been centered for decades along the beaches of the state, most importantly in the area around Mazatlán. For much of the year, the warm waters off the shore of the state's largest city have attracted domestic tourists from the hot interior towns as well as from the United States. The expansion of tourist activities in neighboring states, especially Sonora and Baja California Sur, has undercut the popularity of Mazatlán. In light of that trend, federal and state government efforts have been made to improve tourist facilities for beach tourism along the east side of the Gulf of Cortez. Toward that end, early in his administration, President Vicente Fox (2000–2006) launched a vast project called the Nautical Ladder, which was intended to encompass the entire northwest of Mexico and convert it into a premier tourist area, primarily for visitors from the western region of the United States. The economic troubles of Mexico since then have forced the federal government to drastically scale back the project; Mazatlán nonetheless continues to attract visitors, including large numbers of Americans who often arrive via automobile, using the highway connecting Nogales, Arizona, with Mazatlán (about a 12- to 15-hour drive). Mazatlán is also served by various airlines, including direct flights from U.S. airports. On the other hand, tourism in Sinaloa tends to attract middle-brow, lower-budget visitors, as opposed to the high-end market that gravitates toward Los Cabos and Puerto Vallarta.

The production and distribution of illegal drugs, and their attendant money-laundering activities, represent a third significant component of the economy of Sinaloa. In fact, at this writing, one of the most powerful drug organizations is anchored in the state and is often referred to as the Sinaloa cartel. Built on the production of opium from illicit plantings in the hills of the state, as well as marijuana growing, the Sinaloa cartel has also been involved in making methamphetamines (using the port of Mazatlán as entry point for the import of foreign-made ephedrine and its derivatives). The drug organization also distributes cocaine brought from South America, using the long Pacific coast as a means to bring it into Mexico.

Overlooking Mazatlan and the bay, Sinaloa, Mexico. (Vividpixels | Dreamstime.com)

Asian illicit drug producers also provide another source for the Sinaloa group. The cartel competes with rival drug organizations for control over the entry points into the United States, particularly through Tijuana/San Diego, Nogales/Nogales (Arizona), and Ciudad Juárez/El Paso. This competition has led to violence in recent years at these drug transit points along the U.S.-Mexican border. The Sinaloa cartel launders the profits by investing in legitimate enterprises, from tourist projects and real estate to the buying of farm land. The income from the drug trade amounts to billions of dollars, invigorating the local economies of the hard-scrabble hill towns of the state, where the combination of rainfall, climate, and soil fertility has led to optimum growing conditions for opium poppies (for heroin) and marijuana. The Mexican government's campaign against both crops, however, has pushed the Sinaloa cartel to increase its growing operations elsewhere, including sites in the United States, especially those related to marijuana—the drug trade's most lucrative crop at this time.

The political economy of the state, therefore, has two dimensions: one is legitimate and represented by its agribusiness and tourist industry, but the other is based on an illegal enterprise that pumps billions of dollars into the region. A substantial middle class exists, most of it associated with the lawful economy. Wealthy farmers and businessmen are at the top of the social pyramid of the state, but their affluence is rivaled by the lavish homes, expensive vehicles, and yachts owned by drug-related entrepreneurs. The political system had been largely in the hands of the Partido Revolucionario Institucional (Institutional Revolutionary Party, PRI).

After the 2004 elections, the governorship, six of eight congressional seats, and two of three senators belonged to the PRI. Allegations of political corruption have been rampant for decades, but the infiltration of the drug trade into politics has increased along with the importance of Mexico's northwest corridor in the flow of drugs to satisfy the demand in the United States. Most observers concede that the political system reflects the two dimensions within the economic structure of the state. PRI operatives in many cases are apparently influenced by drug-related interests, but they have essentially left the agricultural and tourist-related economy to operate relatively on its own. However, the rise in drug trade–related crime took a toll on the PRI, allowing the right-of-center Partido Acción Nacional (National Action Party, PAN) to gain a foothold in Sinaloa; the left-of-center Partido de la Revolución Democrática (Democratic Revolution Party, PRD) remains a weak presence. Thus, the 2010 elections reflected the negative impact of the drug trade violence on the PRI; it lost the gubernatorial race. The association of the PRI governor with the drug cartels clearly undermined the party, in contrast to the resurgence of the PRI elsewhere in the country. On the other hand, the extreme violence generated by the competing drug cartels during the administration of President Felipe Calderón (2006–2012) of PAN has seriously undermined public support for his party, including in the state of Sinaloa. The elections of 2012 will provide a major test of the ability of PAN to consolidate its gains in Sinaloa; the results will hold a decisive meaning for the state's politics, and not without implications for the economy of Sinaloa.

Compared to other parts of Mexico, Sinaloa fares relatively well in terms of socioeconomic conditions. Poverty marks the migrant labor used by the state's farmers, though the large agribusiness operations are well mechanized and employ workers to a much lesser extent than in the past. Small farmers often find it difficult economically, but money made from the plantings of poppies and marijuana supplement the income of many landholders of limited means. Unlike the southern states of the country, Sinaloa holds a very small population of indigenous people, and it is not an important immigration sending area.

The soundness of its export-oriented farming activities, combined with its services economy (nourished by tourism- and transportation-related jobs), allows for a significant middling social sector, several institutions of higher learning, and a large number of professionals. Cultural life revolves around its larger cities, but it is a state that carries a dubious fame instigated by the lyrics in the ballads about drug traffickers, so-called *narcocorridos,* that tend to romanticize drug dealing.

Sinaloa stands at a cusp concerning its future. The drug trade, and its political and economic shadow, casts a pall over the state, and the resolution of that issue will have long-term repercussions for life in Sinaloa.

Alex M. Saragoza

See also Agriculture; Drug Trade and Trafficking; North American Free Trade Agreement; Tourism

Further Reading

Aguilar Soto, Oscar. 2007. *Sinaloa en la globalizacion: costos ecologicos, sociales y economicos.* Culiacan: Universidad Autonoma de Sinaloa.

Ibarra Escobar, Guillermo. 2009. *Ensayos sobre el desarrollo economico regional de Sinaloa.* Mexico City: Juan Pablos.

Ingram, Helen, Nancy K. Laney, and David M. Gillilan. 1995. *Divided Waters: Bridging the U.S.-Mexico Border.* Tucson: University of Arizona Press.

Santamaria Gomez, Arturo, Luis Martinez Pena, and Pedro Brito Osuna. 2009. *Morir en Sinaloa: violencia, narco y cultura.* Culiacan: Universidad Autonoma de Sinaloa.

Sinaloa Official State Website. http://www.sinaloa.gob.mx.

Tinker Salas, Miguel. 1997. *In the Shadow of Eagles: Sonora and the Transformation of the Border during the Porfiriato.* Berkeley: University of California Press.

Voss, Stuart F. 1982. *On the Periphery of Nineteenth-Century Mexico: Sonora and Sinaloa 1810–1877.* Tucson: University of Arizona Press.

Soccer

Although it is not officially regarded as the national sport, football (or soccer, as it is known in the United States) is the sport that brings more people to the stadiums in Mexico.

The mines of Real del Monte, factories, and coffee plantations in the state of Veracruz and the fields of the English Casino and the British Club in Mexico City were the places where soccer was first practiced in the late 19th century, in the middle of "The *Porfiriato.*" It was the wealthy Englishmen who first organized soccer in Mexico. In 1900 they created the Pachuca Athletic Club. After its establishment in the capital, their countrymen formed the Reforma Athletic Club, the British Club, and the Mexico Cricket Club, plus a team formed in Orizaba (Veracruz) by the employers of a Scottish textile factory. These five teams competed in 1902 in the first official football competition in the country, which began on October 19.

Soccer in Mexico was exclusively played by British people until 1910, when the first club exclusively for Mexicans was founded: The Club of San Pedro de los Pinos, who won its first championship in 1912, the same year in which "Club España" was created, was one of the most important clubs in the first phase of Aztec football. After the success of those teams, more were created: the Club Unión (antecedent of Guadalajara), Club Asturias, América, Atlas, Veracruz Sporting Club, Necaxa, and Atlante. Most of these clubs still exist.

Despite América being the first Mexican team to make a tour outside its country in 1922, Necaxa formed the first Mexican soccer dynasty, obtaining four league titles in the 1930s, earning the nickname "The 11 Brothers." They formed the national team that played in the World Cup, which was disputed in Italy, in 1934. In 1943 Mexican soccer organizations made the decision to go professional, and in 1946 the Major League of Mexico City decided to open its doors to the provincial

Mexico supporters smiling and cheering at a World Cup soccer match between Argentina and Mexico in Johannesburg, South Africa, 2010. (fstockfoto | Dreamstime.com)

teams. Then in 1950, this group changed its name to First Division. At that time the Revolución stadium, the first stadium made of cement, was inaugurated in Irapuato (Guanajuato), and the stadiums of the City of Sports and the University City were inaugurated in Mexico, Distrito Federal.

The media, especially radio and the press, became the principal disseminators of a sport that was already enjoyed by a big part of the population. However, the early years of professionalism were marked by failures of the National Team, which lost all their games in the World Cups of Brazil 1950 and Switzerland 1954. But in 1958 in Sweden the Mexican National Squad tied one game, which meant the first point in the history of Mexico in the World Cup, and was widely celebrated, although not as much as for their first victory against Czechoslovakia in 1962, guided by a team of players from Guadalajara known then as Campeonisimo.

A period of transition would mark the 1960s, ending in 1970, with the dispute of the ninth Fédération Internationale de Football Association (FIFA) World Cup, which took place on Aztec land and was won by Brazil, a competition in which the hosts showed a team renewed, with young stars such as goalkeeper Ignacio Calderón, Gustavo "Halcon" Peña, and striker Enrique Borja. Unfortunately, Mexicans lost against Italy in the quarter finals. Since then a new phase has began, where the World Cup's furor makes soccer the most important sport in the country. Cruz Azul lived in soccer's golden era, which was supplanted by América, who became the king in the 1980s.

In mid-1982, Colombia decided not to organize the 1986 World Cup, and the FIFA decided to give the championship to Mexico, a decision that put Mexican soccer under the scrutiny of the international sport community. The competition was won by Argentina, guided by Diego Armando Maradona, and Mexico had an important role, winning 2–1 to Belgium, tying in one match with Paraguay, and winning 1–0 to Iraq, which gave them the first place in their group. In the eighth finals, Bora Milutinovic's team beat Bulgaria, but the dream sputtered in Monterrey in quarter finals, when they lost to Germany in penalty kicks.

The post–World Cup period lacked enthusiasm in Mexican soccer, which ended in August 1991 with the arrival of Cesar Luis Menotti (World Champion with Argentina in 1978) as the National Team coach. The "philosopher of football" achieved the desired change in mentality in the Mexican soccer player, which unfortunately was not reflected in the World Cup match in the United States in 1994 and France in 1998, where they could not advance from the eighth finals.

In 1996, when the dominion of Necaxa was ending and the reign of Toluca was beginning, the Mexican soccer executives decide to divide the year into two tournaments, opening the possibility for more teams to aspire to the championship. Mexican clubs also began playing in championships disputed in South America. This brought direct benefits to teams often called "small teams," mainly to Pachuca, which in the past 10 years has won five championships.

The greatest achievement of any Mexican clubs was winning the Copa Sudamericana, obtained by Pachuca in 2006 against the Colo Colo of Chile. Followed by the success of the national under-17 team led by Coach Jesús Ramirez, it was proclaimed champion in the World Championship in Peru in 2005.

Unfortunately, the greatest problem of Mexican soccer is in the stands. The presence of radical groups (paid by the club's directives and influenced by the Argentine "Barras Bravas") have made soccer in Mexico lose its familiar air, to the point that attending matches in some stadiums in the country is a situation of high risk. The civilian and sports authorities do not do as much as the fans desire to stop these criminals disguised as fans, and those who pay the consequences, sadly, are the real fans.

Despite this, Mexican soccer is currently experiencing a period of economic and sportive boom, where the level of the local championship has grown and players are making achievements as members of important international teams.

The most popular team in the country is Guadalajara, also known as "Chivas." This club was founded in 1906 by one of the largest warehouses of the Pearl of the West, where employees started the Union Club, which after two years became the club Guadalajara. The Sacred Herd is the one team that has the most titles in the Mexican league, with 11. Between the years 1956 and 1965, "Chivas" earned the nickname of "Campeonísimo" because of their great success in playing the game and because of their seven first-place division titles. Its most emblematic player was Salvador Reyes, who played with them between 1952 and 1967.

Founded on October 12, 1916, América is one of three teams that has always been in the First Division of Mexico since its emergence. It is the second-ranked professional team for wins in the Mexican soccer league, with 10 titles, and is the Mexican team that has achieved more international titles. Its most fruitful period was during the 1980s, when they won five league titles, with the Chilean Carlos Reinoso as their star player.

Since its emergence in the First Division in 1964, Cruz Azul has played a leading role in Mexican soccer. The Cementers have won eight titles (the last of them in the distant 1997), with their most fruitful period between the end of the 1960s throughout the 1970s, where they won seven league titles. It was famous for its Argentine goalkeeper Miguel Marin, known as "the cat" or "Superman."

During the end of the 1990s and the early years of the 21st century, soccer in Mexico was dominated by Toluca, a club founded in 1917. According to a poll by Reforma (one of the most popular newspapers in the country) this team had the highest increase in fans. In 1998, Toluca won its fourth title and started a golden era, which ended in 2005, when they won their eighth star. Toluca's main star players were the Mexican striker Vicente Pereda and Paraguayan forward José Saturnino Cardozo.

The team of the last golden age of Mexican soccer is Pachuca. "Tuzos" got their first championship in 1999, which began a great journey including five league titles, three CONCACAF (Confederation of North, Central American and Caribbean Association Football) Champions' Cups, and the Southamerican Cup in 2006. Its greatest player is an Argentine naturalized Mexican Gabriel Caballero, who has played with the team in all the competitions the team has won.

The first great Mexican soccer player was Luis de la Fuente, nicknamed "the Pirate," who was born in the port of Veracruz in 1914. His natural playing position was midfielder, but his skills greatly helped his game, distributing accurate passes and becoming a great assist player. His heading and his strength kicking the ball helped him to become the first Mexican to play in Europe, with Spanish Racing of Santander, and also playing in Argentina for Velez Sarsfield. Moreover, in Mexico "the Pirate" also played for Aurrera, España, América, Marte, and Veracruz. He also played in the World Cup celebrated in1934.

Antonio Carbajal, also named "Tota," was a Mexican goalkeeper who played in five World Cups, between Brazil 1950 and England 1966. Carbajal shares the honor of the most World Cups played with German Lothar Matthäus, who participated in five World Cups between 1982 and 1998. At clubs, Carbajal highlighted in León, where he won two league titles and remained a star for 18 years.

Any talk about Mexican soccer will include the mention of Hugo Sánchez, whose achievements have not been matched by any of his compatriots. The striker came to prominence for the Pumas of the Universidad Nacional Autónoma de México (National Autonomous University of Mexico, UNAM) and was picked up by Atletico Madrid, where he was the top scorer in the Spanish League. The

Steven Pienaar of South Africa (l) battles Francisco Rodriguez of Mexico (r) during a World Cup match on June 11, 2010, in Johannesburg, South Africa. (fstockfoto | Dreamstime.com)

following year he was traded to Real Madrid, where he won another four Pichichis (prize for the top scorer in Spain), plus five Spanish Leagues, two Spanish Cups, two nominations as Best Foreign Player in the Spanish League (1987 and 1990), and the Golden Boot for best scorer in European football in 1990. Following his career as *"meringue,"* Sánchez returned to Mexico to play for one year in América and then he played for one year in Rayo Vallecano, closing his career in Spain, where he scored 234 goals. Atlante repatriated him, but he proved lucky once again abroad in the Second Division of Austria, with FC Linz, and then joined the Dallas Burn of Major League Soccer in the United States, and concluded his career in 1997 in Atletico Celaya. Individually, Sánchez was voted as Mexico's best athlete of the 20th century and best Mexican soccer player of the 20th century by the International Federation of Football History and Statistics, who also chose Sánchez Márquez as the best footballer of Northern and Central America in the 20th century and named him as the 26th best footballer in the 20th century around the globe. He also participated in the World Cups of 1978 in Argentina, of 1986 in Mexico, and of 1994 in the United States.

Nowadays, one of the most important Mexican players is defender Rafael Márquez. He emerged from Atlas, the club that traded him in 1999 to Móncaco of France, in exchange for $6 million. In the French League, "Rafa" was proclaimed the best center defender in his first campaign, and he also won the French League, the French Cup, and the French Super Cup. In the summer of 2003, "The Kaiser of Michoacán" was hired by FC Barcelona in exchange for 25 million euros, becoming the first Mexican player in the history of the Catalan club. With Barça, Márquez has won the Spanish league on two occasions, in addition to the Union of European Football Associations (UEFA) Champions League. With the Mexican National team, for which he is currently captain, Márquez Álvarez won the 1999 Confederations Cup and CONCACAF Gold Cup in 2003, as well as appeared in the World Cup in 2002 and 2006.

After four difficult years and three different coaches, Mexico qualified for the 19th FIFA World Cup in South Africa. On the bench the national team had Javier Aguirre, who had coached Mexico in the FIFA World Cup in Japan and Korea and for seven years worked in Spain with Osasuna and Atletico de Madrid. In addition to the strategist, Mexico took to South Africa a representative team full of players working for European teams, labeled as the best Mexican team in the history of World Cups. Mexico had the honor of playing the tournament's opening game against the championship's host South Africa in a match that ended tied at one goal.

For the second game Mexico faced the French national team, winning 2 to 0 with goals by Cuauhtemoc Blanco and Javier "Chicharito" ("Little Pea") Hernández, the last pearl of Mexican football. Two months before the World Cup, Hernández, who played for Guadalajara, was sold to Manchester United for $10 million.

Mexico lost against Uruguay in the first round's last match and qualified for the knockout round, where the team would have to face Argentina, the team that sent them home in Germany 2006. The outcome was the same: Argentina won three goals to one, and the dream of reaching the quarterfinals was diluted once again.

During the next season, all Mexicans were amazed by the performance of Hernández in Manchester United, where he became a starter scoring 20 goals and winning the Premier League and second place in the UEFA Champions League; he also won the Sir Matt Busby award for Player of the Year chosen by the fans.

The progress of Mexican soccer was ratified in the summer of 2011, and the Aztec team hosted and won the FIFA U-17 World Cup, defeating Uruguay 2–0 in the final. In addition, the U-20 national team finished third in the World Cup in Colombia.

Carlos A. Siliceo Bárzana

See also Nationalism and National Identity; Popular Culture; Sports; Television

Further Reading

Club Deportivo Toluca Official Website. www.deportivotolucafc.com.

Club Guadalajara Official Website. www.chivascampeon.com.

Crónica del Futbol Mexicano. 1998. Mexico City: Editorial Clío.

FIFA Official Website. www.fifa.com.

Historia de los Mundiales de Futbol. 2009. Madrid: España.

Rafael Márquez Official Website. www.rafaelmarquez.com.mx.

Social Etiquette

See Family, Friends, and Social Etiquette

Social Structures, Class, and Ethnic Relations

It would be inaccurate and unjust to think of Mexico unreflectively as a society of a vast majority of extremely poor native people from the countryside contrasted with a very few extremely wealthy and cosmopolitan elites of European descent, with very little in between. Certainly there are very poor indigenous Mexicans who are subject to crushing discrimination and minimal access to opportunity for social advancement. And there are also extremely wealthy Mexicans whose global power and influence are considerable. But as any visitor to Mexico realizes, the country also has a considerable middle class, and the majority of Mexicans fall somewhere in between the very rich and the very poor. Nevertheless, Mexico is a deeply divided society, and the divisions are stark. Income inequality can be dramatic, especially between rural Mexico and urban Mexico, and structural impediments to social mobility are real and entrenched, and they affect many people. What is also clear, though, is that the inequality and lack of access to opportunity that does exist in Mexico are connected to race, ethnicity, and even gender in Mexican society. What is the nature of Mexican society? And how do the racial, class, and ethnic dimensions of Mexican society shape Mexico's history and its contemporary reality?

Mexican society is a blend of very culturally and ethnically distinct peoples. The existence of large, settled, and complex pre-Columbian indigenous civilizations and peoples prior to the Spanish conquest has not only made the process of racial and ethnic mixture difficult and troublesome but has also complicated the process of constructing a unique national identity. Many Mexicans still identify less as members of some kind of national community and more in terms of their local or ethnic communities. And efforts to bridge the stark differences that often separate the different peoples of Mexico have been a major part of public policy and intellectual debate.

In fact, during the colonial period, the European settlers and administrators believed that the best way to manage these differences was simply to recognize that they existed; and, instead of trying to encourage a process of either aggressive social integration or elimination, they created two parallel worlds that existed side by side and that were governed primarily by their own conditions and practices. Thus, colonial Mexico evolved as a place where the concept of different worlds defined by ethnicity, region, cultural practices, or economic status was basically encouraged and accepted, or at least not questioned.

Evidence of this was the creation, for instance, of hospitals, schools, and convents that separated Mexicans according to ethnic identity. Social conventions such as the institutions of marriage or property ownership also varied according to the different worlds in which people lived. And while the Spanish colonial authorities established Roman Catholicism as the only officially tolerated form of religious expression, the practice of indigenous and other non-Catholic religious beliefs and rituals continued with minimal interference by the enforcers of religious orthodoxy. The replication of these worlds, differentiated by racial, ethnic, and class lines throughout the colonial period and even up through the present day, has led some to speak of Mexico not in the singular, but in the plural. The phrase "many Mexicos," coined by the Mexicanist scholar Lesley Byrd Simpson, captures this sentiment.

Evidence of the continuing importance and relevance of class and ethnic identity in Mexican society is also present in the country's modern, postindependence society. The independence movement of 1810 was led by the priest Miguel Hidalgo y Costilla and continued by the priest José María Morelos, but it was a movement that not only represented a quest for political separation from Spain but also captured the voice of Mexico's lower classes and indigenous peoples. In the middle of the 19th century, Mexico's first and only full-blood indigenous president, Benito Juárez, seemed to have broken through the confines that kept indigenous Mexico apart from Spanish and *mestizo* Mexico; but whatever chance this presented in the forging of a unified nation was shattered first by the French intervention and occupation of the country, and later by the racist and classist elements of positivism espoused by Porfirio Díaz that thrived on the conceptual discriminations inherent to the notion of "many Mexicos."

And even in the 20th century, the Mexican Revolution divided along the lines of racial, ethnic, and class identity. The agrarian, peasant-based movement of Emiliano Zapata, which resonated with Mexico's indigenous peoples, clashed with the more nonindigenous, popular class faction that constituted the bulk of support for Pancho Villa. And both of these groups clashed with the ultimately victorious revolutionary faction dominated by *criollo* ranching elites from the north in collaboration with the urban working and professional classes.

Yet, the governing consensus that emerged out of the Revolution, and that found expression even in an embrace of Mexico's rich and varied ethnic diversity through the *indigenista* movement, could not overcome the ethnic, linguistic, and cultural divisions inherent to Mexico. The 1994 Zapatista uprising, which claimed to speak on behalf of all of Mexico's oppressed indigenous peoples and poor underclass, is a modern, contemporary manifestation of the different ethnic, class, and socioeconomic elements that continue to define the country's reality.

Mexico's cultural and ethnic diversity is a source of cultural richness and national pride, but it is also a regular and continuous source of social conflict. Such conflict is likely to remain present in Mexico in the years to come, with occasional outbursts of protest and violence among and between Mexico's different ethnic populations. Nevertheless, nearly all Mexicans understand that their existence as a nation depends on finding a way to recognize and embrace the multicultural and multiethnic identities that define them as they also continue to work through the lingering sociopolitical structures that divide them along class and ethnic lines.

James D. Huck Jr.

See also Income; Indigenous Peoples; Nationalism and National Identity; Poverty; Racism

Further Reading

Dion, Michelle. 2010. *Workers and Welfare: Comparative Institutional Change in Twentieth Century Mexico.* Pittsburgh: University of Pittsburgh Press.

Nutini, Hugo G., and Barry Isaac. 2009. *Social Stratification in Central Mexico, 1500–2000.* Austin: University of Texas Press.

Rueda Peiro, Isabel. 2009. *La creciente desigualdad en Mexico.* Mexico: Universidad Nacional Autonoma de Mexico.

Sonora

The official coat of arms of Sonora. (Corel)

Sonora state is located in the northwestern part of Mexico. It is bordered on the west by the Gulf of California, on the east by Chihuahua, on the south by Sinaloa, and on the north by the United States. Along with its capital city of Hermosillo, Sonora is home to the important port city of Guaymas and the border town of Nogales, situated just across from the Arizona city of the same name. According to the 2010 census, the state's population was about 2.66 million. Precolonial Sonora was home to several major native groups, including the Pima, Papago, Opata, Yaqui, and Mayo. Jesuit missionaries worked among Sonora's native peoples during most of the colonial period and then were replaced by the Franciscans during the 18th century. By the middle of the 17th century, Sonora attracted more settlers due to the emergence of gold and silver mining. For Sonora's native peoples, the colonial era was one of decreasing options, as the missionaries and Spanish settlers threatened their lands, their water (a scarce commodity in this arid region), and their autonomy. Many natives responded with rebellion, which remained a part of Sonora's history well into the 20th century.

Sonora became an independent state in 1830, following the Mexican War of Independence. During the 19th century, Sonora experienced some expansion of its economy, as agriculture grew and mining continued to attract investors, both Mexican and foreign. Sonoran wheat became part of a Pacific coast trade, and the port of Guaymas linked Sonora to the United States and beyond. Agriculture increased with the expansion of the hacienda system, and the Yaquis, Mayos, Pimas, and Opatas provided a labor force. Such development was not always peaceful, however, as the Sonoran natives resisted the steady encroachments on their lands and autonomy. At the same time, Sonora struggled to contain the Apache raids that encouraged many Sonorans to leave and that threatened to depopulate the Sonora-Arizona frontier.

Beginning in the 1850s, Sonoran governor Ignacio Pesqueira emerged as an important political figure. He presided over a lengthy campaign to pacify the state and improve its infrastructure. Although Pesqueira successfully resisted continuing American attempts to annex Sonora, his efforts against the Apaches met with mixed results. The Yaqui and Mayo likewise remained resistant, and Yaqui leader José María Leyva Cajeme led a movement to create a separate Yaqui state. The Yaqui rebellion was inherited by Pesqueira's successors and by President Porfirio Díaz, who governed Mexico from the late 19th century until the beginning of the Mexican Revolution in 1910. Under Díaz, the federal government began to aid Sonora in the fight against the Apaches and in attempts to end the uprisings by the Yaqui and Mayo natives. Cajeme ultimately was captured and executed in 1887. However, on the eve of the Mexican Revolution, a war of extermination was still being waged against both native groups. Although the Mayo were effectively subdued by the combined efforts of federal and Sonoran troops, the Yaqui remained a contentious presence. Eventually, many Yaqui were forced to relocate to the Yucatán, where they were put to work on *henequén* (agave) plantations.

In the decades before the Mexican Revolution of 1910, Sonora experienced significant growth, particularly in mining and agriculture. Copper and silver mining attracted foreign, especially American, investment. Federal land policies that tended to encourage land concentration helped stimulate the large-scale production of export crops, such as garbanzos, in the Yaqui and Mayo river valleys. Sonora's growth strengthened its connection to the United States. By the beginning of the 20th century, the Sonora-Arizona border zone was especially well integrated, with family and business networks stretching across the international line. The economic importance of this border area to both countries was especially apparent in 1906, when copper miners in Sonora staged a strike for better pay and working conditions, and Porfirio Díaz suppressed the strike with the help of the Arizona Rangers.

Sonora was a major theater of the Mexican Revolution, and it produced several revolutionary leaders, including Adolfo de la Huerta, Alvaro Obregón, and Plutarco Elías Calles. In the early phase of the revolution, Obregón helped secure the state against the insurgency of Pascual Orozco, which threatened the new national regime of Francisco I. Madero. After Madero was overthrown and killed, Obregón and Calles participated in the rebellion that eventually brought victory to the constitutionalist movement of Venustiano Carranza. Because of leaders like de la Huerta, Calles, and Obregón, Sonora secured for itself a central place in Mexico's postrevolutionary state.

Mobilized to protect their lands since the colonial period, Sonora's Yaqui natives were easily enlisted into the Mexican Revolution. They formed their own

Not far from the port of Guyamas this marina at San Carlos can be found, Sonora, Mexico. (Enrique Gomez | Dreamstime.com)

battalions and contributed their own leaders to the revolutionary armies. Promises that their lands would be restored and their autonomy respected, however, were lost in the aftermath of the revolution, particularly with the growth of commercial farming in the Yaqui River Valley. In 1926 and 1927 the Yaqui staged their last armed uprising, a move that resulted in a brutal massacre and another deportation of Yaquis to the Yucatán. During the 1930s, the Yaqui claimed a temporary victory when they were officially given one-half million hectares of land by the government of President Lázaro Cárdenas. This effectively ended the Yaqui military threat, though it did not guarantee Yaqui autonomy. With the continued growth of capital-intensive commercial agriculture, the Yaqui gradually became dependent on the Mexican government, especially as federal control was established over the waters of the Yaqui River.

The period from Word War II to the early 1980s saw continued economic prosperity. Sonoran agriculture was bolstered by the expansion of irrigation, and new technology contributed to a Green Revolution. The state's cattle industry also benefited from modernization. Wealthy companies and private individuals gained the most from these developments, and many *ejidatarios* (the beneficiaries of land reform) were compelled to sell their lands to those with the resources for large-scale agriculture. In this way, land became concentrated in fewer hands, particularly in the fertile Yaqui and Mayo river valleys. In response to the economic and political monopoly held by a small group of wealthy farmers, leftist groups emerged. President Luis Echeverría reacted to this challenge by building on the work of Lázaro Cárdenas, expropriating more land and establishing more *ejidos*. Nevertheless, large-scale agriculture and cattle ranching maintained their central position in the Sonoran economy.

Like most Mexican border states, since the 1960s Sonora has also been host to the maquiladora industry, in which materials are imported, assembled in Mexican factories, and then reexported. Foreign-owned maquila plants, which take advantage of cheap Mexican labor, are concentrated on the Sonoran-U.S. border, in Nogales, Naco, Agua Prieta, and other cities. The maquiladora industry has attracted Mexican workers to the border zone and provided many with a viable economic alternative. However, the maquila industry has contributed to the environmental deterioration that is now evident throughout the U.S.-Mexican border zone. The twin cities of Nogales, Sonora/Nogales, Arizona, are emblematic of the problem. A steady growth in population and industry has depleted and contaminated the water supply and has resulted in a steady deterioration of air quality. Health problems, including cancer and birth defects, in the Nogales area are a grim reminder of the effects of rapid and unregulated growth. In recent years a number of maquila plants have also been established in Hermosillo, about two hours away from the border in the interior of the state.

During the last two decades of the 20th century, Sonora began to struggle with the consequences of intensive agriculture. The depletion of water and the exhaustion of land threatens the agricultural sector of the state, whose agribusiness firms have benefited substantially from the North American Free Trade Agreement (NAFTA) since its signing in 1993. Sonora's large farmers have been a key source of winter vegetables for the U.S. markets as well as grains for domestic consumption. Sonora has also witnessed the growth of the drug trade (along with its violence and corruption) during the latter part of the 20th century. The state is a transit point for cocaine, marijuana, and other illegal drugs that make their way to the United States on a regular basis. Despite the efforts of both Mexico and the United States to halt this illegal traffic, Sonora remains a center of drug-related activity. Tourism activities have suffered as a result of the drug trade and its attendant violence, and more so with the recession in the United States of 2007–2010, given the importance of American visitors to Sonora's travel industry. Sonoran coastline on the Sea of Cortes has been the site of several tourist developments, including those composed of second homes for U.S. citizens and those largely dedicated to retirees from north of the border. Since much of that tourist traffic arrives by car to such sites, the fears of kidnapping and carjacking has lessened the usual number of vehicles to the tourist areas of Sonora. The public concern over the association of the drug cartels with the old dominant political party, the Partido Revolucionario Institucional (Institutional Revolutionary Party,

PRI) eventually cost it the gubernatorial election of 2009. On the other hand, the drug trade–related violence has continued unabated under the presidency of Felipe Calderón (2006–2012) of PAN, which has contributed to a resurgence of the PRI elsewhere in the country. The elections of 2012 will pose a major test of the capacity of the opposition to the PRI in Sonora to keep the former ruling party at bay.

Suzanne B. Pasztor

See also Borders, Northern and Southern; Drug Trade and Trafficking; Maquiladoras; North American Free Trade Agreement; Tourism

Further Reading

Acuña, Rodolfo. 1974. *Sonoran Strongman: Ignacio Pesqueira and His Times.* Tucson: University of Arizona Press.

Bocanegra Gastelum, Carmen Otilia. 2008. *El Comercio en Mexico y su encuentro con la globalizacion (el caso de Sonora).* Hermosillo: Universidad de Sonora.

Hu-DeHart, Evelyn. 1984. *Yaqui Resistance and Survival: The Struggle for Land and Autonomy 1821–1910.* Madison: University of Wisconsin Press.

Ingram, Helen, Nancy K. Laney, and David M. Gillilan. 1995. *Divided Waters: Bridging the U.S.-Mexico Border.* Tucson: University of Arizona Press.

Sonora Official State Website. http://www.sonora.gob.mx

Tinker Salas, Miguel. 1997. *In the Shadow of Eagles: Sonora and the Transformation of the Border during the Porfiriato.* Berkeley: University of California Press.

Vasquez Ruiz, Miguel Angel. 2009. *Frontera norte: La economia en Sonora, una vision desde perspectiva industrial.* Hermosillo: Universidad de Sonora.

Voss, Stuart F. 1982. *On the Periphery of Nineteenth-Century Mexico: Sonora and Sinaloa 1810–1877.* Tucson: University of Arizona Press.

Sports

Professional sports   Soccer is the most popular sport in Mexico. It does not matter if you are in a big city or in a community affected by extreme poverty, you can always find children and adults dressed with the shirt of their favorite soccer team.

The team Guadalajara (also known as Chivas) is the most popular team in the country and has won the championship 11 times. The team América follows Chivas, with 10 titles, and both play in "El clásico," the most important match of the season, almost considered a national party.

In the past few years, Mexican soccer teams have played in the most important soccer tournaments in America: Copa Libertadores de América (America's Liberators Cup) and Copa Sudamericana (Southamerican Cup). Pachuca won the Southamerican Cup in 2006, and Cruz Azul lost the Copa Libertadores' final in 2001.

Hugo Sánchez (five time lead scorer in the Spanish soccer league, who played in Real Madrid, Atletico de Madrid, and the Mexican national team) and Luis "El

Pirata" de la Fuente (Aurrerá, España, América, Racing of Santander, Velez Sarsfield, Veracruz) are considered the best players in Mexican soccer history.

Another sport of great tradition, much like in the United States and the Caribbean, is baseball. "The King of Sports" is played in two leagues: Mexican League (played in summer with 16 teams, having Diablos of Mexico City, Tigers of Cancún, and Sultanes of Monterrey as the favorites) and Mexican Pacific-Coast League (played in winter with eight teams, with Naranjeros of Hermosillo, Venados of Mazatlán, and Tomateros of Culiacán as the teams with more titles). Mexican baseball teams participate in the "Caribbean Series" with the winners of the winter leagues of Venezuela, Dominican Republic, and Puerto Rico. The national team also plays in the biggest baseball events, such as the Olympic Games and the World's Baseball Classic.

The most important baseball player in Mexican history is Fernando Valenzuela, a left-handed pitcher who played in Major League Baseball between 1980 and 1997 with the Los Angeles Dodgers, California Angels, Baltimore Orioles, Philadelphia Phillies, San Diego Padres, and St. Louis Cardinals.

Basketball in Mexico has been developed at the professional level. The National Professional Basketball League was founded in 2001 with 11 teams. More recently, the 2011 season started with 14 teams, all in different cities spread over the entire country. Halcones of the Universidad Veracruzana campus Xalapa, Halcones Rojos of Veracruz, Pioneros of Cancún, and Toros of Nuevo Laredo are the most important teams in this league. These Mexican teams already disputed the America's Cup, played under the rules of the FIBA (International Basketball Federation) and comprising the best teams from across the continent, especially Mexico, the United States, Argentina, and Brazil, the most competitive leagues. In 2007, Soles of Mexicali lost the final against Peñarol of Mar del Plata (Argentina), and in 2011, Halcones Rojos of Veracruz played in the final four.

Mexicans also feel a great passion for racing. In different cities across the country, the speedways receive thousands of people eager to hear the roar of engines, be it of cars, trucks, or go-karts. Thanks to the success of drivers such as Adrian Fernández (winner of several races in Champ Car Series in the United States, owner of Fernández Racing team, and current competitor in the American Le Mans series), Mario Domínguez (cart series), Michel Jourdain Jr. (cart and National Association for Stock Car Auto Racing [NASCAR] Busch series), and lately Salvador Duran (World Series by Renault, A1GP series), the automobile has become a new highlight in Mexican sports geography. This has generated huge investments in companies that are interested in developing the Mexican talents outside the country (Team Telmex, Corona, Gigante, Tecate, Herdez), either by sponsoring the national serials such as Corona Cup or NASCAR Mexico. In the last months, Mexico came to the forefront of motorsport with the presence of Sergio Pérez in the Sauber Formula 1 team.

Today, Mexico is one of the most powerful countries in the world of boxing. The Aztec nation, historically regarded as the cradle of great boxers, has reaped more than 100 world titles throughout its history, and everything seems to indicate that the figure will continue to grow. The Mexican protagonism has been shown in different categories and organizations, cemented in advance by legends such as "Kid Azteca," Raúl "Ratón" Macías, Ruben "Púas" Olivares, Alfonso Zamora, Carlos Zarate, Salvador Sánchez, Mantequilla Nápoles, Julio Cesar Chávez, and others. Nowadays, the domain of Mexican boxers has increased if it is accepted that many of the most popular and most talented boxers today are Mexicans, including their eight world champions and many great fighters without the belt of champions.

Golf has become very popular because of Lorena Ochoa, a golfer born in Guadalajara (Jalisco), ranked in first place in the Ladies Professional Golf Association (LPGA) tour of the United States until April 2010, when she decided to retire and start her family. Besides her trophies, which will ensure her membership in the Golf Hall of Fame, Lorena established a nonprofit organization named the Lorena Ochoa Foundation, which provides scholarships so more Mexicans can go abroad to seek an opportunity such as the one she had.

Other sports   *Charrería* (similar to rodeo) is considered the national sport of Mexico. Its history goes back to the first colonial society when horses where introduced to Mexico and riding became a sign of social status. With these activities, the 10 *charro* movements were born, consisting of acrobatics on horseback or even lasso of cattle. However, it was not until after the land reform of the early 20th century, when the former landowners migrated to the cities of Guadalajara and Mexico, were they organized into *charros'* associations, which gradually spread throughout the country, founding the National Association of Charros in 1921.

Mexico has 6,911 miles of coastline, split between the Gulf of Mexico and the Caribbean Sea (2,046 miles) and the Pacific (4,865 miles). This has allowed many Mexicans to see the ocean in a unique opportunity: to observe beautiful landscapes and practice sport. One of the most popular is fishing, which has its mecca in Mazatlán, the self-proclaimed world capital of fishing. Here you can catch swordfish, dorado, tuna and yellow fin, and some species of marlin (stripped marlin, blue marlin, black marlin) in tournaments that are held several times a year. In the Gulf of Mexico, Veracruz is the most visited port by fishermen who compete in tournaments with good prizes, including the traditional Chad Silver, which takes place in May. In addition, on the shores of Veracruz sharks, barracuda, and sea bass can be caught. In the Caribbean, Cancún is the paradise of sport fishing, and one can catch sierra, bonito, pargo, mero, chad, and sea trout.

Given the large obesity rates in Mexico, the government and various associations have been devoted to promote sports, especially athletics. They have begun campaigns all across the country inviting people to start a healthier life, and running is a perfect exercise for achieving this goal. This is evidenced by the large number of 10-kilometers races ran across the country, as the International Gulf in Veracruz, or the races organized by Televisa and Television Azteca, the two most important television broadcasters in the country. In addition, the city of Torreón (northern Mexico) hosts the marathon of La Laguna, with a special prize of $1 million for anyone who breaks the world record. Much of this euphoria for athletics has to do with Ana Gabriela Guevara (Sonora, 1977), who was Olympic subchampion and world champion in the 400 meter flat, and thanks to some advertising contracts, she became the most popular athlete of that nation.

Olympic sports   Currently, Mexico has 29 federations for Olympic sports and 22 for the non-Olympic ones. The Mexican Olympic Committee (COM), headed by Felipe "El Tibio" Muñoz, as well as every other federation, reports to the Comisión Nacional de Cultura Física y Deporte (National Commission of Physical Culture and Sports, CONADE), the maximum authority headed by Carlos Hermosillo (former soccer player and holder of the record for must goals scored by a Mexican playing in Mexico).

In the past, the budget for the CONADE was one of the smaller budgets compared to other public entities, because the state did not consider the promotion of sports a priority. President Felipe Calderón, encouraged the goal of using the practice of sports as a preventive mechanism against drugs and violence.

Mexico does not have an emblematic sport. In other words, it is not largely considered dominant in a particular sport. However, endurance sports such as walk-run, the marathon, boxing, and distance running have given international recognition. Among the most relevant Mexican athletes are Humberto Mariles Cortes (show jumping, first gold medal in Mexico's history, London 1948), Felipe Muñoz "El Tibio" (swimmer, gold, Mexico 1968), Ernesto Canto (race walker, gold, Los Angeles 1984), Fernando Platas (diver, silver, Sydney 2000), Soraya Jimenez (weightlifter, gold, Sydney 2000), and Ana Guevara (track and field athlete, silver, Athens 2004).

Given the fact that Mexico is a country that does not win a large amount of Olympic medals, success stories are followed closely.

Paola Arena and Carlos A. Siliceo Bárzana

See also Education; Soccer

Further Reading

Crónica del Futbol Mexicano. 1998. Mexico City: Editorial Clío.

Lorena Ochoa Official Website. www.lorenaochoa.com.

Medallistas Olímpicos Mexicanos. 2006. Mexico, DF: El Universal, CONADE, Comité Olímpico Mexicano.

Mexico Society and Culture Complete Report: An All-Inclusive Profile Combining All of Our Society and Culture Reports. 2010. Petaluma, CA: World Trade Press.

Valero Silva, José. 1989. *El libro de charrería*. Mexico City: Gráficas Montealbán.

Street Children

The magnitude of the problem of street children (ages range from 5 to 16 years) is generally underestimated by official reports. The population of street children is anywhere from half a million to 250,000 in number, depending on the definition used. The evidence indicates that the problem has increased over the past two decades, especially in the nation's major cities. By far the most severe example of street children in the country is found in Mexico City, where the estimates run as high as 18,000 completely homeless street children; but again, the number may be much greater.

Studies indicate that young males represent the majority of street children, approximately 75 percent, and about half of all street children start living in the streets between the ages of 5 and 9 years of age. There are basically three types of street children. First, there are those who have a home, but for a variety of reasons, stay in their homes irregularly, going in and out of their households. These children often work illegally as underage laborers and attend school erratically and often eventually drop out. Second, there are those without homes who literally live on the streets. Third, there are the young people who are in transition from living in a home and to a life in the streets. Given these different forms of children on the streets, the numbers used to describe this population are at best educated guesses, but there is no doubt about the growing extent of this social problem in Mexico.

Reports of street children cite several, usually interrelated, causes for this growing phenomenon, particularly in Mexico City. Familial breakdown is the main reason children leave their homes. Parental alcoholism, violence, drug use, or a combination of these behaviors push children out of their homes. Similarly, a single mother may have a series of casual relations or be involved in prostitution, which creates conditions that provoke a child to abandon his or her home; in many cases, girls who take to the streets are victims of molestation by a sexual partner of the mother, a stepfather, or a family member. It is not unusual for street children to be abandoned by their parents. Again, abandonment is frequently related to the parents' drug addiction, prostitution, or migration, where a parent or both parents leave children behind to fend for themselves (or with a relative or friend, who may tire of the burden and force the children out onto the streets).

Extreme poverty compounds the root causes of homelessness among children. Nearly half of the Mexican urban population is considered poor by official estimates, and about 20 percent live in extreme poverty, creating the social context leading to children living on the streets.

Street children are apt to survive through various strategies, such as working illegally, selling items in the informal sector of the economy, begging, theft, or a combination of these activities. It is not unusual for street children to engage in prostitution to survive or to have sex at an early age; female street children are especially vulnerable to rape, to being forced into prostitution, and to have children at a very young age. Drug use is common among male street children in particular (e.g., using paint thinner, glue, and similar substances as well as marijuana and hard drugs when the opportunity permits). Health problems are rampant among street children, including a high incidence of human immunodeficiency virus/acquired immunodeficiency syndrome (HIV/AIDS); they are also subject to workplace injuries that are unreported, given that they are illegally employed. Although the exact extent is unknown, many street children have learning disabilities of various types or are mentally disabled.

Children of the streets reside in a shadowy, often dangerous world of underground dwellings, door fronts, park benches, playgrounds, freeway overhangs, culverts, and the like. They often congregate in small groups, pool resources, and offer one another support in some way. In such groupings, the older members assume a quasi-paternal role, giving protection to the younger ones in the group. As a consequence, the young, vulnerable members give their fidelity to the older ones, but these relations may also become abusive and exploitative. These groups may evolve into structured social groups, with a hierarchy of authority, codes of behavior, and gang-like activities.

Several public, private, and nonprofit organizations and institutions work to address the problem. Commonly, the initial steps are face-to-face encounters by "streets educators," who attempt to induce the children to participate in diversion activities, to offer medical care, and to provide rewards for entering shelters. The Mexican government has recently initiated efforts to increase the number of orphanages for abandoned children, and private foundations have also stepped up their efforts to raise funds for helping homeless children. Nonetheless, this problem has become a major challenge to social reformers in Mexico, public and private. As the numbers of street children grow, government social agencies and nonprofit organizations will be hard-pressed to remedy this situation, and more so if the Mexican economy falters and poverty persists at contemporary levels.

Pablo Martínez Zárate

See also Crime and Punishment

Further Reading

Camp Yeakey, Carol, Jeanita W. Richardson, and Judith Brooks Buck, eds. 2006. *"Suffer the Little Children": National and International Dimensions of Child Poverty and Public Policy.* Amsterdam: Elsevier JAI.

Cummings, Patricia Murrieta. 2008. *Poder y resistencia: el proceso de permanencia de los niños de la calle en la ciudad de México* [*Power and Resistance: The Permanence of Street Children in Mexico City*]. México, DF: Plaza y Valdés.

Poniatowska, Elena. 1999. *El Niño: Children of the Streets, Mexico City (Niños de la calle, Ciudad de México).* Kent Klich, photographer. Syracuse, NY: Syracuse University Press.

T

Tabasco

The official coat of arms of Tabasco. (Corel)

The state of Tabasco is located in the deep southeastern region of Mexico, at the neck of the Isthmus of Tehuantepec. The east side of the state faces the Gulf of Mexico, with the states of Veracruz and Campeche on the north and south, respectively; the state of Chiapas is southeast of Tabasco, and a short strip of it abuts the boundary between Mexico and Guatemala's Peten district.

Tabasco is relatively small, ranking 24th of 31 states in territorial size, and the state's total number of residents makes it about 20th in the country. Extremes of heat and humidity, as well as rainfall, characterize the climate of Tabasco. For much of its history, the state attracted little attention through 300 years of Spanish colonial rule and for most of the 19th century, given the lack of a valuable economic resource and an unfavorable climate. The extensive rainy season of the area swamps the coastal plains and a mountain range runs along the southern spine of the state, but the vast majority of the geography of Tabasco is basically flat and is subject to long, wet seasons and occasional flooding.

The tropical nature of Tabasco makes it ideal for agriculture tied to products conducive to the region's climatic conditions, where the overwhelming majority of the population finds employment in agriculturally related jobs. Cocoa, cassava, sugarcane, coconuts, and plantains are abundantly grown for both domestic and foreign markets; cattle raising is also important, along with commercial fishing on the coast. Early in the 20th century, oil production played an important role in the economy of the state, but the oil fields of Tabasco have been largely depleted. The Mexican government–run oil company, Petróleos Mexicanos (PEMEX), continues drilling in the area, though productivity has declined drastically compared to past yields. Some manufacturing occurs in the capital city of Villahermosa, yet the scale of production is small even by Mexican standards.

On the other hand, Tabasco lies on the primary coastal route linking the Yucatán Peninsula's popular tourist sites (i.e., Cancún and the Mayan archaeological sites of that region). The commercial traffic on that roadway has been supplemented by petroleum-related transport, which has led to Tabasco possessing a well-developed

Lagoons and part of the city of Villahermosa, the capital of Tabasco, Mexico. (iStockPhoto)

transportation infrastructure; Villahermosa, the capital, has benefited in particular by the movement of goods, services, and people through the state. Relatively few tourists visit the state; most are drawn to the archaeological remnants of Mexico's purported "mother" culture, that of the Olmecs, and its premier site at La Venta, located near Villahermosa. The capital city also often serves as the staging area for those travelers on their way to the spectacular Mayan ruins at Palenque, which actually lies inside the neighboring state of Chiapas. The tourism sector of Tabasco, nonetheless, has contributed only modestly to the local economy.

Agriculture marks most of the state, giving Tabasco a decidedly rural character, with much of the population scattered among innumerable small towns, villages, and hamlets. A substantial portion of the land is controlled by large farming, plantation-type operations, but Tabasco also holds an enormous number of peasant farmers; they often work part time for others as a means of supplementing their meager incomes. Much of the poverty in Tabasco (it is considered to be in the bottom 10 of the 31 states in Mexico) reflects these conditions, where peasant farmers try to eke out a living from their plots in the midst of government cutbacks in support for small farmers since the changes in agrarian policies after 1993.

As was the case for much of the 20th century in Mexico, the political life of Tabasco was dominated by the Partido Revolucionario Institucional (Institutional

Revolutionary Party, PRI). The control of the federal, state, and municipal governments by the PRI allowed it to dole out resources sufficient to keep much of the population economically dependent on governmental programs of one kind or another, such as the farm credits given to agricultural producers, large and small. In exchange, for decades, voters dutifully supported PRI candidates. PEMEX activities in the region added yet another means for the PRI to use oil-related employment as a form of patronage for local political purpose. In short, Tabasco became a prototypical example of the PRI's strength among rural voters (or *voto verde,* the "ag vote," as it is referred to in Mexico). Though the national dominance of the PRI unraveled by the late 1990s, certain states remained PRI strongholds, including Tabasco; in fact, a former PRI governor, Roberto Madrazo, ran for the presidency in 2006, though with disastrous results. At the local level, however, the PRI continues to exercise substantial political muscle. After the 2006 elections, for example, the PRI captured the governorship and all six of the congressional seats, but the Partido Acción Nacional (National Action Party, PAN) salvaged two of three senatorial positions. The left-of-center party, the Partido de la Revolución Democrática (Democratic Revolutionary Party, PRD), made inroads into the PRI's dominance, but the divisions within the national party structure have undermined the PRD's strength in the state.

In many respects, contemporary Tabasco represents a backwater of Mexico, lacking in economic dynamism, political significance, or cultural prominence in comparison with other states of the country. Yet there is an evident stability, a predictable if impassive quality to life in Tabasco. In contrast to other states, very few Tabasquenos migrate to the United States—lending the state a rather placid if not unremarkable character. On the other hand, Tabasco's voters, who have consistently voted for the PRI, will play a key role in the ability of the old dominant party to make a comeback from its near oblivion after the 2006 elections. The PRI's political recovery from 2006, when it placed a distant third in the voting, was in marked contrast with the party's showing in the midterm elections of 2009. Tabasco, therefore, is one of those states the PRI must hold in its column, while the party rebuilds in other parts of the country.

Alex M. Saragoza

See also Agriculture; Peasantry; Politics and Political Parties; Social Structures, Class, and Ethnic Relations

Further Reading

Bernard, Shane K. 2007. *Tabasco: An Illustrated History.* Jackson, MS: University Press of Mississippi.

Tabasco Official State Website. http://www.tabasco.gob.mx.

Vautravers Tosca, Guadalupe. 2008. *Tres enfoques de la migracion en Tabasco.* Villahermosa: Universidad Juárez Autonoma de Tabasco.

Tamaulipas

The official coat of arms of Tamaulipas. (Corel)

The state of Tamaulipas is located in the northeastern corner of Mexico. It is bounded on the north by the tip of the southeastern Texas border, on the east by the Gulf of Mexico, on the west and southwest by the states of Nuevo León and San Luis Potosí, respectively. After the 2010 census, Tamaulipas ranked 13th in terms of population, while the state's land area is ranked seventh in the nation. The capital of the state is Ciudad Victoria, which is adjacent to the crossroads of the two main commercial arteries between the northeast of Mexico and the United States.

The climate of Tamaulipas varies considerably, though most of the state is dry and semiarid, with scant rainfall most of the year. Much of the interior of the state has scorching summers and dry chilly winters; it is separated from the Gulf Coast of the state by the Sierra Oriental mountain range. The coastal area is usually humid and is subject to volatile weather, including hurricane conditions and heavy seasonal rains. The economic geography of the state is divided basically into four parts. The southern portion of the state is dominated by the importance of oil-related industries, anchored by the city of Tampico. The northern edge of the state is dominated by three cities that are marked by their production of goods primarily for the U.S. market: Reynosa, Matamoros, and Nuevo Laredo; the latter is a major portal in the commercial traffic between the United States and Mexico. The interior portion of the state is sparsely populated; the land is largely scrub to semidesert in character, where there is some livestock raising. Agriculture is found in the strips of land along the three key rivers in the state, with the valley of the Río Bravo (named the Rio Grande on U.S. maps) being the most important. The flora and fauna of the state correspond to the distinct climatic zones of the state.

Tamaulipas has a highly diversified economy, and its labor force reflects the distinctive character of the economic geography of the state. About 40 percent of the workforce is occupied in industrial-related jobs, roughly 22 percent in the service sector, and 15 percent are employed by commercial establishments; agriculture absorbs about 9 percent of the state's workers. The border zone has a long history of commercial ties with the state of Texas since the middle of the 19th century and as a crossing point into the United States. The onset of the Border Industrialization Program (BIP) by the Mexican government in 1965 led to the development of industrial parks that served foreign companies, mainly those based in the United States, as production platforms for apparel manufacturing and industrial parts. The BIP attracted firms interested in lowering their production and labor costs, given the incentives provided by the Mexican government, the proximity to the United States, and most important, the abundance of low-wage labor (overwhelmingly female in composition). The North American Free Trade Agreement (NAFTA) of 1993 rapidly accelerated the development of assembly plants in the state (so-called maquiladoras), from about 30 factories in 1988 to about 130 by the late 1990s, employing approximately 150,000 people as of this writing in the cities of Matamoros, Nuevo Laredo, and Reynosa (the latter has the largest number of maquiladoras and it holds about half of the maquila workers in Tamaulipas). The border zone of Tamaulipas is also a key site for several pipelines that take natural gas from fields in Mexico into the United States.

At the southern end of the state, Tampico is the center of the oil-related industry that is controlled by the government-run company, Petróleos Mexicanos (PEMEX). Oil was found in the area of Tampico at the turn of the 20th century, and for a time it was the most productive site in Mexico. Subsequently, the Tampico area became a major oil refining site; currently, the main PEMEX refining facility is specifically located in the city adjacent to Tampico, Ciudad Madero, where a large portion of the crude oil produced in Mexico is converted into gasoline and related derivatives. The oil-related industries of Ciudad Madero and Tampico are served by the nearby deep water port of Altamira, which is also the site of PEMEX's huge petrochemical complex. As a result of the extensive PEMEX facilities in the Tampico area, the government-operated enterprises are collectively the largest employer in the state as of 2010.

Tamaulipas possesses one of the principal roadway corridors that serve the enormous commercial traffic between Mexico and the United States (and Canada). One is the main portal of Nuevo Laredo, across the border from Laredo, Texas, which has the heaviest traffic and carries the bulk of the international commerce, but it is supplemented by two other border points in Tamaulipas, Reynosa (on the other side of McAllen) and Matamoros (across from Brownsville). The significance of Nuevo Laredo is that the city is the terminus of two heavily used highways from the interior of Mexico. Highway 85 serves the eastern corridor of the country, while the other (Highway 57) comes up from central Mexico, and both highways merge at Monterrey, Nuevo León, before entering Tamaulipas and reaching their end point of Nuevo Laredo. Thus, Tamaulipas is located in a very strategic place in the commerce between the NAFTA countries. As a result, transportation-related services represent a key economic sector of the state, from the repair and maintenance of vehicles to hotels and restaurants as well as financial services of various types. Tourism has developed along the Gulf Coast of the state, but its position within the state economy is dwarfed by the importance of the state's oil-related industries and the assembly plants of the border zone.

For decades, the importance of the government-controlled oil-related industries made the state a crucial stronghold of the dominant party, the Partido Revolucionario Institucional (Institutional Revolutionary Party, PRI). Because the oil industry was nationalized in 1938 and organized under the government's PEMEX, the company became a fundamental source of revenues for the federal government, as well

The north wall at the mouth of El Río Pánuco, the entrance to the Port of Tampico, Tamaulipas, Mexico. (Corel)

as for the purposes of political patronage by the PRI, whose dominance spanned from the late 1920s to the late 1990s. It was not until the 2000 presidential election that the political stranglehold of the PRI finally ended. Until that time, the PRI held Tamaulipas in tight political grip. The economic importance of PEMEX gave the PRI tremendous license in the state. The party used its control of PEMEX and its relationship with the powerful PEMEX union to advance the party's apparatus in the state. The unraveling of the PRI at the national level by the end of the 1990s, however, eventually led to a lessening of the power of the party's organization in the state. This shift was facilitated by the rise of the business interests that were generated by the development of the border zone, as opposed to the historic dependence of the state's economy on PEMEX-related activities. Since the 1990s, the conservative Partido Acción Nacional (National Action Party, PAN) has made inroads into the political base of the PRI. As of this writing, PAN holds five of the eight congressional seats, and two of the three senate posts from the state. (The left-of-center party, the Partido de la Revolución Democrática [Democratic Revolutionary Party, PRD], has had little traction in the state.) The PRI, on the other hand, continues to hold on to the governorship, as it has since the 1920s, and PAN's troubles under President Felipe Calderón (2006–2012) suggest a resurgence of the PRI in Tamaulipas. PAN's problems stem in large measure from President Calderón's lack of success in his war against the drug cartels, where Tamaulipas has played a key but very unsavory role.

The largest and most lucrative market for illegal drugs in the world is the United States. Tamaulipas has been and continues to be one of the main crossing sites for the illicit drug trade from Mexico to its northern neighbor and its voracious appetite for methamphetamines, heroin, cocaine, and more recently and most importantly, marijuana. One of the major Mexican drug cartels is the so-called Gulf cartel, which had its origins in the shipment of cocaine from Colombian drug lords in the 1980s. The Gulf cartel's major portal to the U.S. market was through Tamaulipas, where corrupt PRI operatives became allies in the trade. This movement of illegal drugs by the Gulf cartel was facilitated by the leap in commercial traffic generated by NAFTA, given the huge volume of container units that crossed the border, where relatively few were thoroughly inspected by Mexican or U.S. customs. The magnitude of the profits from illicit drugs invited competition from the other drug cartels. By the early 2000s, the rivalries over control of the Tamaulipas corridor for the drug trade led to escalating violence. At the onset of his six-year term as president in 2006, Felipe Calderón promised a war on drugs, and he launched a broad campaign to combat the Mexican drug organizations, primarily through the deployment of federal troops. As a result, the violence in Tamaulipas became endemic and reached unprecedented proportions soon thereafter, casting a very negative light on the performance of the Calderón administration and that of his party, PAN.

U.S. border enforcement policies also played a role in the importance of Tamaulipas in the commerce in illegal drugs. The U.S. Department of Homeland Security initially focused its efforts along the California to Texas border and their main portals (i.e., San Diego/Tijuana, Nogales, Arizona/El Paso [Ciudad Juárez]) in order to suppress undocumented immigration as well as the drug trade. As a consequence, for a time the Tamaulipas portals became comparatively easier for the drug cartels to penetrate as a means of reaching their U.S. destination points. With the surge in NAFTA-related traffic via Nuevo Laredo in particular, the importance of Tamaulipas to the drug trade increased, as the competition among the drug cartels intensified. As a result, Tamaulipas became a site of escalating competition among rival drug crime organizations, and more so when President Felipe Calderón initiated an aggressive campaign to suppress the cartels.

With the rampant violence along the Tamaulipas-Texas border and its primary access routes via Reynosa, Nuevo Laredo, and Matamoros, the stature of PAN deteriorated in the state along with that of President Calderón by 2010. The PRI—despite its historic association with corruption—retained its powerful political position, in spite of earlier gains by PAN. But the PRI has not been immune from the competition among the drug organizations. The initial PRI candidate for the governorship in the 2010 campaign, Rodolfo Torre, was gunned down by cartel operatives in June 2010, shortly before the elections that were scheduled for the following month. The reasons for his murder were unclear, but speculation focused on his stated aim for the PRI apparatus in Tamaulipas to sever its ties with the drug trade; others suggested that Torre had made a deal with one cartel group, and a rival group had exacted its revenge. (Polls showed that he would have been easily elected to office.) Regardless of the reasons for Torre's murder, the assassination of a leading politician of the party most associated with the drug trade indicated the extent of the problems generated by the drug cartels in the governance of the state irrespective of party politics.

The unease created by the drug trade–related violence has cast a pall over the social and cultural life of the state, which is basically clustered in three areas: at the border zone's three key cities; at the southern part of the state, primarily in Tampico; and at the capital, Ciudad Victoria, which possesses the main campus of the leading university and the amenities associated with the city's role as the center of state government. The state as a whole has over a dozen museums, a handful of art centers and first-rate performance venues, and a small number of dance troupes and dramatic arts groups. Outside of the principal urban areas, social and cultural activities are relatively scarce; there are no archaeological sites of much significance, though there is the well-regarded El Cielo biosphere located in the Sierra Madre Oriental mountain range, about 300 miles south of Matamoros. For all of its attractions, as meager as they may seem, the liveliness of the border towns has lessened, and the night life of the principal cities, such as Tampico and Ciudad Victoria, has been negatively impacted by the social anxiety generated by the presence of the drug cartels.

The insecurity created by the violence since 2006, and especially in 2009 and 2010, has led to a decline in tourism, to an erosion of confidence in government, and to a slowing of investments into the state. Worse, the economic downturn in the United States from 2007 to 2010 battered the export sector, given its sensitivity to the business cycles of the U.S. economy. A recovery in the maquiladora sector seemed imminent by the fall of 2010, but thousands of workers had lost their jobs during the recession in the United States. Meanwhile, the Mexican oil-related industry has struggled in the face of declining productivity, in spite of a general rise in petroleum prices with the recovery in the United States from the recession of 2007–2010— given that the United States is the main market for Mexico's petroleum industry. As a result, the social divides in the state have sharpened into even more stark relief.

The social structure of Tamaulipas has a pronounced hourglass shape. At the top are the highly educated professionals associated with the oil-related industries based in Tampico, as well as the managers and owners of the corporate assembly plants of the border cities, such as Reynosa; the directors of important state agencies in Ciudad Victoria round out the elite of the state. In between is a middle class tied to the three key segments of the state's economy, which is joined by the merchants of the larger commercial enterprises generally located in the state's primary urban centers. At the bottom of the social scale are the vast majority of the rural population and the very poor that eke out a living at the border, their shacks often overlooking the maquiladoras. Above them is the diversified labor force of the state that ranges from relatively well-paid mechanics and experienced skilled technicians employed by the maquiladoras, for example, as opposed to the huge number of low-paid menial laborers, from domestics to restaurant workers. And there are about 150,000 or so maquila workers, most of them female, the majority earning anywhere from $500 to $700 a month as of 2010. There is also a sizable informal sector, primarily located at the border, composed of street vendors, day workers, and those selling various types of cheap goods, usually to tourists.

The Human Development Index of Tamaulipas places it among the top 10 in the country, but its high ranking disguises the enormous disparities between the excellent and very high income petroleum engineers working at the PEMEX petrochemical complex, for instance, and the families that roam the garbage heaps of Reynosa looking for anything to use or to sell. In this sense, the concentration of relatively well-educated high income earners associated with the oil industry and the assembly plant sector skews the aggregate figures on the social conditions in the state, but in fact the level of poverty in Tamaulipas is quite high. The statistics on poverty are complicated by the large number of migrants that arrive daily to the border zone, seeking employment in the assembly plant sector or its ancillary economic activities, or to cross unauthorized into the United States. Some estimate that up to 30 percent of the population of the state lives below the poverty line.

For decades, life in Tamaulipas operated basically in two dimensions: one associated with the manufacturing plants at the border as well as the sprawling oil-related industry in the southern portion of the state; and the other the huge, usually low-wage labor force that toiled in the bottom echelons of the bustling sectors of the state's economy. But the Mexican oil industry faces uncertain prospects, as the productivity of PEMEX has sagged, with obvious adverse implications for the Tampico-based petroleum complex. Moreover, the maquiladora sector confronts increasing competition from Vietnam, China, and other low-wage countries, in addition to the negative consequences of any slowing of the U.S. economy (as occurred in its most recent recession of 2007–2010). And finally, the unsettling effects of the illegal drug trade and its attendant violence suggests the persistence of political and social turbulence in Tamaulipas for the near future and perhaps longer. In brief, Tamaulipas will have to address a number of difficult challenges that will test the state's governance and social life over the next several years.

Alex M. Saragoza

See also Borders, Northern and Southern; Corruption; Drug Trade and Trafficking; Energy; North American Free Trade Agreement; Petróleos Mexicanos; Politics and Political Parties

Further Reading

Mendoza, Arturo Alvarado. 2004. *Tamaulipas: sociedad, economic, politica y cultura.* Mexico City: Universidad Nacional Autonoma de Mexico.

Munoz Martinez, Hepzibah. 2010. *The Double Burden on Maquila Workers: Violence and Crisis in Northern Mexico.* Matamoros: Colegio de la Frontera Norte.

Pastrana, Daniela, 2010. "Tamaulipas, Mexico's Black Hole," September 2. http://www.ips.org.

Tamaulipas Official State Website. http://www.tamaulipas.gob.mx.

Telenovelas

Soap opera in Mexico   The genre of soap opera in Mexico has its roots in the melodrama, which is characteristic of a large majority of national cinema, from silent films to those that formed part of the golden age during the first half of the

1940s and those that were still produced in the early 1950s. Although, as noted below, the soap opera genre would develop, during the course of its evolution, subgenera such as comedy, detective, didactic, and historical plots, to mention a few, the melodrama would remain the most prominent thematic, such as those mainly seen by Mexican viewers and broadcast to television stations all over the world.

Soap operas are identified by their excess of passion and the sentimental identification of viewers with the characters. They have plots mainly focused on female characters, Manichaeism, represented by the heroine-victim in opposition to the villains of the story. In addition, and as what is usually prevalent in cinematographic melodrama, there is a moralist tone that follows what is socially accepted as "proper conduct" in the characters' behavior. Only the plot's evil characters could be set apart from proper conduct where in the end, they receive their deserved punishment. In contrast, the virtuous characters are rewarded in the end. Happy endings—like the Hollywood "happily ever after"—would be incorporated into the characters and personalities of the television genre.

Background   Although officially speaking, *Senda prohibida* (Forbidden Path, 1958) is considered the genre's precursor, other examples of live dramatized series contributed to the evolution of telenovelas). *Ángeles de la Calle* (Street Angels, 1951) was first a radio program success that was also adapted to the cinema.

Although some actors limited their histrionic magnetism and performance to the big screen, others joined the new media that recruited well-known actors and directors from the theater. By the 1970s, it was common for novelists and dramatists of that time to accept projects either as writers of original scripts or as adapters of the plays. Renowned novels were performed, especially those published in the 19th century and originally published in the format of serial story, where plots were adapted for soap operas.

At the beginning, Mexican television was considered something for family viewing, a time where family members got together at home in front of the television set. Although soap operas were short lasting (half-hour episodes, aired for just a few weeks, and in black and white), they were originally scheduled in the evening, and only later in the midafternoon. Through the years, program producers considered how to add new viewers to the fan base, adjusting the plots and broadcasting schedules to fit each profile and basing the remaining subgenera according to the traditional melodrama.

The subgenres of soap opera   Historical soap operas were created as a joint effort of Telesistema Mexicano (predecessor to current Televisa), the only existing private television company at that time, and the Social Security Mexican Institute. They were short stories, produced with popular actors, great production resources, and historical research. Along with the fictitious characters, historical events and characters were portrayed, from the Constitution of 1857 to the outbreak of the Revolution in 1910 (*La Tormenta* [*The Storm*], 1967), the fight for Mexico's independence (*Los caudillos* [*The Leaders*], 1968), and the Reform War (*El Carruaje* [*The Carriage*], 1972). The diva of the golden age in Mexican movies, María Félix, participated for the first and only time in this television genre in *La Constitución* (*The Constitution,* 1970). This genre was redeveloped in the 1980s thanks to the producer, Ernesto Alonso, who with more resources and abundant technology, including color television, produced *Senda de Gloria* (*Path of Glory,* 1987), spanning from the 1910 Mexican Revolution to the six-year period of president Lázaro Cárdenas; *El vuelo del águila* (*The Flight of the Eagle,* 1994), a biography of dictator Porfirio Díaz; and *La antorcha encendida* (*The Lighted Torch,* 1996), a new version of the already mentioned *Los caudillos.*

In 1974, Televisa aired *Mundo de juguete* (*Toy World,* 1974), which established the genre of children's soap opera, with plots centered on children's adventures as protagonists. Because it remained on the air for years, it might have caused a temporary lack in interest to the extent that some time had to elapse before the genre was reactivated.

Didactic soap operas appeared with the intent that through relating sentimental stories and family problems, the audience could be motivated toward seeking literacy (*Ven conmigo* [*Come with Me*], 1975), toward family planning (*Acompáñame* [*Accompany Me*], 1977), toward protection of minors and responsible parenthood (*Vamos juntos* [*Let's Go Together*], 1979), as well as toward sexual education (*Caminemos* [*Let's Walk*], 1980).

Soap operas for an adult audience, including male viewers, have their roots in a series being broadcast once a week, after the program *Siempre en Domingo* (*Always on Sunday*), with Raúl Velasco, usually after 10:00 p.m. *Domingos Herdez* presented more audacious, or at least realistic, plots, given its schedule; some of them were taken from the famous short story *Lágrimas, risas, y amor* (*Tears, Laughter, and Love*).

It was, however, the soap opera *Rina* (1977), broadcasted from Monday to Friday at 9:00 p.m., that would captivate adult audiences. Ofelia Medina, in her character of a poor, ugly, vulgar, badly dressed, rude woman with a hunchback, did whatever it took to protect her family, but she had to face the deceit of her boyfriend, a handsome leading man who was trying to deprive her of her huge inheritance. Once this schedule was taken by soap operas—with *Rina* for the first time—it would no longer be given to any other television genre. *Viviana* (1978), the prime time launch of Lucía Méndez, inaugurated the erotic melodrama. A representative figure of soap operas, Angélica María had an enormous failure with *Yara* (1979), absurdly personifying a Tarahumara indigenous woman. It was downgraded to the afternoon schedule category, with *Los ricos también lloran* (1979) taking over its time slot, which was Veronica Castro's first stellar performance. It was successful thanks to the actress's charisma and its elemental and flashy plot. *Colorina* (1980), once again with Lucía Méndez, constituted a scandalous plot. Her protagonist was a prostitute until she was redeemed through motherhood. Although its schedule was adjusted to 11:00 p.m., it was watched by a large number of television viewers.

Between 1976 and 1981, the state channel 13, inaugurated in 1968, took up the Mexican Telesistema's experience of the 1960s of adapting great works in universal literature into short soap operas: the first was *La novela semanal* (*The Weekly Soap Opera*) and then *La historia del mes* (*The Story of the Month*). José María Eca de Queiroz, Fedor Dostoyevski, León Tolstoi, Miguel de Unamuno, Benito Pérez Galdós, Rafael Delgado, Honoré de Balzac, Stendhal, Guy de Maupassant, Henry James, Edgar Allan Poe, and Thomas Mann, among other actors, starred in this soap opera. Most of these productions evidenced the lack of resources and miscasting by hiring Mexican actors who did not match the physical appearance of their characters, given that the original geographic locations of the narrations were maintained. What was interesting about it was that there was a possibility of having Televisa actors participate in them, without the threat of being vetoed by the powerful company. (Channel 13 televised programming that was elitist in nature and not very popular with the audiences.)

The prime schedule at 9:00 p.m. on channel 2 (XEWTV) became the favorite of the genre's followers. *El maleficio* (*The Curse,* 1983) had a mixture of melodrama and horror; but another soap opera, *Cuna de lobos* (*The Wolves' Cradle,* 1986), remained foremost in the minds of the audience, especially because of the legendary character of Catalina Creel, a serial killer who caused trouble for her family and the police.

Without eliminating the romantic melodrama, it was combined in subsequent years with other genres, such as soap operas for children and adolescents. The former aired at 4:00 p.m. and the latter at 7:00 p.m. There was even a direct comical treatment of the genre.

The competition and new schemes involved   The death of Emilio Azcárraga Milmo in 1997 brought about major changes in the company's labor policies when son Emilio Azcárraga Jean took over the company. A large number of exclusivity contracts of actors were canceled, and producers who did not fit into the company's new model left the company. One of them, Víctor Hugo O'Farrill, joined the recently created TV Azteca (which was acquired by Ricardo Salinas Pliego from the government, together with a package of other media), to produce the unsuccessful soap opera *A flor de piel* (*Under the Skin,* 1994).

The pair of actors and producers Christian and Humberto Zurita also migrated from Televisa and produced *La Chacala* (*The Jackal,* 1997) for TV Azteca, with a tone of involuntary humor rather than of horror; *Azul Tequila* (*Blue Tequila,* 1998), a period story; *El candidato* (*The Candidate,* 1999), with political traces;

La calle de las novias (*The Bridals' Street,* 2000), with a popular ambience, in *La Lagunilla;* and *Agua y Aceite* (*Water and Oil,* 2002), a sensational melodrama that touched on the weekly news and directly addressed a lesbian case. The inopportune broadcasting of the last soap opera coincided with the separation of this creative couple from the company.

Elisa Salinas, the aunt of TV Azteca's licensee, Ricardo Salinas Pliego, ventured into the production of soap operas with irregular success; she held the position of director of the production center for such programs at Azteca Digital television stations.

A singular case, worthy of consideration, was that of producer Epigmenio Ibarra. His *Nada personal* (*Nothing Personal,* 1996), where romantic and police plots were combined and had a political resonance, drew strong attention from the audience. From this soap opera and in the soap operas he outsourced for TV Azteca, Ibarra would characterized himself by introducing more ordinary characters, without the dichotomy of traditional melodramas, with longer and fresher dialogues—without the use of an electronic prompter—to fit the longer scenes; the latter were frequently solved by using sequence shot recourse, without camera cuts, emphasizing the effect of naturalness. The artistic talent summoned by Ibarra to his productions combined people from the theater and from the movies who had not yet ventured into television, and actors who had developed their career in Televisa, but who thought that changing television stations was convenient for them. Such was the case of Angélica Aragón, the protagonist of *Mirada de mujer* (*The Look from a Woman,* 1997), which was TV Azteca's greatest success and revolutionized not only the way of doing television, but also strived to influence the point of view of the role played by older women in Mexican society. Among the other titles that Ibarra produced through his company were *La vida en el espejo* (*Life in the Mirror,* 1999) and *Todo por amor* (*Everything for Love,* 2000) stood out where, besides continuing with his style, he addressed prohibited topics in Mexican television, such as male's homosexuality and prostitution.

After his labor relationship with TV Azteca came to an end, Epigmenia Ibarra would undertake projects for Telemundo and even independent projects such as *Cara o cruz* (*Face or Cross,* 2001), *Ladrón de corazones* (*Heart Thief,* 2000), *Gitanas* (*Gypsies,* 2004), and *Los plateados* (*The Silver-Plated,* 2005), scarcely broadcast in Mexico.

Mirada de mujer, el regreso (*A Woman's Look, the Return,* 2003) was considered an artistic failure and disappointment for the audience, since it now lacked the talent of Epigmenio Ibarra; it focused more on political aspects and domestic violence, rather than on the romantic aspect of the first version; whereas *Tan infinito como el desierto* (*As Infinite as the Desert,* 2004), with a format similar to a miniseries, generated eulogistic comments for its technique and narrative as well as for the honest treatment of Juárez's murdered women.

Los Sánchez (*The Sánchez,* 2004), with a tone of comic farce, *Amor en custodia* (*Love in Custody,* 2005), and *Montecristo* (2007) were broadly accepted by the audience to the extent that *Amor en custodia* was ranked second in national rating. The same was true with *Se busca un hombre* (*Searching for a Man,* 2007) and *Mientras haya vida* (*As Long as We Are Alive,* 2007), the latter marking the return of Epigmenio Ibarra to TV Azteca.

From Televisa's side, Ernesto Alonso, "Mister Soap Opera," was producing less and less until his death in 2007. During this stage of Televisa, producer Carla Estrada stood out and took over with soap operas such as *Alondra* (1995), *María Isabel* (1997), *El privilegio de amar* (*The Privilege of Loving,* 1998), *El manantial* (*The Spring,* 2002), *Amor real* (*True Love,* 2003), *Alborada* (2005), and *Pasión* (2007). Estrada specialized in traditionalist and period stories, a guarantee of success for the company.

At that time, besides Carla Estrada's soap operas, Felevisa had rating successes with soap operas such as *Cadenas de amargura* (*Chains of Bitterness,* 1991), *María Mercedes* (1992), *María la del barrio* (*María from the Slum,* 1995), *Cañaveral de pasiones* (*Canefield of Passions,* 1996), *Te sigo amando* (*I Still Love You,* 1996), *La usurpadora* (*The Usurper,* 1998), *Soñarás* (*You Will Dream,* 2004), *Infierno en el paraíso* (*Hell in Heaven,* 1999), *Abrázame muy fuerte* (*Hug Me Tightly,* 2000), *Salomé* (2001), *Las vías del amor* (*Paths of Love,* 2002), *Entre el amor y el odio* (*Between Love and Hate,* 2002), *Velo de novia* (*Bride's Veil,* 2003), *Mujer de Madera* (*Wooden Lady,* 2004), *Rubí* (2004), *Contra viento y marea* (*Against Wind and Tide,* 2005), and *La esposa virgin* (*The Virgin Wife,* 2005).

Soñadoras (*Dreamers,* 1998), *DKDA* (1999), *El juego de la vida* (*The Game of Life,* 2001), *Rebelde* (*Rebellious,* 2004), and *Lola* (2007) followed the line of adolescent soap operas, frequently mixed with music, where Televisa has been by far the leader. *Rebelde* is the clearest example of these types of soap operas that created a marketing phenomenon, including recordings, concerts, and even fashion that imitated the protagonists.

Mexican soap operas nowadays have similarities as well as differences on both major television networks. The former were highly subordinated to ratings, to an extent that stories were prolonged or shortened on air, characters are stressed or taken off camera, psychological profiles are changed or, in many cases, fall into unimaginable situations. International markets were, for both companies, another important niche for selling national soap operas, although paradoxically it was more common for them to be Mexican versions of hits from Venezuela, Colombia, or Argentina. In the case of Televisa, there was also a proliferation of second and third version plots carried over from other television shows, probably since they were already proven formulas. Original scripts were scarce.

There were some exceptions, of course, mainly due to Epigmenio Ibarra's convening power, TV Azteca had the benefit of histrionic reliability, being also outstanding in the cinematographic media. This television network, however, has not been able to retain these actors, whether due to the lack of a large volume of production, contractual differences, or competition both inside and outside of Mexico, which enabled actors to switch to other companies.

Televisa is still launching actors and actresses who have little experience to stardom. Both companies engaged artistic talents from all over Latin America in order to promote them in such a way that when their productions are exported, they were more acceptable for a foreign audience who would identify them through their work as local figures.

Another shared distinctive feature of the soap opera is its defined segmented audience profile, which is not as heterogeneous as before, now expanded to include children, adolescents, housewives, and adults of both genders. TV Azteca's evening soap operas, especially those produced by Argos, used to focus on a more demanding audience both in their stories and histrionic quality. Televisa soap operas, with a greater audience, covered less favored socioeconomic segments, with less demanding viewers who were in contrast with whatever entertainment was offered to them.

Edmundo Gómez Martínez

See also Art Education; Musical Groups and Artists; Television

Further Reading

Smith, Paul Julian. 2009. *Spanish Screen Fiction: Between Cinema and Television.* Liverpool: Liverpool University Press.

Television

The television industry in Mexico has been decisively shaped by two historic factors. First, from the late 1920s until 2000, the federal government was dominated by one party, the Partido Revolucionario Institucional (Institutional Revolutionary Party, PRI). Since the federal government oversees mass communications in Mexico, the influence of the PRI has been crucial to the development of the television industry. Second, because of its historic ties to the PRI, one network, popularly known as Televisa, has come to dominate the industry. Though competitors have challenged that dominance at various points in time, Televisa remains the most powerful presence in the industry and its ancillary activities. Its current major rival, TV Azteca, has struggled to make significant gains in market share since its inception in 1993. It is generally estimated that Televisa controls about 70 to 80 percent of the viewing market in Mexico. The federal government has supported its own nonprofit public broadcasting stations, primarily for educational purposes, but government-sponsored programming has failed to attract any substantial viewing public to date. A large proportion of Mexico's population is poor, which limits the use of cable and satellite systems as alternatives to the two major commercial networks. The end of Mexico's one-party government in 2000 failed to dislodge Televisa from its dominant perch. However, in 2007, the Mexican Supreme Court basically voided congressional legislation that clearly favored the maintenance of the duopoly of Televisa and TV Azteca over television broadcasting. Yet, it is unclear whether greater competition will result from the court's ruling over access to the licensing of any new broadcasting channels. The advantages accrued over time by Televisa, and to a lesser extent, TV Azteca, are likely to make it difficult for any media company to pose a viable challenge to the current two major networks for audience share, advertising revenues, talent, and profitability.

The PRI's presidential candidate was defeated in 2000 by Vicente Fox, the candidate of the Partido Acción Nacional (National Action Party, PAN), which has been consistently probusiness and has championed the privatization of the economy. Thus, despite its longstanding criticism of the television industry's subservience to the PRI, PAN has been reluctant to attack the unbalanced structure of the industry, as Televisa, for instance, has continued to exercise its extraordinary hold over the industry. Since the late 1990s, commercial broadcasters have made notable strides in their impartial coverage of elections and political issues. In the past, commercial broadcasters rarely criticized the PRI or the federal government for fear of losing their licenses or other types of retaliation. Thus, news programming was essentially self-censored by commercial networks, but that situation has changed dramatically in recent years. Still, critics argue that the dominance of the television media by two companies hinders the democratization of Mexican society and access to information vital to the public interest. There have been periodic calls for the dismemberment of Televisa in particular, similar to what took place in the United States in 1943, when the National Broadcasting Company (NBC) was forced to sell one of its two networks to create the American Broadcasting Company (ABC).

Televisa's programming and distribution capability has been key to the company's predominate and durable role in the industry. TV Azteca and Televisa monopolize the production of television shows, everything from game and children's programs to musical and artistic presentations. Mexican programming is sold throughout the Spanish-speaking world, particularly to other Latin American countries. Televisa and TV Azteca also supply the bulk of programming to the two Spanish language television networks in the United States, Univisión and Telemundo. The dominant role of Televisa and TV Azteca in producing shows for television has sparked debates over the content of the industry's programming. Feminists, for example, have often criticized the portrayal of women on television, and critics have lamented the industry's small range of products, limited public affairs programs, and reliance on foreign-created (often from the United States) programs translated into Spanish to supplement programming produced in Mexico and other Latin American countries. On the other hand, televised soap operas (telenovelas) have been very popular and important to the industry, despite the telenovelas' frequent dependence on traditional and predictable story lines. Occasionally, Mexican soap operas have presented characters or plots that challenge traditional roles or values, but these efforts have often been couched in familiar story lines. Mexico's television industry imports some programming from other Latin American broadcasters, such as Brazil's Globo network and Venezuela's Venevisión media conglomerate. News programming has improved noticeably since the mid-1990s, but Mexican television has moved slowly to embrace investigative reporting, news documentaries, and high-quality educational and public service programming. Local affiliate stations have some leeway in producing their own shows, but most of the daily programming for network stations is determined by the corporate headquarters of the two major networks.

In short, the basic structure of the Mexican television industry continues to be marked by its unbalanced nature. In the 2006 presidential electoral campaign, the candidate of the left-of-center party criticized the monopolistic character of Mexico's private sector with a clear reference to the television industry. His defeat by the PAN candidate, however, has made it unlikely that the industry's structure will change in any fundamental manner in the near future. Since the late 1990s, the two major networks have made a deliberate effort to provide more balanced coverage of Mexican politics as a means of deflecting criticism of the dominance of the industry by Televisa and TV Azteca.

Background   Television in Mexico became a controversial issue since its beginnings. The initial request for a television broadcasting license was submitted to the federal government in 1946 by Emilio Azcárraga Vidaurreta, who controlled the country's dominant radio network. The request was denied by Miguel Alemán Valdés, who was subsequently elected president in that same year. The evidence demonstrates that Alemán wanted to own a portion of the new medium for himself. Alemán, however, had no experience in broadcasting, and he stalled Azcárraga's repeated requests for a license. Toward that end, Alemán commissioned a study to consider whether the new medium would be controlled by the state (such as England's BBC) or whether to follow the private commercial model of the United States. The subsequent report recommended the model of the United States. In the meantime, Alemán had developed a close political relationship with auto tycoon and publisher Romulo O'Farrill, who consequently received the first concession to begin televised broadcasting in 1949 (station XHTV channel 4). Under mounting pressure, Alemán finally conceded a license to Azcárraga Vidaurreta in 1951 (station XEWTV channel 2). A third licensing permit was granted in 1952 to Guillermo González Camarena (station XHGC channel 5), the former chief engineer for Azcárraga's radio operations. Alemán's apparent plan was to force Azcárraga to sell his license to the station ostensibly controlled by O'Farrill. González Camarena's bid was probably granted by the Aleman government in part to deprive Azcárraga of his main source of engineering expertise.

The three stations competed brutally against each other for audience share in a pitifully small market. Television sets were expensive at that time, and few people in Mexico could buy one; nonetheless, the competition was fierce. The O'Farrill station, backed clandestinely by Alemán and businessmen tied to the president, struggled to overcome the huge advantages of Azcárraga's station. With his long history of dominating the radio industry, Azcárraga held much of Mexico's entertainers under contract or had their loyalties as well as much of the technical expertise in the new medium. Alemán's influence could not be easily discounted, however, given the privileges granted to ex-presidents even after their tenure in office by the country's dominant party. (Meanwhile, González's station floundered for lack of programming and capital.) In that context, Azcárraga was essentially forced into a partnership with O'Farrill, and by implication, with Alemán. In 1954, the three stations fused to become Telesistema Mexicano. The company basically monopolized the industry for the next several years, using three broadcasting channels to offer various types of programs.

In 1968, Luis Echeverría was elected to office on a reformist platform. Concerned by the dominance of the industry by Telesistema, and as an overture to the powerful business interests of Monterrey, Nuevo León, Echeverría's administration approved the television licensing request of businessmen closely tied to the so-called Grupo Monterrey. The resultant Television Independiente de Mexico (TIM) began broadcasting operations in that year. In 1970, TIM bought a relatively weak regional network of small stations initiated in 1965 by Manuel Barbachano Ponce as a way to expand the reach of TIM in the country. Serious financial problems, however, pushed the TIM network in 1973 to merge with Azcárraga's company to form Televisa.

Critical of the dominance of commercial television, in 1972 Echeverría also invigorated the government's public television capability through the creation of Imevision. Previously, the first public station had been founded in 1958 and was operated by the National Polytechnic Institute, but the government stations failed to offer any real competition to the commercial dominance of Televisa.

The relationship between Televisa and the dominant party changed, as the PRI faced mounting criticism and opposition in the wake of the economic crisis of the late 1970s. Television increasingly became important to influencing the political perceptions of the Mexican public through televised news coverage, or through television's lack of attention to governmental corruption, mismanagement, rigging of elections, and related issues. In this sense, the PRI was forced to rely increasingly more on television as a means of lessening its sagging electoral dominance of the country, especially with the worsening economic problems that plagued Mexico into the 1980s. Televisa used its news broadcasts as a means of trying to boost the PRI's image, as the party confronted the effective challenge of the right-of-center PAN party by the mid-1980s. This growing reliance of the PRI on Televisa produced dividends for the company, as the network's licenses were renewed and its bid to begin satellite transmissions via a government-financed satellite system was approved. As a consequence, Televisa's grip over the television industry tightened still further.

Key to this process was the Emilio Azcárraga Milmo, who took over the reins of the company with the death of his father in 1972. Azcarraga Milmo greatly enhanced his political influence through the use of his network to bolster the flagging political capital of the PRI. Nonetheless, the erosion of support for the PRI continued, as the Mexican economy spiraled to the brink of bankruptcy by the early 1980s. Pressured by international lenders to change course, the PRI retreated from its historic policy of government-led economic development. The onset of the neoliberal economic model led to a surprising move in 1993, when the government sold its main public broadcasting venture (Imevisión) to a private business group headed by Ricardo Salinas Pliego—hence the birth of TV Azteca.

Initially TV Azteca seemed to have the potential not only to compete with Televisa, but also to offer an alternative to the close connection that had developed between Televisa and the government. As it turned out, the formation of TV Azteca reflected the influence of the president's brother. The involvement of the brother of then President Carlos Salinas de Gortari with the winning bid for Imevision by the Salinas Pliego group (no relation) has shadowed the subsequent development of TV Azteca. Though Televisa's near monopoly of the industry seemed to have been dealt a blow by the emergence of TV Azteca, the government in 1994 approved the licensing renewal of Televisa's network of stations and extended their expiration period. In the ensuing battle for viewers, Televisa lost some of its market share to the upstart network, but it has sustained its dominant position.

The television industry in Mexico diversified in the 1990s as the impact of microwave, cable, and satellite transmission lessened the market's reliance on Televisa's channels and those of TV Azteca. The use of cable and satellite systems was greatly constrained by the cost to consumers of such services, as Mexico's large low-income population simply could not afford the price for the installation and maintenance of televised entertainment and news independent of the two major television networks available after 1993.

The sharp recession of 1994 deeply wounded both of the major networks, especially Televisa, because of its debt, while TV Azteca struggled to increase its market share. The problems of Televisa were compounded by the death of Azcarraga Milmo in 1997, and the company edged toward the brink of financial disaster. Equally important, the dominant party's hold over political power plummeted after its presidential victory of 1994. The post-1994 recession undercut the remaining credibility of the PRI, and the party reeled from the sinking value of the peso, a huge rise in inflation, and the constriction of credit. Mexico's middle class was especially hard hit, and the discontent led to the shocking defeat of the PRI in the midterm elections of 1997. For the first time since the 1920s, the PRI had lost control of the Mexican Congress.

The television industry survived the political storm that wrecked the PRI's political monopoly by acknowledging the need for change. Indeed, the industry made a major political shift, led by the new leader of Televisa, Emilio Azcárraga Jean. Young, relatively untested, and under pressure at the time from other family members with interests in Televisa, Azcárraga Jean weathered his shaky start building on a spectacular move. In one of its news programs in 1996, Televisa showed a videotape of the killing of protesting peasants by the PRI governor of the state of Guerrero. The unexpected broadcast of such an obvious criticism of the PRI regime stunned the Mexican public and indicated a decisive break from the past, where the industry would no longer be a tool of the dominant party. In the elections of 2000, the industry for the first time made an evident effort to lessen its biases in the coverage of that historic electoral contest. In light of the past, the change contributed importantly to the defeat of the PRI's presidential candidate.

Nonetheless, the structure of the industry has remained largely the same. Despite numerous calls to lessen the concentration of the control of the two networks, the Mexican Congress has failed to make any substantive move to curtail the dominance of TV Azteca, and, most importantly, that of Televisa. This situation presented a conundrum to President Fox when he assumed office in 2000, given his party's longstanding promotion of neoliberal policies, including the lessening of government intervention in the economy. Hence, Fox refused to reduce the dominance of the two networks. In fact, toward the end of his term in office, the Fox administration approved the expansion of Televisa's network of stations to the dismay of many critics.

It was anticipated that a left-of-center presidential regime would make inroads in the dominance of the two networks over the television industry. But in the 2006 elections, the right-of-center, probusiness PAN party won again by a razor thin margin over the challenge of the leftist candidate.

In that same year, the question of the future of the broadcasting licensing came before the Mexican Congress. Concerns over televised coverage of electoral campaigns pushed many representatives to favor legislation that would leave the industry's structure intact. Few politicians wished to invite the wrath of the two major networks. In fact, much of the new legislation was purportedly written by lawyers associated with Televisa. Congress hastily approved the measure, and newly elected President Felipe Calderón failed to mount any effective effort to block its passage. Critics of the law, however, challenged the legislation before the Mexican Supreme Court. In a stunning decision in the fall of 2007, the Supreme Court ruled that key provisions of the measure were unconstitutional. The eventual outcomes of the ruling remain unclear, but the Court's decision represents yet another step toward the democratization of Mexico. Equally significant, in light of the Court's decision, the Mexican Congress passed legislation that essentially eliminated paid political advertising on radio and television, a significant source of profits to the dominant media companies. In short, the two major television networks face important challenges within Mexico, and the prospects for Televisa and TV Azteca are far from bright, given the increased competition from abroad, for example, in the selling of programming to foreign markets.

On the other hand, the Court's ruling and Congress's ban on paid political advertising are unlikely to have any substantial impact in the short term over the structure of the television industry in Mexico. Time will tell whether Mexican television will reflect greater diversity in its pattern of ownership and content.

Alex M. Saragoza

See also Echeverría Álvarez, Luis; Election, Presidential, 2000; Election, Presidential, 2006; Partido Acción Nacional; Partido Revolucionario Institucional; Popular Culture; Telenovelas

Further Reading

Hernandez Lomeli, Francisco, and Guillermo Orozco Gomez. 2007. *Televisiones en Mexico: Un recuento historico.* Guadalajara, Jal: Universidad de Guadalajara.

Juarez Garniz, Julio. 2009. *La television encantada: Publicidad politica en Mexico.* Mexico City: Universidad Nacional Autonoma de Mexico.

Theater

Since the last half of the 20th century, the Universidad Nacional Autónoma de México (National Autonomous University of Mexico, UNAM) has been a center of theatrical innovation and experimentation, a source of the avant-garde that has challenged the commercial and official theater (the latter refers to works and companies supported by the government's main cultural agencies). In this regard, a crucial movement in the dramatic arts took place in the late 1950s, with the debut of the theatrical productions of *Poesía en Voz Alta* (Poetry Out Loud), which aimed to challenge the established, traditional theater and its reliance on plays in the style of Spanish romanticism and other standard dramas. Though the movement did not prosper and withered away for lack of funding, the impact of *Poesía en Voz Alta* had an enduring effect on that generation of playwrights in terms of their attention to realistic writing, to the use of colloquial language, and to the importance of staging in dramatic works. The famous playwright, Héctor Mendoza, was among those associated with the *Poesía* movement, who broke away from the canon of that time in the Mexican theater, culminating in his production of the play *Don Gil de las calzas verdes* (1966). Mendoza was joined in this move by other directors, such as Julio Castillo, Juan Ibáñez, Ludwing Margules, Luis de Tavira, and Juan José Gurrola; set designers José de Santiago, Gabriel Pascal, Philippe Amand, and Alejandro Luna contributed to the formation of a generation of dramatists shaped by the rupture of the 1950s and whose influence persisted into the 1970s.

During the 1980s, in the context of Mexico's economic and political turmoil of those years, a distinct group of dramatists emerged primarily from independent theatrical workshops. Their thematic elements were dominated by their recurring concerns for the hardships, marginality, and tragedies of everyday life for the country's poor; the technique of these playwrights tended toward realism and the use of testimonials. The plays of this group, however, did not coalesce into a cohesive style or school of drama. Nonetheless, their break from the plays of the 1950s generation led to their inclusion into the so-called New Mexican Dramaturgy, which included Víctor Hugo Rascón Banda, Oscar Liera, Héctor Azar, Vicente Leñero, José Ramón Enríquez, Abraham Oceransky, Jesús González Dávila, Guillermo Alanis, Jorge Esma, Tomas Espinoza, Alejandro Licona, Felipe Santander, Guillermo Schmidhuber, Miguel Ángel Tenorio, Juan Tovar, Tomás Urtusástegui, Gerardo Velásquez, Sabina Berman, Leonor Azarate, Vivian Blumenthd, and Olivia de Montelongo.

The new Mexican theater failed to sustain its vitality, however, and a transitional period ensued, as government funding for the arts declined while the recession of the mid to late 1980s deepened. With the introduction of neoliberal policies, privatization, and the decentralization of governmental cultural policies in the midst of the political and economic troubles of the 1990s, theater in Mexico fragmented into a diverse constellation of companies and stylistic initiatives. Established, publicly funded companies survived the budgetary constraints of the times, notably the Compañía Nacional de Teatro (National Theater Company, founded in 1977), as a number of theatrical efforts arose and then disappeared quickly for lack of finances, audiences, or both. The Taller de Teatro (Theater Workshop) of the University of Sinaloa under the direction of Oscar Liera was among those efforts that achieved a measure of success. In 1982, after the staging of the play *Salmodia,* Liera was invited to lead the drama program at the University of Veracruz. Despite the difficulties faced by the Mexican theater, several stellar plays were written during that period: *Habitación en blanco* (*Room in White*) by Estela Leñero; *Dolores o Felicidad* (*Sorrow or Happiness*) by David Olguín (who, together with actor Daniel Giménez Cacho, founded El Milagro publications, one of the main publishing houses of theater in Spanish); *Lobo* (*Wolf*) by Jorge Celaya; *El motel de los destinos cruzados* (*The Motel of the Crossed Fates*) by Luis Mario Moncada; *El ajedrecista* (*The Chess Player*) by Jaime Chabaud; *Los niños mutilados* (*The Crippled Children*) by Hugo Salcedo; *Los niños de sal* (*The Children of Salt*) by Hernán Galindo; *Deseo* (*Desire*) by Ricardo Pérez Quitt; *El Viejo de la Condesa* (*The Old Man from La Condesa*) by Luis Eduardo Reyes; and *El Tren nocturno a Gregoria* (*The Night Train to Gregoria*) by María Luisa Medina. Amaranta Leyva, writing for children's plays, received critical acclaim for her work using puppets, along with directors Martín Acosta, Carlos Corona, and Mauricio García Lozano.

One innovative trend appeared in the 1990s that became known as theater of the body, spearheaded by the work of Gabriel Weisz, who proposed the body as a means for theatrical material. This approach was embraced and extended creatively by a cluster of female directors, the so-called La Rendija (The Slit) group, which included Rocío Carrillo, Raquel Araujo, and Alejandra Montalvo. Several important plays were produced by the Rendija group and its individual members, such as *Infinitamente Disponible* (*Infinitely Available*) by La Rendija; *Asesino personal* (*Personal Killer*), and *Cuerpo poseído* (*Possessed Body*) by Rocío Carrillo; *Condesa Sangrienta* (*Bloody Countess*) by Raquel Araujo; and *Dibujo de viaje* (*Drawing Trip*) by Alejandra Montalvo.

Building on the theory of the theater of the body, performance artists began to literally enter the stage, giving new meaning to the concept of drama and its presentation in Mexico; these artists included Jorge Vargas, Ricardo Díaz, Rubén Ortiz, Héctor Bourges, and Jean Fréderic Chevallier. Formed in 2001, the independent theater troupe, Project 3, derived from this approach and organized several events to promote its style for the stage. A similar, recent theatrical innovation was sparked by the visits of Le Cirque du Soleil of France to Mexico in the 1980s. The performances of the French troupe, a combination of classic and contemporary pantomime, spectacle, clowns, and circus techniques, inspired a group of Mexican artists concerned with the exclusive nature of the theater. The results were a series of events such as the International Festival Rodará, the International Convention of Circus and Stage, and the Atayde encounter, among others, which explored the uses of circus elements for the arts. These encounters led to the creation of a hybrid of circus and theater groups, for example, Cirko de Mente (Circus of Mind), Rodará or Circo Sentido (Sensible Circus), whose performances usually took place at alternative and independent forums. This movement in theater brought to Mexico well-known trainers of clowns, such as Anatoli Lokachtchouk, and his company El Escuadrón Jitómate Bola (Rounded Tomato Squad). Among those influenced by this coupling of street theater and clown method (e.g., acrobatics, juggling, and pantomime) are Azis Gual and Jesús Díaz, whose works incorporated elements from a variety of sources generated by this fusion of performance artistry.

The vibrancy of the Mexican theater has been sustained by the organization of international events; two annual festivals have been of special importance for the production and performance of drama: the Cervantino Festival of Guanajuato and the Festival of Mexico City. In addition, the Muestra Nacional de Teatro (National Theater Exhibition) has provided an opportunity for dialogue and exchange of ideas among playwrights, actors, directors, as well as a forum for new works. Since 2002, the Festival Internacional de Teatro de Calle (International Festival of Street Theater) in Zacatecas has encouraged that particular genre, in the same way that the Línea de Sombra company has maintained an interest in the theater of the body through its holding of conferences on that genre. Unfortunately, these efforts to maintain the vitality of theater in Mexico have been plagued by a historic problem: the primacy of Mexico City as the site for theatrical production. In spite of attempts to decentralize the arts, it has been very difficult for theater groups outside of Mexico City to thrive without consistent state or local governmental support. Talented playwrights from the north, for example, such as Hugo Salcedo and

Enrique Mijares—both winners of Mexico's top prize for theatrical achievement, the Tirso de Molina Award—have received scant support or acknowledgment for their accomplishments from their native states to date.

The struggles of playwrights, drama directors, actors, and theater companies have been mirrored by the challenges faced by Mexico's university-based drama programs. For example, in 1989 the drama school at the UNAM was finally allowed to grant a degree in theater, despite the long tenure of one of the country's leading dramatists Rodolfo Usigli, generally regarded as the founding figure of modern Mexican theater. The degree program maintained Usigli's insistence on a strong theoretical background to the training in the dramatic arts. In a companion to the drama school at the UNAM, the University Theater at the UNAM's Cultural Center has focused since 1980 on the staging of plays as a training ground for students of the theater.

In addition to the programs at the UNAM, the Escuela Nacional de Arte Teatral (National School of Theatrical Art), founded in 1964, was incorporated in 1994 into Centro Nacional de las Artes (National Center for the Arts, CNA); the main purpose of the school is the training of professionals for the stage. There are also several schools for the theater in Mexico City, such as the Centro de Arte Dramático A.C. (Dramatic Art Center), which opened in 1975 under the direction of the playwright Héctor Azar; and more recently, Carlos Payán and Epigmenio Ibarra have inaugurated a training center for actors for the theater as well as for television and film. Furthermore, Luis de Tavira formed the Casa del Teatro (House of Theater) in 1992, joining another initiative in the same year, the Contemporary Forum Theater. These new theatrical venues allowed for alternative productions, such as *Todo somos Marcos* (*We Are All Marcos*) by Vicente Lenero; *La manta que nos cobija* (*The Protective Blanket*) by Jose Ramon Enriquez; *Sueno mexicano* (*Mexican Dream*) by Osvaldo Dragun, and *Los ejecutivos* (*The Executives*) by Sergio Celis. Outside of Mexico, the drama schools of Patzcuaro, Michoacán, offered notable plays and toured the country in order to bring the stage to marginalized communities. Mention should be made of Jesusa Rodríguez and Liliana Felipé for their valiant efforts to maintain the cabaret theater as a form of political criticism through their performance club El Vicio (the Vice, originally named the Habito).

The work of archiving Mexico's theatrical history has been done by the Centro Nacional de Investigación, Documentación e Información Teatral Rodolfo Usigli (National Center of Theatrical Research, Documentation and Information Rodolfo Usigli) located in the CNA and founded in 1981. The center has been responsible for the preservation and dissemination of information on various aspects of drama production, including set designs, scripts, and documents related to the theater in Mexico. In sum, the theater in Mexico faces an uncertain road ahead, but the resilience of the Mexican dramatic arts has persevered through very difficult circumstances in the past.

Zulai Macías Osorno

See also Cultural Policies

Further Reading

Breining, Daniel. 2007. *Mexican Theater and Drama from the Conquest through the Seventeenth Century.* Foreword by Óscar Armando Garcia. Lewiston, NY: Edwin Mellen.

Leñero, Vicente, ed. 1996. *La nueva dramaturgia mexicana [The New Mexican Dramaturgy].* Mexico City: El milagro, CONACULTA.

Ponce, Armando, ed. 2003. *México, su apuesta por la cultura [Mexico, Its Bet for Culture].* Mexico City: Grijalbo Mondadori.

Schmidhuber de la Mora, Guillermo. 2006. *Dramaturgia mexicana: Fundación y herencia [Mexican Dramaturgy: Foundation and Heritage].* Guadalajara, Jalisco: Universidad de Guadalajara.

Tlatelolco Massacre

Student movement of 1968   The year 1968 was marked by student demonstrations all around the world, and Mexico was no exception. As in other countries such as Czechoslovakia, Poland, or Germany, these protests became a turning point for the political or social future of the country. Mexican college students organized several protests and demonstrations, mainly centered around freedom, democracy, and peace. For many, these events were the first clear indications of discontent with an authoritarian government, and its reaction was a confirmation. The government's massacre in the student demonstration on October 2, 1968, marked the beginning of a more organized and prodemocratic Mexican civil society. Furthermore, it is considered the Mexican peak event of an internationally shared period termed "*Guerra sucia*," where the Latin American and Spanish authoritarian governments persecuted and assassinated opposite social leaders and students.

Background   From 1940 to 1970, Mexico experienced significant economic growth. The gross domestic product increased sixfold and the population only doubled, while the peso-dollar parity was maintained. This gave the Partido Revolucionario Institucional (Institutional Revolutionary Party, PRI) economic stability that strengthened its power position. However, by the 1960s a new generation experienced peace and stability of the regime, but also a lack of political rights and opportunities. It became evident that even though elections were celebrated, they were only a facade, and the regime had repression mechanisms for any opposition movement.

The economy was thriving, and in 1968 Mexico became the first developing country appointed as the venue for the summer Olympic games. This was considered quite an accomplishment for the Gustavo Díaz Ordaz administration (1964–1970). The students, however, used the international attention on Mexico to point out the lack of democratic conditions and the political repression.

A soldier prods a protester with the butt of his rifle in Mexico City's Tlatelolco Plaza on October 3, 1968, after a night of violence between protesting university students and soldiers. Exactly how many died is still hotly contended (with claims between 38 and 300), but the incident brought the repressive tactics of Mexico's government sharply into focus. (AP/Wide World Photos)

The growing tension between Díaz Ordaz and the students The year 1968 started with the repression of some student strikes in the Universidad Nacional Autónoma de México (National Autonomous University of Mexico, UNAM) and the Instituto Politécnico Nacional (National Polytechnic Institute, IPN). Some students were imprisoned or hurt in the riots. Instead of calm demonstrations, the students wrote a statement requesting the release of their comrades, the dismissal of the chief of police and his deputy, punishment for the responsible officials of the bloodsheds, and the repeal of Articles 145 and 145b of the Penal Code (which sanctioned imprisonment of anyone attending meetings of three or more people, deemed to threaten public order).

The students' requests were backed by college authorities. For example, UNAM's rector Javier Barrios Sierra blamed the violent government's irruption on some schools that had declared they would strike by June. In protest, he raised the university's national flag to only half mast. He also presented a speech where he summoned the students into another public demonstration and called on the government to respect the university's autonomy.

Under the pressure of the upcoming Olympic games, Díaz Ordaz was determined to stop the demonstrations. But instead of negotiating, he hardened the police's repression. Both demonstration intensity and the government's reaction increased. In

August, the students publicly insulted President Díaz Ordaz. He responded by sending military tanks to disperse the protest. In September, a month before the beginning of the Olympic games, Díaz Ordaz sent the army to take over the UNAM and, a week later, the IPN. Both colleges were under military control as a result of the failed intimidation strategy toward the students. The army left by October 1, but the students summoned another massive demonstration for the next evening, October 2, at the Plaza de las Culturas, in the Tlatelolco area in Mexico City.

The massacre It is reported by some agencies that around 20,000 students and supporters were gathered in Tlatelolco that evening. The army was closely watching the demonstration. As a matter of fact, there were plain-clothed soldiers among the students. The government was particularly protecting the Ministry of Foreign Affairs building in the surroundings of the plaza.

For apparently no reason, soldiers hiding in the neighboring buildings started firing against the demonstrators. Presumably the soldiers were misguided by a helicopter that overflew the mobilization and fired flares as a warning. It is said by witnesses that the soldiers who were interspersed among the demonstrators believed the shots were coming from the students, so they too opened fire against the mob.

The government stated that 20 people had been killed. It excused these deaths as military mistakes, not as a deliberate planned repression. However, the students argued that the soldiers were clearly obeying the order of killing and persecuting the demonstrators. Students and witnesses stated that when the firing began, most of the students fled to hide in the neighboring buildings. They claimed that the soldiers followed to seize them, entering into private apartments without warrants.

Simultaneous to the events in Tlatelolco, the army was also repressing a public protest at the IPN campus. This has been suggested by some as a proof that the government was really planning a violent repression and what happened in Tlatelolco was not just mere confusion.

Some Mexican writers and witnesses such as Elena Poniatowska and Jorge Castañeda said that there were at least 65 dead students and insinuated that there were probably more.

The Mexican government received international criticism for the massacre. Still the Olympic games were inaugurated just 10 days after the events. During the inaugural speech, some students flew a black dove-shaped kite to symbolize the massacre and the contradiction of carrying out an international peace event.

Gustavo Díaz Ordaz was hated by social groups and international critics. In order to protect him, his successor Luis Echeverría (1970–1976) sent him to Spain as an ambassador. However, in Spain he was criticized and rejected even by the Francisco Franco authoritarian government in that country. With an important social and political rejection, he was dismissed from the embassy and disappeared from the public. He died in 1979, a victim of colon cancer and asthma. He never was named in any legal or judicial procedure for the massacre. During the following decades, until the democratic transition, the case was never opened again.

Tlatelolco's implications   Before the Tlatelolco massacre, the left was scattered in a number of movements, clubs, cells, and other types of organizations without legal recognition. The only opposite institution recognized by the PRI was the Partido Acción Nacional (National Action Party, PAN). The massacre was taken as a unifying banner for most of the left movements. This motivated more serious attempts to form a stronger organization.

Several Maoist groups and the Partido Comunista Mexicano (Mexican Communist Party, PCM) were involved with student demonstrations. Also, in 1994 the leader of the Ejército Zapatista de Liberación Nacional (Zapatista Army for National Liberation, EZLN) insurrection, Subcomandante Marcos, mentioned the 1968 student movement as an influence for his career.

The Tlatelolco massacre and other student repressions that happened in the 1970s served as a wake-up call for the opponents to the PRI's hegemony. Actually, the left movements, even though being considered illegal, had the strength to support a nonregistered candidate for the 1976 presidential election. The votes he received were discarded, but it reminded the PRI of the growth of the opposition and the imminent risk for social collapse by not opening the system. In 1977 the PRI passed the first political reform needed to achieve a democratic transition. This reform allowed the registration of the PCM. The left finally had a legal channel of political participation instead of public demonstrations.

Tlatelolco at the democratic transition   At the 1988 presidential campaign, the claim for justice in Tlatelolco's massacre case was part of dissident and left PRI candidate Cuauhtémoc Cárdenas's campaign. He gathered the left forces and the heirs of the PCM. Among his supporters was the activist Rosario Ibarra, mother of a Tlatelolco victim. Since the massacre, she had become an emblematic left politician and main demander for justice. Cárdenas lost the election in what seemed a widespread electoral fraud, for which the PRI did not reopen the case.

It was not until the PRI lost the majority in the Congress in 1997 that the first governmental actions were taken to clarify the events. Congress created a special committee to investigate and appoint blame. Since Díaz Ordaz was dead by then, the committee interviewed many political participants involved in the massacre, including Luis Echeverría, the former Mexican president who was Díaz Ordaz's minister of the interior at the time of the massacre. Echeverría admitted that the students had been unarmed and also suggested that the military action was planned in advance. Still, no judicial process was opened.

For the 2000 presidential election, Vicente Fox, PAN's candidate, also used the Tlatelolco massacre in one of his campaign promises. He said that during the PRI's government, the case was covered and forgotten, and he proposed reopening the investigations. When he became president, he created the position of special prosecutor for past social and political movements, with the main task of investigating and identifying offenders in the 1968 Tlatelolco massacre and other disappearances during the *Guerra sucia* in the 1970s.

In 2006, Echeverría was charged with genocide in connection with the massacre. He was placed under house arrest pending trial. Just a month later, he was exonerated from genocide charges by the judge, because the statute of limitations had expired.

Juan Manuel Galarza and José Ignacio Lanzagorta

See also Echeverría Álvarez, Luis; López Portillo, José; Partido Revolucionario Institucional

Further Reading

Camacho, Alma Rosa. 2008. *1968: Un archivo inédito* [*1968: A New Archive*]. Producción, Consejo Nacional para la Cultura y las Artes, Dirección General de Publicaciones. México, DF: El Universal.

Poniatowska, Elena. 1991. *Massacre in Mexico,* translated by Helen R. Lane. Columbia: University of Missouri Press.

Tlaxcala

The official coat of arms of Tlaxcala. (Corel)

Located in central Mexico, Tlaxcala is the country's smallest state. The city of Tlaxcala is the state's capital, and other major urban centers are Apizaco, Huamantla, Santa Ana Chiautempán, and Tlaxco. It is dwarfed by the state of Puebla, which nearly surrounds it, and by Mexico's Federal District, with which it shares a border. In 2010 its population was estimated at 1.7 million residents, among the very lowest of the country's 31 states.

In the centuries before Spanish contact, Tlaxcala was home to a variety of indigenous groups. Cacaxtla and Xichoténcatl (just outside of today's capital city) were particularly important ceremonial centers, distinguished by their pyramids and murals, which are still well preserved. Tlaxcala's native peoples fought a constant battle to preserve their independence in the face of challenges from the Aztecs of central Mexico and the Indians of Cholula in neighboring Puebla.

Although they initially resisted the Spaniards, the Tlaxcalan Indians soon forged an alliance with the Europeans, aiding in the final defeat of the Aztecs at Tenochtitlán (today's Mexico City). The Tlaxcalans continued to aid the Spaniards in the colonization of Mexico, and Tlaxcalan settlements emerged in San Luis Potosí, Zacatecas, Durango, and Coahuila. They derived special privileges from their relationship with the Spaniards. They were allowed to preserve their own government and successfully represented Indian demands during the colonial era.

Despite their alliance with the Spanish administration, the Tlaxcalans were increasingly affected by colonization. Population decline (caused by disease and migration to other areas of New Spain) and intermarriage with the Spanish population altered Tlaxcalan society. These same factors also led to the transfer of traditional native lands. Tlaxcala's native peoples did not escape tribute demands, and many were drafted as workers on major projects, such as the construction of Puebla's cathedral. Over time, many natives also became a source of labor on Spanish haciendas and in textile factories owned by Spaniards in the towns of Tlaxcala and Apizaco. Additionally, the Roman Catholic Church touched the lives of some natives, as Franciscan missionaries tried to gain converts.

In spite of the encroachments of the Spaniards, the Tlaxcalan leaders tended to favor the colonial arrangement as a way of protecting themselves against the ambitions of neighboring Puebla, which sought to expand into Tlaxcala. Thus Mexico's struggle for independence, beginning in the early 19th century, was resisted by many native (and nonnative) elites. Tlaxcala remained a federal territory until 1856, when it was finally granted statehood. Political autonomy was only part of the battle, however. The small state also struggled to build a viable economy, and its major products, wool and pulque (a beverage made from the fermented juices of the maguey plant), failed to compete in Mexico's markets. Meanwhile, Puebla's wealthy entrepreneurs acquired haciendas and textile factories in Tlaxcala.

The 19th century also was marked by political instability in Tlaxcala. During Mexico's War of Reform (1858–1861), Tlaxcala was the scene of numerous battles. The competing liberal and conservative factions both established governments in the state—the liberal government in the capital and the conservative regime in Huamantla. The 1860s brought additional disturbances, as invading French forces (who helped establish a French empire in Mexico) occupied Tlaxcala City, forcing the state government to retreat. The French were expelled in 1867, and Tlaxcala was reclaimed by the insurgent forces of Miguel Lira y Ortega, who then became the state's governor.

The last decades of the 19th century saw greater stability and prosperity in Tlaxcala. Under the leadership of Lira y Ortega and of Próspero Cahuantzi, Tlaxcala's economy grew. Although some Tlaxcalans lost their lands during this period, the state did not experience a great movement of land into the hands of a wealthy few (as was the case in many areas of Mexico). Taxation, rather than loss of land, therefore was a more important factor in creating the opposition that led to rebellion and revolution. Under Cahuantzi, landowners struggled against increasing taxes. In 1899 thousands of small landholders protested yet another increase in property levies and were violently repressed. Cahuantzi's selective application of taxes also caused a division among the elites.

When the Mexican Revolution began in 1910, the movement sparked the discontent of Tlaxcala's campesinos and workers, particularly in the densely populated (and heavily indigenous) central-southern region of the state. Isidro Ortiz

A small shrine just outside the city of Tlaxcala (seen in background), Mexico. (Corel)

and Juan Cuamatzi were among the earliest leaders of the Revolution and were influenced by the radical ideas of Aquiles Serdán in Puebla. Cahuantzi's government soon fell, along with the national regime of Porfirio Díaz. Antonio Hidalgo became governor and attempted radical reforms, including the return of communal lands. He met elite resistance, which intensified after the overthrow of the Madero government. The state's revolutionaries regrouped under Máximo Rojas, Domingo Arenas, and Pedro Morales. Arenas, a textile worker, emerged as a leading champion of land reform. He helped to redistribute land in both Tlaxcala and Puebla before his death in 1917. His followers, including his brother Cirilo Arenas, continued their rebellion against Venustiano Carranza, who resisted radical reforms.

In the aftermath of Carranza's own demise, and during the 1920s and 1930s, Tlaxcala experienced a period of social reform. Rafael Apango, Ignacio Mendoza, Adrián Vázquez, and Isidro Candia (all leaders who represented the popular classes of rural Tlaxcala) redistributed lands and used agrarian reform to co-opt Tlaxcala's campesinos. Land reform eventually affected the pulque haciendas of northern Tlaxcala, which had been particularly resistant to reform. Apango, Mendoza, Vázquez, and Candia also strengthened the state's ties with the central government and organized workers. After 1940, as Mexico shifted away from its period of revolutionary change, Tlaxcala's leaders became more conservative, neglecting the continuing demands for land reform that persisted into the 1980s and that worsened with population growth and overexploitation of resources. Instead, the state's leaders focused on developing industry, and industrial zones emerged (including the Tlaxcala-Puebla industrial corridor).

The last decades of the 20th century were characterized by increasing urbanization and by the migration, particularly of native peoples, to the cities. Environmental problems, including water pollution and the encroachment of urban zones into agricultural areas, accompanied such change. Tlaxcala's economic modernization also resulted in an erosion of the state's indigenous cultures. Beginning in the 1980s, however, the state government embraced a plan to preserve Tlaxcala's rich indigenous heritage.

In light of recent political and economic conditions, the electoral context of the state has moved from its previous conservative bent toward PAN in the 2004 race for the governorship. Instead, a PRI candidate won the 2010 gubernatorial elections, indicative of an ebbing of confidence in the leadership of the right-of-center party. Both parties basically share power after the 2010 elections, with each possessing 12 seats in the state legislature. The declining popularity of President Calderón (2006–2012), a member of PAN, has clearly undermined his party's base in Tlaxcala, opening the door for the PRI's comeback. Meanwhile, support for the left-leaning PRD has eroded dramatically among the state's voters, consistent with national trends, as it won only 2 seats in the 2010 legislative election, 8 less than it had after the 2007 electoral round. Tlaxcala represents a key political battleground as the Mexican presidential election looms in the year 2012.

Suzanne B. Pasztor

See also Immigration and Emigration; Indigenous Peoples; Partido de la Revolución Democrática; Peasantry

Further Reading

Flores Hernandez, Aurelia. 2010. *A las mujeres por la "ley" no nos tocan las tierras: genero, tierra, trabajo y inmigracion en Tlaxcala.* Tlaxcala: Universidad Autonoma de Tlaxcala.

Rendón Garcini, Ricardo. 1996. *Breve historia de Tlaxcala.* Mexico City: El Colegio de Mexico.

Sanchez Munoz, Bertoldo. 2001. *Desarrollo economico y cambio demografico en Tlaxcala.* Tlaxcala: Universidad Autonoma de Tlaxcala.

Tlaxcala Official State Website. http://www.tlaxcala.gob.mx.

Tourism

The tourism industry of Mexico represents a key sector of the economy, generating both an important source of foreign earnings for the country as well as domestic spending by Mexican tourists. As an economic activity, tourism involves the flow and social composition of tourists, the origins of those travelers, the services generated for those travelers (food and drink establishments, lodging, entertainment and recreation, etc.), and the various types of tourism and their effects on the environment, local economies, and infrastructure. Tourism is generally among the top three or four sources of revenues for Mexico; the travel industry ranks only behind oil and remittances as a means of foreign currency earnings since the 1990s. In recent years, safety concerns related to the swine flu outbreak in 2009 and drug-related violence have dampened some enthusiasm for tourist visits to Mexico, but tourism continues to be relatively strong for the country.

Tourists are composed of two basic types: domestic and international travelers. Domestic tourism represents about three-fourths of total spending in the Mexican travel industry, but international tourists generally spend much more money per capita on a daily basis, and they earn Mexico a significant amount of foreign earnings as a consequence. It should be emphasized that the numbers for international tourists are distorted for Mexico because of the significance of visitors who cross the U.S.-Mexican border. Thus, while by official statistics about 100 million tourists on average visit Mexico, in fact more than 80 percent of those visitors are border tourists; about 16–20 million tourists actually traveled in the interior of Mexico or visited via boats over the last several years; figures vary from one year into the next.

The tourist industry in Mexico is marked by imbalances of various sorts, due in large part to the fact that the overwhelming majority of international tourists are from the United States. Thus, the geographic distribution of major destination points corresponds to the proximity and demand of North American tourists. Moreover, the social character of those sites tends to reflect North American tastes. As a consequence, particularly since the 1970s, the Mexican government has fostered a tourist policy oriented largely toward international tourists, most of them from the United States. Thus, a disproportionate number of international tourists visit just a handful sites in Mexico, notably Mexico City, Cancún, Puerto Vallarta, and Los Cabos. North American tourism also exhibits a distinct dimension, called border tourism; however, the majority of tourists who arrive via air or boat, as well as via automobiles, into the interior of Mexico are also North Americans.

Nonetheless, the travel industry also recognizes the obvious significance of domestic travelers and their needs. Unlike American tourists, Mexican travelers exhibit a much more dispersed pattern of destinations, and they reflect a wider social spectrum, from the budget tourist (who spends modest amounts of money per day) to the very upscale traveler who spends lavishly on lodging and other amenities. Domestic tourism often involves visiting recreational areas in the interior of Mexico close to major cities, where water parks, picnicking, boating, and the like can be enjoyed and which are commonly combined with cultural tourist activities, such as visiting museums, shopping for arts and crafts, and viewing historic sites. For example, every weekend a stream of residents from smog-choked Mexico City visits the nearby hillside town of Cuernavaca, about an hour away by automobile,

A local fisherman opening his catch of oysters below a shrine for the Virgin of Guadalupe on a beautiful Acapulco beach filled with tourists. (Uli Danner | Dreamstime.com)

to stay a night or two at one of its hotels, dine at its restaurants, do a bit of sightseeing, and then return to the city on Sunday evenings. In brief, tourism in Mexico follows well-established routes, routines, and practices and is among the most highly developed sectors of the Mexican economy.

In the case of Mexico, tourism, both domestic and international, is dominated by three types of destinations: border, beach, and cultural sites. In several destinations, as described below, the latter two elements are combined. Ecotourism also takes place in Mexico, but that component of the travel industry remains somewhat underdeveloped in comparison to other places in Latin America, such as Costa Rica. Time-shares and second homes—a variation on traditional tourism—have spread rapidly in recent years, and the location of that trend has tended to mirror primary tourist sites in Mexico.

The Mexican government has played a crucial role in the development of the tourist industry. Since the late 1920s, the federal government actively promoted travel to Mexico. Initially, much of that policy impetus focused on Mexico City and its monumentalist heritage, such as the city's colonial architecture and its pre-Columbian archaeological ruins, as the government established standards for the ratings of hotels, improved roadside amenities for tourists, authorized tour guides, licensed food establishments and their ratings, and advertised Mexico's attractions in foreign publications, especially in the United States.

Beach-oriented tourist policy emerged with the development of Acapulco in the 1940s, and that trend was greatly accelerated in the 1970s with the formation of a new government agency, Fondo Nacional de Fomento al Turismo (FONATUR; National Trust Fund for Tourism), created to develop planned resorts primarily for foreign visitors. The agency initially moved to create tourist complexes at Loreto, on the Gulf of California in the state of Baja California Sur; Huatulco and Ixtapa, on the Pacific coast; and Cancún, on the Caribbean tip of the Yucatán Peninsula. The latter site turned out to be the most successful by far, as it quickly outstripped the popularity of the other FONATUR-built resorts. The Mexican government held a tight rein on major destination sites for foreign visitors through FONATUR and basically funneled international travelers toward the agency's premier resorts. Indeed, for a time FONATUR provided financing and construction related to tourism and even operated a chain of upscale hotels among its many efforts to promote travel to Mexico.

However, a new stage in Mexican tourism appeared in the 1980s, as the Mexican government began to relax its regulations on tourist development, particularly for beachside resorts, and facilitated greater foreign investment in the travel industry. FONATUR lessened its grip over tourist-related development and began to focus primarily on infrastructure projects to attract attention to the industry from domestic and foreign investors. As a consequence, other sites expanded and modernized their tourist complexes to supplement the established destinations for foreign and domestic tourists, such as Puerto Vallarta, Los Cabos, and the so-called Mayan route along the main coastal highway south of Cancún. The reduction of FONATUR's role and controls over the travel industry encouraged privatization and further development, but this trend has also been subject to corruption and/or violations of ecological rules and regulations.

Yet another trend in the travel industry increased rapidly in the 1990s and into the present: the growth of the second-home market, time-shares, and retirement communities. Most of this travel market was oriented toward Americans. These sites tended to be close to established tourist areas, such as the coastal towns along the upper reaches of the Gulf of California (i.e., close to the populous cities of Phoenix and Las Vegas and the inland areas of southern California). While domestic tourists have consistently participated in these trends, a large proportion of Mexican travelers continued to visit secondary sites that are less likely to attract foreign tourists, such as Manzanillo, Veracruz, and Acapulco, just to name a few.

One other, but unfortunate trend in Mexican tourism has been the infiltration of capital from the drug trade into this sector of the economy. Tourist development has been used by drug lords as a form of legal investment, as well as a means to launder the profits of drug trafficking. Puerto Vallarta and resort complexes in and around Cancún in particular have drawn the monies of drug lords, often through legitimate channels, making it difficult to trace the connections between drug traffickers and tourist development—a process linked to a time when politicians of the Institutional Revolutionary Party (PRI) facilitated the entry of drug monies into the structure of the Mexican travel industry. Moreover, the violence that has accompanied the drug trade holds negative consequences for tourism, such as to the border and certain beachside destinations, most notably Acapulco.

Thus, the configuration of Mexican tourism reflects the long history of involvement of the Mexican government in the industry. While new investment, domestic as well as foreign, in the tourist industry has greatly increased, much of it remains tied to the framework laid down in the past. For example, relatively few foreign tourists visit the interior of the country outside of the traditional destinations, such as the colonial circle of cities of central Mexico, including Guanajuato and San Miguel de Allende. As a result, southern Mexican states—other than Oaxaca and its celebrated archaeological ruins and Day of the Dead festivities—receive very few foreign or domestic tourists compared to other areas of the country. A similar pattern holds for several other states that are off the beaten path of the established tourist circuits. In short, Mexican tourism continues to bear the mark of the centrality of the federal government in the development of the travel industry.

Border tourism   The overwhelming majority of international tourists are in fact Americans who cross the U.S.-Mexican border to shop, eat, and enjoy themselves in various ways. On average, about 80 million visitors have crossed the boundary between the two countries every year since the 1990s. Perhaps the most prominent example of this type of tourism is the San Diego, California–Tijuana corridor, where Americans by the thousands visit the area, usually for very short periods of time. This type of tourist activity also takes place along the rest of the border between the two countries, principally at Nogales, El Paso, Laredo, and Brownsville and their "sister" Mexican cities of Nogales, Ciudad Juárez, Nuevo Laredo, and Matamoros, respectively. The Tijuana-based border tourism also allows for visitors to access the beachside areas south of the Mexican border city, particularly in the vicinity of Ensenada. Border tourists are often "weekenders," but a large proportion of border tourists do not even stay overnight in Mexico but simply go back across the border to the American side at the end of their visit. Nevertheless, given the huge volume of such visitors, border tourists represent a major source of revenues for the Mexican economy.

Mexicans mirror the activities of their North American counterparts, though not in the same numbers nor with a similar level of financial impact. Still, large numbers of Mexicans cross the border to visit the United States to shop or to enjoy themselves at sites near enough to the border to be accessible by automobile. Mexican tourists from Tijuana frequent San Diego, California, for instance, in the same way that Mexicans from Chihuahua visit Tucson, Arizona. Furthermore, the relatively brief flights from Mexican cities to American destinations near the border permit

Mexicans of means to travel easily to the United States for touristic purposes. For example, Mexican tourists from Monterrey, Nuevo León, and its surrounding area have become commonplace in upscale hotels and shopping centers in Houston, Texas, which is a couple of hours away by air from that northeastern Mexican city.

Beach tourism A very large proportion of international and domestic travelers visit Mexican beaches on both sides of the country. International tourists congregate primarily in the area dominated by Cancún, along the Caribbean coast, where a resort corridor has spread southward along the coastline of the Yucatán Peninsula all the way to the boundary between Mexico and Belize. While most of those tourists are from the United States, many Europeans also visit Mexico's main Caribbean resort complex. On the Pacific side, Puerto Vallarta and Los Cabos have become especially popular with Americans, and the latter beachside vacation site has begun to challenge the primacy of Cancún as a foreign tourist destination, particularly for American high-budget travelers.

Beach tourism in particular is characterized by social and economic segmentation, ranging from very expensive all-inclusive hotels to budget lodging for young people and the like. Cancún, for example, has a reputation, not entirely deserved, as a place of constant partying, largely by American college students, especially during so-called spring breaks. In contrast, the coastal highway south of Cancún proper is studded with out-of-the-way boutique hotels as well as by expansive resorts that cater to the very wealthy, who are usually older and prefer a more sedate atmosphere. Similar distinctions take place at all of Mexico's primary beach destinations; the more upscale tourist sites tend to draw fewer domestic tourists, though well-heeled Mexicans can be found at the most exclusive of tourist sites. Beachside destinations tend to attract younger visitors, leading to a wide array of leisure and recreational activities, from parasailing and waterskiing to dance clubs and water parks.

There has been an effort by Mexican government tourist planners to combine beach tourism with cultural activities. Tour guides in Cancún, for instance, offer trips to nearby Mayan archaeological sites from the beachside resort area. Oaxaca will soon have a highway to facilitate tours to the Zapotec ruins in Oaxaca City from the beachside site of Huatulco, one of FONATUR's original resorts.

Domestic tourists tend to visit secondary beach sites to a much greater extent than do foreigners. Mexican travelers are much more likely to vacation in beachside destinations like Veracruz on the Gulf of Mexico, and on the Pacific side, Manzanillo, Ixtapa, Acapulco, and Mazatlan attract large numbers of domestic visitors.

A variant of beach-oriented travel is the popularity of Mexico for cruise-ship tourism. Both coasts have attracted cruise-ship companies, though a clear circuit has developed that basically coincides with established beachside resorts. This includes the Caribbean circuit anchored by Cancún and encompassing Cozumel and Playa del Carmen for cruise ships most often leaving from Miami. The Pacific circuit, generally beginning in Los Angeles, usually incorporates Ensenada, Los Cabos, Mazatlan, Acapulco, and Puerto Vallarta.

Cultural tourism   From the beginnings of the Mexican tourist industry, the country's spectacular archaeological and historic architectural sites have drawn large numbers of tourists. Especially since the 1940s, travelers have also been drawn to Mexico to visit sites representative of its artistic patrimony, modern art galleries, and excellent museums.

Among the most popular of those destinations for cultural tourists are the pyramids near Mexico City and the architectural wonders of the Mayan culture in various places in the Yucatán Peninsula, as well as those of the Zapotec civilizations of the valley of Oaxaca. Archaeological ruins, however, can be found throughout central Mexico in particular, given the density of the indigenous cultures of that region prior to European contact. In addition, many travelers also seek the well-known folkloric arts and crafts of Mexico, such as its pottery, textiles, and jewelry among many other items, whose designs and methods can generally be traced to indigenous artisans since before colonial times.

Particularly since the 1920s, the Mexican government has actively promoted cultural tourism through its various agencies, most importantly the *Instituto Nacional de Antropología e Historia* (INAH, or National Institute of Anthropology and History). This agency and its allied institutions have been at the forefront of maintaining the country's artistic production, from the murals of Diego Rivera to the art studio of Frida Kahlo—both sites attract thousands of visitors per year. The crowning monument to this cultural policy is the magnificent Museum of Anthropology in Mexico City, a vast and incredibly rich collection that features artifacts from the country's pre-Columbian heritage.

The long period of Spanish colonialism (1521–1821) produced a host of architectural monuments, most notably religious monuments, plazas, and government buildings. The national cathedral of Mexico City, the myriad of churches in the nearby city of Puebla, and the colonial architecture of the city of Guanajuato are among the most popular of the hundreds of sites reflective of Mexico's colonial era and the wealth generated during that time by its mines, agriculture, and labor.

Ecotourism and adventure tourism   In recent years, Mexico has made an effort to develop and promote ecotourism and adventure tourism. Developed primarily by private interests, these efforts have included touring the country's southern states, such as Chiapas, with its dense jungles that possess an astounding array of flora and fauna. In Baja California, ecotourists have frequented the marine reserves off the coast of the peninsula. The Usumacinta River valley in the state of Chiapas, along the Mexico and Guatemala border, has received attention from ecotourists, and the Yucatán has attracted adventure tourists to its caverns and underwater caves. The infrastructure for these types of tourism is in the process of further development and has yet to reach levels that generate substantive revenues. Still, the promise for these types of tourism is clearly evident though largely untapped, given the richness of Mexico's geography and locales conducive to draw ecotourists and their adventurous counterparts.

Future prospects   The tourist industry in Mexico faces a number of challenges in the coming years. The asymmetries of the past will be difficult to change, as much of the structure of the industry has become deeply entrenched. The primacy of Cancún persists in terms of beach tourism, though Puerto Vallarta and Los Cabos have become important rivals to the Caribbean resort; these three destinations account for a disproportionate share of the foreign earnings derived from international tourists. The dependence on tourists from the United States suggests that this pattern in beach tourism will continue, leaving large stretches of Mexico's coastline relatively unaffected by international tourist development.

There is also an uneasy dimension to recent tourist developments that emphasizes the separateness of resorts for foreign tourists (overwhelmingly from the United States), such as all-inclusive expensive hotels and similar enclave sites. In the early history of tourism in Mexico, the travel industry focused on creating a "Mexican" experience for the visitor, which invariably meant the presence of tourists at museums, archaeological sites, historic buildings, markets, and, in the evenings, at local attractions. Enclave-type tourism isolates the tourist from the everyday life of the country and its cultural differences. Indeed, upscale travelers in particular often desire a "bubble" experience that minimizes interaction with the local area and its people. In effect, these travelers are primarily interested in replicating their "home experience" in another locale and are relatively unconcerned with the opportunity to learn about the cultures that surround the hotel and its amenities. This type of tourism thrives in the form of all-inclusive hotels with spas, gyms, multiple in-house restaurants, exclusive golf courses, and related services that essentially insulate the visitor.

On the other hand, the benefits of the travel industry are not without costs, and the environmental degradation of well-traveled sites poses a serious threat to various destinations. Acapulco in this regard has long been a warning sign to these concerns, as the rapid expansion of that resort in the 1940s and 1950s fouled the ecology of Acapulco Bay almost beyond repair. Despite such lessons, there are many areas endangered by unchecked and/or poorly planned tourist development, such as the coastline of the Yucatán Peninsula, where much damage has been done to coral formations, to the habitat of rare species, and to the water quality of underground aquifers by the overbuilding of resorts.

At the other end of the country, the breakneck pace of the travel industry on the Baja California peninsula not only menaces flora and fauna but has also strained the scarce water sources of the region. The construction of desalinization plants and conservation efforts notwithstanding, the fast building of hotels, time-share complexes, retirement communities, and second-home housing, as well as golf courses for tourists, puts huge pressures on the delicate ecology of the region. Furthermore, the expansion of the industry invariably produces the need for housing to accommodate the workforce that services tourist activities, adding yet another necessary stress on the environment.

A major challenge for both international and domestic tourism has been the negative impacts of the illegal drug trade and its attendant violence. Media reports and travel advisories by the U.S. State Department in 2009 and again in 2010 led to the perception of endemic violence in Mexico that seriously undermined the travel industry. More recently, however, tourist activity has mounted, as more travelers realize that the drug-related violence is largely confined to a few areas of the country. Puerto Vallarta and Los Cabos, for example, have been relatively untouched by the killings and kidnappings that have plagued traditional destinations such as Acapulco, but border tourism continues to be depressed by the shootings that have regularly taken place as the drug cartels vie for control of the entry points into the United States. Despite the bad publicity related to the murderous drug trade south of the border, the economic downturn in the United States since 2007 has made Mexico a bargain for financially strapped American travelers. Recent evidence suggests that the negative impact of the U.S. recession on Mexican tourism has lessened considerably, particularly for Cancún, but also for other beachside destinations. Domestic tourism, however, has yet to rebound from the uncertainty generated by the violence associated with the drug trade; in large part, this is due to the propensity of Mexican travelers to rely on cars, making them vulnerable to carjacking and kidnapping.

Finally, the trends in global tourism do not favor a major increase in the flow of international visitors to Mexico. The aging of American society, combined with its income inequality, means a likely ebbing of tourists, especially high-budget travelers, from the United States to Mexico's main resort destinations, with a corresponding decline in those resorts' profitability. On the other hand, the trend toward second-home and retirement complexes, primarily for Americans, will continue to expand, especially in those areas of Mexico in close proximity to the United States. It is also probable that Mexican tourism will rely increasingly on its domestic market to generate more revenue for the travel industry and will have an increasing proportion of foreign visitors remain in tourist enclaves.

Alex M. Saragoza

See also Archaeological Sites; Baja California Sur; Economy, U.S.-Mexican Border; Environmental Issues; Jalisco; Oaxaca; Quintana Roo; Sonora; Yucatán

Further Reading

Berger, Dina, and Andrew Grant Wood. 2010. *Holiday in Mexico: Critical Reflections in Tourism and Tourist Encounters.* Durham, NC: Duke University Press.

Goertzen, Chris. 2010. *Made in Mexico: Tradition, Tourism, and Political Ferment.* Oxford: University of Mississippi Press.

Transportation

Geographic background and history   Mexico's geography is extremely diverse. The country is marked by two mountainous chains that roughly parallel each other along the curve of the coasts of the Atlantic and Pacific oceans, with a high plateau in between. These two mountain ranges along the north-south axis of Mexico are traversed by a chain of mountainous terrain in the central region of the country. During the first centuries of the nation's independent life, the complexity and division of this geography made national integration a real challenge. In the 19th century, transportation across the territory was scarce and unreliable, mostly short rural roads, which made travel uncomfortable and insecure. Often, the roads themselves presented a greater danger than the abundant road bandits that could assault the traveler during the trip. For the same reasons communications were equally difficult. During the hectic 19th century, in which Mexico suffered many civil wars (including the War of Independence), the war news traveled so slowly that often, by the time one region of the country heard of the events happening in another region, the war was almost over. Economic development was also hindered greatly by this lack of integration and swift transportation within the country. Economic historians have often said that Mexico's geography conspires against its development.

The first unified attempt to conquer the nation's resilient territory was made by President Porfirio Díaz. He became president of Mexico in 1876, and would remain so (with a brief interruption) until 1910. Díaz understood the importance of a transportation network that would cover the territory for both political and economic reasons. With the help of abundant foreign investment, he set forth on the task to build a massive transportation infrastructure that would connect the country. True to his time, Díaz had a fascination for trains. He believed that the fastest and most efficient way to connect the country was to build a comprehensive net of railroads that would link the country's business and financial centers with the maritime ports and the northern border. This would encourage trade from abroad and would foster economic and social development. When Díaz seized power, Mexico had fewer than 500 kilometers (km) of railroads, but by 1910 railroads measured more than 20,000 km. The most important routes built in this period were the Mexico City–San Juan del Río (1880), Mexico City–Paso del Norte (1882), Mexico City–Ciudad Juárez (1884), Mexico City–Tehuacán (1891), and the Transismic Route that united the Gulf of Mexico with the Pacific Ocean across the 215 km of the Isthmus of Tehuantepec (1894). Along with the construction of railroads came that of telegraphic lines. Using the same routes, communications across these locations were now possible.

However, when Díaz was exiled by the Revolution, the civil war damaged the infrastructure that had cost the country so much. Ten years of revolts not only stopped the maintenance of the railroads, but also maimed them severely as the rebels actively destroyed them as a war strategy. The Revolution brought with it more than a change of president; it brought a new paradigm. For Díaz, foreign investors were paramount to the country's development, and they should be respected and protected to encourage necessary capital inflows. Whereas for the revolutionaries, foreign investors were essentially the enemy, as they profited from the nation's resources and expatriated their earnings to their home countries. These new revolutionary ideas led to a wave of nationalizations that would span most of the 20th century.

In 1912 British and American railroad companies were bought out almost entirely, and the Mexican government took over the administration and building of railroads. From this date to the late 1980s, private investment in transportation infrastructure would be heavily regulated, confined to Mexicans, and essentially used only when the government could not manage the enterprise alone. The final blow to foreign investors came in 1937, when Lázaro Cárdenas expropriated the National Railroad Company and expelled foreign capital from it completely.

The 20th century   The 1920s brought important changes to the Mexican transportation sector, as well as to the Mexican political system. As the oligarchic spawn of the Revolution, the Institutional Revolutionary Party (PRI) consolidated its inner structure and tightened its grip on political power, automobiles and air transportation became popular. This shifted the focus from railroads to airports and highways. The government inaugurated the highway connecting Mexico City and Pachuca, an important industrial location in the adjacent state of Hidalgo, in 1926; the highway from Mexico City to Acapulco in 1927; and the highway from Mexico City to Oaxaca in 1930. Parallel to the development of highways, the first bus companies started operations during the same decade. In 1925 Flecha Roja started transporting passengers throughout the territory, using the old roads as well as the new ones. By 1940 Mexico had 9,929 km of federal roads.

However, the nation's territory was still highly fragmented. In sum, Porfirio Díaz was right; transportation infrastructure and development were closely linked. Despite the efforts to build roads to span the territory, huge regions were left unattended. The only coastal city of any economic significance on the Pacific Ocean was Acapulco. The rest of the coast was essentially unchanged by the 20th century. The same thing happened to the region of southeast Mexico, to a large portion of the northern desert, and even to some isolated areas in central Mexico.

Airlines also emerged during this period. In 1928 the first route traveling from Mexico City to the northern border town of Laredo started its operations, managed directly by the Ministry of Transports. In 1929 this route started from the newly opened Mexico City airport. International air travel would have to wait until 1934, when the first route from Mexico City to Los Angeles was opened. This same year marked the birth of the first Mexican airline, Aeronaves de Mexico, flying at first only to Acapulco. Transatlantic travel came in 1948, with the first route being Mexico to Madrid.

However, the true boom of air transportation came with the opening of the Benito Juárez International Mexico City Airport in 1950. The leading airline at the time was Aeronaves de México, whose shares belonged mostly to U.S.-based Pan Am Airlines. Aeronaves de México was nationalized in 1957.

Maritime transportation attracted less attention in the first decades of the 20th century. Despite the fact that roughly 80 percent of international trade came by sea, the government paid little attention to the development of ports during this period. This changed when President Lázaro Cárdenas stated that the country's lack of a merchant marine was a huge obstacle to development. This statement was particularly true at the time because the nationalization of oil, and the subsequent expatriation of foreign capital, left the country with the sole responsibility of the export of crude. The task fell upon PEMEX, the newly created national oil company, to develop a maritime transportation system and coordinate exports. A few years later, this measure effectively centralized all maritime trade in the country. It became evident that PEMEX could not manage this kind of activity, and the Autonomous Marine Department was created. In 1949, the government finally permitted private enterprises to enter the market. This led to the foundation of the Company of Maritime Services.

The next key shift in government policies concerning transportation came about with President Carlos Salinas de Gortari. From the first months of his tenure, it became evident that, unlike many presidents he welcomed private enterprise and foreign capital. The government's blatant incompetence in the management of transportation, communications, and banking was becoming evident as the 1980s came to an end. In 1989, Salinas set forth an ambitious plan to build 4,000 km of state-of-the-art highways with the help of private investment. The federal government invested $300,000 million in this project. These measures allowed for the vast improvement of well-traveled roadways, including the notoriously dangerous route, Mexico City–Acapulco, as well as the Guadalajara-Colima and Constituyentes–Reforma-La Venta highways. During this period, there was also a major liberalization of the assignment of automobile transportation routes. Salinas gave more than 70,000 permits to private contractors in previously controlled routes.

Current situation   The transportation sector has increased its relative weight in national economic activity. In 1980 only 8.3 percent of gross domestic product (GDP) came from transportation; in 2007 this figure had climbed to 13.4 percent. However, the sector faces important challenges in the coming years. As of 2007, 80 percent of the volume of transports was made through roads, the least efficient means to cover long distances. Throughout the world, railroads have been gaining importance as the costs of railroad transportation have diminished greatly relative to other means. However, the infrastructure demand for this kind of endeavor is very large. The logistics sector has been developing new ways to combine transportation means within a given route to minimize costs.

The Mexican railroad network has been losing significance for the last two decades. Less than 20 percent of the volume of transportation is done through this means. This is in spite of its relatively low cost. Today, railroads are mostly privately owned, with the government having a small stake in the companies involved.

Something similar is happening to maritime transportation. Port technology and efficiency are becoming more and more important in the choice of an export route. Mexican ports lack the efficiency necessary to manage the massive amounts of cargo that would otherwise come through the country. However, investments are being made to modernize port infrastructure.

The air transportation sector has suffered a major transformation in the last years. The introduction of low-cost airlines has diminished the cost of an airplane ticket by about 40 percent. Low-cost airlines are currently competing for the bus transportation market, as they offer low fares and a faster means of travel. The traffic of air cargo has not undergone this transformation. Whereas the traffic of passengers is growing at a steady rate, cargo has stagnated. Less than 5 percent of all transportation volume is done through air travel.

The Mexican logistics sector is relatively inefficient compared to that of other countries. Recent studies indicate that the Mexican logistics sector is ranked 30 within the 45 countries evaluated. This is due to the fact that costs are still very high in spite of the country's privileged location. Mexico has direct maritime access to the United States, Asia, and Europe, and a short land route to the United States. These advantages are being underexploited by the difficulty faced by Mexican transportation companies, particularly in multimodal services.

President Felipe Calderón launched an ambitious infrastructure plan that aims to correct these inefficiencies. With 100 projects defined, the plan includes highways, airports, and other modernizing infrastructure. The plan estimates an investment of $300 billion.

Juan Manuel Galarza and José Ignacio Lanzagorta

See also Economy, U.S.-Mexican Border; Foreign Trade; Mexico City; North American Free Trade Agreement; Urbanization

Further Reading

Graizbord, Boris. 2008. *Geografía del transporte en el area metropolitana de la ciudad de Mexico.* Mexico City: El Colegio de Mexico.

Ojah, Mark I. 2002. *Truck Transportation through Border Posts and Entry: Analysis of Coordination Systems.* College Station: Texas Transportation Institute, Texas A&M University.

U

Universidad Nacional Autónoma de México

The prestigious Universidad Nacional Autónoma de México (National Autonomous University of Mexico, UNAM) combines facilities for senior high school, higher education, and research and cultural dissemination. It is one of the most outstanding institutions in the international arena. In terms of its own legislation, the UNAM "is a public corporation—an organization decentralized from the State—endowed with full legal capacity and whose purpose is to provide higher education to form professionals, researchers, professors and technicians that serve society; organizing and carrying out research mainly addressing the national situation and problems, as well as expanding, as much as possible, the benefits of culture" (Article 1, Organic Law of Mexico's National Autonomous University).

Since its founding more than 450 years ago, the UNAM has set the stage and taken national leadership in cultivating and developing almost every scientific and humanistic discipline, as well as artistic production and culture dissemination. Many of the most distinguished characters in science, humanities, culture, and the arts of Mexico and Latin America were educated here. For example, three Mexicans who were awarded the Nobel Prize took classes at the UNAM: Alfonso García Robles, Nobel peace prize in 1982; Octavio Paz, Nobel literature prize in 1990; and Mario Molina, Nobel chemistry prize in 1995.

History It was during the first half of the 16th century that the initiative of having a university in New Spain—the Real y Pontificia Universidad de México (The Royal and Pontifical University of Mexico)—arose. It was founded upon royal decree issued on September 21, 1551, following Archbishop Fray Juan de Zumárraga's initiative of founding a university, to which Viceroy Antonio de Mendoza joined.

The university was organized, in the beginning, following the European university models, in particular that of Salamanca. During the subsequent centuries, schools and colleges of science, humanities, and arts were incorporated. In the 19th century after surviving the Mexican Independence, the institution was named Universidad Nacional y Pontificia (National and Pontifical University), and further on the name Universidad de México (Mexico's University) remained.

The immediate background of the modern Mexican university dates back to 1881, when the legislature of the already independent country outlined a project to reform it, this time following the North American and European liberal

The main building at the National University of Mexico, Mexico City, 2009. (Carlos Sanchez Pereyra | Dreamstime.com)

models; in the following years, the idea grew stronger until the institution was officially refounded in 1910 as the Universidad Nacional (National University), comprising the National High-School, the School of Jurisprudence, the School of Medicine, the School of Engineers, the School of Fine Arts, and the School of Higher Studies. The young university lived its first days in the middle of the outbreak of the Mexican Revolution, when the country was going through an era of disturbance to which the university was not exempt.

In 1921 José Vasconcelos, an outstanding member of a group of intellectual young people named "El Ateneo de la Juventud," proposed the institution's emblem and motto—"The Spirit Will Speak on Behalf of the Race (*Por la raza hablará el espíritu*)"—which is still in place today. After occupying for several centuries the timeless buildings where, during the colonial period, its different schools and colleges were established, by the end of the 1940s, a project to build a new campus for the university became official, giving birth to the construction of Ciudad Universitaria, built on the expropriated properties in Pedregal de San Ángel, to be officially handed over in 1954.

After transferring the different academic entities making up the university to these facilities, the institution's fundamental task was to consolidate the pieces of the new university, providing it with a wide and complex administrative structure to meet its growing needs in a more responsive and efficient manner. During this process, the relationship between the university and the State assumed major importance since a large percentage of the UNAM's resources come from federal subsidy. During this stage the university became the major vehicle for social mobilization in the metropolitan area of Mexico City and even in states around the country, from which hundreds—even thousands—of young people migrated to the capital city with the aim of getting an academic degree and to subsequently practice a profession in their home towns. The university of the 1950s, "with its own unique characteristics, became an event without precedent in the country's cultural history, since the university's offer had never had the coverage it had, and it had never created such an expectation before."

By the middle of the 1960s, during the era called *desarrollo estabilizador* (stabilizing development), the university played a preeminent role by creating a pool of professors, researchers, and professionals that, during subsequent years, would occupy leading positions in science, health, industry, and other areas that had an impact on the country's progress. This impact was achieved by means of these professionals' integration to the labor market, as well as by the university implementing several special programs covering a wide variety of areas.

Once its model was consolidated, the UNAM became the educational institution with the longest academic and cultural tradition in the country, whose model was gradually adopted by other public institutions throughout Mexico. By the beginning of the 1960s, the university faced adverse situations despite its explosive growth in enrollment.

During the 1960s the university went through a period of upheaval, when the Mexican economy experienced an economic boom. During this time, the UNAM strove to emulate the higher educational models of industrialized countries, which became a reference for the institutional projects that ruled the university in subsequent years. In the first years of the decade, several student movements arose to address concerns over, among other issues, the succession processes for the directorships of schools and faculties, which led to an outbreak of violence in 1968.

Among the multiple factors involved in this historical moment was the exponential growth of the UNAM's student population, which had already exceeded 100,000 students. By then, the Mexican political system and the development model imposed by it were already evidencing the first signs of depletion. The economic currents of that time supported the concept of human capital, with which the Mexican State clearly identified itself by promoting intellectual investment to revitalize education, with a clear approach toward production. Mass universities—like the UNAM—spoiled the educative project based on such theories.

After a number of convulsive years, Dr. Ignacio Chávez resigned from the rectorship of the university, ushering in a period characterized by a strong impetus toward core reforms under the leadership of Javier Barros Sierra. Barros Sierra worked to inhibit the students' movement and ensure the institutional continuity of the reforms initiated by his predecessor by making use of open, democratic dialogue within the UNAM community. Barros Sierra's conciliation policy positioned him as the natural antagonist of Mexican president Gustavo Díaz Ordaz, who called upon the nation's armed forces to violently repress a student demonstration, resulting in a massacre on October 2, 1968. After the student movement was suppressed by this violent episode, the federal government continued punishing the university's authorities and the institution itself, particularly by cutting down its federal subsidy to a bare minimum.

Although the years of the 1970s were not free from student mobilizations and social upheavals throughout the country, the decade was marked by a coincidence of ideas between the UNAM and the government, which became more open to diverse ideological trends in an attempt to heal the social fractures caused by Díaz Ordaz's regime. During this time university classrooms welcomed a wide variety of trends, as countless academicians, from almost every area of knowledge, sought asylum in Mexico from dictatorial regimes in Latin America and Europe. This influx of political refugees was reminiscent of a similar situation in the late 1930s, when the university opened its doors to outstanding Spanish intellectuals, humanists, and scientists who came to Mexico to escape the civil conflict in Spain.

The last two decades of the 20th century were marked by the quick progression of new technologies and their corresponding demands in generation and transmission. During this period the university produced many of its most distinguished alumni in science, humanities, culture, and the arts of Mexico and Latin America, including its three Nobel Prize recipients. The UNAM was the pioneer in Mexico of scientific research in such fields as genomics and ecology and in the humanistic and social disciplines, including philosophy of science and regional studies.

Current organization Since gaining its autonomy in 1992, the university has the right to organize itself as it deems best to its interests. This fundamental principle constitutes the genesis of the UNAM's complex government structure and grants a solid nature of plurality to it, since it supports full participation by members of every sector—academicians, students, workers, and authorities—in the decision-making processes. Representatives from the various sectors have a voice and vote in the deliberative bodies of the UNAM, which range from internal councils at each entity level to the University Council, which is the ultimate representation and decision-making body of the institution. The University Council exercises the power to provide education and to develop its research priorities based on the principle of full academic freedom. Unlike those public education entities that are not autonomous, the UNAM issues its own study certificates, degrees and diplomas, and grants for academic purposes. It also validates studies made at other educational institutions, whether nationally or abroad.

The UNAM authorities are organized as follows:

1. The Governing Board
2. The University Council
3. The rector
4. The Board of Governors
5. The directors of faculties, schools, and institutions
6. The technical councils of faculties and schools, as well as those of Scientific Research and Humanities

The university's substantive functions are those of teaching, research, and culture dissemination. In order to perform these tasks, its structure is divided into three subsystems. The subsystem of teaching includes high school studies, professional studies, and postgraduate studies; that of research is organized by means of scientific research and humanities coordination departments; and that of the cultural dissemination subsystem is organized into different managing departments according to the different cultural activities: Cinematographical Activities, Plastic Arts, Music, Publications and Editorial Promotion, Television, Radio, Dance, Literature, and Theater. The structure of the cultural dissemination subsystem includes 138 libraries, 13 museums, 18 historical buildings, 152 murals, 800 sculptures, 86,000 graphic works, 1 film archive, 2 culture houses, 33 bookstores, and 194 periodical publications, among other cultural assets.

During 2010–2011 the UNAM had 316,589 students and 36,162 academic personnel. The university offered 40 postgraduate programs, 33 specializations, 91 undergraduate programs, 4 technical degrees, and 3 bachelor's degree study plans.

Jorge Jiménez Rentería

See also Art Education; Cultural Policies; Culture and the Government; Education; Science and Research; Tlatelolco Massacre

Further Reading

Cultural Topics at UNAM. http://www.cultura.unam.mx/.

Domínguez Martínez, Raúl. 2001. *La Universidad de México: Un recorrido de la época colonial al presente,* Renate Marsiske, coordinator. Mexico City: Centro de Estudios sobre la Universidad, UNAM.

García Cantú, Gastón. 1987. *Años críticos: La UNAM, 1968–1987.* Mexico City: Coordinación de Difusión Cultural, Dirección de Literatura, UNAM.

La Universidad en el espejo. 1994. Mexico City: UNAM.

Legislación Universitaria. 2006. Oficina del Abogado General. Mexico City: UNAM.

Planning Policies for the University. http://www.planeacion.unam.mx/.

Scientific Studies and Research at UNAM. http://www.cic-ctic.unam.mx/cic/index_cic.html.

UNAM siglo XXI. 2001. *Espíritu en movimiento.* Mexico City: UNAM.

Universidad Nacional Autónoma de México. http://www.unam.mx/.

Urban Culture

Defining the contemporary "urban" culture of Mexico is a difficult and complex task, but it is clear that one city encapsulates the depth and breadth of this topic: Mexico City, a megalopolis of more than 20 million people with a history dating back more than 500 years. The Mexican capital embodies the heterogeneity of the country's urban spaces and its cultural expressions, and suggests the future trajectory of the other expanding urban centers of Mexico, such as Guadalajara and Monterrey. Mexican urban centers tend to spread outward, rather than upward, and more so in the last 30 years, as the rural exodus from the countryside has accelerated the growth of metropolitan areas. With few exceptions, Mexico's principal urban areas date back at least to colonial times. Thus, as urbanization has expanded and engulfed what were distinct communities, they reflect concentric circles of settlement that have gradually merged into one urbanized landscape, belted by slums as well as enclaves of upscale and middle-brow neighborhoods. A seemingly endless accumulation of partially constructed dwellings is pockmarked by gated, exclusive enclaves that refuse to participate in the spatial agglomeration of the city. For the latter denizens of Mexican cities, their cultural world revolves around a lifestyle oriented toward American upper-class behaviors. Meanwhile, middle-income sectors increasingly flee to suburban homes, seeking a safe refuge for their families and belongings, while young people rediscover aging areas of cities and invigorate the sagging, ragged remnants of formerly desirable neighbor-hoods, or *colonias* in Spanish. In this sense, some groups expose themselves to the burgeoning urban realities, while others systematically try to avoid them. This basic spectrum of difference sets the tone for the production and consumption of urban culture in Mexico. More so than other cities of the country, Mexico City is punctuated by extremes, by vast differences that mirror the social asymmetries that reflect so much of the nation itself.

However, this almost stereotypical description of the wide range of differences of Mexican urban culture does not mean that it is impossible to make some sense of contemporary city life in Mexico. In comparison to other contemporary mega-cities, especially in East Asia, Mexico City seems to maintain the spatial and cultural character of a huge and colorful patchwork of jarring variations. Thus, the tallest skyscraper in Latin America, the imposing Torre Mayor (inaugurated in 2003) at the Paseo de la Reforma near the Chapultepec castle, stands in stark contrast to the chaotic and vivid culture at the street level far below the tower's top floors, where energetic taco vendors in their plastic tents and vast numbers of *ambulantes,* or street sellers, vie with the hypermodern design of the building above them.

Such contrasts capture the contradictory configuration of Mexico City's urban culture, which is essentially reproduced in the country's other metropolitan centers, where highly commercialized zones clash with areas at different stages of deterioration and/or revitalization. A description of Mexico City's urbanized and urbanizing spaces perhaps best captures the urban culture of the country.

In the center of the city, an area declared a world heritage site by UNESCO, there are historic zones like La Merced, which are in decay but at least preserve historical and aesthetic values indicative of the Spanish colonial city. On the other hand, recent large-scale development, such as that at the southern edge of the venerable Alameda park, symbolically marked by a Starbucks coffee shop, glaringly demonstrates the globalization of the city's culture that, in effect, excludes the low-income people who live and work in the surrounding area.

Nonetheless, the shift in the cultural policies of the city's government since 1997 has fostered a revitalization of the cultural uses of the historic central zone. The Festival del Centro Histórico (Festival of the Historical Center), for example, has become an annual event that brings people of all social strata back to the core of the city, including those who would normally avoid the downtown area and its past association with chaos, violence, and urban decay—a cumulative process that was accelerated by the relocation of the Universidad Nacional Autónoma de México (National Autonomous University of Mexico, UNAM) in the 1950s to the new university campus (Ciudad Universitaria) in the southern part of Mexico City. The departure of the thousands of students who had animated downtown Mexico City led to a period of neglect and deterioration of the urban core. But, with the change in city policies of the 1990s, the historic center has been enlivened by book fairs, live concerts, and temporary exhibition projects (such as the notorious mass nude "happening" in the central plaza arranged by Spencer Tunick in May 2007), which has produced an evident renewal of the downtown urban zone.

The residential expansion of the early 20th century, leading to districts like the Colonia Roma or Colonia Cuauhtémoc, including the infamous Zona Rosa (Pink Zone), have become urban spaces of showy, glittering cultural life, oscillating between fancy bars, junk food restaurants, and avant-garde art galleries. While the construction of the huge subway station "Insurgentes" in the 1970s radically changed the former bohemian character of this zone, recent trends in urban development by the city government and investors have led to a reinvigoration of the area, drawing an eclectic, lively mix of people and countering what had been a fading, decadent place. A similar process of revitalization has taken place in and around the nearby Plaza de Rio de Janeiro, which has become a breeding ground for new artistic expression.

An even more chic and vital urban cultural space, especially for the educated and "creative" sectors of society, is the Colonia Condesa, a zone comparable to Greenwich Village in Manhattan. The Condesa, as it is commonly referred to, boomed in the 1990s and became densely punctuated by an enormous array of restaurants, bars, boutiques, designer shops, and other symbols of a globalized hip cultural outpost in the 500-year-old city. In the Condesa, contemporary urban culture is embedded in the architectural scene of art deco buildings and the two adjacent parks (Parque México and Parque España), which offer plural leisure activities evocative of the diverse character of the city and its people.

While the Condesa undergoes a near overdose of commercialization—comparable to what happened to the Village and Soho in New York City—the Colonia Nápoles still maintains vestiges of its 1950s atmosphere, as opposed to the jarring height of the huge, hulking World Trade Center, a high-rise building finished in the 1990s that stands in obvious contrast to the surrounding neighborhood. The skyscraper, a startling spire covered by a shimmering blue glass curtain wall, offers one of the most striking views of the city and its cultural fragmentation, as reflected in the architectural quilt that marks the urban culture of the megalopolis. From that lofty view, the agglomeration of the city of 20 million people seems clearly at odds with the constellation of islands, such as the neighborhoods of

Condesa or Roma, that sustain a traditional *colonia* urban culture almost lost in the vast extensions of endless streets, residential housing, office buildings, industrial sites, and storefronts.

This paradigmatic contradiction between macro and micro scales of Mexico City, and its counterparts elsewhere in the country, is particularly witnessed in the former village of Coyoacán, in the southern part of the city. A Spanish colonial street grid overlays the area, which is marked by buildings dating back to the arrival of the first Europeans, along with late 19th-century villas and a number of 20th-century neocolonial-style houses, creating an illusion of the beautiful preindustrial small town or village. The microcosmos of Coyoacán forms an inviting atmosphere for strolling through its center and its select restaurants, cafés, and galleries, highlighted by the colorfully painted house of the celebrated artist Frida Kahlo, where early feminist art is juxtaposed with traditional Mexican pottery as well as portraits of Stalin and Mao.

Nearby is San Ángel (a type of Mexican Montmartre), another of those urban "pockets" in which the local ambience clashes with the dull gray of the megalopolis. The *colonia* San Ángel boasts the amateur art market on San Jacinto plaza in apparent accordance with the preserved studio of Diego Rivera, which is located in the neighborhood. Finally, there is the historic area of Tlalpan, in the south of Mexico City, which functions as a site for tourists to catch a glimpse of preindustrial Mexican urban culture.

Topographically close, but conceptually distant from these three main pockets of historic colonial landmarks, is the Ciudad Universitaria (CU in common parlance, or University City), which holds upward of 300,000 students, professors, administrative personnel, and campus workers. (The original central area of campus was declared a world heritage site in 2007.) Moreover, the Centro Cultural Universitario (University Cultural Center) in the southern part of CU has become a nucleus for cultural activities that rival those funded by the federal and city governments. The university's cultural programming, from its symphony orchestra and concerts to works of theater, dance, and film, has had a considerable impact on the cultural life of the city. Indeed, it has become a cultural garden of sorts, symbolized by the ecological reserve that surrounds the university's cultural center.

A cultural mapping of Mexico City reveals that the south possesses a higher density of cultural infrastructure, while the northern parts of the city are dominated by industries and poor housing. In the eastern section of the city is found its worst elements, where garbage dumps and vast illegal shantytowns cast a harrowing shadow over urban Mexico. In the recently suburbanized western part of the metropolis, chaotically planned, upscale, and contemporary suburban developments, like the Santa Fe district, collide with the presence of nearby slums, calling into question the sustainability of such romantic refuges as Coyocán or Condesa as living, vibrant urban cultural sites.

This rough topographical description suggests a surreal, almost absurd city of irreconcilable contrasts and overwhelming problems; yet this configuration of the city disguises its stimulating potential for those willing to engage its visual, acoustic, tactile, and even odorous realities, rather than following the established paths of tourist guides and magazines. Such a trek may be a painful experience filled with banal shopping malls, devastatingly impoverished places, and occasional violence, but urban cultures redefine themselves constantly and generate new, fascinating aesthetic spaces, even in the midst of decay.

In this sense, exploring urban culture in Mexico City provides insights into the future of the country, especially its ability to sustain a coherent notion of a city and, in a sense, the possibility of a cohesive society. This challenge for Mexico City is shared with its counterparts; that is, it remains to be seen whether Guadalajara and Monterrey, for instance, will be able to negotiate their transitions to megacities and yet maintain the vitality of their collective urban cultural spaces.

Peter Krieger

See also Architecture; Earthquake in Mexico City, 1985; Environmental Issues; Mexico City; Universidad Nacional Autónoma de México; Urbanization

Further Reading

Gallo, Rubén, ed. 2004. *The Mexico City Reader.* Madison: University of Wisconsin Press.

Hernandez, Daniel. 2011. *Down and Delirious in Mexico City: The Aztec Metropolis in the Twenty-first Century.* New York: Scribner.

Krieger, Peter de, coordinator. *Megalópolis: La modernización de la ciudad de México en el siglo XX.* 2006. Mexico City: Universidad Nacional Autónoma de México, Instituto de Investigaciones Estéticas: Instituto Goethe-Inter Nationes.

Mraz, John. 2009. *Looking for Mexico: Modern Visual Culture and National Identity.* Durham, NC: Duke University Press.

Prakash, Gyan, ed. 2010. *Urbanisms: Dystopic Images of the Modern City.* Princeton, NJ: Princeton University Press.

Urbanization

Over the last 50 years, Mexico has become an intensely urbanized country, far removed from its historic association with an agrarian-based culture of tradition-bound small rural communities. As Mexico enters the 21st century, three out of four Mexicans live in cities, and projections indicate that about 90 percent of the nation's population will be in urban areas by around 2030.

The pace of urbanization in Mexico accelerated notably after 1940 with the onset of the country's move toward government-led industrialization at the expense of the agricultural sector of the economy. In the pursuit of an economic development model to promote and protect native industry, government policies relegated agriculture to providing raw materials for the manufacturing sector and to supplying low-cost food staples for the burgeoning population of industrial workers and their families, as well as for the business sector that paralleled the increase in urban populations. Public investments in agriculture lagged, especially in those regions with dense rural populations. Squeezed by price controls on their products and dwindling income, an exodus of peasants and small landholders from the Mexican countryside ensued, swelling the country's urban areas. Higher wages in cities added to the incentives for rural dwellers to migrate, particularly young adults. In this era, a handful of cities became symbolic of the country's fast urban growth, such as Monterrey (Nuevo León), Guadalajara (Jalisco), and Acapulco (Guerrero)—but none was more dramatic than the enormous expansion of the metropolitan area of Mexico City.

This process of urbanization continued even after the end of the old development model and the move toward economic liberalization in the 1980s. The turn in economic policies was accompanied by the emergence of new poles of urban growth, such as those cities located in the northern border zone (which had benefited from the rapid expansion of assembly plants since the 1960s), or those that became popular tourist sites, as well as those with economies bolstered by international and/or oil production activities. As a consequence, the urban character of the country changed, as the overwhelming primacy of Mexico City lessened significantly with the rise of cities such as Aguascalientes, Nuevo Laredo, Ciudad Juárez, Tijuana, Veracruz, and Toluca, among others.

The proliferation of newly urbanized areas generally meant the expansion of higher educational institutions, the greater diffusion of human capital, and the widening of the location of investments, all of which served to lessen the disproportionate role of Mexico City in the country's economic development. In this context, Mexican cities have become crucial engines of economic growth, making urban areas the main source of the country's gross domestic product.

Nevertheless, growth rates in these cities have created huge agglomerations, as distinct towns have been engulfed by the extension of primary urban centers, leading to the creation of megacities (more than 10 million residents) that retain separate municipalities of more than one million people. There are about 55 metropolitan zones in Mexico that as a whole hold more than half of the national population. The multiplication and expansion of these areas presents complex challenges in terms of urban governance that require efficient intergovernmental coordination and an adequate administration of those metropolitan zones. Fast-growing populations have also intensified the pressure on local authorities to consolidate and augment the infrastructure and services needed to satisfy the demands of these new urban inhabitants. Municipalities, large and small, have faced difficulties in providing necessary services: around 10 percent of urban Mexicans do not have running water, about a quarter are devoid of sanitation services, about the same proportion live in irregular settlements, and more than 60 percent reside in neighborhoods where the street system is unpaved.

The challenges posed by Mexico's urban growth are profoundly deepened by the lack of competent city administration. The inept management of cities compounds the frequent scarcity of resources needed for urban areas and their expansion. Turnover in elected municipal authorities undermines the ability of city officials to develop and implement long-term urban-planning programs. This problem is made worse by the push-and-pull of distinct municipalities within large metropolitan zones that compete for resources and services. The lack of coordination of policies between cities and the federal government adds to the difficulties of urban planning in Mexico. Moreover, urbanization generally means consumption patterns that pressure the use of resources, worsen congestion, and increase the production of waste and pollution. For example, it is estimated that daily domestic waste production in the country is nearly 100 tons, of which more than three-fourths is produced by cities.

Large cities also tend to suffer from high rates of the social ills associated with crowding, such as crime, violence, and loss of social capital. Broken families are much more apt to be in urban areas, as the overwhelming majority of single-headed households are found in cities, with a corresponding concentration of street children. Poverty in Mexico is increasingly found in cities, as more than half of the country's poor are found in urban areas. Small- to medium-size municipalities (15,000 to 50,000 inhabitants) in the country's metropolitan areas have the heaviest concentrations of poverty-stricken households, since such communities generally possess fewer resources to serve the growing numbers of the urban poor. Furthermore, the poor tend to settle in the peripheries of cities, creating in effect cities within cities; and informal settlements (i.e., shantytowns) become sites for extremely poor people, as shoddy residential clusters often dot urban landscapes. Studies suggest that as many as a quarter of urban households settle in an irregular manner, without benefit of legal title (urban squatters), and are frequently composed of ill-constructed shacks without access to potable water, sanitation, roads, or utilities. These shantytowns are often located in areas prone to landslides, flooding, fires, and the like. While local, state, and federal government measures have made efforts to ameliorate the problem, the vast number of such irregular settlements makes any real progress at best a slow and uneven process. The cost of land and materials for adequate housing makes it nearly impossible for very poor families to access formal housing.

On the other hand, urban areas also boast the greatest concentration of Mexico's wealthy, as the country has one of the highest levels of income inequality in the hemisphere. As a consequence, cities reflect intense class segregation, with gated communities that include palatial homes on estates. Shopping malls studded with exclusive boutiques and commercial zones marked by expensive restaurants stand in stark contrast to the flea markets, informal eateries, and street vendors that occupy modest neighborhoods—middle-class residential areas are intermixed among the pockets of enormous wealth and large stretches of poor homes. Yet, cities generally offer greater opportunities for social and economic mobility, better schooling and educational choices, and social amenities, such as parks, amusements, and leisure activities.

It is likely that urbanization will continue to mark Mexico's population growth, although signs of accelerated suburbanization have appeared in the country's major cities. Thus, Mexico faces an enormous challenge of improving the quality of life in its urban core areas, while balancing the proliferation of suburban growth.

Claudia Acuña

See also Agriculture

Further Reading

Giugale, Marcelo, O. Lafourcade, and Vin H. Nguyen, eds. 2001. *Mexico: A Comprehensive Development Agenda for the New Era.* Washington, DC: World Bank.

V

Veracruz

The official coat of arms of Veracruz. (Corel)

The state of Veracruz stretches along the elbow of the eastern coast facing the Gulf of Mexico. It is bordered by several Mexican states, including Tamaulipas to the north; Tabasco, Chiapas, and Campeche to the south; and Hidalgo, Puebla, and San Luis Potosí to the west. Among Mexico's states, Veracruz ranks 3rd in population and 11th in size. The state covers an extensive territory with a very diverse topography, from the sweltering savannahs along its coastal edge to the cool highlands of its interior mountains. As a result, the climate of Veracruz varies considerably, but all of the state receives ample rainfall, as it is subject to storms off the Gulf of Mexico; hurricanes have often wreaked havoc on the state. The diversity of the state's geography reflects a wide social range, from small villages strewn among the hills and valleys of the interior to the bustling, modern, and dynamic urban life of the city of Veracruz. The state holds a large indigenous population, ranking third among Mexican states in the number of Indian groups, most of which live in small, rural communities in the region's mountainous interior. At one time, Veracruz had a sizable African-origin population due to the use of African slave labor during the colonial period, and remnants of African influences persist in various regional forms, including in music and dance. Over time, migration and immigration into the region, particularly to the city of Veracruz, have led to the state's distinctively multicultural character.

Although the capital of the state is Xalapa, the port city of Veracruz has dominated the area since colonial times, and to this day it is Mexico's principal oceanic import-export conduit. In addition to its shipping importance, the city of Veracruz has been associated with the country's oil industry from its beginnings at the turn of the 20th century and still possesses several of the country's major refining plants. The economic prominence of the state's port city has meant that Veracruz has played a major role throughout Mexico's history. As the main seaport of the country, the city of Veracruz has been a key strategic site in Mexico's internal conflicts as well as for foreign interventions, including the occupation of the port by the United States in 1914 during the Mexican Revolution.

The economy of the state encompasses a broad range of agricultural, industrial, and service-oriented activities. The state's different microclimates, rates of precipitation, river valleys, shipping and transportation services, and energy resources make for a highly complex economy centered in the port city of Veracruz. Agricultural pursuits characterize the interior of the state, as its combination of rainfall and topography allow for the growing of various types of tropical products, such as mangos and bananas; coffee is grown in the highlands of the state and citrus in its interior valleys. The raising of livestock is also an important aspect of the state's agriculture. Land distribution is like that in much of the rest of the country—a mix of huge estates, marked by the use of modern means of production, and a multitude of small farming units, often relying on cooperatives and traditional methods in the marketing of their products.

Although agriculture represents a major aspect of the state's economy, Veracruz is best known for its association with shipping and oil-related industries.

The nationalization of the oil industry in 1938 contributed to the centrality of Veracruz as the primary site for the refining and distribution of oil-related products for both domestic and international consumption. One of the first rich oil deposits was found initially in the town of Tuxpan, Veracruz, in 1910, and that discovery would be followed by the even larger Poza Chica oil field in 1932, making the state the leading source of oil in the country for several decades until the exploitation of the Cantarell oil field off the coast of the state of Campeche in 1976. The first major refining complex of Mexico was built in Veracruz at Minatitlan as early as 1906, adding to the reputation of the state as an oil-producing center. (The refinery has undergone a series of improvements and expansions since its founding.) The establishment of PEMEX, the government's oil company after 1938 in Veracruz, increased still further the economic importance of the state. About 10 percent of Mexico's export earnings (depending on the international price for oil) comes from oil-related products. Equally important, with nationalization, the oil industry provided the federal government with a lucrative source of revenue, with estimates as high as 37 percent of total federal government receipts. (Mexico has a very low rate of income-tax collections.) Given the one-party dominance of the country from the late 1920s to the 1990s, oil-generated revenues became a decisive asset for the party in power, as it used the largesse to reward its loyalists and to fund its political activities. Thus, Veracruz holds crucial national political significance, which has also accrued to the influence of the oil workers' union. PEMEX therefore has assumed a prominent role in the state in several ways.

The former dominant party, the Institutional Revolutionary Party (PRI), remains a powerful presence in the state, though it has been challenged by the right-of-center National Action Party (PAN); the leftist-oriented Democratic Revolution Party (PRD) has had trouble establishing a foothold. In the elections of 2007, the

Rolling hills and vegetation in Veracruz, Mexico. (Scaramax | Dreamstime.com)

PRI made a strong showing, capturing nearly half of the mayorships in the state, and winning 30 of 50 congressional seats. The PRI's continuing strength derives to a large extent from the investments made in the state in the past, when the party controlled the federal government and lavished spending on PEMEX and allied activities. The economic troubles that have plagued the presidential administration of PAN's Felipe Calderón have served to erode support for his party, and the PRI has reaped the rewards of the president's travails. In the 2010 elections, the PRI continued its control of the governorship, but by a slight 4 percent margin over PAN. It is likely that the PRI will hold on as a major political actor in the state, in contrast to the weakening of the left-oriented PRD. For the near future, it appears that only PAN will have the means to challenge the grip of the old dominant party on the politics of Veracruz. On the other hand, as was the case in three states in the 2010 gubernatorial elections, a coalition between PAN and the PRD successfully displaced the PRI; in Veracruz such an alliance could take the governorship from the PRI, given its thin margin of victory in the most recent electoral round. But the PRI's strength in Veracruz will be very difficult to overcome, according to most political analysts. In that regard, economic conditions in the state will be a key factor in the competitive partisan politics of Veracruz.

The oil industry and its importance have sustained the historic role of the city of Veracruz as Mexico's major seaport, making the port city a vast transportation hub. Trucks and rail bring goods from various parts of the country for transshipment to export markets, and a large volume of imports come through the port as well for shipment to other parts of the country. Much of the service industry of the state is tied to oil and shipping-related sectors of the economy, such as the repair of trucks, port facilities, and ships. Moreover, the state of Veracruz has long held one of Mexico's largest breweries, originally named Moctezuma, and the state also possesses the huge steel-pipe making plant, TAMSA, which relies to a large extent on the demand for piping from PEMEX.

The state of Veracruz therefore holds a prominent place in Mexico, given the diversity and significance of its economy. As a result, the state has a robust middle class, with an extraordinary number of professionals (engineers, hydrologists, geologists, and the like) and a substantial agribusiness sector composed of wealthy farmers. On the other hand, the state is ranked among the four poorest in Mexico, with over one-third of its population living in poverty. Much of the poverty rate is related to the lack of educational opportunities in the rural areas of Veracruz and the number of small farmers and landless peasants in the state—a large proportion of whom are indigenous groups. In this light, the state of Veracruz contains glaring differences in income, living standards, and access to modern amenities among its population and has led to a sizable migration of young people from the state's interior rural areas to Mexican urban centers and/or to the United States. Social life in Veracruz reflects the stratification within its population; some social sectors enjoy a modern lifestyle, while a substantial portion of the state's residents live a vastly different way.

The social distinctions noted above frame the cultural life of the state. In general Veracruz's indigenous culture is officially celebrated, as some of Mexico's most important archaeological sites are located in the state, including the UNESCO-designated World Heritage site of El Tajín. Among the established tourist attractions of Veracruz are the traditional "flying men" of Papantla, who perform a type of acrobatic dance with four men who are tied by ropes at the ankle and slowly circle downward from a tiny platform at the top of a pole 50 feet or so in height. But in fact, the treatment of the state's indigenous population still displays much of the prejudice of the past dating back to the colonial era. The recognition of the region's traditional culture contrasts with the reality of everyday life for the Indians of Veracruz, whose policies have long neglected the state's rural dwellers, many of whom are primarily of Indian descent.

Alex M. Saragoza

See also Archaeological Sites; Energy; Indigenous Peoples; Petróleos Mexicanos; Transportation

Further Reading

Cordova Plaza, Rocio, et al. 2008. *Migracion internacional, crisis agricola y transformaciones culturales en la region central de Veracruz.* Mexico City: Plaza y Valdes.

Nutini, Hugo G. 2005. *Social Stratification and Mobility in Central Veracruz.* Austin: University of Texas Press.

Veracruz Official State Website. http://www.veracruz.gob.mx.

Visual Arts

The origins for the development of contemporary art in Mexico are varied, jointly forming fertile grounds for different artistic proposals. The term "visual arts" encompasses all artistic practices that, beyond such traditional techniques as sculpture, painting, and engraving (known as plastic arts), make use of multidisciplinary strategies to formulate conceptual discourses and visual poetics of different approaches. Practices such as the in situ installation, performance, interventions, artistic projects, and their processes and documentation, which are fundamental parts of the work, are included in the term "visual arts."

The replacement of the qualifier "plastics" for "visual" to designate arts is related to the inability of the former to include proposals such as installations, happenings, actions, video arts, and advertising graphics, among others. In Mexico, people started using the term visual arts by the end of the 1960s. Some of the factors leading to this name change were: (1) inefficiency of the Mexican cultural institutions (national institutions, schools, galleries, and rooms) to embrace artistic projects that were not pictorial, sculptural, or graphical; (2) the artistic rigidity that arose from the nationalism of the canonical Mexican School of Painting, established with the mural paintings in 1921; (3) the political authoritarianism, seen in the censorship to address content relating to social issues, denial of freedom of expression, and repression of social and student movements and protests; (4) the need of young artists to experiment with new languages and topics; and (5) conceptualistic influences coming from abroad.

The primary event that set a practical and conceptual rupture in Mexican art took place in 1968, shortly before the Olympic Games in Mexico City. Two circumstances are crucial in this respect: the student repression that culminated in the slaughter at Tlatelolco on October 2, and the denial of several of the artists to participate in the Solar Room (Salón Solar), a government proposal to exhibit Mexican art in the settings of the Olympic Games. These artists, citing as an argument the orthodoxy and unsuitability of this room for their art, decided to create an Independent Room, inaugurated on October 15. Fewer than 40 artists participated; in a "democratic" manner, they displayed paintings, sculptures, object art, installations, and graphics, while also closely working with independent filmmakers and drama directors.

The influence of the Independent Room with respect to the opening of artistic practice in Mexico was felt during the 1970s. Collective work was used as a formula to consolidate nonobject or conceptual art projects created by the so-called groups. Groups such as Proceso Pentágono, Mira, Suma, Tepito Arte Acá, Arte Otro, Taller de Investigación Plástica, and No-Grupo made installations, performances, and urban interventions, juxtaposing low- and high-level Mexican culture, between 1976 and 1983. Some of these groups used art as a means for political accusation, exhibiting work commenting on such topics as the guerrillas, torture, and censorship. The behavior of other groups was more experimental and was directly related to technical-conceptual poetics.

Likewise, the influence of international artistic trends and discourses little by little strongly positioned the so-called conceptual art brought to Mexico by artists who temporarily lived in Europe, such as Felipe Erehnberg, Ulises Carrión, and Martha Hellion. This trend is notoriously seen in the actions, object-art, and neographics of Felipe Erehnberg, who designated himself as a neologist instead of an artist in order to stress his condition as a philosopher and the importance of the artistic idea over the object itself.

During the 1980s there was a resurgence of the languages and subjects that have been addressed previously, but superficially, by the artistic groups. Several painters and sculptors went back to issues such as nationalism, posed from a personal point of view, including gay and female perspectives. Likewise, some artists combined installation and performance with elements of Mexican and borderline popular culture.

During the last years of the 1980s and the first years of the 1990s, performance art acquired new vigor with which to criticize nationalistic fundamentalisms from both sides of the U.S.-Mexican border. Cities like Los Angeles, California, and Mexico City became the venue for groups of performers who were trying to reorganize cultural networks internationally. Spaces sponsored by the government, such as X'Teresa Arte Alternativo (today ExTeresa Arte Actual), headed by Eloy Tarcisio, gave shelter to the works of these creators.

Together with the performance phenomenon, some other artistic proposals came about in Mexico City. The defining characteristics of these proposals were their multidisciplinary nature, the importance of their conceptual processes and record, and their independent nature apart from governmental patronage. In 1989 Guillermo Santamarina, in cocuratorship with Gabriel Orozco and Flavia González Rossetti, summoned Mexican and foreign young artists to participate in the exhibition named *A propósito, 14 obras en torno a Joseph Beuys.* Carried out in the former convent of the Desierto de los Leones, the exhibition paid homage to this important contemporary artist. The exhibit included the presentation of works, in situ installations, and actions that led toward a practical and conceptual split of what had been done in Mexico to that date. *A propósito, 14 obras en torno a Joseph Beuys,* is nowadays considered a milestone for Mexican visual arts.

Since this expo and throughout the 1990s, the aesthetic discourses being produced posed problems relating to the modernization and social deterioration of the country. Mexico City provided not only the scenario but also the ideal object for contemporary artistic practice. Artists used international languages in vogue to produce discourses about a metropolis for which they professed fascination. Topics such as consumerism, recycling, crowding, the disposable, media ideologies, pornography, insecurity, poverty, and urban violence were explored from very different points of view.

The topic of death was another of the urban and borderline issues that artistic groups such as SEMEFO, founded by Teresa Margolles, addressed. By means of the visual poetics of horror and subversion, these artists faced the audience with violence and eroticism. In 1992 the InSite project emerged from the Mexican border with the United States, bringing artists of both countries together to make urban interventions and artistic projects in San Diego and Tijuana. Year after year, InSite became stronger, becoming by 1994 one of the most important artistic events worldwide in which 78 artists from all over the world, including Allan Kaprow, Dennis Oppenheim, Yukinori Kaniagui, Anya Gallacio, Silvia Gruner, Abraham Cruz Villegas, and Enrique Yezik, participated.

Needing to show their works, artists became cultural representatives and undertook the opening of alternative spaces. The multimedia art, actions, and installations of the first years of the decade were displayed in the artists' own studios, in abandoned spaces, or in marginal locations of the city. This provided a greater experimentation and transgression of the artistic arena. As an example of the freedom provided by these ordinary spaces, mention can be made of "Intervención en Flora 9," under the responsibility of Mauricio Rocha, who drilled the walls of this space or, even more so, the "Galería quemada con gasolina," project by Santiago Sierra, which consisted of setting the exhibition space on fire.

The participation of independent curators and the circulation of magazines and newsletters published by young artists and critics provided international visibility for the Mexican artistic proposals. During the second half of the 1990s, the recognition of such Mexican artists as Gabriel Orozco and Rubén Ortiz was consolidated, as well as of those foreign artists who became known by their works developed in Mexico: Tomas Glassford, Francis Alys, and Melanie Smith. The personality of the Mexican artist has, since then, been that of a global artist, a nomadic artist who does a little bit of everything and only discourses on Mexican topics. Likewise, during the last 10 years, major Mexican contemporary art exhibitions have been presented in spaces such as P.S.1 Contemporary Art Center in New York, the Institute of Contemporary Art in Boston, and the Tate Modern in London.

In the 21st century, visual arts in Mexico followed the paths opened during the 1990s. Urban, borderline, and global topics were addressed from multidisciplinary perspectives. Conceptual art is the one with more spaces in the artistic circuits. Mexican contemporary art positions itself conclusively in the international arena. Major European, North American, and Asian fairs and galleries promoted such Mexican artists as Damián Ortega, Minerva Cuevas, Dr. Lacra, Diego Teo, Gabriel Kuri, Eduardo Abaroa, Miguel Calderón, Jonathan Hernández, Daniel Guzmán, among others. In 2005 Mexico was the guest country of honor invited to the widely recognized International Art Fair, ARCO, in Madrid, becoming the first Latin American country invited to this cultural event.

Luis Vargas-Santiago and Silvia D. Zárate

See also Art Exhibitions; Arts, Alternative Venues for; Painting

Further Reading

Debroise, Olivier, and Cuauhtémoc Medina. 2006. *La era de la discrepancia: Arte y cultura visual en México, 1968–1997,* translated by Joëlle Rorive y Ricardo Vinós and James Oles. Mexico City: Universidad Nacional Autónoma de México.

Medina, Cuuhtémoc. 2009. *What Else Could We Talk About? 53. International Art Exhibition. La Biennale di Venecia,* works and images by Teresa Margolles. Mexico City: Editorial RM S.A. de C.V.

Orozco, Gabriel, and Ann Temkin. 2009. *Gabriel Orozco.* New York: Museum of Modern Art.

Polkinhorn, Harry, et al., eds. 1991. *Visual Arts on the U.S./Mexican Border.* Calexico, CA: Binational Press.

Voters

During the decades of the hegemony of the Institutional Revolutionary Party (PRI) (1929–2000), the Mexican electorate was practically irrelevant in the political arena. Its main purpose was to give legitimacy through the ballots to the PRI's next president. Although elections were celebrated, they were not competitive. Through one of the PRI's political machineries called *clientelismo* ("clientism"), the hegemonic party offered benefits to labor unions as well as more land redistributions to peasant organizations in exchange for their votes. Thus, elections were virtually designed to guarantee PRI's victory. The electorate was a mass that could be easily controlled by the government through corporative networks, where almost every labor union or rural organization was linked to the PRI.

Before the political reforms of the 1990s, there were few political events where the electorate showed strength enough to challenge a nondemocratic regime. This was particularly the case in the 1976 presidential election. José López Portillo was the only officially registered candidate. However, left groups supported Valentín Campa as a candidate. His candidacy was considered illegal because the laws did not recognized radical left groups as political parties. Still, the electorate cast their votes for him, and by the end of the election, they claimed to have received more than a million votes. López Portillo won the election, but for the first time a strong opposition was not satisfied with the authoritarian conditions. The electorate force made the government launch the first political reform needed to achieve a democratic transition. By 1977 the social groups that supported Valentín Campa got official recognition; a proportional representation rule was created for the Congress in order to give some degree of political power to all minorities in elections, and a new electoral authority was named, but it was still directly controlled by the executive branch.

The other critical event for the evolution of the Mexican democracy was the 1988 election. Cuauhtémoc Cárdenas, PRI's dissident and son of the famous President Lázaro Cárdenas (1936–1940), registered as an opposing candidate from a left-wing coalition called Frente Democrático Nacional. He rapidly became a popular figure, and became the first opposing candidate to seriously threaten the PRI. The Ministry of Interior (through its Federal Electoral Commission) was the institution in charge of the electoral process. This institution installed a modern computing system to count the votes. However, the night of the election, after a "systems shut-down," the minister of the interior declared Carlos Salinas de Gortari as the official winner, even though several national and international surveys indicated Cárdenas as the winner. The social agitation could have been strong enough to collapse the political system, but Cárdenas finally accepted Salinas as president, although he never recognized his own defeat in the election.

The 1988 election showed that the political system did not match the electorate interest. It became obvious that Mexico was not a real democracy and that the electorate could not express their choices through voting. The PRI had the option of keeping the political system as it was, and risk a coup d'etat or social revolution, or of opening the system to real competitive and democratic election. So it chose the political reforms path and in 1990 created the Federal Code for Political Institutions and Electoral Procedures (COFIPE), which founded the Instituto Federal Electoral (Federal Electoral Institute, IFE) and the Federal Electoral Tribunal (TRIFE). Other reforms needed to achieve autonomy, impartiality, and objectivity for the IFE were legislated in 1994 and 1996. The IFE also created nonfalsifiable photograph identification, and international and citizen observers were invited for the election process.

The presidential election of 1994 was not fully democratic. However, it is said that there was no significant electoral fraud and that the PRI's candidate, Ernesto Zedillo, won cleanly. It is presumed that the assassination of the PRI's former candidate, Luis Donaldo Colosio, as well as the Zapatist Army for National Liberation (EZLN) uprising and a seemingly good performance by the Salinas administration, gave the electorate fear to vote for the opposition and confidence for the incumbent.

The real empowerment of the electorate was to be seen after the final political reforms of 1996 in the 1997 midterm election, which, for the first time in its history, the PRI lost the absolute majority in the Chamber of Deputies. The first presidential alternation happened in the 2000 election, where the National Action Party's (PAN) candidate was declared winner without any questions or doubts about the electoral authority.

Alejandro Moreno, a Mexican political scientist, opinion leader, and director of *Reforma* newspaper's polls, published in his book *El votante mexicano* (The Mexican Voter) an analysis of the behavior of the electorate in the 2000 election. Moreno revealed the different political values and interests of the electoral segments. Through several polls and surveys, Moreno claimed that 4 of every 10 voters in 2000 voted for a change, for an alternation of parties in the presidential seat. This meant that the electorate, after 70 years of having the same party in power, was probably only measuring its own ability to change governments, to prove that the democracy was working. Four out of 10 had no interest in the different policies or ideologies presented by the candidates, just alternation in power of political parties.

Votes in the 2000 election also showed the cleavages in the Mexican electorate. Apparently older voters, those with less education, those from rural areas, and those with more authoritarian values wanted the PRI to stay in government. Young voters, with higher levels of education and from urban areas, were prone to vote for an opposition party (mainly PAN or the Democratic Revolution Party [PRD]). This could be explained by noticing that young voters, born between 1977 and 1982, had only lived through crises, political instability, and the decadence of PRI's hegemony, as well as the political and economic reforms of the 1990s. Older voters might have nostalgia for the "Mexican miracle," the decades in which the PRI led Mexico into important economic growth rates and political stability.

The evolution of the electorate's party identification was also key in the 2000 election and, later, for the 2006 presidential election and the political crisis it left. Through the last 15 years of the 20th century, the PRI started losing partisans in a cyclical but constant way. It was clear by the 1988 election that it had lost a significant number of partisans, but, as it has been seen, that was not the case in the 1994 election. After the economic crisis of 1995, the PRI lost another significant bundle of voters. Moreno describes a "conversion and replacement" phenomena in the Mexican voters regarding the PRI: some mature voters changed their adhesion from the PRI to another party (conversion), but more significantly, every three years new young voters are seen with new political preferences reflected in the ballots (replacement). However, still today, the PRI is the political party that can retain a higher number of strongly partisan voters compared to as its main opponents.

At the 2000 election, according to Moreno, voters were more sensible to Vicente Fox's charisma than to a clear ideological affiliation with PAN, while the PRD supporters expressed their sympathy with the left ideology and the political party that represents it. Taking into consideration a socioeconomic cleavage, the PRD is more closely identified with the low-income social classes, PAN with the middle-income class, and the PRI with the less-educated classes.

What Vicente Fox apparently did in the 2000 election campaign was to become the catch-all candidate by building an electoral coalition with the main purpose of defeating the PRI, forgetting ideologies and party identification. He even concentrated more votes from left-wing supporters than Cárdenas. The electorate moved PAN to a more central ideology, and the PRI moved to the right wing due to its authoritarian practice. However, the 2000 election registered an abstention of 36 percent of the electorate. Moreno estimates that most of that percentage belonged to PRI supporters who thought their vote was not needed. It is possible that with lower abstention rate the PRI would have won the election.

The 2006 election showed, however, a completely different electorate. This time, the PRI lost a much more significant number of voters to the strong competition between PAN's candidate, Felipe Calderón, and a charismatic left leader, Andrés Manuel López Obrador, of the PRD. In this election, PAN was identified with a right-wing ideology and was no longer a catch-all party. The PRD received the highest number of votes in all its history, concentrating most of the left-wing voters. The polarization of the contest, and a strong internal struggle in the PRI, caused PRI voters to divide their support to the other parties: the PAN and PRD. In the official result Calderón won with 35.89 percent of votes, followed extremely closely by López Obrador, with 35.59 percent of the votes. Roberto Madrazo (PRI) came in third place with 22.26 percent of the votes. However, it was clear that voters were strongly influenced by the candidates, more than the parties, because in the simultaneous legislative election, the PRI's coalition almost equaled the PRD's coalition with approximately 28 percent of the votes.

The PRD's protest against the results and its accusation of a "structural fraud" that favored PAN, forced a new political reform in 2007. PRD claimed that there had been an unfair campaign in electronic media (mainly on television and radio). The new political reform, besides removing three electoral councilors from the IFE, including its president, Luis Carlos Ugalde, also banned the political campaigns in television and radio, out of the official prime times regulated by the IFE. This was particularly delicate, considering Moreno's study reveals that 6 out of 10 adults consider television to be the media outlet offering the best information about the presidential candidates. Two-thirds of the electorate follows television news during campaigns, and 8 out of 10 actual voters affirm that they receive their political information through television. The impact of the 2007 political reform to the electorate and the way in which voters generate their decisions is yet to be seen in the upcoming federal elections.

Moreno's study expresses that Mexican society feels more satisfied in the 2000s than it did in the beginning of the 1980s. Most of the electorate affirms that nowadays people have more freedom to chose and control their own decisions. Most of the Mexicans believe in democracy. However there is still a high percentage of people who distrust Mexican political institutions, which were designed to have the PRI in power.

The Mexican democracy needs to be evaluated in terms of its own performance as a political system, the practice of democratic principles and ideals, and its ability to represent Mexican voters and their interest. Still, structural institutional reform needs to be done in order for the Mexican political system to function as a representative democracy.

Juan Manuel Galarza and José Ignacio Lanzagorta

See also Election, Presidential, 2000; Electoral Institutions; Partido Acción Nacional; Partido de la Revolución Democrática; Partido Revolucionario Institucional

Further Reading

Hagopian, Frances, and Scott P. Mainwaring. 2005. *The Third Wave of Democratization in Latin America: Advances and Setbacks.* New York: Cambridge University Press.

Moreno, Alejandro. 2003. *El votante mexicano: Democracia, actitudes políticas y conducta electoral.* Mexico City: Fondo de Cultura Económica.

Y

Youth Culture

Mexican youth is a broad social category that has been of enormous symbolic importance to Mexican society, given the demographic character of the country—Mexico is a "young" society, unlike the United States, for instance, which has a much larger proportion of an aging population. Indeed, the youth of Mexico has received much attention from the country's leading intellectuals since at least the 1940s, and more so after the student-led protests of 1968. The question of youth in Mexico and their collective welfare in the 1940s symbolized the broader issue of the direction of Mexico as the revolutionary generation—those who had experienced the Mexican Revolution of 1910 and its aftermath—aged and passed on, and the first postrevolutionary generation emerged by the 1940s. Similarly, the 1960s witnessed the maturation of the second generation of the revolutionary years, raising once again the issue of the future of Mexico.

The concept of youth in Mexico encompasses a very wide spectrum of people, as young Mexicans choose, under very distinct circumstances, the set of beliefs and practices that identifies them as "young." In fact, the very definition of youth in Mexico is not just about age, as it was only after World War II that adolescence became a social reality for many young people. Previously, only the well-off could afford to send their children to secondary schools and to have them avoid working toward basic household necessities. The social life associated with "teenagers," therefore, included a very small proportion of those between the ages of 14 and 21, as the majority of the population of Mexico lived in the countryside, where young people were expected to work at an early age. Most young people in rural Mexico went from childhood to adulthood without pause, and most did not attend school beyond the elementary level. With the impacts of rapid industrialization and the parallel increase in urbanization during the World War II era and its aftermath, by the 1960s a much larger segment of Mexican young people became part of a youth culture—they attended secondary school and had the means to participate in those activities associated with being unmarried, living at home, and not working full-time for one's livelihood. After the 1960s, distinguishable youth cultures had emerged, especially in urbanized areas of the country.

The plural term of youth cultures is used here to underscore the diversity of the experience of young people in contemporary Mexico. There are several youth cultures that coexist in present-day Mexican society, but two basic groups have become discernible due to the stereotypes that have been largely engendered by

Middle-class youth in Mexico today. (iStockPhoto)

government agencies and the media. Lower-working-class youth as a social group has often been associated with the stigma of "gangs"; in contrast, the term "youth culture" has been ascribed to those from middle- and upper-class backgrounds, which is indicative of the class cleavages among young people in Mexico, but also a reflection of the prejudices that surround the description of subgroups among the country's young people. The dress, the music, the language, the meeting places, and the general lifestyle of each youth social group form the visible signs of distinction among the different youth cultures. The significance of each group's outlook is usually expressed in some form or another, such as through hairstyle, attire, or personal embellishment of one kind or another, including tattoos, makeup, hair coloring, and the like. It is important to mention that the media and/or advertising industries will focus in a superficial way on these styles that may bring particular notoriety to a specific youth social group.

Regardless of social background, Mexican young people must contend with the contrast between the beliefs, values, and expected behaviors of their parents and families and those generated by living in the midst of the cosmopolitan social and cultural practices of present-day Mexico. Personal and socioeconomic factors play a crucial role in the meanings attached to the individual rights and responsibilities of a young person. From a traditional perspective, each social class has a series of activities that young people might, can, or should engage in, and they can be shaped by the interplay of local, regional, national, and even international influences. For example, the terms used in Mexico for certain youth subgroups correspond to those utilized in the United States, such as *rockeros* (hard-rock enthusiasts), goths and punks, *skatos* (skaters), or hippies, all with the same connotations as in the United States. On the other hand, there are those terms ascribed to Mexican youth subcultures that possess a distinctly Mexican inflection; the term *fresa* (in English, literally "strawberry"), for instance, is commonly used to describe socially privileged young people with a conventional if not conformist lifestyle. In contrast, the term *emos* (derived from the term for "emotional") refers to a youth subculture that tends toward an effeminate look among males and a spiked, colored hairstyle for females, and both males and females will use heavy mascara and wear dark clothing, yet they are also likely to be of the middle sectors of Mexican society. *Emos* are often described as young people who are drawn to music that speaks of depression, despair, and emotional displays of anger—hence the descriptive term for the group. Generally speaking, youth of a higher income status have more flexibility to experience and/or experiment with alternative lifestyles. Nonetheless, familial pressures continue to exercise considerable weight on the choices made by young people in their forms of social identification, and more so among middle- and upper-income youth. Lower-income young people, not surprisingly, have fewer options, as their economic position does not allow for easily accessible alternatives.

The country's largest cities, most notably Mexico City, offer the greatest variety of economic and cultural avenues for young people to create or seek lifestyles that correspond to their needs or interests. The cultural influences of the large urban centers, diffused by the media into the country's smaller towns and rural areas, mean that multiple youth subgroups are to be found in most parts of Mexico. And for young people living in close proximity to the U.S. border, the cultural spillover from the "other side" adds and reinforces the adaptation of American youth lifestyles onto those in Mexico. A similar effect takes place for Mexican young people living in areas heavily traveled by Americans, such as Cancún and Puerto Vallarta. In sum, Mexico possesses a number of different youth cultures that reflect a society becoming more complex, subject to outside influences, and complicated by social stratification as well as the impacts of globalization.

Mariana Domínguez

See also Family, Friends, and Social Etiquette; Family and Marriage; Urban Culture

Further Reading

Cornelius, Wayne A., et al., eds. 2010. *Mexican Migration and the U.S. Economic Crisis: A Transnational Perspective.* La Jolla, CA: Center for Comparative Immigration Studies.

Flores, Luis, and Arline Kaplan. 2009. *Addressing the Mental Health Problems of Border and Immigrant Youth: A Culture and Trauma Special Report from the National Child Traumatic Stress Network.* Los Angeles: National Child Traumatic Stress Network.

Hernandez, Daniel. 2011. *Down and Delirious in Mexico City: The Aztec Metropolis in the Twenty-first Century.* New York: Scribner.

Nilan, Pam. 2006. *Global Youth? Hybrid Identities, Plural Worlds.* Hoboken, NJ: Taylor and Francis.

Yucatán

The official coat of arms of Yucatán. (Corel)

The state of Yucatán is located in the peninsula of the same name, and it is bounded by the states of Campeche to the southwest and Quintana Roo on the east and southeast. The Gulf of Mexico lies to the north and northwest of Yucatán. According to the census of 2010, the population of Yucatán ranks 21 out of 31 states; in terms of its land surface, the state ranks 20th in the nation. By far the most important city is the capital of Mérida, and its metropolitan area of about one million people represents nearly half of the population of Yucatán. The main port of the state and second largest city is Progreso, which is situated 25 miles north of Mérida.

The state's rural residents are dispersed among a multitude of small towns and villages. Yucatán has a large indigenous population of Mayan origin, and about a third of the population speaks in some dialect of the Mayan language, though the vast majority of the Mayan-speaking population also uses and understands Spanish.

The climate of the state is generally warm and humid, with a seasonal rainfall of approximately 45 inches a year. However, the land is primarily limestone (like the rest of the peninsula), so that much of the rainwater seeps down into underground aquifers, and the top soil is thin. Large-scale agriculture therefore is difficult; much of the agricultural production of the state takes place on relatively small, intensively cultivated plots. The land is generally covered with scrub, trees, and some tropical forest and flora, with corresponding fauna. The state contains several wildlife preserves, including the spectacular Celestun biosphere and the Los Largitos preserve, among others. Because of its location on the Gulf of Mexico, the state is vulnerable to hurricanes and strong tropical storms.

For a time in the late 19th and early 20th centuries, the main export of Yucatán was sisal (also known as hemp or henequen), a fiber made from a type of maguey plant. The strong fiber was used primarily for cordage of various sorts, as well as for the making of burlap sacks and similar products. The so-called henequen boom led to the development of extensive plantations. The fiber was shipped to markets abroad from the port of Progreso, and much wealth was generated by the henequen boom for a small number of landowners that dominated its production. To this day, the huge houses on Montejo Boulevard in Mérida stand as symbols of that gilded bygone era (although most of the old palatial homes are no longer used as residential housing). The henequén boom basically ended with World War I, as the growing use of metal wire products and synthetic materials deflated the market for the fiber.

For several decades afterward, Yucatán remained essentially isolated from the rest of the country, as most of its population lived off subsistence agricultural pursuits. An important step in the economy of the state took place in the 1960s, with the construction of a major highway from the interior of the country to Mérida and Progreso. The building of a modern airport in Mérida in that decade also reduced further the relative isolation of the state. Then, two decisive events radically changed the contemporary structure of the economy: the development of the seaside resort of Cancún in the late 1970s in the neighboring state of Quintana Roo, and 20 years later, the surge in the establishment of assembly plants in Yucatán following the signing of the North American Free Trade Agreement among Mexico, Canada, and the United States in 1993.

The spectacular success of Cancún meant a substantial increase in tourism to Yucatán, although the resort is actually located in the neighboring state of Quintana Roo. However, the construction of Cancún stimulated the economy of Yucatán in various ways. For example, a large amount of the materials to build and to sustain the enormous complex came through Progreso and/or through Mérida. Also much of the labor to build Cancún came from Yucatán, given the very sparse population of Quintana Roo at the time of the early development of the beachside resort. In addition, the volume of tourists that began to flow through Cancún boosted enormously the number of visitors to Yucatán's famous archaeological sites, most importantly that of Chichén Itzá, but also that of Uxmal. Soon after the appearance of the first major hotels at Cancún, tour operators began offering visits to the archaeological ruins located in Yucatán. And as a byproduct of this influx of travelers, an increasing proportion of them—mostly foreigners—also began to visit Mérida and to use the city as a launching point to lesser known archaeological sites in Yucatán. The improvement in the roadway between Méida and Cancún, combined with the expansion of services at both the Mérida and Cancún airports, also contributed to Mérida becoming an important gateway to the archaeological sites of Palenque and Tikal to the south of Yucatán in the nearby Chiapas and at the northern edge of Guatemala. Thus, the extraordinary flow of tourists to Cancún and its growth through the 1990s held an important benefit to the economy of Yucatán.

The signing of NAFTA had an immediate impact on Yucatán, as the number of assembly plants (maquiladoras) jumped from about 30 to more than 130 between 1994 and 2000. Most of the new plants produced various types of apparel and textiles, but factories also appeared that made different types of goods for export to the United States and Canada, such as furniture. The deepwater port of Progreso facilitated the shipment of the products from Yucatán's maquiladoras to U.S. and Canadian markets. By the year 2000, the tourist trade and the quick growth of

Tourists visit the ancient Mayan city of Chichen Itza, Yucatán, Mexico. (Pierdelune | Dreamstime.com)

assembly plants had reconfigured the economy of Yucatán and its workforce. Yet, those economic shifts have also made the state's business sector even more vulnerable to economic conditions in the United States, as well as to competition from other low-wage countries, like China and Vietnam. Thus, since 2000 Yucatán has faced swings in its economy and corresponding ups-and-downs in its employment figures, largely as a consequence of the business cycle in the United States and the global economy. For example, the recession of 2007 to 2010 in the United States led to an erosion of jobs and plants in the maquiladora sector; this loss of employment and industrial production was worsened by the movement of several plants to other countries that offered lower labor costs, such as China. Thus, like so much of Mexico, globalization has added to the sensitivity of Yucatán to the international economy, a lesson that the state knows well from its experience with the henequen boom a century earlier. How Yucatán will handle the challenges as a result of its dependence on global economic trends will be a key question for the political leaders of the state in the coming years.

Political conditions, however, have changed much less quickly or dramatically than the economic shifts in the state. In 2001 the Institutional Revolutionary Party (PRI) lost the governorship for the first time in seven decades. The defeat to the conservative National Action Party (PAN) echoed the results at the national level of a year earlier, when the PRI lost the presidency to PAN. It appeared that the PRI's domination of Mexico's political system had ended. But, six years later, the resurgent PRI recaptured the governorship of Yucatán, and as of 2010 controlled 10 of the state's 15 congressional seats; PAN has two of the three senatorial posts. And more recently, the mayoral race of the state's most important and largest city, Mérida, went to the PRI candidate. In contests for the state legislature, the PRI won 15 seats, while PAN settled for 6 posts, down from the 9 positions that it had won in 2007. In short, PAN's gubernatorial victory of 2001 failed to dislodge the PRI from its stronghold in Yucatán. (The lackluster polls of President Felipe Calderón [2006–2012] underscored the public's sagging support for PAN, and Yucatán has not been an exception. The left-leaning Democratic Revolution Party [PRD] has been unable to establish a strong base of followers in the state.) On the other hand, the economic slowdown in Yucatán since 2007 has served to undermine the electorate's confidence in the PRI. Regardless, both parties face a diverse constituency and a range of demands and expectations. The PRI is clearly rebuilding its political strength in the state, but its future success in that respect remains an open question.

Severe poverty marks the rural areas of Yucatán, where a disproportionate number of the poor are of indigenous origin. The Human Development Index, an indicator of the overall socioeconomic conditions in the state, ranks Yucatán 21st in the country out of 31 states. At the other extreme of the social scale are the well-educated and relatively well-paid managers of the maquiladora and tourist sectors, and the wealthy owners of the state's largest commercial establishments. The middle class of the state is overwhelmingly located in the metropolitan areas of Mérida and Progreso. The incomes and lifestyles of the relatively small upper and middle classes in Yucatán are in stark contrast to the economic and social conditions of the working class. The maquiladora labor force is composed primarily of females who earn a modest income, at best. Given the importance of tourism, a large proportion of men and women are employed in servicing restaurants, hotels, and related enterprises, in which most earn a meager income. Out-migration has increased as young men and women move out of their poverty-stricken villages and towns to seek better employment opportunities, frequently seeking jobs in the tourist corridor next door in the state of Quintana Roo and its so-called Mayan Riviera. In recent years, however, a growing number of young people have begun to migrate to the United States. Outside of the low-wage jobs available in Mérida and Progreso, there are scarce opportunities for much of the young, undereducated population of the state.

Economic developments since the 1980s have reinforced the dominance of Mérida in the social and cultural life of the state. Virtually all of Yucatán's quality museums, theaters, art galleries, and other cultural amenities are found in Mérida, along with the most important institutions of higher education, including the Universidad Autonoma de Yucatán, the state's public university. Nonetheless, compared to many other capital cities, Mérida retains much of its old charm. The city does not have the level of frenetic congestion that tends to afflict so many of the country's larger cities. Nor does Mérida possess the vast shantytowns that often encircle Mexico's major metropolitan centers, although Mérida is not without areas of substandard housing and evident urban poverty. Still, the overall character of the city suggests a slow, casual rhythm, nearly provincial in character. In glaring contrast to Mérida, the rural towns and villages of the state have few amenities. The poverty of the countryside affords little more than traditional forms of entertainment and diversion. Many villagers that live close to archaeological zones earn a modest income from the making and selling of arts and crafts to tourists. Indeed, due to the migration of much of the younger generation, an increasing number of Yucatán's rural towns are disproportionately populated by the elderly and children, as many adolescents and young adults have left to seek a livelihood elsewhere. Government efforts to alleviate rural poverty in the state are helping, but the magnitude of the problem is deeply entrenched; improvements in schooling remain uneven and the job opportunities in the state continue to depend overwhelmingly on the demand for low-wage labor.

Yucatán is subject to events and forces beyond its immediate control. International flows of capital and labor may undercut the sustainability of its assembly-plant manufacturing sector; competition from Asia in particular has already had a dampening effect on the expansion of the maquiladoras in the state. Global economic conditions also influence travelers, with obvious implications for the state's tourist industry. Mexico is highly dependent on North American markets, especially that of the United States; Yucatán is no exception. Prospects for the state hinge therefore on its ability to attract tourists and industrial investment; those goals will pose the basic challenges facing the state and its leaders, as Yucatán wrestles with promoting greater social and economic equity for its citizens.

Alex M. Saragoza

See also Archaeological Sites; Environmental Issues; Immigration and Emigration; Indigenous Peoples; Maquiladoras; North American Free Trade Agreement; Quintana Roo; Tourism

Further Reading

Cornelius, Wayne, et al. 2007. *Mayan Journeys: The New Migration from Yucatán to the United States.* La Jolla: University of California, Center for Comparative Immigration Studies.

Valdéz, Nelson. 2001. *The Caste War of Yucatán.* Rev. ed. Palo Alto, CA: Stanford University Press.

Yucatán Official State Website. http://www.Yucatán.gob.mx.

Z

Zacatecas

The official coat of arms of Zacatecas. (Corel)

The state of Zacatecas lies in north central Mexico, surrounded by the states of Durango and others; it is the eighth largest state in the country and has 56 *municipios,* which are similar to counties in the United States. The capital is the city of Zacatecas and ranks among the most important cities in the country for its historical and economic importance. Although the state is named in the Náhuatl language after an indigenous society, the overwhelming majority of the contemporary population is of non-Indian descent. Much of the original indigenous population was used as a source of labor with the introduction of Spanish colonialism in the 16th century and subsequently suffered horrific levels of mortality due to overwork, exposure to European diseases, and malnutrition. The rapid decline of the indigenous peoples of the area was accelerated by the discovery of silver deposits in the middle of the 16th century, when the local Indian population became the initial source of mining labor.

Since that time, mining has been a mainstay of the state's economy, especially in the area dominated by the city of Fresnillo. Mexico is the largest producer of silver in the world, and the mines of Zacatecas are among the most important; the second most-productive silver mine in Mexico is in the state, along with several others known for their silver deposits. Lead and zinc are also significantly mined in Zacatecas. Although mining remains central to the state's economy, as a source of labor the sector has waned over time, particularly with the introduction of new technology that has lessened the demand for workers.

Manufacturing has expanded in the state, including the establishment of assembly plants producing textiles, auto parts, and electrical components. The city of Zacatecas also has one of Mexico's largest breweries. Transportation services represent another important economic activity in the state, as the capital sits at the junction of major railways and roads that link the northern and southern parts of the country.

Agriculture plays a prominent role in the state's economy, but it has been marked by two very different components. One sector is characterized by extensive, modern, highly capitalized farming operations for domestic and export markets that produce beans, corn, peaches, and mangoes. A second agricultural sector, however, is composed of small farmers, who have found it difficult to sustain a decent standard

An aerial view of Zacatecas, Mexico. (Jesús Eloy Ramos Lara | Dreamstime.com)

of living, especially with the reduction of government-funded supports since the changes in farming policies of the 1990s. For much of the state's rural population, therefore, migration has become an alternative to staying on the land and trying to eke out a living wage. As a consequence, the state has become a major sending area of immigrants to the United States. Los Angeles, Atlanta, and Chicago are key destination points for immigrants from Zacatecas. It is estimated that roughly half of the people born in Zacatecas are in the United States at any given time. Not surprisingly, remittances from immigrants in the United States have become an important element in the economy of the state and to the livelihood of much of its rural population. Thus, any downturn in the U.S. economy holds very negative effects for those communities that have become dependent on remittances. Poverty afflicts about one-third of the population, much of it in the rural areas of the state. Drug-trafficking activity has increased in the region, as poor youth in particular have been lured into the drug trade as a quick way out of their impoverished conditions.

In recent years, the left-of-center party, the Democratic Revolution Party (PRD) has become a major political force in the state, winning the gubernatorial race in 2004. And four of the state's five deputies subsequently belonged to the PRD. But the national PRD party structure became deeply divided after the 2006 presidential election, jeopardizing the strength of the party in the state. Since then, the old dominant party, the Institutional Revolutionary Party (PRI), has regained support among local voters and cut significantly into the political power of its left-leaning rival in the state. Thus, not surprisingly, the internal splits of the PRD facilitated the victory of the PRI candidate in the July 2010 election for the governorship, a major blow to the left-of-center party. To what extent the PRD can recover from this defeat remains unclear, but the signs do not auger well for the party of the Left. In mayoral races, the PRI won 28 contests, while the PRD was victorious in 17, down from the 29 that it had taken in 2004.

The capital city of Zacatecas attracts large numbers of tourists due to the beauty of its colonial architecture, reflective of the wealth generated by the region's silver mines during Spanish rule. Largely as a result of its colonial architectural patrimony, the city was named a world heritage site in 1993. Zacatecas is dominated by its capital, where nearly half of the state's population is located, along with the state's main concentration of universities, galleries, museums, and cultural life. It is the site of a very popular and major festival every year that features renowned international musical artists and attracts thousands of visitors to the city. The capital also is known for various local holidays, including a dramatized battle between "Christians and Moors" that recalls the city's Spanish colonial roots. In sum, the state reflects the contrasts that mark contemporary Mexico, a region with a deep-seated colonial past facing an uncertain political and economic future.

Alex M. Sargaoza

See also Agriculture; Immigration and Emigration; Mining; Partido de la Revolución Democrática

Further Reading

Burnes Ortiz, Arturo. 2009. *Zacatecas: dEsarrollo economico regional.* Zacatecas: Universidad Autonoma de Zacatecas.

Hernandez Chavez, Alicia, and Mariana Teran Fuentes. 2010. *Federalismo, ciudadania y representacion en Zacatecas.* Zacatecas: Universidad Autonoma de Zacatecas.

Jones, Richard. 1995. *Ambivalent Journey: U.S. Migration and Economic Mobility in North-Central Mexico.* Tucson: University of Arizona Press.

Volker, Hamann. 2002. *The Impact of NAFTA on Agricultural Development in Mexico.* Bochum, Germany: Department of Sociology, Ruhr-University Bochum.

Zacatecas Official State Website. http://www.zacatecas.gob.mx.

Zapatist Army for National Liberation and the Indigenous Movement

See Ejército Zapatista de Liberación Nacional and the Indigenous Movement

Zedillo Ponce de León, Ernesto

Ernesto Zedillo, who served as the president of Mexico during 1994–2000, was the last president to hold office during the hegemonic period of the Partido

Revolucionario Institucional (Institutional Revolutionary Party, PRI), which lasted 71 years in power. During Zedillo's term, the last democratic political reforms in order to make elections competitive were achieved. Zedillo also dealt with one of the largest economic crises in recent Mexican history and with the uprising of the Zapatist Army for National Liberation (EZLN), as well as two massacres in rural communities of southern Mexico. By the end of his period the economy was stabilized and all political conditions were gathered for a real transition to democracy.

Background and arrival to the presidency   Zedillo was not the PRI's original candidate. Carlos Salinas de Gortari handpicked Luis Donaldo Colosio as his candidate for the presidential election of 1994. However, Colosio was killed during an official campaign in the city of Tijuana. Just a few days later, Zedillo was named candidate.

Colosio's assassination has never been clarified. Some suggest that the choice of Zedillo was interpreted as Salinas's way of retaining real power, since Zedillo was not really a politician but an economist (like Salinas), who apparently lacked the president's political talent and influence.

The election was known as the cleanest of the century. This contrasted with the previous election, where it was widely claimed that the Ministry of the Interior committed electoral fraud in favor of Salinas. For the 1994 election, international observers were invited to the election.

This time Cuauhtémoc Cárdenas, who ran again as a presidential candidate, did not collect enough strength to challenge Zedillo; neither did the National Action Party's (PAN) candidate, Diego Fernández. It was presumed that the electorate feared for a change in the regime after recent events, such as the uprising of the EZLN, the assassination of Colosio, and the assassination of Francisco Ruiz Massieu, another PRI leader.

Economic policy   The whole Zedillo administration was framed by the economic crisis that began the first weeks of his term. In keeping with the PRI election-year tradition, Salinas launched a spending spree to finance popular projects, which translated into a historically high deficit. This budget deficit was coupled with a current account deficit, fueled by excessive consumer spending with an overvalued peso.

These events, together with the increasing current account deficit fostered by government spending, caused alarm among Mexican and foreign *tesobono* investors. Dramatic capital flight depleted the already low central bank reserves (which eventually hit a record low of $9 billion).

At the beginning of his term, Zedillo, after a series of inexperienced decisions from his minister of finance, decided to let the peso float. Whether the effects were aggravated further or not, the result was that the peso crashed under a floating regime from 4 pesos to the dollar (with the previous increase of 15 percent) to 7.2 to the dollar in a week.

President Zedillo also had to face the possible bankruptcy of the Mexican banking system. To avoid the threatening consequences, the Zedillo Administration launched a rescue plan for banks: the Bank Fund for the Protection of Savings (Fobaproa). The government would absorbed the unpaid debt, capitalized the financial system, and guaranteed savers' deposits in commercial banks, with a cost of approximately $552 billion. The project was financed partly by taxpayers' money, but also with foreign debt and aid, mainly from the International Monetary Fund, the United States, and Canada.

The Fobaproa was later strongly criticized by the opposition as fraud to the nation. In retrospect, one of the main factors that caused the 1994 economic crisis was the rapid expansion of credit as well as the government's policy of spending financed by debt. The use of a semi-fixed exchange rate monetary policy as a means of stabilizing the economy while attracting considerable amounts of foreign capital to finance the credit expansion eventually gave way to an unsustainable flight of capital.

Political reforms   The Congress reformed the Federal Code for Political Institutions and Electoral Procedures (COFIPE), creating the citizen-driven Instituto Federal Electoral (Federal Electoral Institute, IFE). The 1995 and 1996 reforms consisted of eliminating any governmental influence over the electoral authorities. The councilors of the IFE needed to be citizens proposed by the executive branch and approved by two-thirds of the votes in Congress. This gave independence to the IFE, making possible cleaner and democratic elections.

The midterm 1997 election was the indicator of the PRI's future loss of the presidency. For the first time in its history, Mexico City elected its mayor. In the 1997 election, Cuauhtémoc Cárdenas of the Democratic Revolution Party (PRD) won as a mayor of Mexico City. Also, in the federal legislative elections, the PRI lost absolute majority. In the second half of his term, Zedillo was bound to rule with the first divided government in PRI's history, and an opposite government in Mexico City. The new electoral laws and an elevated number of protest votes for the economic crisis and the social instability started to undermine the PRI's electoral strength.

Social issues   During the Zedillo administration, social movements claiming social and economic justice persisted. Zedillo dealt with the EZLN insurrection through his whole period and could not contain it. Several rounds of negotiations were installed in Chiapas, and several negotiators were appointed by the government. However, the EZLN movement continued taking over some Chiapas municipalities and declared them autonomous.

Also, during Zedillo's term, two important social issues spotted his administration: the massacres of indigenous people in the southern communities of Aguas Blancas and Acteal. Both were related to guerrilla groups and local political struggles with remaining authoritarian practices in rural areas of southern Mexico.

Although the press and public opinion did not directly blame Zedillo of severe acts of repression, top officers within Zedillo's cabinet were pointed out.

Foreign affairs   With the coming into effect of the North American Free Trade Agreement (NAFTA), Zedillo started a more pragmatic foreign policy. His foreign affairs were generally related to economic matters with China, Japan, and the United States. Actually, both the United States and Mexico started the closest relations since the Manuel Ávila Camacho administration during World War II, causing Cuban leader Fidel Castro to criticize Zedillo. Traditionally, the Mexican governments had condemned the U.S. policy toward Cuba and supported Castro's government. After NAFTA, Mexico started to lessen diplomatic relations with Cuba.

The end of the PRI's hegemony   In 2000 Zedillo also faced the democratic transition at the very beginning of the presidential campaigns. He was the PRI's first president that could not handpick his successor. The strong pressure from the opposition forced the PRI to organize its first primary election for nominating its presidential candidate. The primary election was won by Francisco Labastida, who was said to be the president's favorite. Labastida was not capable of winning the 2000 presidential election, making Zedillo the last president after 71 years of PRI hegemony.

The night of the election, Zedillo announced the PAN's candidate, Vicente Fox, as the winner. He congratulated Vicente Fox's victory and offered him all his support in the transition. This was strongly criticized by factions of the PRI, who accused him of betrayal to the party. For others, Zedillo's quick response was considered an act of political responsibility, facilitating a peaceful transition.

Since leaving office, Zedillo has held many jobs as an economic consultant for various international companies and organizations. He is currently director of the Yale Center for the Study of Globalization, where he is a teacher, researcher, and consultant.

Juan Manuel Galarza and José Ignacio Lanzagorta

See also Economic Crash of 1994–1995; Election, Presidential, 2000; Partido Revolucionario Institucional; Salinas de Gortari, Carlos

Further Reading

Domínguez, Jorge I., and Alejandro Poiré, eds. 1998. *Toward Mexico's Democratization: Parties, Campaigns, Elections and Public Opinion.* New York: Routledge.

Selected Bibliography

Aguayo Quezada, S. 1998. *1968: Los archivos de la violencia.* Mexico City: Grijalbo.

Aguilar Medina, J. I. 2008. *Adolescencia, identidad y cultura: El caso de la ciudad de Mexico.* Mexico City: Instituto Nacional de Antropologia e Historia.

Alvarez, R. R. 2005. *Mangos, Chiles, and Truckers: The Business of Transnationalism.* Minneapolis: University of Minnesota Press.

Anderson, J. B., J. Gerber, and L. Foster. 2008. *Fifty Years of Change on the U.S.-Mexico Border: Growth, Development, and Quality of Life.* Austin: University of Texas Press.

Andreas, P. 2009. *Border Games: Policing the U.S.-Mexico Divide.* Ithaca, NY: Cornell University Press.

Ashbee, E., H. B. Clausen, and C. Pederson, eds. 2007. *The Politics, Economics, and Culture of Mexican-U.S. Migration: Both Sides of the Border.* New York: Palgrave Macmillan.

Bacon, C., ed. 2008. *Confronting the Coffee Crisis: Fair Trade, Sustainable Livelihoods, and Ecosystems in Mexico and Central America.* Cambridge, MA: MIT Press.

Brewster, C., and K. Brewster. 2010. *Representing the Nation: Sport and Spectacle in Post-Revolutionary Mexico.* London: Routledge.

Brown Grossman, F., and L. Dominguez Villalobos, eds. 2010. *Mexico: Desigualdad economica y genero.* Mexico City: Universidad Nacional Autonoma de Mexico.

Bruhn, K. 2004. *Taking on Goliath: The Emergence of a New Left Party and the Struggle for Democracy in Mexico.* University Park: Pennsylvania State University Press.

Carrillo Trueba, C. 2009. *El racismo en Mexico: Una vision sintetica.* Mexico City: Consejo Nacional para la Cultura y las Artes.

Castaneda, J. G. 2011. *Manana Forever: Mexico and the Mexicans.* New York: Knopf.

Cerutti, M., M. C. Hernandez, and C. Marichal, eds. 2010. *Grandes empresas y grupos empresariales en Mexico en el siglo XX.* Mexico City: Plaza y Valdes.

Cornelius, W. A., D. S. Fitzgerald, and S. Borger, eds. 2009. *Four Generations of Norteños: New research from the Cradle of Mexican Migration.* La Jolla, CA: Center for Comparative Immigration Studies, University of California, San Diego.

De Hoyos, R. E. 2007. *Accounting for Mexican Income Inequality during the 1990s.* Washington, DC: World Bank, Development Prospects Group.

Díez, J. 2006. *Political Change and Environmental Policymaking in Mexico.* New York: Routledge.

Domínguez, J. I., and R. Fernández de Castro. 2001. *The United States and Mexico: Between Partnership and Conflict.* New York: Routledge.

Domínguez, J. I., and C. Lawson, eds. 2003. *Mexico's Pivotal Democratic Election: Campaigns, Votes, and the 2000 Presidential Race.* Stanford, CA: Stanford University Press/Center for the U.S.-Mexican Studies, University of California, San Diego.

Dominguez-Rubalcava, H., and I. Corona, eds. 2010. *Gender Violence at the U.S.-Mexico Border: Media Representation and Public Response.* Tucson: University of Arizona Press.

Edmonds-Poli, E., and D. Shirk. 2009. *Contemporary Mexican Politics.* Lanham, MD: Rowman and Littlefield.

Eisenstadt, T. A. 2004. *Courting Democracy in Mexico: Party Strategies and Electoral Institutions.* Cambridge: Cambridge University Press.

Ewell, G. F., ed. 2005. *Mexico: Migration, U.S. Economic Issues and Counter Narcotic Efforts.* New York: Nova Publishers.

Fitting, E. M. 2011. *The Struggle for Maize: Campesinos, Workers, and Transgenic Corn.* Durham, NC: Duke University Press.

Gallagher, K. P. 2004. *Free Trade and the Environment: Mexico, NAFTA, and Beyond.* Stanford, CA: Stanford Law and Politics.

Garcia-Cadena, C. H., ed. 2006. *Psychosocial and Cultural Research on Poverty in Mexico.* New York: Nova Science Publishers.

Gonzalez, A. 2010. *Afro-Mexico Dancing: Between Myth and Reality.* Austin: University of Texas Press.

Gonzalez Gutierrez, A. 2011. *Protection of Maize under the Mexico Biosafety Law: Environment and Trade.* Akron, OH: University of Akron Press.

Haber, S., et al. 2008. *Mexico since 1980.* Cambridge: Cambridge University Press.

Hanson, G. H. 2005. *Globalization, Labor Income, and Poverty in Mexico.* Cambridge, MA: National Bureau of Economic Research.

Hellier-Tinoco, R. 2011. *Embodying Mexico: Tourism, Nationalism and Performance.* New York: Oxford University Press.

Hernández-León, R. 2008. *Metropolitan Migrants: The Migration of Urban Mexicans to the United States.* Berkeley: University of California Press.

Herrera, O. U. 2008. *Toward the Preservation of a Heritage: Latin American and Latino Art in the Midwestern United States.* Notre Dame, IN: Institute for Latino Studies.

Hind, E. 2010. *Femmenism and the Mexican Woman Intellectual: From Sor Juana to Poniatowska.* New York: Palgrave MacMillan.

Holo, S. 2004. *Oaxaca at the Crossroads: Managing Memory, Negotiating Change.* Washington, DC: Smithsonian Books.

Katz, E. G., and M. C. Correia, eds. *The Economics of Gender in Mexico.* Washington, DC: World Bank.

Kay, T. 2011. *NAFTA and the Politics of Labor Transnationalism.* New York: Cambridge University Press.

Kennedy, D. 2010. *Oaxaca al Gusto: An Infinite Gastronomy.* Austin: University of Texas Press.

Lamas, M. 2011. *Feminism: Transmissions and Retransmissions.* New York: Palgrave MacMillan.

Latapí, A. E., and S. F. Martin, eds. 2008. *Mexico-U.S. Migration Management: A Binational Approach.* Lanham, MD: Lexington Books.

Lawson, C. H. 2002. *Building the Fourth Estate: Democratization and the Rise of a Free Press in Mexico.* Berkeley: University of California Press.

Levy, S. 2006. *Progress against Poverty: Sustaining Mexico's Progresa-Oportunidades Program.* Washington, DC: Brookings Institution Press.

Levy, S., and M. Walton, eds. 2009. *No Growth without Equity? Inequality, Interests, and Competition in Mexico.* New York: Palgrave Macmillan.

Loewe, R. 2010. *Maya or Mestizo: Nationalism, Modernity, and Its Discontents.* Toronto: University of Toronto Press.

López, A. A. 2007. *The Farmworkers' Journey.* Berkeley: University of California Press.

Lopez, R. A. 2010. *Crafting Mexico: Intellectuals, Artisans, and the State after the Revolution.* Durham, NC: Duke University Press.

López-Acevedo, G. 2006. *Mexico: Two Decades of the Evolution of Education and Inequality.* Washington, DC: World Bank, Latin America and the Caribbean Region, Poverty Reduction and Economic Management Division.

López-Acevedo, G., and A. Salinas. 2000. *How Mexico's Financial Crisis Affected Income Distribution.* Washington, DC: World Bank, Latin America and the Caribbean Region, Economic Policy Sector Unit, and Mexico Country Office.

Lopez-Calva, L. F., and N. Lustig, eds. 2010. *Declining Inequality in Latina America: A Decade of Progress?* Washington, DC: Brookings Institution Press.

Magaloni, B. 2006. *Voting for Autocracy: The Politics of Party Hegemony and Its Demise in Mexico.* New York: Cambridge University Press.

Massey, D. S., ed. 2008. *New Faces in New Places: The Changing Geography of American Immigration.* New York: Russell Sage Foundation.

Mexican Fine Arts Center. 2006. *The African Presence in Mexico: From Yanga to the Present.* Chicago: Mexican Fine Arts Museum.

Middlebrook, K. J., ed. 2004. *Dilemmas of Political Change in Mexico.* London: Institute of Latin American Studies, University of London/Center for U.S.-Mexico Studies, University of California, San Diego.

Middlebrook, K. J., and E. Zepeda, eds. 2003. *Confronting Development: Assessing Mexico's Economic and Social Policy Challenges.* Stanford, CA: Stanford University Press/Center for U.S.-Mexico Studies, University of California, San Diego.

Najera-Ramirez, O., N. E. Cantu, and B. M. Romero, eds. 2009. *Dancing across Borders.* Urbana: University of Illinois Press.

Nevins, J. 2008. *Dying to Live: A Story of U.S. Immigration in an Age of Global Apartheid.* San Francisco: Open Media/City Lights Books.

Orme, W. A., Jr. 1996. *Understanding NAFTA: Mexico, Free Trade, and the New North America.* Austin: University of Texas Press.

Orrenius, P. M. 2008. *Why Stop Here? Mexican Migration to the U.S. Border Region.* Dallas, TX: Federal Reserve Bank of Dallas.

Oxley, H., F. Colombo, and M. L. Gil-Lapetra. 2005. "Mexico." In *OECD Reviews of Health Systems,* 17–138. Paris: OECD.

Pastor, R., Jr. 2011. *The North American Idea: A Vision of a Continental Future.* New York: Oxford University Press.

Pick, Z. M. 2010. *Constructing the Image of the Mexican Revolution: Cinema and the Archive.* Austin: University of Texas Press.

Preston, J., and S. Dillon. 2004. *Opening Mexico: The Making of a Democracy.* New York: Farrar, Straus and Giroux.

Rich, J. G. 2003. *Environment and Development in Mexico: Recommendations for Reconciliation.* Washington, DC: Center for Strategic and International Studies.

Rivera, J. M., S. Whiteford, and M. Chávez, eds. 2009. *NAFTA and the Campesinos: The Impact of NAFTA on Small-scale Agricultural Producers in Mexico and the Prospects for Change.* Scranton, PA: University of Scranton Press.

Ruiz, R. E. 2010. *Mexico: Why a Few Are Rich and the People Poor.* Berkeley: University of California Press.

Ruy-Sanchez, A., and M. de Orellana, eds. 2004. *Tequila: A Traditional Art of Mexico.* Washington, DC: Smithsonian Books.

Sabet, D. M. 2008. *Nonprofits and Their Networks: Cleaning the Waters along Mexico's Northern Border.* Tucson: University of Arizona Press.

Santibáñez, L., G. Vernez, and P. Razquin. 2005. *Education in Mexico.* Santa Monica, CA: RAND Corporation.

Sayer, C. 2009. *Days of the Dead & Other Mexican Festivals.* Austin: University of Texas Press.

Schneider, S. 2010. *Mexican Community Health and the Politics of Health Reform.* Albuquerque: University of New Mexico Press.

Smith, R. C. 2006. *Mexican New York: Transnational Lives of New Immigrants.* Berkeley: University of California Press.

Soloaga, I., J. S. Wilson, and A. Mejía. 2006. *Moving Forward Faster: Trade Facilitation Reform and Mexican Competitiveness.* Washington, DC: World Bank, Development Research Group, Trade Team.

Stephen, L. 2007. *Transborder Lives: Indigenous Oaxacans in Mexico, California, and Oregon.* Durham, NC: Duke University Press.

Tello, A. 2010. *La musica de Mexico: Panorama del siglo XX.* Mexico City: Fondo de Cultura Economica.

Trejo Delarbre, R. 2010. *Simpatia por el rating: La politica deslumbrada por los medios.* Mexico City: Cal y Arena.

Tulchin, J. S., and A. D. Selee, eds. *Mexico's Politics and Society in Transition.* Boulder, CO: Lynne Rienner Publishers.

Verner, D. 2005. *Poverty in Rural and Semi-Urban Mexico during 1992–2002.* Washington, DC: World Bank, Latin America and the Caribbean Region, Environmentally and Socially Sustainable Development.

Walker, C. J. 2009. *Heritage or Heresy: Archaeology and Culture on the Maya Riviera.* Tuscaloosa: University of Alabama Press.

Wilson, S. 2010. *The Boys from Little Mexico: A Season Chasing the American Dream.* Boston: Beacon.

Zavala, A. 2010. *Becoming Modern, Becoming Tradition: Women, Gender and Representation in Mexican Art.* University Park: Pennsylvania State University Press.

About the Editors and Contributors

The Editors

Alex M. Saragoza is a professor of history in the Department of Ethnic Studies at the University of California, Berkeley. His research has focused on the social and economic history of Mexico since the Mexican revolution of 1910.

Ana Paula Ambrosi studied for her BA in international relations at the Instituto Tecnológico Autónomo de Mexico (ITAM). She earned her MA in Latin American studies at the University of California, Berkeley. She also received a postgraduate certificate in strategic political analysis at the Centro de Investigacion y Docencia Económica (CIDE) in Mexico. During her professional career, she worked in the Foreign Affairs Ministry and the Presidential Communications Office in Mexico as a political communication analyst during the first years of the Fox administration. She also worked for the California-Mexico Health Initiative and the Center for Latin American Studies at UC Berkeley. Her research has focused on Mexico's politics and Mexican immigration to the United States.

Silvia D. Zárate is an independent art and culture specialist. She earned her MA in arts and humanities education at New York University and is working on her dissertation to obtain an art history master's degree from the Universidad Nacional Autónoma de México (National Autonomous University of Mexico, UNAM). During her professional career she has worked in various cultural projects and institutions both in Mexico and the United States. She was a project leader in the creation of a museum about economy sponsored by the Central Bank of Mexico and has represented artists as part of a renowned art gallery in Mexico City.

Contributors

Cecilia Absalón is a documentary and iconographic researcher. She received her MA in art history at the Universidad Nacional Autónoma de México (National Autonomous University of Mexico, UNAM). She is currently writing her PhD dissertation at UNAM on Juan Guzmán's photography.

Claudia Acuña earned an MSc in social policy and planning in developing countries at the London School of Economics. She worked for three years as an adviser to the vice minister of urban and territorial development and for five years as a housing microfinance analyst at the Mexican Development Bank for Housing Finance (Sociedad Hipotecaria Federal). In March 2011 she started her own consultancy firm, FIVASE Consultants, which provides professional advice in urban and housing issues.

John A. Adams Jr. has been actively involved in international trade, with an emphasis on emerging industrial and financial markets in Mexico. He has served as a delegate to the General Agreement on Tariffs and Trade (GATT) negotiations and an adviser to the World Trade Organization and has provided congressional testimony on infrastructure issues involving the U.S.-Mexican border. He has also been an adjunct professor of international banking and finance at Texas A&M International University in Laredo and is the author of *Bordering the Future: The Impact of Mexico on the United States* (Praeger, 2006), among other books.

Rita Alazraki earned her master's degree in art history form the Facultad de Filosofía y Letras at the Universidad Nacional Autónoma de México (National Autonomous University of Mexico, UNAM). She is the coauthor of the book *Historia de la cultura y el arte* (Editorial Alhambra). She has also been a professor of art history at the Instituto de Cultura Superior and of the Diplomado "Sensibilización y expresión creativa" at the Universidad Iberoamericana in Mexico City. She was curator at the Unidad de promoción Cultural y Acervo Patrimonial of the Secretaría de Hacienda and was also a curator at the Museum of the Ex Palacio Arzobispal.

Fernanda Álvarez Gil is a children's art teacher and visual artist in Mexico City.

María Álvarz earned an MA in Modern European Literature from the University of Sussex. She was editor of *Sabor* a culinary magazine in Mexico City. She has published extensively in different Mexican magazines.

Linda Allegro has taught at the University of Tulsa and specializes in immigrant issues. Among other works, she has contributed to *Borderlands: An Encyclopedia of Culture and Politics on the U.S.-Mexico Divide* (Greenwood, 2008).

Paola Arena holds a master's degree in marketing. She has been an independent writer for several newspapers and periodical publications. Sports have always played an important role in her personal and professional life.

Steven M. Bell is the chair of Latin American studies at the University of Arkansas and has written about Mexico for numerous publications as well as coauthored *Culture and Customs of Mexico* (ABC-CLIO/Greenwood, 2004).

Dolores Bernal received her master of arts degree in Latin American studies from the University of California, where her research focused on law enforcement in Mexico.

Italia Boliver is a writer and a PhD researcher at King's College, London, where she also teaches a course on language and critical thinking. She has worked for several publishing houses and publications including, *Editorial Clío, Letras Libres, Contemporary Magazine, The Journal of Latin American Studies,* and, more recently, Stacey Publishing.

Stephany A. Cadena studied at the Instituto Tecnológico Autónomo de México. She has participated in projects in different areas of the public sector, including the Instituto Nacional de Migración (National Institute of Immigration), the Presidencia de la República Mexicana (Presidency of the United Mexican States), the Secretaría de la Función Pública (Secretariat of the Public Function), and, currently, the Secretaría de Relaciones Exteriores (Secretariat of Foreign Affairs) in Mexico.

Rodrigo Cano received his MA in economics from New York University. He is interested in monetary policy topics, and his master's degree thesis was titled "An Empirical Study of the Transmission Mechanism of the Monetary Policy: The Case of Mexico."

Don M. Coerver is professor of history at Texas Christian University, Fort Worth. His published works include *Revolution on the Border: The United States and Mexico* and *Tangled Destinies: Latin America and the United States.* He is the coauthor, along with Suzanne B. Pasztor and Robert M. Buffington, of *Mexico: An Encyclopedia of Contemporary Culture and History* (ABC-CLIO, 2004).

Mariana Domínguez teaches linguistics and intercultural communication at Universidad Modelo in Mérida, México. She conducts social science research and is currently creating and coordinating cultural project related to media and minority linguistic rights promotion.

Deborah Dorotinsky Alperstein has a BA in cultural anthropology from UC Berkeley and an MA and a PhD in art history from the Universidad Nacional Autónoma de México (National Autonomous University of Mexico, UNAM). She is a full-time researcher in the Instituto de Investigaciones Estéticas, UNAM, and a professor of the historiography of art, the history of photography, and visual culture and gender topics in the Art History Graduate Program, which she had coordinated at UNAM since 2011. She has published extensively in Spanish on the topics of visual imagery and ethnic identity, indigenismo and photography, and, more recently, visual culture and gender in Mexico during 1920–1950. She was academic coordinator of the visual culture and gender area in the Gender Studies Program at UNAM (2008–2010). She edited with Renato González Mello the book *Encauzar la mirada: Arquitectura, pedagogía e imágenes en México, 1920–1950* (UNAM, 2010). She is the proud mother of two girls and a member of the Collage Art Association.

Minerva Escamilla is a historian specializing in the colonial and 19th-century history of Veracruz. Since 2006 she has served as director of extended learning at the Universidad Critstobal Colon in Veracruz. She has an MA in history from the Universidad Nacional Autónoma de México (National Autonomous University of Mexico, UNAM) and is a contemporary history doctoral candidate at the Universidad del Pais Vasco.

Juan Manuel Galarza has a degree in economics from the Instituto Tecnológico Autónomo de México and a master's degree in public administration from Columbia University. He worked at the World Bank from 2004 to 2006 as an economic analyst for Latin America at the Global Information and Communication Technologies Department in Washington, D.C. In 2006 he was invited to the consulting firm Grupo de Economistas y Asociados in Mexico City as a partner in charge of the infrastructure projects. In 2009 he was named CEO of FONATUR Operadora Portuaria, a subsidiary of FONATUR (Trust Fund for Tourism Development) in charge of the ports and nautical projects of the fund. Currently he is the chief commercial officer of FONATUR, responsible for marketing and sales strategies.

Ana Garduño earned her PhD in art history at the Universidad Nacional Autónoma de México (National Autonomous University of Mexico, UNAM). She is a researcher at the Cenidiap/INBA (National Institute for Fine Arts) and is a professor in the graduate programs in art history at the UNAM and of museology at the National School of Conservation, Restoration and Museography of the National Institute for Anthropology and History. She has contributed to numerous publications on museums, art collecting, and cultural politics of the 20th century.

Edmundo Gómez Martínez is a comunicologist specializing in film and publicity. He holds an MA in publicity from the Centro Avanzado de Comunicación Eulalui Ferrer (CADEC, AC). Since 2006 he has worked as a professor and coordinator of cultural affairs at the Universidad Cristobal Colón in Veracruz.

Erin Graham is a doctoral candidate in Latin American history at the University of Houston. She was awarded the 2008–2009 Women Studies Program Dissertation Fellowship for work on her dissertation, "Bordering Chaos: Mothers, Daughters, and Neoliberalism."

Angus M. Gunn is professor emeritus at the University of British Columbia, Vancouver, Canada, and is the author of a number of books on education and environmental science. His publications include *The Impact of Geology on the United States* (Greenwood, 2001), and *Encyclopedia of Disasters: Environmental Catastrophes and Human Tragedies* (Greenwood, 2007).

Anisha Hingorani is a graduate of the University of California, Berkeley, where she studied international relations.

James D. Huck Jr. is assistant director and graduate adviser at the Stone Center for Latin American Studies at Tulane University, New Orleans, Louisiana. His published works include articles and papers on contemporary Mexican foreign policy, diplomatic history, and general Latin American international relations. He is the author of *Mexico: A Global Studies Handbook* (ABC-CLIO/Greenwood, 2008).

Jorge Jiménez Rentería is a lawyer by the Universidad Nacional Autónoma de México (National Autonomous University of Mexico, UNAM). He has been a professor and academic official at diverse areas in the fields of teaching, research, and administration at UNAM, linking his academic activities with diffusion and cultural promotion in media.

Peter Krieger is research professor at the Institute of Aesthetic Research at the Universidad Nacional Autónoma de México in Mexico City, vice president of the Comité International d'Histoire de l'Art (International Committee of Art History, CIHA), and editor of the art historical magazine *Anales del Instituto de Investigaciones Estéticas* (www.analesiie.unam.mx). He has done research in and written publications about political iconography, aesthetics, and ecology of the megacities.

José Ignacio Lanzagorta earned degrees in political science from the Instituto Tecnológico Autónomo de México (ITAM) and in social anthropology from the Iberoamericana University (UIA). He is in the process of building a multidisciplinary academic career. Currently his research interest is the social use of urban space. Mr. Lanzagorta is a political analyst at GEA, Grupo de Economistas y Asociados, where he deals with public surveys, consulting on projects for public and private enterprises, and the analysis of the Mexican political situation.

Anthony LaRose is an associate professor of criminology and criminal justice at the University of Tampa. Dr. LaRose was a 2004 Fulbright scholar, and his research background includes police value systems, ethics in the criminal justice system, and comparative studies of American and Mexican legal systems. Among other publications, he contributed to *Crime and Punishment around the World* (ABC-CLIO/Greenwood, 2010).

Citlali López Maldonado studied history at the Universidad Nacional Autónoma de México (National Autonomous University of Mexico, UNAM). She works with themes related to visual culture and 20th-century Mexican art history and has experience in cultural dissemination in art museums and in iconographic research. In addition, she coordinates a mobile contemporary art library in Mexico City.

Sophia Luber received her bachelor of arts degree at the University of California, Berkeley, and is a graduate of the School of Law of San Diego University.

Gabriel Macías Osorno has a degree in Latin American studies from the Universidad Nacional Autónoma de México (National Autonomous University of Mexico, UNAM). He is currently studying etnomusicology at the Escuela Nacional de Música at UNAM. He is also a flamenco music player and researcher.

Vania Macias Osorno is a researcher at Arkheia, the Documentation Center of the Museo Universitario de Arte Contemporáneo (MUAC) in Mexico City. She earned her MA in art history at the Universidad Nacional Autónoma de México (National Autonomous University of Mexico, UNAM), with emphasis in photography. She has realized several exercises of independent research and curatorial practices.

Zulai Macías Osorno has a degree in psychology and an MA in philosophy from the Universidad Nacional Autónoma de México (National Autonomous University of Mexico, UNAM) and also studied contemporary dance in the Ollin Yoliztli school.

Acacia Maldonado is an independent researcher with a master's degree in art history, with specialization in modern and contemporary photography in Mexico. She currently works at the Universidad Nacional Autónoma de México (National Autonomous University of Mexico, UNAM) Extension School in Canada (ESECA).

Erin Maloney, a student at the University of Tampa, focuses her research on domestic and dating violence in Latin America. With Anthony LaRose, she contributed to *Crime and Punishment around the World* (ABC-CLIO/Greenwood, 2010).

Luis M. Martínez Cervantes is professor and researcher at the Communication and Engineering Department at Universidad Iberoamericana in Mexico City. He has extensively published about engineering design and the digital convergence panorama in Latin America.

Josué Martínez Rodríguez is an art historian focusing on the links between pictures and literature. He holds an MA in Mexican literature from Universidad

Veracruzana (UV). In 2008 he worked at Fundación Cultural Televisa conducting research for two photography books. Since 2009 he has lectured at the Schools of Arts and Literature at UV.

Pablo Martínez Zárate is a lecturer in literature and communications at several universities in Mexico City. He has published academic and literary work in Mexico, Europe, and the United States.

Arnoldo Matus is on his final year of a DPhil in geography and environment in the Environmental Change Institute at the University of Oxford. His research is on adaptation to climate change in the Mexican Caribbean tourism sector. Arnoldo is a cofounder of Climate & Biodiversity Nexus (www.cbnex.com). He also holds an MSc in renewable energy and environment from Reading University, an MSc in environment and resource management from BTU-Cottbus, and a BA from McGill University.

Octavio Mercado is an associate professor of design at the Universidad Autonoma Metropolitana. His most recent publication is "Territorios del arte y el diseño en la obra de David Consuegra" in David Consuegra's *Pensamiento Gráfico* (Universidad Nacional de Colombia, 2011).

David Antonio Morales is an archaeologist and museographer specializing in the cultures from the Gulf and central regions of Mexico. Since 2005 he has been the director of musuems for the Instituto Nacional de Antropología e Historia (INAH) in the state of Veracruz.

Eréndira Muñoz Aréyzaga is a profesor of archaeology at the Universidad Autónoma del Estado de México (UAEM). Her focus is on the social perception of cultural heritage, and she currently conducts analysis of production and reception for the Museo Nacional de Antropología.

Alejandro Navarrete graduated from the Universidad Nacional Autónoma de México (National Autonomous University of Mexico, UNAM) Escuela Nacional de Artes Plásticas with a focus on the theory and practice of photography. He is currently studying at the Utrecht School of Art at Utrecht University in the Netherlands.

Christelle Pages Patron studied political science and international relations in Mexico City. She worked at the Mexican National Population Council from November 2008 to May 2010 as an assistant to the secretary-general. Since August 2010 she has been working as an associate assigned to public affairs management at a private consulting group named Solana Consultores.

Suzanne B. Pasztor is associate professor of history at Humboldt State University, Arcata, California, specializing in Mexican history. She is the coauthor, along with Don M. Coerver and Robert M. Buffington, of *Mexico: An Encyclopedia of Contemporary Culture and History* (ABC-CLIO, 2004); the author of *The Spirit of Hidalgo: The Mexican Revolution in Coahuila* (University of Calgary Press, 2002); and a contributing editor to the *Handbook of Latin American Studies* (University of Texas Press, 1999).

Aarón Polo López is a professor of film history and painting in colonial Mexico at the Escuela Nacional de Antropología e Historia in Mexico City. He has written about Maria Callas and her stay in Mexico, the history of opera in Mexico, and Mexican Cinema. He works at the Universidad Nacional Autónoma de México (National Autonomous University of Mexico, UNAM) in the Instituto de Investigaciones Filológicas.

Lenice Rivera Hernández is an independent researcher interested in the images and the cult of the Virgin Mary on which she has published articles and cocurated exhibitions. She has been a researcher at the Museum of the Basilica of Guadalupe in Mexico City.

Carlos A. Siliceo Bárzana started his career as a sports journalist in 2006. Nowadays he is the coordinator of sports information in Grupo FM Multimedios in Veracruz.

Gonzalo Soto is a reporter at the *Reforma* newspaper in Mexico City, covering the macroeconomics and public finance beat. Previously he worked at the British Embassy in Mexico and as an analyst for a lobbying firm. He studied international relations at the Instituto Tecnológico Autónomo de México and Stockholm University, where he was a member of the Stockholm Association of International Affairs.

Peter Standish is professor of Spanish at East Carolina University, Greenville, North Carolina, and has published widely on Mexico. Among other works, he is the author of *The States of Mexico: A Reference Guide to History and Culture* (ABC-CLIO/Greenwood, 2009) and coauthor of *Culture and Customs of Mexico* (ABC-CLIO/Greenwood, 2004).

Cristina Vaccaro earned her master's degree in art history at the Universidad Nacional Autónoma de México (National Autonomous University of Mexico, UNAM), where she specialized in modern architecture. Today she is studying for her PhD at the UNAM on the theme "The Sublime in Modern Architecture."

Neli Varela Martínez received a master's degree in graphic design from the Metropolitan Autonomous University (2009). She also holds an MA in creativity and design from the National Institute of Fine Arts (2010). She is currently a PhD student at the Metropolitan Autonomous University. Her main research interests are in history and theory of design.

Lina María Vargas is a Mexican art historian based in Veracruz. She has worked in cinema and audiovisual productions in the Department of Art and is mainly interested in multitask activities and business-related contemporary culture, art, music, and fashion.

Luis Vargas-Santiago is an art historian specializing in Mexican and U.S. Latino art. He is currently pursuing his doctoral degree at the University of Texas at Austin. His research focuses on the migration and reproduction of Mexican national imaginaries. He has published extensively in journals and catalogs in Europe, Latin America, and the United States.

Olivia Vidal López is a graphic designer and has a master's degree in art history from the Universidad Nacional Autónoma de México (National Autonomous University of Mexico, UNAM). She is dedicated to independent investigation of sociopolitical phenomena in contemporary art.

Ian Wilson is a graduate of the University of California, Berkeley, where he majored in Latin American Studies.

Index

Abortion, **1–2**, 119, 283
Acapulco, 330–335, 639
Accused, rights of the, 160–161
Active School of Photography, 524
Adolescents
 alcohol consumption among, 27–28
 culture of, 673–676
Adventure tourism, 642–643
Aeromar, 26
Aeroméxico, 20–25
Aeroméxico Connect, 26
African influences, 661
Agave cactus, 379
Agencia Federal de Investigacion (AFI),
 156, 159
Agrarian reform, 5–7, 123–124, 218,
 316, 328, 343, 392, 395–398, 424,
 437, 446–447, 460, 512, 635–636.
 See also Land distribution and land
 reform
Agribusiness, 80, 128–129, 598, 664
Agriculture, **2–18**, 461
 agrofoods, 12–15
 in Baja California, 81
 in Chiapas, 122–123
 in Chihuahua, 129
 in Durango, 215–216
 ejido system and, 392, 395–397, 446,
 461, 512–514, 598
 in Guanajuato, 326
 in Hidalgo, 340
 NAFTA and, 10–12, 14, 466
 in Nayarit, 460
 in Oaxaca, 475, 476
 peasantry and, 510, 513–515
 population growth and, 7–10
 in San Luis Potosí, 578

 in Sinaloa, 584
 in Sonora, 596, 597–598
 in Tobasco, 605, 606
 in Veracruz, 662
 in Yucatán, 676–677
 in Zacatecas, 681–682
Agrofood sector, 12–15
Agroindustry, 150, 510
Agua miel, 340
Agua Prieta Plan, 218
Aguacatecos, 367
Aguas Blancas massacre, 334
Aguas frescas, 97–98
Aguascalientes, 7, **18–20**
Aguilar, Antonio, 450
Aguilar Zinser, Adolfo, xxxii, 302
Aguirre, Javier, 592
Aguirre Velázquez, Ramón, 328–329
Agustín, José, 406
Ahome, 583
Air Force, 46, 48
Air pollution, 270, 276
Airlines, **20–27**, 646–647, 648
Airports, 646, 647
Alameda Art Laboratory, 420
Alameda Central, 432
Alamillo, Trinidad, 149–150
Alcoholic beverages, 100–103
Alcoholism, **27–28**
Alemán, Miguel, xxv, 152, 322, 403
Aleman Valdés, Miguel, 621–622
Alfaro Siqueiros, David, 40, 71, 483
All Soul's Day, 567
Allende, Ignacio, 326
Alliance of the Countryside, 6
Alonso, Ernesto, 618
Alternative Spaces Salon, 63